"This is a unique and creative book. Gilhool laborate in detailing their complex, intense journey. Their account of their interactions, ... rigorous examination and recontextualizing of psychoanalytic history, their brilliant integration of interdisciplinary fields, and their meticulous documentation of psi phenomena should lead to a reassessment and expansion of every clinician's theory and technique. This highly valuable work will stir controversies energizing, enriching and developing the psychotherapeutic field."

> —**Robert J. Marshall, PhD,** ABPP in Clinical Psychology,
> author of *Resistant Interactions: Child, Family and
> Psychotherapist* and *The Transference-Countertransference Matrix*

"A vivid picture of the unconscious resonance that occurs in psycho-analysis. Gilhooley and Toich, having both endured the traumatic death of a loved one, create a 'magnetism of loss' in an analysis facilitating intersubjective rapport, where pasts never spoken of can be intuited and futures, as yet unlived, can be predicted. The physical theory of quantum entanglement grounds this concept of a nonlocal and transpersonal unconscious less in magic than in science. A must read for anyone who has ever experienced an unsettling confrontation with the uncanny."

> —**Lucy Holmes, PhD,** author of *The Internal
> Triangle* and *Wrestling with Destiny*

"Dealing with concepts essential to the nature of psychoanalysis—death, time, timelessness and the nature of reality—this book is an original and captivating combination of theory and clinical practice. Weaving fictional characters through historical accounts of psychoanalysis and quantum physics, Gilhooley and Toich create an ambiance of nonlocality. As a demonstration of clinical intersubjectivity, the authors reveal that within our unconscious mind we dwell outside time and locality, accessing timeless and space-less dimensions."

> —**Angeliki Yiassemides, PhD,** author of *Time and
> Timelessness: Temporality in the Theory of Carl Jung,*
> editor of *Time and the Psyche: Jungian Perspectives*

Psychoanalysis, Intersubjective Writing, and a Postmaterialist Model of Mind

In this in-depth and unique collaboration between a patient and his psychoanalyst, *Psychoanalysis, Intersubjective Writing, and a Postmaterialist Model of Mind: I Woke Up Dead* examines the unconscious mind by analyzing the patient's novel written during his treatment as the focus. Using the patient's creative writing and their intersubjective relationship as evidence, Dan Gilhooley and Frank Toich show how psychoanalysis fits within a postmaterialist model of mind.

In this ground-breaking exploration, Gilhooley and Toich together demonstrate how a nonlocal unconscious can reshape the psychoanalytic conception of the mind. Split into four parts, Intersubjective, Quantum, History and Collaboration, Dan introduces three themes in the first: recovery from death, the intersubjective nature of therapeutic work and the role of creative imagination, combining these themes with analysis of Frank's work and short, related stories from his own life. Part II, Quantum, introduces the concept of nonlocality to describe the mind and draws on the appearance of quantum physics in Frank's science fiction, before moving onto Part III, History, which examines the emergence of psychoanalysis out of animal magnetism, looking at rapport, telepathy and love in psychotherapy. Finally, Collaboration discusses their ongoing psychotherapeutic experiment, the role of imagination, dissociation and the cosmic mind in psychological growth. Interweaving creative writing, psychoanalytic theory and real-life stories, the book re-contextualizes the history and future of psychoanalysis.

Due to its multidisciplinary nature, this book will appeal to psychotherapists and psychologists in practice and in training. It would also be a vital resource for academics and students of counseling, consciousness studies, psychoanalysis, psychotherapy and psychology.

Dan Gilhooley is a psychoanalyst, artist and teacher. He has published papers on therapeutic process, dreams, and creativity, and is a practicing visual artist. He is a training analyst, supervisor and teacher at the New York Graduate School of Psychoanalysis and the Center for Modern Psychoanalytic Studies, with a private practice in Manhattan and Bellport, New York.

Frank Toich is a writer living in Woodstock, New York. He is the author of *The Journey West* and is currently working on a second novel entitled *The Way of Change*. He is also a composer of transcendental and house music which he's recorded with the musical group, Shining Path.

Art, Creativity, and Psychoanalysis Book Series
George Hagman, LSCW
Series Editor

The *Art, Creativity, and Psychoanalysis* book series seeks to highlight original, cutting edge studies of the relationship between psychoanalysis and the world of art and the psychology of artists, with subject matter including the psychobiography of artists, the creative process, the psychology of aesthetic experience, as well as the aesthetic, creative and artistic aspects of psychoanalysis and psychoanalytic psychotherapy. *Art, Creativity, and Psychoanalysis* promotes a vision of psychoanalysis as a creative art, the clinical effectiveness of which can be enhanced when we better understand and utilize artistic and creative processes at its core.

The series welcomes proposals from psychoanalytic therapists from all professional groups and theoretical models, as well as artists, art historians and art critics informed by a psychoanalytic perspective.

For a full list of all titles in the series, please visit the Routledge website at: https://www.routledge.com/ACAPBS.

Psychoanalysis, Intersubjective Writing, and a Postmaterialist Model of Mind

I Woke Up Dead

Dan Gilhooley and Frank Toich

Routledge
Taylor & Francis Group

LONDON AND NEW YORK

First published 2020
by Routledge
2 Park Square, Milton Park, Abingdon, Oxon OX14 4RN

and by Routledge
52 Vanderbilt Avenue, New York, NY 10017

Routledge is an imprint of the Taylor & Francis Group, an informa business

British Library Cataloguing-in-Publication Data
A catalogue record for this book is available from the British Library

Library of Congress Cataloging-in-Publication Data
A catalog record has been requested for this book

ISBN: 978-0-367-33533-5 (hbk)
ISBN: 978-0-367-33535-9 (pbk)
ISBN: 978-0-429-32044-6 (ebk)

Typeset in Times New Roman
by Swales & Willis Ltd, Exeter, Devon, UK

Contents

Acknowledgments

Dan Gilhooley

I'm thankful for George Hagman's support of my work first in his book, *Art, Creativity and Psychoanalysis: Perspectives of Analyst-Artists*, and then for his endorsement of *Psychoanalysis, intersubjective writing, and a postmaterialist model of mind* for the Art, Creativity and Psychoanalysis Book Series he edits for Routledge. Thank you, George, for supporting this creative project undertaken by Frank and me. At Routledge I thank the publisher Kate Hawes, and editors Charles Bath, Heather Evans, Martin Pettitt and Adam Bell for their interest in our work and their patient and skillful guidance.

I thank Faye Newsome, editor of *Modern Psychoanalysis*, for her permission to publish my chapter, "I woke up dead." An earlier version of this essay was published as "The third" in *Modern Psychoanalysis*.

I'm indebted to my first psychoanalyst, Howard Boskey MD, who had a formative and lasting influence on me. My love for psychoanalysis originates with him. Though he might disagree with parts of this book, he was committed to helping me become the person I needed to be. I dedicate this work to him in deep appreciation for everything he gave me.

I've appreciated the friendship and support of my colleagues at the Center for Modern Psychoanalytic Studies and the New York Graduate School for Psychoanalysis which has been my home, as a student and teacher, for the past thirty years. Phyllis Meadow, Theodore Laquercia, Lucy Holmes, Lynne Laub and Mimi Crowell have memorably contributed to my psychoanalytic development. I'd like to thank our librarian, Laura Covino, for her tireless efforts supporting our research. I've appreciated working with students at CMPS and NYGSP, many of whom contributed to the ideas appearing in this book. Finally, I'm indebted to my patients who are my first teachers.

I'm grateful to the following readers of this work whose questions, suggestions and support were helpful in shaping our final product: Joan Lippincott, Robert Marshall, William Hurst, and Fredrika Stjarne. If Joan Lippincott and Bob Marshall had not originally encouraged me to document these experiences, this book would never have been written.

I'd like to thank members of the Studio Study Group for their ongoing engagement with the ideas discussed in this book. This group has included Barbara Goldberg, Jennie Colbert, David Waxman, Margo Goodman, Raul Plasencia, Tony Geralis, Lois Paley, and Cathie Guiffre. This group provided us with a nurturing and illuminating environment.

Thanks to Michele Fitzpatrick, Melissa Costanza Sallah, Carlita Field-Hernandez and Emily Finch, my students at Suffolk County Community College who appear in this book. Thank you for allowing me to include our classroom experiences in this story. I've appreciated the support of my faculty colleagues, Jim Byrne, Tom O'Brien and Matthew Gehring who've each read and responded to portions of this book.

I'm grateful to have had the support of my family throughout this creative process. I appreciate the continuing love of my sister, Georgia, with whom I shared a traumatic childhood. My wife, Pat, and our children Nonnie, Zach and Cameron are depicted in the book, as is our grandson, Yirdaw. I've benefited from endless discussions of the ideas in the book with Cameron who has significantly affected my thinking. I'm thankful, too, for the loving support of our granddaughters, Jocelyn and Zoe, and our son-in-law Michael Rivera.

Finally, I'm indebted to Frank. This book couldn't be the product of one mind. Knowledge is created intersubjectively. It took two of us and *Nous* to the make this book. Thank you, Frank, for proving this to me.

Frank Toich

Out of a great chasm I would come each week to a small office on the lower east side of New York and spend fifty minutes with Dan Gilhooley. Each week fifty minutes, fifty minutes that changed my life. He is the doctor and I am the patient. Neither of us had a clue as to the enormity of the transformational process that was going to take place over the next few years. There, in that office, I began to reveal to Dan short pieces of an allegorical tale that was to become my novel, *The journey west*. After a few years he too revealed a work about my work, our relationship and some extraordinary philosophical musings. Thus, doctor and patient became one. I'm still sending vignettes and he still receives them with as much enthusiasm as that first day. I will forever be indebted to his kind, patient and loving spirit.

I thank members of the Studio Study Group for being my first audience and for being so supportive and not minding becoming characters in new vignettes: Barbara Goldberg, Jennie Colbert, David Waxman, Margo Goodman, Raul Plasencia, Tony Geralis, Lois Paley and Cathie Guiffre. Barbara, while sharing coffee and a light-filled morning overlooking Long Island Sound, you made me believe my allegories weren't just personal. Thanks.

Even before I was made aware of him and his theories, Hugh Everett's Many Worlds interpretation of quantum mechanics fueled much of my writing imagination. So, at least in one world, Hugh and I were acquainted. Thanks, Hugh.

It all starts with my son, Anders Larson-Toich. There isn't enough space to list what a remarkable human he was. All I will say is that he showed me the true meaning of the word courage. Journey well my son, journey well.

Less than a year has passed since my beloved wife succumbed to cancer, Signe S. Larson, a constant, my gravity, my love. She filled my life with enormously powerful yin energy. My being has been diminished by her passing. A brilliant doctor of pediatrics, a talented violist, a caring mother and a loving wife. Give Anders a kiss for me, my love.

Contributors

Dan Gilhooley is a psychoanalyst, artist and teacher. Born in 1950 in Racine, Wisconsin, he graduated with an MA in Fine Art from Hunter College. Receiving his psychoanalytic training at the Center for Modern Psychoanalytic Studies, Gilhooley earned master's and doctoral degrees in psychoanalysis from the Boston Graduate School of Psychoanalysis. In 2007 he was a research fellow in the Yale Psychoanalytic Research Training Program. Gilhooley has published papers focusing on the therapeutic process. He practices in Manhattan and in Bellport, New York.

Gilhooley has exhibited nationally as a visual artist for the past forty years. He was elected to the National Academy of Design, and he has received a Gradiva Award for Art Contributing to an Understanding of Psychoanalysis. He has been a dean and professor of visual art at Suffolk County Community College on Long Island for thirty-seven years. He is a training analyst, supervisor and teacher at the New York Graduate School of Psychoanalysis.

Frank Toich was born in 1950 in Astoria, New York, one of two children, to Frank and Valia Toich. He spent his formative years in a modest two-family house, the ground floor occupied by his grandparents. The light was bright; the food was exceptional; there was love everywhere. He had no idea what was waiting for him.

Attending a small private college, he majored in mathematics and minored in philosophy. All in all, he managed to survive a world of flower power, lending his talents to projects funded by the government. Bored with it all, he was shocked to meet a medical student, Signe Larson, who became the love of his life for the next forty years.

During the intervening years, they had a wonderful and talented son, Anders. He ran marathons and found solace in playing ice hockey and forming lifelong bonds. When his son was taken at age twenty-three, Signe was his rock. A supremely wonderful doctor and loving wife, they created the Anders Larson-Toich Foundation to help young artists. They would continue on together offering each other mutual love and support.

A year after Anders' passing, Signe was diagnosed with breast cancer. She fought valiantly and long but in the end the war was lost. Now he will stumble on picking up their banner and charging into impossible odds.

Introduction

Psychoanalysis, intersubjective writing, and a postmaterialist model of mind is an in-depth look at a patient's unconscious experience through a close reading of a free-associative document—a novel written by the patient—that became the focus of treatment. The book is unique in two ways: Firstly, it is a collaborative effort of the patient and analyst, an alliance that grew naturally out of the patient's creative writing. It is rare in the history of psychoanalytic case studies for a patient and analyst to participate as partners. Second, the book re-contextualizes both the history and future of psychoanalysis. It shows how psychoanalysis was Freud's rebranding and positivist reduction of Mesmerism. Although psychoanalysis was created in the context of materialism, the future of analysis lies in a postmaterialist conception of nonlocal consciousness (Baruss & Mossbridge, 2017) born out of quantum physics. Psychoanalysis is a misfit within materialism. Psychoanalysis' main tenant, mind transforming the body, is impossible in the materialist paradigm. Using the patient's creative writing and our intersubjective therapeutic relationship as evidence, *Psychoanalysis, intersubjective writing, and a postmaterialist model of mind* describes how psychoanalysis fits within a postmaterialist model of mind.

Here's an overview of the book. The patient, Frank's, twenty-three-year-old son dies of cancer. A month later Frank and his analyst, Dan, both dream of "waking up dead." Frank declares this mutual dream is a turning point and starts writing a dreamy noir detective novel, *The journey west*. The novel is set in a timeless space in which the protagonist, having woken up dead, struggles to find eternal life. Frank's character slips through space and time. He is a nineteenth-century silk merchant in India, a turn of the century detective in New York City, a Spirit Boxer fighting in the Chinese Boxer Rebellion, a marine at the Battle of Guadalcanal, and a Nazi murdering Polish Jews in the Warsaw ghetto.

Frank's novel weaves religious and philosophical conceptions from the ancient world with concepts from contemporary quantum physics. Parallel universes, quantum entanglement, and time reversal mix with ancient religious themes of Eternal Recurrence and Pre-Socratic Greek philosophy. Frank's fiction questions the nature of reality, knowledge, and the role of the divine in life. In despair, his creative work reaches across the history of thought and belief as he tries to understand how to live with the death of his son.

Psychoanalysis, intersubjective writing, and a postmaterialist model of mind contains an arresting cast of characters. Frank's fiction features a hardboiled detective and his old college friend, Friedrich Nietzsche; a Freudian analyst whose insane patient repeatedly hurls him out the window to his death; an ancient Chinese magician who is actually God; and a one-eyed ex-CIA assassin guided by angels. Frank's fictional characters mix with a collection of Pre-Socratic philosophers like Pythagoras, Parmenides, Zeno, Anaxagoras, and the hardnosed Heraclitus. Who knew, for example, that Pythagoras possessed a detailed memory of four previous lives, made frequent trips to the underworld, was capable of bilocation and worked for the divine? Telling the history of psychotherapy and the development of quantum physics puts the reader in contact with historical figures like Mesmer, Puysegur, Charcot, Janet, Breuer, Freud and Jung; patients like Victor Race, Friedericke Hauffe and Anna O.; along with scientists Newton, Einstein, Schrodinger, Everett, Wheeler and Godel.

Although Frank had no knowledge of his analyst's life, his writing depicted several significant events from Dan's personal history. These become the basis for examining the intersubjective nature of their psychoanalytic work and provide a clinical example of a transpersonal model of mind. As Frank wrote his novel it became clear he had unconscious access to Dan's thoughts and memories. For example, when Frank and Dan have parallel dreams of "waking up dead" they both begin writing. Although it will be years before he'll learn of Dan's writing, Frank's stories repeatedly have twin authors writing the same text. Then Frank writes about a life-threatening experience two months before Dan has it. Following an intense period of Dan ruminating over two premonitory experiences, Frank writes about successive premonitions. Frank writes of a boy raised by a shell-shocked war veteran whose unrelenting memory of combat disables him and contributes to his suicide. This was Dan's story growing up with his father who suffered a traumatic brain injury in WWII, and who committed suicide. Frank writes about a psychoanalyst placing a pistol to his head and killing himself. This was the reason why, as a young man, Dan entered analysis. He believed it was inevitable his life would end as his father's had. Because Frank had no conscious awareness of Dan's personal history, Dan regarded the many parallels between his life and Frank's writing to be examples of unconscious thought transference.

Psychoanalysis, intersubjective writing, and a postmaterialist model of mind examines rapport and thought transference in psychological therapies during the past two centuries. Telepathy was a common feature of Mesmerism and the hypnotic tradition that emerged from it. Freud believed in telepathy but couldn't integrate it into a psychoanalysis rooted in mechanistic materialism. Since 1950, with its focus on countertransference and the Kleinian concept of projective identification, thought transference has become a staple of contemporary psychoanalysis (Brottman, 2011). Nonetheless, telepathy can't be explained within a materialist model of reality. So, historically these experiences have been culturally suppressed only to continuously reappear. Today thought transference is recognized as a feature of a postmaterialist model of nonlocal consciousness. Within this new paradigm, mind is dominant, and matter derives from mind. The conflict between materialism and nonlocal consciousness is a contemporary iteration of the philosophical tension between materialism and idealism which is encountered throughout the book.

In a model of reality where consciousness is primary, mind affects matter. In fact, psychoanalysis was born out of the idea that mind transforms the body. Mesmer was ridiculed for curing patients' physical ailments by imagination. Charcot demonstrated ideas created paralysis, and Anna O. showed that talking eliminated paralysis. Mental actions modified physical states. Mesmer and Charcot were professionally disgraced for their public demonstrations proving their assertions. Why? Science was frightened by the mind, particularly the unconscious, and suppressed evidence of its power. Within the materialist conception of reality there are only physical causes, so something as immaterial as a thought couldn't affect matter. But in a contemporary model of nonlocal consciousness mind *creates* matter. In this new paradigm, imagination stimulates human growth and produces therapeutic change. Imagination and belief transform life.

Psychoanalysis, intersubjective writing, and a postmaterialist model of mind is written in the genre of creative nonfiction. This book attempts to describe reality in an imaginative, personally expressive, and collaborative way. In fact, the authors propose this form of writing is closer to the nature of psychoanalytic inquiry, and the development of psychoanalytic knowledge about the unconscious mind, than the medico-scientific style of thinking and writing that has dominated the field of psychoanalysis for the past century. Indeed, analyst Mikita Brottman (2011) proposes the scientistic style of psychoanalytic thinking insulates analysts from their fears of unconscious irrationality, implicitly affecting how they think. Our form of presentation will be creative and unsystematic. We'll study the irrational realities of psychoanalytic experience. We hope to convey the experience of doing psychoanalysis, so the reader can integrate information as patients and analysts do.

In psychoanalysis there aren't any facts, there are only descriptions of human experience. So, psychoanalysis is a collection of stories and these stories are inescapably subjective. Therefore, we employ the personal essay or short story as our form of psychoanalytic discourse. Of course, this isn't an original idea. We are inspired by Therese Ragen's (2009) *The consulting room and beyond: Psychoanalytic work and its reverberations in the analyst's life* which is a masterpiece of psychoanalytic writing.

New psychoanalytic knowledge emerges *within* human relationships. That knowledge is intersubjective, appearing in the intersection of human lives. So, recording it requires a description of two or more lives. Therefore, the analyst of this writing couple, Dan, is compelled to write about himself *with* his subject. Because the development of psychoanalytic knowledge is intersubjective, it must be collaborative or be incomplete. The analysand of this writing couple, Frank, employed fiction as his means of describing himself and his therapeutic experience. Frank's writing was a creative form of sustained free association. Our book tries to weave together both voices to tell an intersubjective psychoanalytic tale. In the Collaboration section of this book we ask, "When has the patient ever had a voice? How would the history of psychoanalysis have differed if Anna O. had been an active participant in authoring her case history?" The creation of this book has been a five-year experiment answering that question.

New psychoanalytic knowledge springs spontaneously from our unconscious mind and sometimes it takes extraordinary telepathic and precognitive forms (Mayer, 2007; Simmonds-Moore, 2012). It always arrives unexpectedly and involuntarily. Because it's the product of intuition, and not the result of logical deliberation, its origin is irrational and inexplicable. It is surprising, unexpected, and sometimes unwanted. It can be frightening, reassuring or inspiring. Psychoanalytic knowledge occurs in the shower, in a dream or when you're half asleep. Often it appears when you're doing something else. It doesn't necessarily occur in the consultation room. Doing psychoanalysis, as a practice of mind, is unbound by space and time. So, we write stories depicting psychoanalytic knowledge where it arises: in a dream or in a classroom, walking in the woods, driving to the train or sitting in a queue of traffic. This knowledge often emerges from the unconscious appearing first in imaginative activity, only to be followed by conscious, reflective thought. We'll employ that format—unconsciously fueled imaginative action followed by conscious reflection—repeatedly throughout the book.

Finally, psychoanalytic knowledge arises episodically, and revelation occurs in identifying and connecting these experiences. Therefore, the first two sections of the book are organized as collections of stories which are associatively, but not systematically, connected. Knowledge doesn't unfold in a systematic way. Rather, we create meaning by linking associated experiences. Readers can learn about the unconscious by making connections among our stories. We believe this is a *realistic* representation of psychoanalytic experience.

This book is divided into four parts: Intersubjective, Quantum, History and Collaboration. Part I, Intersubjective, contains seven chapters introducing three themes: recovery from death, the intersubjective nature of therapeutic work and the role of creative imagination in therapeutic change. Four chapters summarizing and analyzing Frank's fiction combine with three short stories describing related experiences in Dan's world. Together they provide a basis for examining the intersubjective nature of analytic work.

Here's an important example of that intersubjectivity. Uncannily, Frank's novel appears to incorporate several events from Dan's life. In the most surprising of these depictions, Frank seems to write about an automobile accident two months before Dan experiences it. On that occasion Dan, a college professor, had a premonition of a flat tire twenty minutes before nearly killing a man changing the left rear tire of his car on a road with no shoulder in twilight. This premonition associated with a life-threatening event had a profound effect, altering Dan's conception of himself in space and time. Meanwhile, Frank's novel describes a college professor, who authored a paper proposing a dramatic re-conception of our place in space and time, accidentally killing a man changing the left rear tire of his car on a road with no shoulder in twilight.

Dan can't dismiss the striking similarity of these two events as coincidental. Frank's story appears to be a premonition of Dan's premonitory experience. Dan asks, "What conditions would have to exist for Frank to be able to write about an experience in my life two months before I have it?" Trying to solve the mystery of this strange intersubjective event fuels the research in the next two sections: Quantum and History.

Quantum investigates three aspects of quantum physics drawn from Frank's science fiction: parallel universes, quantum entanglement, the nature of time and time reversal. These scientifically oriented chapters combine with a personal essay and two short stories depicting related events happening concurrently in Dan's life outside the consultation room. Dan's stories deal with the subjects of premonition, Jung's concept of synchronicity, and believing one is alive and dead simultaneously.

The Quantum section introduces the concept of nonlocality to describe the mind. While consciousness seems rooted in locality and is bound by the arrow of time, the unconscious mind appears to be nonlocal, existing in multiple spaces/times simultaneously. While consciousness adopts the scientific metaphor of materialism as its explanatory model, the unconscious is better explained by the metaphor of quantum entanglement. Quantum physics proves materialism is false and insists on a form of philosophical idealism as a truer model of reality. Finally, this section introduces a way to think scientifically about mind/matter interactions.

Part III, History, describes the central role of thought transference, *rapport* and intersubjectivity in psychologically based therapies during the past two-hundred-fifty years. By the end of the nineteenth century, the somatic cures produced by Mesmer's *rapport* were believed to be caused by an intersubjective state: the *mutual* hypnosis of patient and practitioner (Hudson, 1893). In a mutually altered state of consciousness, physical conditions in the patient's body were changed. While Freud believed in telepathy, he was personally uncomfortable with the contaminating nature of *rapport*, so he took steps to eliminate it from his practice. But, like previous attempts to suppress thought transference, Freud was incapable of eliminating it from psychoanalysis.

Since 1950, thought transference in the guise of "projective identification" has again become the basis of intersubjective treatment (Brottman, 2011). Transpersonal states of mind evident in thought transference are an attribute of a nonlocal unconscious. Thought transferential experiences can be frightening because of the inherent loss of personal identity. These dissociative experiences cause us to realize the unconscious mind is filled with voices which we mistake as our own. People regrettably connect these momentary losses of identity with insanity, stimulating the universal fear of the unconscious mind. This is a reoccurring theme in the book. It is the basis for the perpetual suppression of exceptional experiences.

The final section, Collaboration, describes how Frank and Dan came to collaborate in writing this book. By the conclusion of Frank's novel his main protagonist, Nigel, and his twin Raymond, have joined "to meet their fate as one." Their fictional relationship serves as a model for Dan, guiding his therapeutic and literary collaboration with Frank. This unique collaboration is based on the inspirational work of psychoanalytic researcher, Robert Stoller (1988). For the past five years their collaboration has been an ongoing psychotherapeutic experiment. This section addresses how Frank's therapy was affected by working together on this project. The reality of publishing their collaborative work caused Frank and Dan to reconfigure their therapeutic relationship to include life outside the consultation room. As part of this process, Frank has participated with five other therapists in Dan's ongoing psychoanalytic group studying imagination and therapeutic change.

Finally, we should mention another unusual feature of this book. Although the book will be told in Dan's voice, three of Frank's fictional characters spontaneously provide commentary in the Quantum, History and Collaboration portions of the book. The most prominent of these characters is Max Besessen, a sensitive and painfully introverted architect whom Frank describes as "obsessional and emotionally unstable." Max is an enthusiastic if unruly reader of our book. Sometimes he can't help interjecting his opinions, particularly when he disagrees. Occasionally his assessments are regrettably harsh. A couple of times, he wrestles with the narrator for control of the text. This might be distracting for the reader, for which we apologize in advance. Nonetheless, overall, we believe Max's unusual insights make a valuable contribution to our tale. We hope readers will agree.

Dan Gilhooley and Frank Toich

References

Baruss, I., & Mossbridge, J. (2017). *Transcendent mind: Rethinking the science of consciousness.* Washington, DC: American Psychological Association.

Brottman, M. (2011). *Phantoms of the clinic: From thought-transference to projective identification.* London: Karnac.

Hudson, T. (1893). *The law of psychic phenomena: A working hypothesis for the systematic study of hypnotism, spiritism, mental therapeutics, etc.* Chicago, IL: A.C. McClurg.

Mayer, E. (2007). *Extraordinary knowing: Science, skepticism, and the inexplicable powers of the human mind.* New York, NY: Bantam Books.

Ragen, T. (2009). *The consulting room and beyond: Psychoanalytic work and its reverberations in the analyst's life.* London: Routledge.

Simmonds-Moore, C. (Ed.). (2012). *Exceptional experience and health: Essays on mind, body and human survival.* Jefferson, NC: McFarland & Company.

Stoller, R. (1988). Patients' responses to their own case reports. *Journal of the American Psychoanalytic Association, 36,* 371–391.

Part I

Intersubjective

I woke up dead

Ben and I worked together for several years and developed a close connection. Then he was hurt by something I said. Ben turned hateful and today I felt threatened by his anger. I need better defenses. I'm struggling to regulate his destructiveness. Ben and I are in a bad place.

My next hour is with Frank. "I miss him so much," he said of Anders, his twenty-three-year-old son who'd died of cancer last year. Frank consulted me four years ago to get help for Anders who was depressed. Frank believed if Anders was less depressed, he could fight his cancer more effectively. Anders didn't want to speak to a therapist, so I never met him. But Frank stayed to talk about the despair and anger associated with his son's illness.

Anders had been fighting a cancer first discovered as a lump beneath the surface of his cheek when he was sixteen. He'd had ten surgeries and a nearly continuous stream of chemotherapy. He lost his eye and the facial nerve on the right side of his face. For most of the last year, his face was disfigured by a large tumor. Anders suffered intensely, and so did Frank. During some periods Anders showed improvement, but nothing could stop the cancer which always returned, eventually spread to his brain and killed him.

Frank said he'd always been an angry guy, but Anders' illness threw him into rages of terrifying proportions. He'd collide with a shopper in a supermarket and shove him into a rack of potato chips. He'd be bumped by someone on the street talking on a cell phone and he'd explode. He'd get into an argument over a cab and nearly end up in a fistfight. He was bitter to be losing his son. While his son's friends grew into adulthood, Frank watched Anders' broken body stagger from toilet to bed. When the cancer reached his brain, Anders began to have seizures causing him to sprawl convulsively on the floor. These seizures were proof that Anders' condition was out of control. In the final months when he was home alone caring for Anders, he dreaded the possibility of a seizure.

During that last year of his son's life Frank talked often about killing himself. He wanted to buy a gun and blow his brains out. The realization he was losing his son was unbearable. After Anders' death, Frank's suicidal wishes intensified. Having endured six years of suffering he wanted to put an end to the pain and join his son in death. Frank picked out a shotgun and studied it online. I told Frank he couldn't have a gun. He once went into a store and placed his hand on a rifle stock and left quickly out of fear. Another time as he was driving home, he began turning into the parking lot of a gun shop, only to veer back onto the highway. When he told me this he said, "I think Anders and you took control of the steering wheel and pushed me back out onto the highway, away from danger." Frank knew his son wanted him to stay alive. On the last day of his life Anders made Frank promise he'd recover and grow strong again.

Saying his son and I both took control of the steering wheel made me realize Frank identified me with the son who wanted to keep his father alive. Frank was not aware my father had shot himself in the head when I was fifteen. I knew the pain of a boy losing his father, and Frank was experiencing the pain of a father losing his son. I certainly knew suicide inside out. I knew what it was like to keep a gun out of the hands of a killer. As a boy, I'd taken a rifle from my father, unloaded and hidden it when he threatened to kill my mother, sister and me. I wondered about the coincidence of Frank ending up with me as a therapist. He said,

I don't think I'd kill myself with a gun. In fact, I don't think I'd kill myself because then I'd never see Anders again. That's my belief. What worries me is an accident, stepping off a curb into a bus, the sort of thing my unconscious might do before I can see it coming.

Like the altercations he got himself into with strangers. Frank reported an interchange with a junkie in a small shop in Chinatown. Though of European descent, Frank feels a strong affinity with Chinese culture. He suspects he was Chinese in a previous life. Early one Saturday morning, just as the shop was opened by a pair of young Chinese girls who spoke little English, Frank arrived to make a purchase. While he was there a young man came in and asked to use the restroom. In a state of incomprehension, the girls said, "No." The man persisted. The girls resisted.

Frank intervened, "Listen, they've told you 'no' several times. The answer is 'no.' I think you should leave."

"What business is it of yours?" the young man responded belligerently.

"I'm making it my business. I think you should get the fuck out of here," Frank said. The junkie responded in kind. Frank stepped closer to the young man. Standing toe-to-toe, about a foot apart, Frank slowly raised his right arm. Staring into the junkie's eyes he said dispassionately, "This, my friend, is the right hand of death. If you don't leave it's going to cut your fuckin head off." The junkie stepped back incredulous.

"What are you talking about? What's going to cut my head off?"

"This hand, and the sword hanging at my side." The junkie looked at Frank's torso; obviously there was no sword.

"Sword? What sword? You're crazy, old man," the junkie said and walked out.

"That's right," Frank said smiling, trailing him out the door, "And if I ever see you in this store again, I'm going to kill you."

Telling me this story, Frank was pleased his craziness had propelled the man out the door. I thought Frank was trying to provoke someone to kill him. I pointed this out to him. This was another way his unconscious was pushing him toward death. Sometimes Frank wanted someone to put him out of his misery.

I needed to protect Frank. I'd failed to protect my father. I hadn't seen it coming then. This time I saw it coming. I had a real understanding of what Frank's suicide would do to his family, and to me. I was surprised to find I had a strong desire to redeem myself. If I could drag Frank away from death's door, I'd pay for the father I'd lost through inattention. I found myself driven by forty-year-old feelings of guilt I'd forgotten I possessed, and a primitive talion principle of a life-for-a-life. I began to realize I depended on Frank for this opportunity for redemption.

Around this time, it also occurred to me that I was living inside a corpse. It's not that I felt dead. In fact, just the opposite. I felt energetic and alive. But I began to feel I was moving within this husk, a dead invisible hulk that seemed to envelop me, its material substance (the grainy texture of its walls) just out of sight. It felt like I was inside an organic version of the Nautilus, a small submarine from 1800. It didn't weigh me down. But it subtly constrained me, keeping me submerged. At first, I thought this corpse fantasy was a representation of my father, and that I was living continuously within his dead body. Then I wondered if this corpse was Anders. Maybe a husk of death enveloped both Frank and me.

I worried a lot about Frank. In the period following Anders' death he'd often be late or not show for his appointments. This frightened me. When he missed an appointment, I'd call each of his phone numbers and leave a message at one of them. If he hadn't called back in a few hours, I'd call again. Or, I'd wait until the next day and then I'd call. I felt uncomfortable about making these second calls. On the one hand, Frank was teetering at the edge of life, and I felt I had to "go get him." But I also believed these second calls revealed an urgent redemptive need to save him. I was ashamed of this shadow peeking out from my past outlining the shape of my own loss and guilt. I tried to avert my eyes from it. I certainly didn't want Frank to see this painful reflection of me. One morning Frank didn't show up for his appointment, and I called and left a message on his phone. Not hearing back from him, at three that afternoon I called his cell phone. He answered.

"What happened this morning?" I asked.

"Oh, hi. Oh, ah, I forgot. I forgot what day it was."

"Where are you now?"

"Where am I? I don't know. I'm in a bookstore looking at rows of books. I've just been wandering. I don't know where I am." He sounded out of breath, in a fog. "I had a presentation at work. I got out at one and never went back. I've just been wandering around since then. I don't know where I am." It sounded like he was looking around trying to get his bearings. He paused. "Look, I don't think I can do this. I can't talk about this. It's just too painful."

"I know it's too painful, but I think talking is the only thing that's going to get you through this," I said. But I wondered if he was right. Maybe he was better off not talking.

"I don't know. I don't know. I guess you're probably right. It's just so unbearable. It's unbearable to talk about." Frank took a deep breath and then was silent. "Ah, okay, I'll see you next Friday," he said, and as an aside before signing off, "Thanks for calling."

Frank couldn't bear talking, yet his actions made me feel as isolated, lost, disoriented and frightened as he was. We were completely adrift with no shore in sight. I was angry with Frank for filling me with feelings of desperation, for his part in spilling out this shadow from my past and forcing me to see this humiliating shape of myself. I knew Frank must be angry at me for the same thing, for forcing him to experience feelings of loss and despair in my presence, and to be confronted by this pathetic image of himself.

I was angry Frank wasn't doing therapy the way I prescribed; not following what I knew in my heart would be a path toward life. He was doing it his way. But his way had me believing there was no path, no way out. Frank filled me with feelings without showing up or saying a word. His method of communication was exquisitely efficient. Perhaps these enactments were a better way for him to do therapy. But I was having a difficult time with it. At some point during his next session when the topic of last week's absence came up, I said, "Look, this is impossible. I can't stand this. You come in here and tell me you're worried about your unconscious pushing you into an oncoming bus. . ."

"And then I don't show up for my appointment," Frank completed my sentence with a smile.

"How do you expect me to react?" I said.

Frank responded, "No, you're right."

"And you're smiling about it," I said with frustration.

"I see what you mean. I think it's kind of funny. It's not funny, of course, the position I put you in. It's not right," he said.

"That's right, it's not right." It wasn't right according to me. The pleasure he seemed to take in my discomfort wasn't right. But to Frank, it seemed just right.

The next week Frank reported a dream he'd had in which he opened the front door of his country home one Saturday morning and found me there having arrived as a weekend guest. Frank pointed out it was the reverse of a well-known movie in which a patient followed his analyst on vacation. In this case, the analyst was following the patient. We laughed about it together. But the image left me feeling humiliated.

"Do you make house calls?" Frank asked. "I could introduce you to my friends as my live-in analyst, always on call."

"I do seem to be chasing you down with those phone calls."

"No, that's good. You're keeping an eye on me. That's what I need you to do. I'm so out of it sometimes." Frank thought of me as someone looking out for him, ever present. I was comforted by the image in the dream of Frank bringing me into his home. But I was embarrassed by that picture of me standing at Frank's doorstep. I'd become the dependent therapist clinging to his patient. I couldn't let him go. It was too dangerous to let him go.

Frank's dream conveyed that he was unconsciously aware of my dependency on him, and I think he was aware of my discomfort and humiliation about it. It also occurred to me that Frank helped create these feelings between us because he felt uncomfortably dependent on me and humiliated to be seen in his desperately weakened state. To be seen by me as incapacitated, not knowing which way to turn, was humiliating. Frank seemed to find relief in knowing that I was uncomfortably dependent on him, and that I felt humiliated and powerless. Frank needed this symmetry. This fundamental sameness was becoming the foundation of our relationship: what psychoanalyst Hyman Spotnitz (1985) called a narcissistic transference, or what Harold Searles (1979) described as a therapeutic symbiosis. Frank and I were clinging to each other, uncomfortable in our mutual dependency, pulled together by a magnetism of loss.

A couple of weeks later I had a dream in which I woke up dead. In fact, those words, "I woke up dead," echoed in my mind announcing the beginning of the dream. I hovered above my body lying motionless in bed. I circled it, checking for signs of life. Was I breathing? I reached out to lift my hand, to prod myself in order to rouse me. My body lay there unresponsive under a white sheet. I concluded I really was dead. For being dead, I felt fine, literally care-free. I seemed to move about effortlessly. It was easy being dead, and I was surprised that I wasn't a bit upset about my death. I guessed it must have happened in my sleep.

I woke from the dream and sat up, swinging my legs over the side of the bed. I thought, "I really am dead in the mind of Ben." Weeks earlier, in a fit of anger, Ben had dramatically ended treatment. "Why do I have such difficulty accepting the reality of my death in his mind?" I wondered. "I'm dead in this case. Get it, I'm dead. It's the part I play," I told myself as I got up.

But Ben's leaving wasn't a painless death like I experienced in my dream. In Ben's case I felt dismal. His leaving felt like a life sentence as a failure. "That's part of the transference," I thought as I trudged downstairs to make some coffee.

Later that day I discussed the dream in analysis and struggled with the emotional injury of losing Ben. At the end of the week during his session Frank again described his despair at the loss of his son. "He's in my thoughts all the time," he said weeping. Near the end of the session Frank said, "I had a strange dream this week. I dreamt I woke up dead."

I came to life. Frank explained this was a turning point, a signal from his dead son Anders who, having achieved angelic status, was now guiding Frank's mourning. Frank said, "I think it means a kind of transition, a moving on. I think Anders is showing me the way." His dream was about life after death. Frank felt his son had transcended the cycle of mortal pain and had moved on to heaven. Anders' role now, Frank said, was to help him recover from his son's death.

"When did you have this dream?" I asked.

"It was the beginning of the week, Monday or Tuesday," he said. "Why do you ask?"

"Monday night, I dreamt that I woke up dead," I told him. Frank glanced over at me out of the corner of his eye.

"Really?" he said.

"Really," I responded. "I've never had a dream like that." Frank looked at me with disbelief, perhaps suspicion. I thought he didn't really believe me. Or, he didn't know what to make of this.

"I suppose that's possible, that you're just connected up with all this," he said. "It makes sense."

It didn't make any sense to me. How could I have had such a parallel dream? Where did it come from? Why now? But by concluding, "It makes sense," Frank appeared to arrest further exploration. We didn't say another word about it. The revelation about my dream seemed to upset him. It interrupted and confused him. So, I never described my dream to him, and he never discussed his dream with me. Instead, Frank focused on the meaning his dream had for him, how it was a message from his son.

Frank was right. This dream was a turning point. Frank began writing a story about life after death that begins with the protagonist, Nigel, announcing, "I woke up dead," the very phrase that heralded the beginning of my dream. The story, which he entitled "So long," is a dreamlike noir detective tale set in a timeless space between life and death, in which Nigel tries to find the path to eternal life. Every week Frank wrote more of the story and read segments to me. The story was a relief from the painful realities of mourning. Each week a portion of the session would be spent with the story. Frank would describe the plot unfolding. He literally was making it up as we went along. I was surprised by his lively and inventive ideas.

Frank's protagonist, Nigel, is in pursuit of Dr. Mekes. Nigel hopes Mekes can clarify an arcane question about the Egyptian *Book of the dead*. Mekes works as an assistant to a Chinese magician named Ching Ling Foo who is really God. Together Mekes and Foo create the holographic experiences we each call life. Nigel believes they hold the key to eternal life. Nigel never meets Mekes, but deals repeatedly with Mekes' associates Khu, Ba, Ka, and Ren, each a name for a different part of the human soul in Egyptian mythology.

Mekes appears to be modeled after the ancient Greek philosopher Pythagoras who traveled to Egypt and the Near East, studied the Egyptian *Book of the dead*, and appropriated Egyptian religious beliefs on the transmigration of the soul (Huffman, 2014). Part philosopher, scientist and shaman, Pythagoras dedicated his life to the service of the divine, making frequent trips into the land of the dead. Recalling Frank's educational grounding in mathematics, he seemed to be placing Western culture's original mathematician at the center of his story.

As Frank read portions of his story to me each week there were curious surprises. For example, one of the main characters was a German architect named Max who went progressively mad contemplating one of Zeno's paradoxes. Max's growing realization that no two lines could ever converge meant the architectural forms he created (his entire life's work) were nothing but an illusion. Max came to realize the manmade structures in the world were held together by a mysterious collective unconscious, a kind of adhesive hallucinatory force that was now weakening. Max could see the fissures, the fault lines beginning to form in New York City's buildings. His growing awareness of this weakening adhesive force drove him insane.

For some time, Max had been seeing a Freudian psychoanalyst. They met twice weekly in the doctor's fifth floor, Bauhaus decorated office. Max contended they couldn't be on the fifth floor because the building was an illusion. The doctor formed a diagnosis of Max as obsessional and paranoid. The analyst disagreed with Max's "convergence theorem," and declared the architect's belief in an adhesive mental force holding together the world was a delusion. This interpretation threw the architect into a fit of despair. In retaliation Max hurled the doctor out the office window to prove to him the illusory nature of physical reality. Moments later, standing over the doctor's dead body lying on the pavement five stories below, Max said, "See what I mean. Get up!" Prodding the psychoanalyst's motionless body, he said, "Quit playing dead."

Listening to this I glanced over my shoulder at the office window, "It's lucky I'm on the ground floor."

"Yeah," Frank laughed. "You're safe." I was struck by the image of a man standing above a dead psychoanalyst, trying to rouse him, disbelieving his death. It was just like my dream of waking up dead in which I circled my dead body prodding myself. As the story develops, Max and his psychoanalyst—who, being trapped in a space between life and death, never really dies—share an apartment. They're destined to reenact the same scene of living, dying and resurrection again and again. Weeks later I remembered the phrase I told myself when I awoke from my dream: "I'm dead in this case, get it. It's the part I play," and I realized how perfectly that phrase fit the part of the doctor in Frank's story who dies again and again.

How could I explain Frank and me both dreaming of waking up dead? Did we both really dream the same dream? Or, did one of us telepathically experience the other's dream? As Sigmund Freud (1933) says, "Sleep seems particularly suited for receiving telepathic messages" (p.37). On the other hand, maybe the dream existed independently of each of us. Maybe the dream was dreamt by a third mind to which Frank and I were linked, and therefore the "dream dreamt us." Who knows? It was mysterious, impossible to decipher. Edmund Gurney (1886) and his colleagues Frederic Myers and Frank Podmore describe five mutual dreams, four of which involved death. In ancient Chinese culture a mutual dream was believed to reveal the hidden mysteries of life, often prophesizing the future (Li, 1999). Was there something about being both awake and dead that related to our futures?

Maybe Frank and I dreamt the dream together, *as one mind*. Has some new identity been born through our therapeutic symbiosis, a convergence of shared aspects of our characters bound together by an adhesive hallucinatory force of our collective unconscious? By working together, have we grown some form of shared mental structure, some portion of our minds which is "us" rather than Frank or me?

Thomas Ogden (2004) describes the analyst's and patient's co-creation of a "third" subjective representation in each of their minds which is used for the purpose of psychological growth. Through this newly created "third" both participants are able to experience thoughts, feelings and perceptions previously outside their realm of experience. In Frank's story Max the architect goes mad and then engages his psychoanalyst in a pattern of repetitive symbolic reenactments of death and rebirth. For Max, going crazy appears to be the first step in the therapeutic process. Perhaps the symbiosis that has developed between Frank and me is an encapsulated mutual madness created through telepathically communicated unconscious processes, creating a therapeutic healing space. At times, our two minds appear to be working in unconscious synchrony. Are Frank and I unconsciously writing this story together?

How can I make sense of Max and his analyst in Frank's story, "So long?" I suspect the story represents Frank's unconscious understanding of the therapeutic symbiosis developing between us. At first, Max's obsession with Zeno's paradox appears to be nonsensical, a confusing mixture of two ideas drawn from ancient Greek philosophy. Max seems to confuse the geometer Euclid's postulate that parallel lines never converge with the numerous paradoxes of the philosopher Zeno. To my knowledge, none of Zeno's paradoxes involve parallel lines converging though many involve space, time, and infinity, and all conclude with the suggestion that reality isn't what it appears. Furthermore, the fact that parallel lines never converge does nothing to undermine the integrity of architectural structures. So, what's Max getting upset about?

Yet Max is deeply distressed by the impossibility of convergence. Max's delusion does make sense in terms of the psychological convergence associated with our therapeutic symbiosis. Zeno's paradoxes are believed to have been authored as proofs in support of the Parmenides' notion that "plurality is an illusion," and that really "all is one" (Huggett, 2004). For Max, the integrity of man's structures is threatened by the impossibility of convergence. For Frank, the integrity of his mental structure is threatened by the same impossibility. It appears Frank unconsciously believes that without a therapeutic symbiosis which eliminates plurality and mixes us together as one, the structure of his mind will fracture and disintegrate.

Just as Max believes man's physical structures are held together by a hallucinatory adhesive force of our collective unconscious, the symbiosis that has developed between our minds—this intersubjective third we've created—is bound together by a similar adhesive. This caused me to think again about my fantasy of living within an invisible husk that envelops both Frank and me. I began to wonder whether this container is a three-dimensional representation of the third we've created.

How does this relate to my defenses as an analyst? Everyone shares conflicting desires to be seen and known, and to remain safely hidden (Aron, 1996). Being seen is risky. Bad things can happen if you're seen. But being known and understood brings with it a pleasure unlike anything else in life, so each of us struggles against our most natural fears and takes risks to be seen. But don't underestimate these powerful, deeply rooted fears about being seen. Remember, we've evolved from people who for thousands of years stayed alive by remaining hidden most of the time.

In psychoanalysis, the patient is seen a little bit at a time and slowly becomes known, while the analyst tries to remain hidden. The analyst's technique is primarily a method of hiding, defending against the patient's intrusive vision. This is a good thing as far as it goes, but these defenses probably work only at a conscious level. It's unclear what protection they provide against unconscious processes, and therapeutic treatment involves a deeply unconscious mixture of the unconscious minds of the patient and analyst. Freud (1912) advises the analyst to "turn his own unconscious like a receptive organ toward the transmitting unconscious of the patient," adjusting himself to the patient's transmissions, "so that the doctor's unconscious is able, from the derivatives of the unconscious which are communicated to him," to understand his patient (pp.115–116).

Employing Ogden's model of the third, patients need access to the analyst's unconscious to grow and to heal, and this can only happen if the conscious analyst can sit still (hour after hour) and allow that to happen. But this means analysts have to endure a sustained level of anxiety over being seen, and this may be too much to endure. So, I think analysts' consciously employed technical defenses really serve as a form of "local anesthesia" allowing them to consciously believe they're fully hidden, while their unconscious becomes accessible to the patient. Anonymity appears to be a necessary self-deception fostering the analyst's participation.

What's the role of enactment in developing this therapeutic symbiosis? Frank needed to penetrate my defenses. He needed me to cast out this shadow of myself that was so similar to him. He didn't need to know very much about me, but he needed to know this specific part, and it was important to him that I was consciously defended against giving it up. This was, of course, a mirror image of Frank's position. Frank was just as consciously defended against revealing his painful and shameful parts.

Frank's enactments were natural experiments designed to circumvent my conscious defenses to obtain specific information about me. I think Frank believed knowledge he acquired through actions, where my feelings of redemption, fear, and humiliation were revealed, was truer and more reliable than anything I could have said to him. Importantly, if I hadn't been defended against providing this information, it would have had much less significance for Frank.

Psychoanalysts would say Frank developed a narcissistic transference, but that only tells half the story. Phyllis Meadow (1996) describes a narcissistic transference as the patient's regression to an infantile state of undifferentiation where there is an inability to distinguish self from other. Yet our apparently mutual dream of "waking up dead," and Frank's descriptions in his story so closely paralleling my dream, stretches the conception of narcissistic transference, suggesting that Frank and I have developed a mutual narcissistic transference. Creating this symbiotic state appears to have required the active participation of both of us. Though I was insulated by my consciously manipulated defenses, my unconscious was obviously permeable, perhaps easily accessible during Frank's skillfully crafted enactments. The symbiosis that developed between Frank and me was formed from slivers of sameness drawn from a much larger world of differences that distinguish us as separate people. Frank seemed to have been searching for sameness in areas of vulnerability, and in these spaces Frank and I appear to have achieved a Zeno-like undifferentiated state where "all is one."

From the point of view of the analyst's defenses, it's important to acknowledge that this merger reflects a mutual psychotic transference. More than anything, analysts feel the need to protect themselves from their own and their patient's insanity. This seems to be a mistake. Freud (McGuire, 1974) cautioned Carl Jung about the dangers of countertransference: "It is best to remain reserved and purely receptive; we must never let our poor neurotics drive us crazy" (pp.475–476). Yet, this case suggests that the analyst and patient going partially crazy together is the first step in a curative process. Karen Maroda (1994) writes, "to some extent the analytic therapist must 'go mad' with her patients in order to promote their independence and growth" (p.33).

Naturally, it's frightening to experience and difficult to acknowledge these crazy states. For example, the esteemed psychoanalytic researcher Robert Stoller (Mayer, 2001) wrote a paper describing a number of telepathic dreams that were similar to our dream of waking up dead, though he never submitted the paper for publication out of fear it would damage his career. It is easier to accept this process of mutual madness if we conceive of psychosis as an imaginative movement toward health—as a person's attempt to bring a discordant internal state into the world for potential integration—that should be embraced, rather than seeing psychosis as the end-product of an organic disease that needs to be disavowed, arrested or eliminated.

Finally, why did I initially attribute my "waking up dead" dream to my painful difficulties with Ben? There's a sensible as well as a speculative explanation for this. As things developed, it became apparent that my dream had a lot more to do with Frank than Ben, and that my initial associations to Ben appear to have been a mistake. I think this reflects the significant split between my conscious and unconscious mental states and highlights my defenses. As my conscious mind first looked at my dream, it related its content to my most pronounced emotion at that moment: the painful feeling of having been injured by Ben. Consciously I instantly tried to protect myself by making sense of the dream in a way that would help me cope with this injury. For example, I comforted myself with the thought, "that's part of the transference." Interpreting my dream in this way was like reflexively covering a bruised knee. Later, I realized a deeper and more complex meaning could be made of the dream with Frank.

That's the sensible explanation, now here is a speculative alternative. Although my initial associations connecting my dream to Ben appear mistaken, many aspects of my dream and Frank's subsequent story could also apply to Ben, and these lead to another possible explanation. For example, feeling perpetually trapped in a space between life and death, the image of a figure standing over Ben's body wondering whether he's alive or dead, and the role of "playing dead" are all narratives that make sense in Ben's life. What meaning can be made of this? Are these themes so universal that they apply to all of us? Or, on that Tuesday morning, did Ben *also* have a dream of waking up dead? Of course, we'll never know. But it raises questions about how an analyst simultaneously experiences multiple symbiotic states with several patients. Furthermore, if Frank and I were drawn together by the magnetism of loss, who is to say that magnetism wouldn't have pulled Ben along in its wake. Perhaps in our symbiotic state, Ben's personal history also contributed to the shape of my dream.

Around this time, I had an odd experience. I hadn't scheduled a new patient into Ben's hour in the hopes that he might return to treatment. So, each week during that hour I'd sit in my empty office often reading and thinking about Ben. Near the end on one of these empty hours, and before the arrival of a string of successive patients, I used the bathroom in the waiting room. As I was standing over the toilet I glanced over to my right and saw Ben standing next to me. He was a young version of Ben, a small boy about six or seven. Although he looked younger and smaller, he had the same blonde hair and I had no doubt it was Ben. He said nothing but looked at me with curiosity and some expectation. Because I could see right through him, I realized he was both there and not there, and I laughed out loud in amazement. What a remarkable experience! I was pleased to see Ben, but then I was struck by the inappropriateness of him standing next to me in the bathroom. Feeling intruded upon, I spoke to Ben as I would to a young child, "Go on, get out of here. You don't belong in here. Go on." At first Ben didn't move. I glanced down at the toilet then back toward Ben. He was gone. I felt relief at the resumption of material reality but delight with this brief apparition.

That was the last I ever saw of Ben, and a couple weeks later I filled his hour with another patient. Was this vision of Ben what the third in my mind creates out of his actual absence? Or, was this apparition the product of the third in *both* our minds? In other words, was this a mutually created event? Had Ben stopped in as a final goodbye? Was it important for us both to reconstrue the end of our relationship as me gently shooing out an intrusive child to replace the image of his dramatically destructive departure?

In our session today, Frank described a new kind of dream of Anders. This was the first dream in which his son was healthy. In the last year Frank has typically dreamt of Anders as still sick and in the hospital. But in today's dream Anders had regained his health. Frank said:

> This dream was different. For some reason, he never looks at me in these dreams. I think it's just too much for him to see me in such pain. He said, 'Dad, will you shut the door?' He was on the other side of the doorway. I wouldn't do it. I don't know why. The dream just ended.

Frank was momentarily overcome with feeling. Then he referred to a character in his novel, a turn-of-the-century Cornish police officer who serves as a guardian of a portal which allows the protagonist to traverse across time between worlds. Frank said, "That's what I'm going to have the guardian figure say, his last line, it will be, 'Will you shut the door?'"

Frank wiped tears from his eyes. Today as I often do, I announced the end of our session with the statement, "That's all the time we have for today." Frank laughed as he rose from the couch. "You know, *that's* going to be the last line in this story. I don't know how I'm going to work it in, but that's the last line. 'That's all the time we have for today.'" Frank rose from the couch. Looking back over his shoulder he said, "See you next week," before closing the door behind him.

References

Aron, L. (1996). *A Meeting of minds: Mutuality in psychoanalysis.* Hillsdale, NJ: The Analytic Press.

Freud, S. (1912). Recommendations to physicians practicing psychoanalysis. *Standard Edition.* London: Hogarth Press, 12, 109–120.

Freud, S. (1933). Dreams and occultism. *Standard Edition.* London: Hogarth Press, 22, 31–56.

Gurney, F., Myers, F. & Podmore, F. (1886). Dreams. *Phantasms of the living,* volume 2 (pp.380–448). Cambridge: Cambridge University Press.

Huffman, C. (2014). *A history of Pythagoreanism.* Cambridge: Cambridge University Press.

Huggett, N. (2004). Zeno's paradoxes. *Stanford Encyclopedia of Philosophy.* http://plato.stanford.edu/entries/paradox-zeno/ (Accessed August 5 2009).

Li, W. (1999). Dreams of interpretation in early Chinese historical and philosophical writings. In D. Shulman & G. Stroumsa (Eds.), *Dream cultures: Explorations in the comparative history of dreaming* (pp.17–42). New York, NY: Oxford University Press.

Maroda, K. (1994). *The power of countertransference: Innovations in analytic technique.* Northvale, NJ: Jason Aronson.

Mayer, E. (2001). On "telepathic dreams?": an unpublished paper by Robert Stoller. *Journal of the American Psychoanalytic Association,* 49, 629–657.

McGuire, W. (Ed.) (1974). *The Freud/Jung letters: The correspondence between Sigmund Freud and C. C. Jung.* Princeton, NJ: Princeton University Press.

Meadow, P. (1996). The preoedipal transference. *Modern Psychoanalysis,* 21, 191–200.

Ogden, T. (2004). The analytic third: Implications for psychoanalytic theory and technique. *Psychoanalytic Quarterly,* 73, 167–195.

Searles, H. (1979). Concerning therapeutic symbiosis: The patient as symbiotic therapist, the phase of ambivalent symbiosis, and the role of jealousy in the fragmented ego. *Countertransference and related subjects: Selected papers* (pp.172–191). New York, NY: International Universities Press.

Spotnitz, H. (1985). Narcissistic transference. *Modern psychoanalysis of the schizophrenic patient: Theory of the technique*, second edition (pp.186–217). New York, NY: Human Sciences Press. (Original work published 1969)

Chapter 2

You're dead

Cuffs of creased wool pants rested on shiny black shoes. Sitting across from me Anne silently uncrossed her legs. "This coffee's running right through me," she said. Leaving on tiptoes, her salt-stained spiked heels barely grazed the cream-colored oriental beneath her feet.

Edna sat next to me on the couch. Taking my hand, she said to the others, "We had a conversation upstairs a few minutes ago. Danny felt he should have done something to have prevented it. That's natural, isn't it? Don't we all feel that way?" They murmured incoherently, twisting in their seats, not wanting to speak. Your death felt contagious. Disease spread with every word. I stared down at the rug, my eyes following the swirling sinew of vine covering its surface, each branch ending in a brilliant red blossom. My vision clouded as if my head had sunk underwater. Tears streamed down my face, burning my skin before dropping onto my shirt and ending in a cluster of small spreading stains. I sat motionless, not breathing, never looking up.

Beneath me is where you did it. Below the couch, beneath the floor, under the wooden beams supporting arteries of electrical conduit and water pipes, sitting at a wooden table in the basement around midday. With sun filtering through the windows casting shadows of withered ivy across the table's white surface, to the sound of a rumbling old furnace pumping hot water to radiators above, sitting with the sleeves of your flannel shirt rolled to your elbows, you did it with the lights out. Afterward you fell out of your chair onto the floor. Blood trickled around your ear, at first puddling in the hollow of your neck before dripping onto the threadbare rug. Your pack of Lucky Strikes slipped from your pocket and slid slowly across your soft shirt landing on the floor above your shoulder where its cellophane wrapper became lightly spattered. You didn't bleed for long.

She was late, and Barry had no hat. We waited by the gym doors bending our bodies against the cold, occasionally stomping our feet. Barry covered his ears with gloved hands. Across the street the brittle light of streetlamps reflected off the frozen metal surfaces of automobiles. Finally, a car pulled up, though not ours. Mother waved from the window. Climbing into the darkened backseat we drove away. We dropped Barry off first, upset that he was late. Then mother, glancing in the rearview mirror, tilted her head back and looked at me out the corner of her eye.

"Danny, today your father took his life."

"What?"

"Today your father took his life."

"You mean, he's dead?"

"Yes, he took his own life."

"He killed himself?"

"Yes, he shot himself."

Numbly, I walked into the house. Georgia stood at the landing. I looked at her to see if this was really happening. She nodded. I climbed the stairs to my room. With the lights out, I laid down on my bed and stared upward.

It was freezing. Large heaps of snow edged the roads in West Lawn Cemetery. They'd cut a hole in the frozen earth. This is where they meant to put you. Reflecting off the snow, daylight was brilliant and blinding. Everyone squinted. The light was inescapable. We stood in a row, mother, Georgia and me, each caught in the light. Motionless. A hatless minister spoke a foreign language. His lips moved over stained teeth emitting clouds of frozen air. Mother stood by glacially, February's own. Later when I saw a photograph of Mrs. Kennedy and her two children at the grave of the president, I thought maybe we looked like that. Mother never cried. The cold burned the skin of my face. I was glad of the pain, comforted by it. The needlelike breeze punctured me and then cut me with lengthening incisions until I turned inside out. No longer contained by skin, I became the cold. My heartbeat rose and fell measured by breaths escaping, and then in seconds evaporating.

Afterward, back at the house they lingered, alternately absent and giddy. Wearing black clothes with chalk white skin blotched red, they joked among themselves in small groups. Death was bad, but your suicide threw them. It struck home. You could kill yourself. The newspaper printed the obituary, just like mother wrote it, saying you'd died suddenly of a heart attack. But on another page, in a small random spot, the paper reported you'd died of a twenty-two-caliber gunshot wound to your head, pronounced dead at the scene. Friends were furious at this insensitive duplication. But I was mute. Submerged, suspended in fluid, breathless, unable to rise to the surface.

Then it was night. The skin of the house stretched tautly around the three of us, current passing rhythmically through its walls: Triplets. In bed, wrapped in layers of fabric, I waited for sleep. I made only the slightest movements, hoping to pass undetected, hoping to awake reborn. Could I survive now that you were gone? You'd been the barrier, the protective wall, the first line of defense. You're dead; I'm next. In carefully measured breaths, I slipped from consciousness, quietly caressed by the pulse of hundred-year-old walls.

Chapter 3

Buried alive

My father, Tom Gilhooley, waded ashore at Omaha Beach on the morning of June 10, 1944, the fifth day of the Allied invasion of France. The fighting at Omaha Beach on the first day had been horrific, but four days later the fiercest combat had shifted inland. One hundred and twenty thousand American soldiers had staggered through these same waters in the days before Tom arrived. Twelve thousand had been wounded and three thousand had died, many of them drowning in the same water Tom just stepped into.

The scale of the Allied invasion was enormous. On the first day the Allies ferried one hundred and sixty thousand men in seven thousand vessels across the Channel, landing them at six locations along the French coast. By the time Tom arrived, nearly three hundred thousand troops had landed, and by July fourth the total would reach a million.

The sense of mortal danger felt by these men, their German adversaries and the local French citizens was incapacitating. Landing that first morning on Omaha Beach was catastrophic. An iconic photo of soldiers plunging into the water off Omaha Beach is entitled "Into the Jaws of Death." Although his odds had improved over men who'd leaped into these waters four days earlier, as Tom waded ashore, he still stood a one-in-ten chance of being killed or crippled by the end of June.[1]

My father was a member of "A" Company of the 297th Army Combat Engineers, whose job would be destroying enemy fortifications, repairing roads, building bridges, and both clearing and planting mines. In the chaos of the invasion, Tom's portion of "A" Company had gotten split-off from the rest of the 297th which landed with their equipment and vehicles further west at Utah Beach. So, after collecting themselves, my father's group set out to find the rest of their battalion.

Although the Germans had retreated from the beachhead, they now pummeled coastal areas with artillery fire. Walking in light rain west along the Route de Carentan, Tom periodically ducked for cover from deafening artillery explosions. Then Tom's group was strafed by a low flying German plane, its cannon fire ripping up the earth in front of him. Diving into a steamy ditch alongside the road, Tom landed face-to-face, staring into the giant brown eye of a dead cow. Recoiling, rolling over, he was surrounded by the stiff bodies of dead soldiers—both German and American. Climbing onto the road, Tom shook uncontrollably. He'd just buried himself in a ditch of dead men. A breath away from death itself, he'd breathed death in. Climbing out he couldn't control his retching reaction to the smell of rotting flesh and the earth-shattering explosions. Tom's body shook violently, melding with the earth around him. Tom had stepped into a world unlike anything he'd ever known.

By the second day Tom's group caught up with most of the 297th in the village of St. Mere Eglise. "A" Company was attached to a succession of infantry units in the First Army, VII Corps. For eleven months they worked under fierce combat conditions at the front edges of the invasion advancing through France, Belgium and Germany. Tom's outfit carried a lot of dynamite and mines that made them especially vulnerable during bombing or artillery attack. Engineers often died when their explosives were detonated by enemy fire.

Along with frequently working on roads and bridges under intense gunfire, my father and his comrades were ferocious fighters. They hunted and killed snipers, they captured prisoners, they made frequent reconnaissance missions into enemy territory, they laid mines, and they were experts at sneaking into enemy areas at night to plant improvised booby traps that would kill German soldiers when they resumed their combat positions in the morning. Nothing could have prepared my father for the killing at Normandy. He'd never been a hunter. He'd had no experience that prepared him for his savage murder of fellow human beings. But now, in an instant, he had to perfect this skill or die.

Men who fought alongside Tom described him as possessing intelligence, leadership, and fearless aggression in the face of enemy fire. When serving as a sergeant he never sent men on a dangerous mission that he didn't lead himself. Sharing risk earned him the respect of his fellow soldiers. On the other hand, Tom's fearlessness was itself frightening, and sometimes seemed crazy. For example, it would be my father who'd recklessly race forward to hurl a grenade while his partners wisely held back. And there was his drinking which brought out an ugly belligerence that often got him into trouble. One of his fellow engineers told me, "if there was ever someone who shouldn't drink, it was your father." When intoxicated Tom would pick fights, and sometimes he'd strike an officer resulting in a temporary demotion in rank.

On June 13, when "A" Company moved from St. Mere Eglise and joined the rest of their battalion at Orglandes, the drinking began in earnest. A thirty-five-gallon barrel of Calvados brandy was commandeered and consumed over the next two days. The 297th's commanding officer remarked that he didn't mind the occasional bottle in camp, "but for God's sake keep the barrels out" (de Polo, 1945, p.14). For the next few weeks drinking and killing went hand-in-hand. In the assault on the port city of Cherbourg an infantry private who was stewed to his ears and armed only with a forty-five-caliber automatic pistol captured a German strongpoint single-handedly (Beevor, 2009).

When the 297th entered Cherbourg on June 26, they came across an enormous cache of brandies, wine and champagne. This large supply of liquor was loaded onto captured vehicles that would travel with the Army VII Corps across Europe (Man, 1994). Cherbourg was taken with my father firing a rifle with one hand while drinking from a bottle of cognac held in the other. A military history of the 297th Combat Engineers (de Polo, 1945) reports half the battalion was drunk during this battle, much of which was fought street-by-street, house-by-house. This seems shocking. But I wasn't there shaking uncontrollably, infused with death, knowing any second, I too could die. Looking back, Tom's fearlessness was probably fueled by alcohol.

Sitting in our darkened living room fifteen years later, my father told me war stories while sipping straight bourbon from a water glass. I was ten or eleven then. Some of the stories were tragic, like an engineer on guard duty one night accidentally shooting to death his best friend. Other stories told of common miseries like enduring relentless artillery shelling while huddled in a flooded foxhole on a rainy night. Once during a shelling some guy unexpectedly jumped or fell into Tom's foxhole with him. There wasn't room for two, and in an instant this guy on top of him was killed. My father wanted to run, wanted to get away from this dead man, but he couldn't. He was trapped, the guy's blood running all over him. Pouring another glass of bourbon my father said, "Don't tell your mother I'm drinking this. She doesn't think it's good for my health."

As he told me stories, I'd wear his dog tags around my neck and run the tips of my fingers around the edges of holes drilled into his skull leaving quarter-sized indentations under his silky-smooth hair. On November 25, 1944, in the small German village of Zweifall, Tom's platoon had just completed the second of two Bailey Bridges—a one hundred-foot-long steel structure atop a timber frame. As Tom drove a jeep across this bridge, a German plane dropped from the sky and strafed my father and his passenger. Tom was struck in the right shoulder by the plane's machine gun fire. His jeep crashed and flipped over fracturing Tom's skull. Hours later army surgeons on the hospital ship, Larkspur, saved his life by drilling holes in his skull to relieve the pressure on his swollen brain. He was in a coma for days.

This head injury ended my father's war. Tom returned to the United States to a seven-thousand-bed military convalescent hospital in Texas. In February, 1945, he was discharged from the army and transported to Hines Veteran's Hospital outside of Chicago. It was uncertain how Tom would recover from his traumatic brain injury. At first, it seemed he'd remain in a Veteran's hospital for the rest of his life. Struggling against that prediction, he left the hospital later that year in the care of his two sisters, Dorothy and Evelyn, both nurses who'd also served in the war.

During the first year, Tom recovered his ability to walk and to talk without slurring his words. That year, as he staggered along a street, people who knew him figured Tom was just drunk. In 1947, he began a career with a small advertising firm in southern Wisconsin. He married my mother and fathered his first child, my sister Georgia. In 1950, I was born.

In time, Tom appeared to achieve a complete physical recovery. But on several occasions during my childhood he'd check himself into a Veteran's Hospital or the Mayo Clinic in Minneapolis because he felt certain there was something wrong inside him. Physicians who examined him found no illness. But there were weird events like discovering him late at night drunk, hiding in bushes outside our home, believing he was being pursued.

Then when I was fourteen, I came home in the early afternoon on a hot August day. I heard my mother call for help from my father's bedroom. Tom was drunk. He'd moved his dresser in front of the door barricading himself into his room. He had a rifle and said he'd kill whoever tried to enter. My mother called his physician, Dr. Faber, who spoke to my father through the closed door, and then bravely stepped into the room. He injected Tom with a sedative, called an ambulance, and left to arrange for his admission to a hospital outside of Chicago.

My mother asked me if the rifle was loaded. I looked. The safety was on, but there was a shell in the chamber. He meant it. He meant to kill us. My father meant to kill me. I was different after that. Mother told me to unload the rifle and hide it. I took it to the attic hiding the gun and cartridges in separate locations. I was surprised I thought to do that. Afterward, I realized I meant to give us extra time to escape if Tom came to and found the gun.

Then she needed help picking my father's naked body up off the floor and placing him back on the bed. Tom had urinated on himself and she was trying to dress him in clean clothes before the ambulance arrived. Having gotten him out of his soiled clothing, when my mother turned away to grab some clean clothes, he'd accidentally rolled off the bed and become wedged between the bed and wall. It took two of us to pull him back up onto the bed. My mother knelt on the bed and pulled on one arm while I grabbed his other arm and ankle. We dragged him onto the bed, and he rolled over on his side. He was unconscious but still moving. The whiteness of his flesh shocked me. This was the only time in my life I saw my father naked.

I left the room while my mother dressed him. I don't recall the ambulance arriving. Tom, who moments earlier had been in a state of complete dissolution, was dressed by my mother and driven away unconscious, but in a freshly laundered shirt. He stayed in the hospital a little over three months, returning home for Thanksgiving. Tom was apparently cured of alcoholism. Now the real trouble began.

Tom spent the next months trying to put his life back together. Embarrassed by his long hospitalization, and concerned about advertising's culture of drinking, he quit his job at the agency. He felt humiliated without a career. He went from being a successful executive to making school lunches while his wife went to work. He'd always been depressed, but without drinking it was difficult for him to cope. Sitting at a folding card table in our living room he wrote a play about the strains of the civil rights movement. A Barry Goldwater Republican, or a George Wallace Democrat, he became increasingly angry and racist before our eyes.

When my father got angry, mother would whisper, "Is the gun where you hid it?" Several times each week I'd secretly check to see if the rifle and cartridges were still hidden, giving us a measure of safety.

Tom was edgy. He'd explode at the slightest infraction. One rainy Sunday afternoon Georgia returned home and sat on the couch across from him. I was at the other end of the room reading the newspaper. From behind his card table my father said he didn't like the smell of my sister's stinking wet feet. I remember glancing over at her dark cordovan penny loafers. She must have said something to him because he erupted in rage and sent the card table flying. In an instant he was hitting my sister. Georgia was screaming. My mother came running from the kitchen and tried to get between them. "Tom, Tom, stop!" she yelled trying to reach her arms around him.

Mother told us to get upstairs to our bedrooms. At the bottom of the stairs, I tried to get past Tom who was standing over Georgia. She'd fallen. Crying, she was crawling up the stairs on her hands and knees. As I tried to get past him, he slugged me with his fist. I couldn't believe he'd hit me. I thought, "He doesn't know who I am."

Georgia and I each got up the stairs to our rooms. But then Tom was upstairs in Georgia's room. My sister, mother and father were all in there screaming, my mother was again trying to restrain him. I was lying on my bed staring at the ceiling.

It was quiet. Georgia was sobbing in her room, my mother trying to calm her. I looked over and saw my father standing in my doorway, about three feet away. Trembling, fists clenched at his sides, breathing hard. I looked away. No eye-contact. Staring at the ceiling, I listened to each breath, heard the racing of his heart, and wondered if he'd kill me.

Tom killed himself a few months later, shooting himself in the head with a pistol we didn't know he had. An hour after finding his body my mother called the husband of a friend, a veteran, and asked him to come over and check our car to make sure that it wasn't booby-trapped. She feared Tom would take us with him.

My mother, my sister and I were devastated by his death. Each of us spent years trying to recover. Like my father in the foxhole, I wanted to run. I wanted to get out from under the weight of his dead body, his blood all over me. Though Tom's death occurred twenty-one years after the end of World War II, the Veteran's Administration determined he'd died from war-related injuries. I received veteran's benefits that paid for my undergraduate education. I also became the sole-surviving son of a deceased veteran which kept me out of the draft for the war in Vietnam, sparing me that trauma and perhaps saving my life.

But when my father shot that bullet through his head, he shot us both. He killed the boy in dog tags who delicately ran his fingertips through his hair, round the edges of those holes drilled in his skull. Carrying that dead couple inside me—that boy and his father—I'd never be the same.

For as long as I can remember, on nights as I begin to fall asleep, and in that liminal state between this world and the next, I have the following sequence of thoughts:

I hear myself say, "Get the gun!" I hear someone call out, "He has a gun!" Then I point my gun toward the closed bedroom door waiting. I fire several times through the door and on either side of the door frame hoping to kill them before they enter.

I worry about their returning line of fire, so I lay on the floor behind and beneath the bed. I know if the grenade they throw into the room reaches the back wall I'll perish. But if it rolls only halfway into the room, the bed will protect me from the explosion. My fate rests with where the grenade lands, like a rolling dice. When they enter following the grenade blast, I shoot them. Then I run through the doorway. I jump through a window and crouch in a clump of bushes checking, listening. "God, my ankle."

I'm behind the line. It's night. More are running toward the house. Undetected I go over a wall and run low, hobbling along a row of hedges. "My ankle!" I scream in my head. "Is it broken?" German trucks are opposite me in the road. I'm motionless. "Jesus, how do I get out of here? Which way?" I try running away from that house, my brain on fire. I pass into sleep.

For years I never gave a thought to this sequence of images as I fall asleep. But now I'm struck by how foreign they seem. I've never been in combat and I dislike guns. I realize the parallels between these nocturnal images and my traumatic experiences with Tom. He was the one expecting to shoot people standing on the other side of a closed bedroom door. He was the person lying on the floor beneath a bed, out of reach, and hiding in the bushes trying to escape pursuers. He was the one behind the line. He was even the one lying on the bed barely conscious.

In these images, I realize I've become my father, reliving parts of his past. It's as though in his moment of extremity, when I grabbed his ankle and pulled his naked body back onto that bed, Tom grabbed me and slipped through my skin. Still alive inside me, each night he meets me at the edge of sleep.

Note

1 World War II was the deadliest conflict in human history. Sixty million people, nearly three percent of the earth's population, perished. The Normandy invasion was a particularly dangerous phase of the war. While the overall casualty rate for Allied forces during the war was less than three percent, ten percent of those participating in the Normandy campaign were wounded or died (Astor, 1994). Landing at Omaha Beach on the first day, half of the 299th Combat Engineers (297th's sister unit) were killed or wounded (Ryan, 1959). After three weeks of fighting, allied casualties stood at 58,732, and Germany had suffered 80,783 losses (Beevor, 2009). The first day of the invasion 3,000 French citizens perished, killed mostly by Allied bombing, and by the end of August 19,000 French civilians had died in the battle. So, during those three weeks in June about 150,000 people in Normandy were killed or seriously wounded.

   Between June, 1944 and September, 1945 811 men served in my father's battalion. Of these, 37 were killed (de Polo, 1945). No record exists of those who were wounded.

References

Astor, G. (1994). *June 6, 1944: The voices of D-Day*. New York, NY: St. Martin's Press.

Beevor, A. (2009). *D-Day: The battle for Normandy*. New York, NY: Viking.

de Polo, T. (1945). *Bridging Europe*. Unpublished history of 297th Combat Engineers. Munich: Bruckmann Printing.

Man, J. (1994). *The D-Day atlas: The definitive account of the Allied invasion of Normandy*. New York, NY: Facts on File.

Ryan, C. (1959). *The longest day: June 6, 1944*. New York, NY: Simon & Schuster.

Chapter 4

Conversations with Schrödinger's Cat

Frank believes his dead son guides his mourning. Having an education in mathematics followed by a technical career, Frank had never been creative. Anders, on the other hand, had been an aspiring artist. After Anders' death, Frank became inspired. He appeared to "breathe in" his son's creativity. Frank says his newfound creativity fends off death and transforms his nuclear rage into something life-affirming. As he reads his vignettes to me each week, I've come to think of Frank's stories as symbolic representations of his therapeutic process. Frank is guided by the spirit of his dead son, and I'm guided by Frank.

In the first chapter, "So long," the crazy architect's convergence theorem becomes Frank's metaphorical description of our minds being bound together by an adhesive hallucinatory force. Max believes he's trapped in perpetual madness because he fails to converge: His life is a "hell of nonconvergence." So, convergence is the first and most essential therapeutic act. Expanding on this theme, Frank wrote a second chapter entitled "Convergence." Over a period of seven or eight weeks, Frank read me a succession of hand-written fragments that ultimately came together into a single tale. He rarely revised anything. Frank said his story seemed to be writing itself.

Frank described a world of parallel dimensions in which one universe is converging with another. An adjunct mathematics professor named Watson Page is haunted by having accidently killed a young man in an automobile accident. Six years earlier, Dr. Page had published a brilliant though controversial paper on quantum decoherence entitled, "Conversations with Schrödinger's Cat." His paper postulated the existence of parallel noncommunicating universes. In the language of quantum theory's famous thought experiment, Schrödinger's Cat really was both alive and dead at the same time, just in different universes.

Page's paper generated professional animosity among a group of Danish scientists committed to preserving a more conservative interpretation of the universe. They worked successfully to undermine his career. In the midst of this professional controversy, while driving on a dimly lit road, the distracted mathematician accidentally sideswiped and killed a young man changing a tire on his broken-down car. The combination of his professional demise with this tragic accident caused Page to suffer a nervous breakdown. He was hospitalized for two months and thereafter began treatment with Dr. Distanziert, the same psychoanalyst seen by Max in the first chapter.

Now, six years later and living with a broken mind, Page is a shadow of his former self. His early intellectual promise has resulted in a part-time teaching position he feels lucky to have. Page begins to be visited by a man named Graf who claims to live a block away on Waverly Place, but in another universe. Graf mysteriously appears and disappears. Because Graf is seen only by him, Page assumes this apparition is hallucinatory and evidence of his increasing insanity.

Graf is a doppelganger, Page's double. Graf exists simultaneously in multiple universes. In one universe he's Max Graf, a musicologist in Vienna and friend of Sigmund Freud. But now, as Page's double, Graf claims to be a mathematician who has also written "Conversations with Schrödinger's Cat." In Graf's universe, this controversial paper has earned him the respect of a growing body of related thinkers. Graf tells Page the calculations contained in their article are correct, but he alerts his twin to an unforeseen consequence of these mathematical formulas: They predict a catastrophic collapse of Page's universe under a statistically unique but inevitable circumstance of two parallel universes converging.

Graf warns Page this convergence is already underway. Page's universe is disintegrating incrementally, being swallowed up by the universe Graf inhabits. This disintegration is appearing first in the minds of the elderly where their memory loss isn't the product of a disease called Alzheimer's, but rather is caused by the incremental elimination of reality itself. Evidence of disintegration appears in little ways: Small objects like keys, a comb, or a book are misplaced. Then one walks into a room and forgets why. What looks like a failure of memory actually occurs because the individual has just encountered a tear in the fabric of time. At that instant the adhesion of past and present fails, causing time itself to partially dis-integrate. What appears to be millions of momentary cognitive failures are actually millions of accurate perceptions of a disintegrating reality! The alarming dissolution of our universe goes undetected because it's misin-terpreted as unrelated individual instances of mental illness. The pattern is unseen because of a failure in our gestalt. By focusing on the part, we're blind to the whole.

It's characteristic of Frank's stories that the protagonist slips seamlessly between dream and wakefulness, so the reader rarely knows whether he's conscious or unconscious. One of the final meetings with Graf begins this way, with Dr. Page walking out of his apartment building on his way to a dinner engagement. As he steps out onto the sidewalk the reader doesn't realize that Page has stepped into a dream where he participates in two cinematographic representations of previous deaths.

First, he experiences his death in 1896 when he is killed in a mugging by an Irish street gang. In this dramatic sequence, similar to my dream of "waking up dead," Page dies and then watches his body being lifted into a hansom cab where he finds himself like Schrödinger's Cat in an inde-terminate state between life and death. Sitting in the cab, Graf explains to Page that he is taking him to meet someone significant, a Chinese magician named Ching Ling Foo.

Foo, who in real-life was a turn-of-the-century magician and colleague of Houdini, appears in most chapters of Frank's novel. Foo exemplifies the Chinese proverb, "Life is a dream walking, death is going home." Foo is omniscient and occupied with two things: magic and transcendence. Knowing everyone's future and past, Foo is the magical creator of the reality each of us experiences. Along with his assistant Mekes—a master of technological invention—Foo creates holographic realities we each unwittingly inhabit. Foo is the Chinese god, Yeng-wang-yeh, who judges each soul at the time of death to determine its future: rebirth into a life of pain, or heavenly transcendence.

Unable to tell dream from psychotic episode, Page begs Foo to bring an end to this nightmare hallucination. Foo, resplendent in flowing red robes, tells the mathematician he has slipped into a gap between moments in time. Page is at the edge where dreaming ends and reality begins. They stand in an indeterminate state, at the point where all universes converge. Having been warned by Graf of impending disaster, Foo invites Page to cross a bridge connecting universes, to leave his imperiled world for another. Following Foo's instruction, Page passes through a door into a movie-like reconstruction of another one of his previous lives. Page stands in a dense tropical jungle in 1942 and observes himself moments before his death in the Battle of Guadalcanal. Rather than walking into a different future, Foo has led him into two different pasts.

Page wakes from his dream. The experience of meeting Ching Ling Foo was too intense, and Page believes he's no longer capable of distinguishing dream from reality. He concludes he's completely lost his mind. Page schedules an emergency appointment with his psychoanalyst. He voluntarily commits himself to the analyst's sanatorium where Dr. Distanziert injects Page with a hypnotic sedative. Page begins to remember a parallel life he's led as an intelligence analyst for the Department of Defense. This is a life from which he'd been totally dissociated, and of which he was completely amnesiac. Page now remembers that Distanziert also works for the DOD, where for years the doctor has been his supervisor.

The Freudian analyst points a pistol at Page and demands to know what Graf has been telling him. Page and his psychoanalyst begin a conversation in which each levels with the other. Distanziert explains that Page's paper, "Conversations with Schrödinger's Cat," has shaken the foundation of our understanding of the physical world. Page has proven there are multiple times, each time having a beginning and an end. Local time, the time of this world, is deteriorating and losing coherence because the adhesion holding together the fabric of time is weakening.

Page tells the doctor of Graf's warning about the two converging universes. Then, in a rush of intuition, Page realizes he and Graf are both "travelers," they're both doors or conduits between universes. This is what Ching Ling Foo had seen in him: There is no door connecting continuums, rather *he is the door!* Graf and Page both have the ability to jump between worlds, so that they'll be spared inevitable destruction. But the doctor has no way out. Hearing this, the psychoanalyst raises the pistol to his head and kills himself.

Page walks out of his psychoanalyst's office and into a dream, or another universe. There he's greeted warmly by Graf. The young motorist, whom he'd accidentally killed six years earlier, wraps his arm around him. The Freudian analyst, alive again, hands him a drink with a smile. "I hope you like Old Fashioneds," the doctor says. "Welcome home."

Chapter 5

Nonlocal time

I leave my home in Bellport each Friday morning at 4:30 to catch the 5:12 train from Babylon. My first patient in New York is at 7:00. I see Frank at 9:00. On this particular winter morning there's a light snow blowing onto my windscreen as I drive along Sunrise Highway. There hasn't been any accumulation, so the roads aren't slippery, but my vision is obscured by the snow caught in my headlights, dancing across my windshield. Traveling at about sixty mph I move to the center lane of the three-lane highway so that I won't have a problem with merging traffic. There are hardly any cars on the road.

After driving about five minutes I get a feeling I'm in danger. I'm struck by how odd this feeling is since I see nothing dangerous, and I can't recall anything currently happening in my life that would contribute to this feeling. I think, "Slow down and move over into the right lane." Then I wonder why I would even think this. Should I actually move over in response to such an irrational thought? What's the difference? I figure I have nothing to lose by moving over into the right lane. I change lanes and slow down to be more cautious.

The snow keeps blowing, limiting what I can see ahead of me. I drive about a mile further and approach a white van traveling in the middle lane with a mattress tied to its roof. The front of the mattress is buffeted by the wind, lifting it up off the truck's roof. As I approach the van, the mattress blows off the truck and lands on the ground right next to me, right where my car would have been if I hadn't changed lanes. I'm startled by the mattress hurtling to the road and so narrowly missing me. In my rearview mirror, I watch it sliding along the empty highway behind me and I wonder if a car will end up hitting it.

I'm rattled by this near-miss. Feeling unsteady, I'm even more upset thinking about the premonitory feeling I'd had a minute earlier. My self-assurance linked to my conception of time is shaken in this moment. This event defies a basic assumption about my indelible place in time. How could I know about a future event?

Could I have sensed the driver's anxiety about the safety of the mattress on top of his van? Maybe. But if the driver had known what was happening to the mattress on top of his truck, wouldn't he have pulled over? There weren't any signs of apprehension. Instead, he appeared to have no idea what was happening with the mattress.

Discarding the idea that I had intuited the driver's feeling, I considered a more radical interpretation. I wondered whether a part of my unconscious mind had already experienced my future. Was this unconscious part of my mind alerting my conscious mind to a dangerous event ahead? In the moments following this event I shifted. Mentally, I changed lanes.

About a year later I had a similar experience on my early morning drive to the Babylon train station. On this late autumn morning, I step onto the porch and think, "Flat tire." I wonder, "Do I have a flat tire?" Even with the porch light the yard is pitch black so there really isn't any way to tell if the tires on my car are flat. I figure if I have a flat tire the car will be listing slightly, but as I walk around the vehicle it seems level. Then I think, "I'll just roll down my window and listen for that sick sound of a flat while I back out of the driveway." I back out and hear nothing, concluding I don't have a flat tire.

I head west toward the train station. There aren't many cars on the road, and the drive is uneventful. When I turn off Sunrise Highway to merge onto Route 231, a two-lane highway heading south to Babylon, there's a problem. Coming around the cloverleaf turn at about fifty mph I start to merge onto 231. To my surprise there's a car immediately to my left blocking me, going the same speed. We travel side-by-side for a second. The driver of that car isn't moving over to let me in. In fact, he doesn't seem to know I'm next to him. With some alarm I think, "Buddy, what are you doing?" He isn't budging. I think of accelerating but get a panicky feeling. Straight ahead of me are the flashing taillights of a parked vehicle at the edge of the cloverleaf, about fifty feet in front of me. I step hard on the brake and tuck in behind the other car to merge onto 231. In an instant, I'm passing a broken-down car. There's a guy kneeling down changing the left rear tire. In the dark I hadn't seen him.

If I'd accelerated, I'd have hit him. In my headlights, I catch his face looking up at me as I whiz by. There's no shoulder on the cloverleaf, so his body was sticking out into the highway. I was five feet from killing him. "Close call," I think. "What a terrible place to change a tire."

I wonder how it could be that twenty-five minutes earlier I had thought of a flat tire, and now I just miss hitting a guy changing the left rear tire on a broken-down car precariously positioned at the edge of the road. What a strange coincidence.

In my head, I calculate the time it takes me to change a tire—everything from finding the jack and wrench, pulling out the spare, loosening the lug nuts, jacking the car, adding time for working in the dark. I figure twenty minutes. That means, if the guy knows how to change a tire, it's unlikely he had a flat tire twenty-five minutes ago when I left the house. So, assuming that's true, how could I have known I'd encounter a flat tire before it happened? I can't explain it. I again wonder whether a part of my unconscious mind might exist in the future. Maybe a part of me had already made this drive and was warning another part of me—my conscious mind—about danger ahead.

For weeks, I thought about this sequence of events. In fact, I couldn't stop thinking about it. I'd think, "It's impossible. We remember the past. We don't remember the future." I kept playing it over in my mind, and my understanding of my place in time seemed less and less secure. I considered an alternative explanation questioning my location in space. If the fellow with the flat took longer than twenty-five minutes working on his tire, so that he had the flat at the same moment or before I had my intuitive thought "flat tire," then my knowledge of the event might be explained by a reconsideration of my spatial location. Maybe on an unconscious level of awareness, when I stepped onto my porch I was in Babylon and Bellport simultaneously.

Of course, if a part of my unconscious mind is untethered in time, where am I spatially, anyway? Am I located where my conscious mind is attending to reality? If I'm "in" multiple locations simultaneously, are location and time only determined by conscious attention? Is it possible that in my unconscious I could be in multiple times, in multiple locations? This is certainly how it looks. What makes consciousness the focus of reality? It's a tiny sliver of mental life, and the handmaiden of the unconscious. I spent weeks pondering this. These two events caused me to question fundamental aspects of reality and who I am.

Seven months later, as I'm writing this essay, I'm reading a copy of Frank's chapter "Convergence." After months of reading me bits of writing from his notebook, Frank has given me a typed copy of his first two stories. Now, having the opportunity to study his story, I discover the part about the mathematician accidentally killing a young man changing the left rear tire on a broken-down car. I'm struck by the parallel with my flat-tire experience.

In Frank's story the police never charge Watson Page with a crime, and instead attribute the accident to "twilight, poor visibility, and too small a shoulder." Those attributes were all true in my near-miss, in fact there was *no* shoulder where the car pulled over. The guy was changing his tire *on* the highway, which is what made it so dangerous. I have no exact record of when my flat-tire experience happened. I estimate it was in the first weeks of December, 2010, from my recollection of the temperature, amount of daylight, and the fact that I would discuss the experience in a class I was teaching at the end of December.

In our next session, I asked Frank when he wrote "Convergence." I didn't mention anything about my experiences. He guessed he'd begun writing it in late August and finished it in October, 2010, a couple of months before my flat-tire experience. It appears Frank wrote about a life-altering experience with a flat tire in a story involving a dramatic re-conception of our place in space and time two months *before* I had my near-miss involving a flat tire—a near-miss that caused me to seriously reconsider my place in space and time.

I'm struck by the eerie quality of these twin events happening in our two lives. These parallels remind me of the relationship between Graf and Page in Frank's story where—living in parallel universes—they both write the same paper about Schrödinger's Cat. I realize Frank and I are writing versions of the same paper. I'm writing about his writing, using his work as the basis of my own. Then, in a close reading of Frank's first chapter, I realize both Max and his Freudian analyst claim to have written the same paper, "The Myth of Mental Illness." For Max, the crazy archi-tect, to have written a paper about the myth of mental illness is ironically amusing. For the psychoanalyst, on the other hand, the success of this publication earns him a dozen speaking engagements and a keynote pre-sentation at the Jakarta Conference on Global Anger (equally amusing). Frank wrote this *before* I began writing about Frank. Perhaps the die had been cast in Frank's first chapter.

I'd asked Frank about the date of writing "Convergence" to determine what came first, my flat-tire experience or his story, looking for some causal relationship between these two events. One thing must precede another to be considered its cause. But the sequence didn't make any difference in this case. Frank's reading me portions of this story in the preceding months may have predisposed me to interpret events in a particular way. But that couldn't explain my actual experience of thinking "flat tire" and twenty-five minutes later encountering a dangerous situation with someone changing a tire. When looking at these two events in chronological sequence, first Frank's story and then my experience, I couldn't see any causal relationship between them.

Then I looked at them the other way around. Frank appears to write about an experience two months before I have it. His story looks like a premonition of my precognitive experience. Is this illusory, or could my future experience *be the cause* of this portion of his story? That's supposed to be impossible. The future can't cause the present, or can it? Anyway, how could Frank even have knowledge about my future? It's weird enough to have premonitory experiences. But it's impossibly strange to think that Frank could write about my experience two months before I had it.

On the other hand, if I presume that Frank has some access to my unconscious, does his story "prove" my future exists within my unconscious? Where else could Frank get this information about my future except from my unconscious? On the other hand, maybe I'm mistaken thinking my unconscious is "mine." Maybe my future and past—and everyone else's—is available in a collective unconscious. Thinking this way makes my head spin.

If my unconscious mind has access to my future, then this affects my behavior. When I have a feeling of danger and think, "Move over to the right lane," and thereby avoid being hit by a mattress flying off the roof of a truck, my behavior appears to be affected by my knowledge of a future event. Similarly, thinking about a flat tire twenty-five minutes before encountering one primed my perception, increasing the likelihood I'd react quickly to a dangerous situation.

If this is true, then on those two occasions *both* future and past events were causes of my behavior. Again, if this is true, it's a significant revision of our traditional conception of causality.

Chapter 6

Premonitions

Frank continued to bring his notebook to sessions and read fragments of his stories. Writing was liberating and freed him temporarily from the massive weight of grief. His dazzling imagination could take him anywhere. A history buff, he liked to weave his stories around real people and events, so his fantasies mixed with reality. He'd spend hours conducting research and he was obsessed with historical accuracy.

Frank's third story, "The path," continues to develop his theme of convergence. In "The Path" convergence permits one to see the future, and the plot zigzags back and forth in time. The story is set in the Weimar culture of Berlin in the early 1930s with its ominous apocalyptic future just over the horizon.

Frank begins the story with a dramatic device taken from *film noir* in which the opening image is actually the final scene. Time is reversed, and only as the story unfolds does the reader come to realize that the beginning is really the end, and what looks like the present is really past. So, just as the 1950 noir classic "Sunset Boulevard" begins with a dead body floating in a swimming pool, "The Path" begins with police fishing a dead boy's body out of an icy river, his delicate face captured in the harsh light of the police photographer's flash. The dead boy is Willy Herold and the reader eventually realizes the disorienting image witnessed at the beginning is the inevitable ending that awaits him. During the story, there will be repeated breaks in temporal sequence when Willy gets glimpses of the future.

Willy is a sensitive transvestite nightclub singer who has a tender relationship with his father, a veteran broken in the Battle of Verdun. Before the war, Willy's father, Eric, had been a talented architect working for Walter Gropius. Eric had contributed to Gropius' design of the famous glass curtain-walls for the Faguswerk factory, an important piece of modernist architecture. But the war changed everything. The German siege of the French city of Verdun in 1916 was a trench-warfare nightmare lasting ten months in which the majority of the seven-hundred-thousand casualties were inflicted by forty-four million artillery shells. The relentless bombardment leveled forests and churned the earth's surface into a hellish pockmarked wasteland where soil mixed with the blood and bone of a hundred-thousand bodies.

Eric's mind was ruined at Verdun and he returned home a shadow of his former self. Now, fifteen years later, he's unemployable and tormented by inner visions of war. Willy's mother is the daughter of a wealthy merchant, and she's critical of Eric, whose promising future dissolved in the war. Her father pays for the psychiatric care Eric receives, but it's done him little good. While she's disappointed with her husband, Willy is Eric's sympathetic confidant. Willy and his father share a deep love, but they each find themselves at odds with an intolerant world.

Living in the apartment next door to Willy is a venerable old doctor who is part criminal, medical genius, and oral historian. The doctor tells stories that weave across centuries, and Willy listens with respectful reverence. One evening Willy knocks on the doctor's door to request a sleeping pill. The elegant gentleman welcomes Willy into his apartment and shows off a Ming dynasty porcelain cup recently given to him by Big-Eared Du, a Chinese mobster. A few years earlier the doctor had been running an osteopathic clinic in Shanghai where he sold a homemade opium tonic to his European clients. One of the doctor's specialties is experimentation and small-scale manufacture of mind-altering chemicals. When Big-Eared Du got wind of this, he insisted on becoming the doctor's business partner and receiving sixty percent of the profit on sales of "Li's Wonder Tonic."

The doctor's potion is named after the ancient Chinese magician, Li T'ieh-kuai, who lived in the sixth century BCE. One of the Taoist eight immortals, Li is traditionally described as an irascible old clown and fierce defender of the sick. Li cured illness by dispensing life preserving medicines, some of which could revive the dead. Li himself was sometimes mistaken for dead when he would leave his body for days to explore celestial realms.

When Willy requests a sleep medication the doctor gives him two tablets of Nembutal, along with a brief lecture on the history of anesthesia.

Handing Willy the pills, the doctor becomes a modern incarnation of the ancient magician. Along with the medicine, the doctor gives Willy a warning. This drug is dangerous: In small doses it's an effective sedative, but larger doses can be fatal.

Willy returns to his apartment, takes the medicine and falls asleep. Perhaps owing to magical properties contained in the pills, Willy has a prophetic dream in which he wakes up in the cabin of a cruise ship. In his dream, as Willy steps onto the deck of the ship two transvestites in high heels greet him, one placing a garland of orchids around his neck. The other offers him a flute of champagne while kissing his cheek and wishing him a safe journey. As the ship pulls away from the pier, Willy and other passengers throw red streamers back toward the throng of well-wishers lining the dock. At the last moment, Willy's streamer is caught by a man stepping into the sunlight and reaching up from the crowd. The man's face becomes illuminated and Willy recognizes it's his father.

At the nightclub where Willy works as a singer the smallest dressing room is used by an old Chinese magician named Ching Ling Foo. Foo's strange magic act is usually greeted with confusion and catcalls from the nightclub's intoxicated audience. Foo is exotic but not especially entertaining. One evening Willy enters Foo's dressing room and stands behind the magician who was applying make-up. Foo looks into his mirror and sees the reflection of Willy behind him. Their eyes meet in the mirror and Willy feels himself drawn into a "vortex of convergence." Willy closes his eyes and has a brief premonitory vision of the nightclub and the surrounding area of Berlin in ruins, the horizon lit with flashes of flame.

On another occasion, when Willy travels to visit his parents, upon entering their home he glances in a mirror where he mysteriously sees Foo. Again, their eyes meet, and this convergence launches a similar image, this time it's his family's home in smoldering ruins. Both these apocalyptic visions are premonitions of the ominous future that awaits them: the disastrous battle of Berlin which will occur in 1945. Through hypnotic convergence with Foo, Willy is able to see the future.

As the story unfolds, Foo asks Willy to join him in his dressing room on a third occasion to "see what might have been in another iteration." Willy closes his eyes and finds himself standing on a sunny California beach embracing his new lover, the English author Christopher Isherwood. A neighbor and probable acquaintance in Berlin's sexual underworld, Isherwood was a romance Willy would never enjoy. This was a relationship from an iteration of Willy's life that he'd never experience. Somewhere in Willy's past he stepped off one path onto another, and in 1933 Isherwood leaves Berlin without him.

Willy's performance each night at the club includes American jazz standards made popular by Libby Holman. He ends each set with a rendition of "The Woods of Verdun" in honor of his father. Willy doesn't have much of a voice, but he enjoys singing. He loves the copy of the Elsa Schiaparelli gown he'd sewn for himself which he's wearing this evening. He adores Schiaparelli's designs and tried unsuccessfully to be hired into one of her houses.

As he looks out into the audience, Willy sees two friends sitting at a table immersed in animated discussion. After his act Willy joins them at their table. His friends are both in their final years at university, both on the verge of careers in architecture and psychiatry, and both drinking Old Fashioneds. They are Max Besessen and Daniel Distanziert, the mad architect and his psychoanalyst from the first chapter. Frank introduces them now as "Max and Daniel, Daniel who interpreted King Nebuchadnezzar's dream, and the king in return made him ruler over the whole province of Babylon and chief over all wise men of Babylon."

Max and Daniel are a matched set of opposites. As grimly agitated as Max can be, Daniel is aloof and calmly optimistic. After completing his medical studies Daniel hopes to travel to Vienna to study with a colleague of Dr. Freud. Even in these early years Distanziert is interested in delusional thinking, in the power of an obsessional idea to overwhelm the natural gestalt and alter the shape of reality. Distanziert is driven by an intuitive belief that ideas create physical reality. When young Max declares, "My theories are about the end of all we know, the breakdown of the absolute structure of nature," Distanziert replies, "Max you will make a wonderful patient, one I expect to parlay into a long career." From Distanziert's perspective, Max's deep-seated paranoia will take a career to correct.

While the nature of delusion and anxieties about the breakdown of the natural order are topics that personally preoccupy Daniel and Max, Frank presents them in the context of the ascendance of the Nazi Party and Adolf Hitler, whose own compelling delusions will lead ordinary Germans to commit acts of genocide and propel the world into war. Sitting in that nightclub in 1932, these three friends are living in a world tilting into madness.

The story begins and ends with premonition. Willy learns that his father Eric has died in a traffic accident, a likely suicide. Willy sees his father one the last time in a freezing hospital morgue, Willy's "breath forming jets each time he exhaled." Willy kisses his father lightly on the forehead realizing the irrepressible images of Verdun have "finally stopped playing behind his eyes."

Two weeks after his father's funeral, Willy gives the best singing performance of his life leaving the audience cheering for an encore. He then enters Foo's dressing room. Again, their eyes meet as reflections in the mirror and Willy drifts into the vortex of convergence. He closes his eyes and sees his own dead body sprawled on the bank of a river, weeds forming a garland around his neck. This image is a repetition of the opening scene of the story. We've come full circle. Figures move around his body with a mindless grace at tasks all too familiar. In the cold brilliant light of the police photographer's flash his anonymous body is transformed into a harbinger of the carnage to come. We're reminded that Willy's last name is Herold, a version of herald—a messenger who reveals the future. Beauty has been defiled; the deluge has begun.

When Willy awakes from this image, he realizes he has already walked halfway home. He encounters three drunken men in brown shirts who identify him as homosexual, beat him senseless, and toss him into a river to drown. Willy's Foo-inspired premonition comes true. Willy wakes up dead and walks to the foot of a gangplank leading up to a large cruise ship. Willy appears to be back in the middle of his earlier Li-inspired dream of being on a ship. Two transvestites in high heels greet him, one placing a garland of orchids around his neck, the other offering him a glass of champagne while kissing his cheek and wishing him a safe journey. At the top of the gangplank he's met by the ship's steward who escorts him to his cabin. Again, we appear to have come full circle: In the dream Willy had left his cabin and now he heads back toward it. In his cabin Willy meets his impeccably dressed father, his face illuminated in warm sunlight. In the earlier dream Willy's father had been on the dock watching Willy depart, but now they're sailing together.

The reader is left to wonder whether the father too had had a premonition. Perhaps having sensed his son's imminent death, the father's suicide may have been an attempt to pass with him or meet him on the other side. Maybe the streamer Willy had tossed his father was the thread connecting them in another realm.

The story ends as all others in Frank's novel, where a death is followed by an apparently random birth. In this case, a baby girl is born to a pair of Scandinavian parents in Sioux Falls, South Dakota. The reader is left to wonder what association she will have with Willy. I happen to know that the young girl, Signe, will grow up to become Frank's wife and mother of their son, Anders.

Chapter 7

Convergence

In each of these stories, Frank's and mine, people meet at the seam separating life from death. Combat kept my father at the edge of death, and then nearly killed him. To escape death, he buried himself alive in a ditch of dead men. In the last year of his life, Tom kept our family suspended at the edge of life, each of us fearing he might find a hidden rifle and kill us. In the years since Anders' death, Frank has felt like a dead man walking, fearing he might step accidentally into death. Frank and I both dreamt of "waking up dead," a state in which we were dead and alive simultaneously. My two premonitory experiences while driving to Frank's sessions both involved life-threatening situations, either for me or a fellow changing a tire.

Many characters in Frank's stories straddle life and death. For example, Ching Ling Foo exists between moments in time, and in his capacity as Yeng-wang-yeh he greets the deceased and returns them to life reincarnated. The ancient magician Li T'ieh-kuai revives the dead, and the psychoanalyst Daniel Distanziert is cyclically killed and resurrected. In all these stories, characters are each like Schrödinger's Cat, suspended in an indeterminate state between life and death, where it's fifty-fifty. It could go either way. Silently running through the fabric of these stories is the thread of probability. Recognizing the parallels between Frank's fiction and my life, I find myself asking, "What are the odds?"

Frank's novel weaves religious and philosophical conceptions from the ancient world with concepts from contemporary quantum physics. Parallel universes and the fabric of time mix with questions posed by Pre-Socratic philosophy. In despair, Frank reaches across the history of human thought and belief trying to understand how he can live with his son's death. He asks, is he still alive when he knows he's dead?

How should I interpret the meaning of convergence in Frank's three stories? If these stories are metaphors describing therapeutic symbiosis, how do our minds intersect to create such a union? Frank had majored in mathematics and physics in college, followed by a technical career. This specialized knowledge informs his writing. My education was on the other side of the curriculum in art and the humanities. I struggle to keep up with Frank.

In Frank's first story, "So long," the obsessional architect Max Besessen despairs over the physical impossibility of convergence. Convergence is depicted as life-saving but elusive. In the story Max seems to symbolically represent Frank's desperate unconscious wish for intersubjective convergence, the creation of a symbiotic state that will restore the integrity of his mental structure. When Max says spatial structures are held together by a "hallucinatory adhesive force of our collective unconscious," he may be speaking for Frank's unconscious belief that our two minds are bound together by an adhesive force of mutual hallucination. If Max is the maker of physical structures, then Frank and I are makers of mental structure. Frank suggests our shared hallucination is a homegrown "sticky gestalt" that overwhelms the physical reality separating our minds.

In a broader sense, Frank appears to be saying our perception of the world is fundamentally hallucinatory. Frank seems to have a lot of questions about consciousness reflected in the deep uncertainties of Max, the crazy architect. Max's madness is epistemological. He's preoccupied with questions raised by the Pre-Socratic philosopher Parmenides and his disciple Zeno. Parmenides was deeply skeptical of sensory perception. He tried to parse out the differences between perceiving, thinking and knowing; contending that people mistakenly believe their perceptions are real, when they're actually false (Curd, 1998). This is Max's problem in a nutshell.

In Max's view, perception is no mirror of nature. For Max, perception never transcends representation, and the fact that he's incapable of directly apprehending material reality makes him nervous. Everyone agrees that certainties about the physical world are the only reliable truths—yet no one directly apprehends the world, so what's there to be certain about? We subjectively experience partial and uncertain mental representations of the physical—we never experience material reality itself. Moreover, from

Max's perspective, a world view based on matter that excludes mind, perception, and the hallucinatory adhesion of our thoughts (gestalts) is incomplete and therefore false. For Max, reality is bound together by thoughts. So, mind and matter are two sides of a single coin—one doesn't exist without the other. To Max, the cultural denial of mind in nature is dehumanizing, and the source of his depression.

Apart from seeing his analyst twice a week, Max spends time obsessively using a laser tool to measure his environment. Max is consumed by the epistemology of measurement. He's concerned about the relationship between measuring and knowing. To begin with, Max doubts the physical world exists independent of the act of measurement. So, existentially speaking, maintaining existence requires perpetual measurement. Then there are endless questions about accuracy and error. Much of Max's repetitive measurement relates to questions about the reliability of his instrument, and his ability to consistently obtain numerical ratios that mirror the proportional relationship between length, width and depth of the objects he's studying. It's significant that Max's counterpart in the story is named Distanziert, German for "distant." Distance or space is what Max is constantly examining.

As an architect, Max makes two-dimensional drawings representing physical forms. In a perspectival rendering of a building, parallel lines converge toward a vanishing point to create an *accurate illusion* of a three-dimensional form receding in space. In the actual three-dimensional structure these parallel edges of the physical form always remain equidistant; the edges never actually converge. So, as an architect Max is routinely confronted with the fact that an accurate representation of reality is illusory and differs in fundamental ways from physical reality.

Max's problem therefore—really an epistemological crisis—occurs at this gap between his experience of representations of reality, and reality itself. For Max this gap is an abyss, an epistemological limit that is literally "the end of all we know." Max's existential anxiety over this fundamental fact is the defining feature of his madness. He realizes no one else worries about such details, but he can't get them out of his head.

Experiencing this gap causes Max to reject the "cultural delusion of materialism." But that gets him in trouble. In everyday parlance, his rejection of materialism is a "failure of reality-testing," society's definition of insanity. So, people around Max consider him crazy. Max is just on the wrong side of a philosophical problem. As a subscriber of philosophical idealism, sanity is a metaphysical rather than psychiatric issue, and the conception of mental illness as an organic disease is a fiction used to prop up the vacuous theory of materialism: Hence, his essay, "The myth of mental illness."

Max's failure to converge is linked to the murder of his psychoanalyst. In his paranoid state, Max kills the analyst as an assertion of non-convergence and as a deflection of self-destruction. Paranoia appears to arise as a fearful response to the awareness of convergence and symbiosis. But what are we to make of the fact that the analyst is repetitively resurrected? Does this simply represent Frank's persistent wish that time could be reversed, and his son's death could be undone? That looks like a good explanation.

On the other hand, could it be that Frank is telling us something about time in the unconscious? When the protagonist enters a dream, or an altered state of consciousness, Frank describes him as "suspended between moments of time." Is this the reason the analyst's death can be repeatedly undone—in an altered state of consciousness the analyst *exists outside of space and time*? Are space and linear time products of consciousness while in our unconscious the past, present and future all occur simultaneously? I asked Frank this question and this is his answer: "In this dream state, past, present and future collapse into one, so characters are alive and dead simultaneously." For example, in one story Ching Ling Foo hires a private investigator to track down Nigel, the meddlesome protagonist, who appears intent on altering Foo's plans. When the investigator asks if Foo wants Nigel killed, Foo laughs and responds, "Why, this man is already dead!" After all, the novel begins with Nigel proclaiming, "I woke up dead." In each of Frank's stories, being dead is part of being alive.

While in his first story convergence is the protagonist's only salvation, in the second story convergence propels the protagonist toward apocalyptic destruction. Here the imminent convergence of two parallel universes is causing time to collapse leading to the disintegration Watson Page's world. Frank appears to be saying that therapeutic convergence, though necessary to maintain the integrity of self, is dangerous because it requires a loss of self. For example, convergence causes the elderly to lose their memories, their personal histories, and therefore themselves. Where spatial structures are cracking apart in "So long," in "Convergence" it's time that's coming undone. Frank again employs the metaphor of "weakening adhesion" to describe the cause of disintegration. The failure of mental adhesion, the capacity of thoughts and feelings to bind material reality together, is his basic concern.

In his first two chapters, Frank uses Zeno's paradoxes and multiple universes to address two sides of the same existential coin. In his first chapter Frank introduces Zeno's paradoxes to present Parmenides' notion that "plurality, change and motion are mere illusions," and that "reality is one, immutable, and unchanging" (Salmon, 2001, p.6). For Max the crazy architect, this "one immutable reality" is what the entwined nature of mind and matter reveals. Frank's second chapter, "Convergence," uses multiple universes to present the opposite proposition: The single universe in which we believe we live is really an illusion. We actually exist simultaneously within an almost infinite number of parallel dimensions.

At the end of "Convergence" the psychoanalyst injects Page with a hypnotic serum causing him to remember he is an intelligence officer working for the Department of Defense. He has led a parallel life from which he is completely dissociated. It turns out Page has multiple personalities each possessing different histories. Living within parallel dimensions means the protagonist sometimes encounters an alternate version of himself, a doppelganger. For example, sitting in a coffee shop Watson Page encounters Graf who exists in another dimension where he has written the same paper as Page, "Conversations with Schrödinger's Cat."

With these two stories, "So long" and "Convergence," Frank sketches his broad paradoxical outline of life. One is simultaneously alive and dead, and one lives in states of symbiotic relatedness with others while also existing in multiple versions of one's self. Life takes place within these bipolar states: being alive *and* dead, being one *and* many. Awareness of the simultaneity of these bipolar states occurs exclusively through contact with our unconscious mind. Consciousness fiercely defends itself from such knowledge. This becomes the fundamental conflict of life woven into the metaphysics of materialism: *Conscious rejection of unconscious awareness.*

In Frank's third chapter, "The path," transcendent knowledge of one's future occurs episodically through another form of convergence, a hypnotic merger with the divine. This represents the third and fourth bipolar dimensions of the unconscious mind. Within the unconscious one lives between moments of time where the past, present and future coexist. Frank's stories suggest our unconscious contains awareness of multiple futures for each of our various selves, a truly dizzying conception.

Willy's repeatedly merging with Foo represents the spiritual foundation for Frank's work. Frank believes he's able to connect with God through a process of hypnotic convergence. In fact, this is what his creative writing process is all about. In Frank's view, within our unconscious our human, mortal, unknowing self is linked with a preternatural, eternal, all-knowing god. Where conscious perception is inherently flawed, knowledge of true reality is obtained through an unconscious connection with the divine. Therefore, truth travels the avenues of the unconscious. For Max, the crazy architect, the denial of the divine power within our minds is what makes materialism morally corrosive. Materialism denies the essence of humanity, and therein becomes the source of cultural dissolution.

It's remarkable that Frank writes a chapter about premonitions right after my flat-tire experience. The fact that I never discussed with Frank any aspect of my life, nor my ideas about convergence or premonition, supports my belief that our minds are telepathically linked. From the beginning Frank took a position of complete disinterest in me personally. In my recollection, Frank asked me only one question about myself: "Do you have experience with death?" I answered simply that I did. Frank associates me with the Freudian psychoanalyst in his novel, Daniel Distanziert. An English translation of "distanziert" is distant, emotionally detached, reserved, aloof, and self-contained. If merging is a central feature of our relationship, then measuring the emotional "distance" between us may be a fundamental concern. In the chapter "The path," Willy's assessment of Daniel Distanziert is that he is "cold." I don't feel either cold or emotionally distant from Frank, but that may be how he sees me.

This makes it all the more remarkable that Frank creates stories with such parallels to my life. First of all, Frank and I both begin writing following our mutual dream of waking up dead. Frank makes repeated references to twin authors writing the same paper. In the first chapter Max and Distanziert both declare they are authors of the article, "The myth of mental illness." Then Page meets Graf, his double from a parallel universe, who has also written "Conversations with Schrödinger's Cat." Frank's novel suggests we are so entwined that we're writing the same story.

Frank describes Page accidentally killing a man changing a flat tire two months before I experienced a very similar event. Following my intense period of rumination over the two premonitory experiences I had while driving to the Babylon train station, Frank writes a story about successive premonitions in which he declares the psychoanalyst Daniel Distanziert to be the interpreter of the king's dream who is rewarded by becoming master of the wise men of Babylon. It may be obvious for Frank to give his fictional psychoanalyst my first name, but it seems uncanny that my interpretation of the "waking up dead" dream should be rewarded with my ascendance over the "wise men of Babylon," the village where I had recently experienced my near-miss with a man changing a flat tire. Coincidentally, I have two male patients who live in Babylon, and both hold administrative positions in the village.

Considering that a father/son relationship is a theme in our work together, Frank writes about a boy raised by a shell-shocked war veteran whose memory of combat disables him, renders him unemployable, and contributes to his suicide. This was my experience growing up with my father. In Frank's story the son is the father's sympathetic confidante, just as I had been with my father. Willy's mother comes from a prosperous family, is uninterested in her husband's war experience and disappointed with his disability, just as my mother had been. In "The path," Willy's last image of his father occurs in a freezing morgue where Willy's "breath formed jets each time he exhaled." Compare this to my description at my father's internment (written in 1994) where I say the minister's "lips moved over stained teeth emitting clouds of frozen air," and say of myself, "I became the cold. My heartbeat rose and fell measured by breaths escaping, and then in seconds evaporating." The parallel images of the sons' frozen breaths are compelling.

Then there is the psychoanalyst placing a pistol to his head and killing himself. This was the very reason why, as a young man, I entered psychoanalysis. I was depressed and believed it was inevitable that I, like my father, would place a pistol to my head and kill myself. This was my deepest trauma and a future I desperately wanted to avoid. Considering the remarkable similarities between Frank's story and my life, what are the odds these parallels are purely coincidental, and not a product of our shared mind?

References

Curd, P. (1998). *The legacy of Parmenides: Eleatic monism and later Presocratic thought*. Princeton, NJ: Princeton University Press.

Salmon, W. (2001). *Zeno's paradoxes*. Indianapolis, IN: Hackett Publishing Company. (Original work published 1970)

Part II

Quantum

Chapter 8

Many Worlds

Frank's character of Watson Page in "Convergence" appears to be modeled on the life of Hugh Everett (Barrett & Byrne, 2012; Byrne, 2010). Knowing about Everett's work is important to interpreting Frank's story.

Everett was a brilliantly gifted mathematician who attended Princeton University in the mid-1950s. Attracted to Princeton by the presence of scientists like Albert Einstein and John von Neumann, Everett was drawn to the world's most sophisticated thinking in physics. As a young man, Everett was a big thinker trying to solve big problems. He was independent and intensely driven. For his doctoral dissertation Everett developed a creative and mathematically sophisticated solution to a major snag in quantum theory called the "measurement problem." As physicist and Jungian scholar Harald Atmanspacher and his colleague Wolfgang Fach (2015) note, "One of the central problems, if not *the* problem, of quantum mechanics is the process of measurement" (p.198). This is quantum physics' version of Max's measurement problem, an epistemological crisis occurring at the intersection of perception, representation and reality. Hugh Everett's controversial solution to the problem, though dismissed in 1957, is today thought to be as significant as Newton's theory of gravity and Einstein's theory of relativity (Lockwood, 2008).

Here's the measurement problem Everett set out to solve. At an atomic level, the location of an electron is indeterminate and can't be known precisely. The electron can be described as a cloud—as in, "the electron is in there somewhere." All that can be known about an electron's location is a distribution of probabilities which evolves over time. Erwin Schrödinger developed a mathematical equation describing this probability wave for which he was awarded a Nobel Prize. For eighty years his equation has proven to be consistently accurate in predicting physical reality (Greene, 2011). Schrödinger's equation is the basis for concluding, "Quantum theory is the most successful physical theory of all time" (Kaku, 2005, p.153).

But here's the rub. The electron's location remains a set of probabilities until the moment of measurement. Then, in the language of quantum theorist Niels Bohr, the probability wave "collapses" and the electron is identified at a specific location. After the moment of measurement, the electron returns to its cloud of indeterminacy. Bohr boldly asserted the act of measurement created reality. This is a remarkable statement, though one that Max, Frank's crazy architect, certainly agreed with. For Max, the world takes form through our perception of it. In Max's delusion, the world maintains its structure through the adhesion of our collective perceptions. So, Max figured Bohr's thinking was spot-on.

This act of measurement was understood by Bohr to occur at the juncture between two worlds, between the microscopic world of the electron and the macroscopic world of measuring instruments and consciousness. It's this boundary between nature and observation, between material and immaterial, that Max Besessen found so compelling. Bohr's conception is the quintessence of philosophical idealism. In the words of philosopher David Chalmers (1996), it "offers us a picture of reality that leaves out the world!" where "all that exists are our perceptions" (p.342).

The electron's shift from an indeterminate haze to a specific location, and its return to indeterminacy, made no sense to anyone. In the face of this confusion, Bohr maintained we simply had to keep these two worlds separate: Employ Newtonian physics at our human scale and quantum physics at this microscopic scale. We can't explain nature, Bohr said, we can only measure it. We can hear Max applauding in the background.

Albert Einstein found this measurement issue deeply perplexing and he rejected Bohr's suggestion that reality is observer-created. Agreeing with Einstein, in 1935 Schrödinger developed his famous thought experiment to underscore this apparently irrational element in quantum theory. Although Schrödinger was a key figure in the development of quantum physics, like Einstein his scientific perspective was conservative. He was so uncomfortable with the reality revealed by quantum physics, he regretted contributing to its development. In fact, Schrödinger once snapped at Bohr, "I should be sorry I ever got involved with quantum theory!" (Kumar, 2008, p.223).

Schrödinger designed his virtual experiment to mimic the measurement problem, to connect the large-scale human world with the atomic scale of the electron. In this thought experiment the fate of a cat depends on what happens to a single radioactive atom. Placed into a sealed steel box are a cat and a tiny bit of radioactive material that has a fifty-percent chance of decaying within the next hour. If the atom decays, a Geiger counter will detect the emerging radiation triggering a hammer to fall breaking a glass vessel releasing a poison that will kill the cat. So, the fate of the cat hinges on the future of a single atom. It's fifty-fifty. According to quantum theory the cat exists in an indeterminate state until the box is opened, at which point Bohr claims the probability wave collapses, and the cat is found to be either dead or alive.

But, there's more to it. Quantum physics *actually* maintains that before the box is opened the cat *is both* dead and alive. This is the real problem. It seems impossible for a cat to be both dead and alive. Schrödinger and Einstein agreed this is ridiculous. We could choose to ignore this affront to common sense, except we know quantum theory to be the most accurate mathematical representation of reality ever discovered. So, we know mathematically it's almost certainly true, yet how can it be?

Max interjects, "This quantum reality was described twenty-five-hundred years ago by Heraclitus who declared 'opposites are always equally true!'" For the philosopher Heraclitus, it's a logical certainty the cat is both alive and dead (Kahn, 1979). Heraclitus wrote, "And as the same thing there exists in us living and dead and the waking and the sleeping and young and old" (Robinson, 2008, p.490). The more Max learned about quantum physics, the more obsessed he became with Zeno and his colleagues.

Actually, Max's views were shared by Schrodinger's colleague Werner Heisenberg (1958) who wrote that Heraclitus realized

> the strife of the opposites is really a kind of harmony. For Heraclitus the world is at once one and many, it is just "the opposite tension" of the opposites that constitutes the unity of the one.
>
> (p.62)

In previous chapters Max has been dismissed as a nut, but now we find his opinions echoed by both Bohr and Heisenberg, central figures in the quantum revolution. Maybe quantum physics and Max are equally nutty.

Max's fictional partner, Daniel Distanziert notes, "The melancholic Heraclitus also described the essence of reality as 'flux,' something akin to the indeterminacy at the heart of quantum theory." A bit of a stretch, but Distanziert often supports Max's eccentric ideas. At university, Max and Distanziert had been attentive students of ancient Greek philosophy. Turns out, Heisenberg attended the same school!

Anyway, this is where Everett comes in. Recall that Frank's mathematician Watson Page and his double, Graf, both wrote controversial papers entitled, "Conversations with Schrodinger's Cat." We might think of their papers as versions of Everett's dissertation. Everett discarded Bohr's notion of breaking the world in two, into a large-scale world of Newtonian physics and an atomic world of quantum physics. Everett claimed Bohr looked at quantum physics as ancillary to Newtonian reality. Everett reversed this perspective, saying quantum reality was foundational from which Newtonian physics must naturally emerge. Everett rejected Bohr's notion that the act of measurement brought clarity to an otherwise indeterminate state. Everett reasoned that we and our measuring equipment are made up of atoms and are therefore subject to the same quantum laws as the other particles in the probability wave. He chose not to privilege the position of the observer, and instead imagined the human observer to be in the same quantum soup as the electron, and therefore described by the same mathematical equation.

Conceptually, Everett (1973b) reckoned the belief in an "outside" observer was pure illusion. He writes "there is no place to stand outside the system to observe it" (p.142). In fact, Everett argued the observer and the atomic particles were highly correlated mathematically. In the language of quantum physics, they'd become "entangled," so the very "basis of Everett's interpretation is the endemic phenomenon of entanglement" (Barbour, 1999, p.222). Where Bohr conceived of an isolated outside observer "looking in," Everett said it was more realistic to imagine multiple observers interacting in the midst of the probability wave.

So, if you're in the middle of this probability wave what happens? Everett's answer was simple: All possible outcomes occur, each in separate dimensions so each outcome sees only itself and remains unaware of other outcomes occurring invisibly around it. According to Everett, in Schrödinger's virtual experiment reality splits creating one universe in which an atom of radioactive material decays causing a cat to die, while in a separate universe the material doesn't decay and the cat lives. The observer also splits so that in one dimension as he opens the box, he discovers a dead cat, while in another dimension another version of the observer opens the box to find the cat alive and well. Both outcomes are equally real, and both occur simultaneously.

Returning to the image of an observer looking for the electron and finding only a cloud of indeterminate locations, Everett again reverses the picture. His theory claims that if the electron were looking for the observer, the electron would find the observer in a similar cloud of indeterminate locations. The observer's location is as uncertain as the electron's because the observer also exists simultaneously in many universes.

Admittedly, this sounds bizarre, but Everett's theory is a mathematically elegant, conservative and a logical elaboration of Schrödinger's equation. Part of its appeal is its straightforward mathematical formalism and its comprehensiveness: It explains the microscopic world of quantum physics and the macroscopic world described by Einstein's theory of relativity. In Everett's view, his theory is the simplest and most complete formulation of quantum mechanics (Barrett & Byrne, 2012). As John Gribbin (2009) writes, "The best reason for taking the Many Worlds interpretation seriously is that nobody has ever found any other way to describe the entire Universe in quantum terms" (p.31). Everett's theory has gained acceptance among many physicists (Deutsch, 1997; DeWitt and Graham, 1973; Greene, 2011; Kaku, 2005; Tegmark, 2007) because of its mathematical clarity and an increasing amount of experimental evidence supporting it. Everett claims his theory is an accurate mathematical representation of the world, and the fact that we can't believe it doesn't mean it isn't real. Mathematician David Deutsch (1997) writes:

> The quantum theory of parallel universes is not the problem, it is the solution. It is not some troublesome, optional interpretation emerging from arcane theoretical considerations. It is the explanation—the only one that is tenable—of a remarkable and counter-intuitive reality.
>
> (p.51)

Obviously, Everett's theory is at odds with our lived experience. Bryce DeWitt, the editor of the journal which published a condensed version of his dissertation, questioned Everett noting that he didn't feel himself splitting and branching off into another version of himself. In a letter to DeWitt, Everett replied that this was the same objection raised against Copernicus when he offered a mathematical proof that the earth revolved around the sun. Everett (2012) quipped, "I can't resist asking: Do you feel the motion of the earth?" (p.254). Of course, we don't feel ourselves spinning in space, but that doesn't mean it isn't happening. In fact, almost all physical events in the universe occur outside our awareness, so our subjective state can't reasonably be used as a measure of a theory's accuracy.

Everett's multiple universes bears striking resemblance to the fiction of Argentinean author, Jorge Luis Borges (1998). In 1941 Borges wrote a short story entitled "The garden of forking paths" which plays out in the context of a mysteriously infinite labyrinthine novel written one hundred years earlier by the protagonist's relative, Ts'ui Pen. In Pen's novel, when a protagonist encounters diverse alternatives, he chooses all of them simultaneously, creating multiple futures with multiple times. Each future itself forks and proliferates. Though Borges doesn't seem to have known much about quantum physics, and his story was published sixteen years before Everett's dissertation, he nonetheless describes the multiple universes Everett claims quantum science reveals.

In fact, Everett's dissertation advisor, John Wheeler (1998), employs the same "forking paths" metaphor to describe Everett's Many Worlds conception:

> Think of yourself driving down a road and coming to a fork. According to classical physics, you take one fork, and that's that. According to the conventional [Bohr's] interpretation of quantum mechanics, you might take one fork or you might take the other, and which one you take will not be known until something happens to pin down your location, such as stopping at a gas station or restaurant, where some outside observer ascertains your location. There is something ghostly about even the conventional quantum interpretation, since it assumes that you travel "virtually" (as opposed to "really") down both roads at once, until it is established that you "really" traveled down a particular fork. According to the Everett interpretation, you go down both roads. If you later stop for gas on the left-fork and someone observes you there and you are yourself aware of being there, that doesn't mean that there isn't another "you," uncoupled from the left-fork you, who stops and eats on the right fork, is observed by people there, and is aware of being there.
>
> (p.269)

What's so difficult to accept about Everett's conception is that it leads to an infinite number of co-occurring "yous." As Nobel laureate Frank Wilczek writes, "We are haunted by awareness that infinitely many slightly variant copies of ourselves are living out their parallel lives and that every moment more duplicates spring into existence and take up our many alternate futures" (Kaku, 2005, p.244). With each worldly transaction a person splits into another version of himself creating a continuous pattern of branches from an original source. In Everett's (1973a) theory, a person doesn't have a lifeline, he has a "life tree." But after a split, which version of you is "you?" While Everett contends we have no awareness of parallel versions of ourselves, and that we are only aware of the outcome but not the process of splitting, when it comes to the question of identity Everett's conception is ambiguous. In the near term, "you" may be a collection of highly similar versions of yourself sharing a nearly identical set of memories and an almost identical physical environment, but after a time most versions of "you" and the physical environments in which you exist become much less similar.

From my conversations with Frank, I think he believes the version of "you" that you end up experiencing—your continuous *conscious* awareness of self—is just a matter of chance. In another dimension his son Anders never got cancer and he and Frank continued their life together. It was just bad luck that Frank ended up living the version of Frank in which his son died.

Everett's creative and mathematically elegant solution to the measurement problem was controversial and caused him a lot of trouble. It altered the course of his life. Everett's paper claimed Bohr's idea of a probability wave "collapse" was misguided. Bohr was a man of titanic proportions in quantum physics and he was admired by Everett's thesis advisor, John Wheeler. Wheeler had spent a year doing postdoctoral research with Bohr, and several years later helped Bohr work out the details of nuclear fission which would lead to the development of the atomic bomb. Attempting to find a middle ground between his student and Bohr, Wheeler required Everett to repeatedly revise his dissertation to make it less contentious and provocative. Everett's single publication in quantum physics, based on a truncated version of his original thesis, was dismissed by Bohr's Copenhagen group. Bohr and his colleagues found Everett's thesis to be heretical, and their complete rejection ended Everett's career in quantum physics. This was a personal and professional injury from which he never recovered.

Everett went to work for the Pentagon researching nuclear war. He developed statistical models predicting the effects of nuclear attacks, which at the time were misunderstood by military and political leaders. His professional career became devoted to mathematically mapping out the apocalyptic end of the human race. Everett struggled to convince political leaders that nuclear conflicts couldn't be used to produce tactical military advantage. During the Cold War he became a central figure in promoting a nuclear strategy of "assured mutual destruction" as the only sane way to avert nuclear catastrophe. Since his premature death at the age of fifty-one, Everett's original theory predicting multiple universes has been accepted as one of several competing quantum interpretations of physical reality.

Bryce DeWitt (1973), an early and ardent supporter of Everett's theory, associated the Many Worlds conception with schizophrenia. He writes,

> I still recall vividly the shock I experienced on first encountering this multiworld concept. The idea of $10^{100}+$ slightly imperfect copies of oneself all constantly splitting into further copies, which ultimately become unrecognizable, is not easy to reconcile with common sense. Here is schizophrenia with a vengeance.
>
> (p.161)

In fact, are aspects of schizophrenia and multiple personality (dissociative identity disorder) attributable to a Many Worlds phenomenon?

I recall a long-term schizophrenic patient of psychoanalyst Harold Searles named Joan Douglas who regularly announced she was seeing multiple of versions of him before her eyes. Was she seeing recently split-off versions of Searles? Mrs. Douglas was similarly aware of thousands of versions of herself, staff members, fellow patients and even the psychiatric hospital in which she resided. As people around her developed different feelings, or as she had different feelings about them, Mrs. Douglas saw these individuals split into multiple versions of themselves. When a collection of new thoughts came into her mind, she believed she possessed a different head than the one she was wearing moments before. Searles (1979) writes,

> She felt accused unfairly by all persons about her for her more destructive acts which, she was convinced, her malicious doubles had done. She once protested, "Well, there were nine hundred and

ninety-seven tertiary skillion women [i.e., projected components, or 'doubles' of herself] associated with Chestnut Lodge; so why should I be blamed for everything that everyone did?".

(pp.200–201)

If Mrs. Douglas' mental condition could be attributed to a Many World phenomenon, her problem would be the result of faulty "decoherence." Decoherence is a buffer insulating each of Everett's parallel dimensions. To travel from one dimension to another, as Graf does in "Convergence," requires him to pass through a buffer of decoherence in which the atomic particles making up Graf and his universe slip out of phase with one another, their structures dissolving into a form of static.

Nobel laureate Steven Weinberg compares Everett's Many Worlds conception to our everyday experience of radio. The spaces in which we are sitting are filled with invisible radio waves. These waves are heard only if one has a receiver tuned to a particular frequency. The many other frequencies invisibly present are not heard because they have decohered and are no longer in phase with one another (Kaku, 2005). One receiver hears only one frequency and is insulated by decoherence from hearing other frequencies. Employing this analogy Everett might conclude that Mrs. Douglas' mind was a room filled with numerous radios playing simultaneously, each tuned to a different frequency permitting her access to the many parallel universes surrounding her.

David Chalmers (1996) and Michael Lockwood (1996) are two philosophers who interpret Everett's continually bifurcating self as occurring *within the mind* rather than within the physical world. From this perspective, Chalmers says "if there is any splitting it is only in the minds of observers. As superpositions come to affect a subject's brain state, a number of separate minds result. . .each of these perceives a separate discrete world" (p.347). Where Everett's theory is called the Many Worlds interpretation, Lockwood's theory is known as "Many Minds." Chalmers and Lockwood adapt Everett's theory in a way that maintains one physical world with innumerable parallel universes occurring within each of our minds. These parallel universes apparently exist within our unconscious, outside conscious awareness. In this Many Minds model, the psychological process of "dissociation" is what we call the "decoherence" isolating one universe from another. Within the Chalmers/Lockwood model, our unconscious contains a nearly infinite number of dissociated split-off lives, doppelgangers like Frank's character Graf, each existing in a self-contained parallel universe.

Quantum physicists have focused on the role of conscious observation in the creation of reality. But I'm unaware of their ideas about *unconscious* thought. Over the past fifty years cognitive science has demonstrated the vast majority of mental life from perception to remembering, from learning to decision making, is unconscious. Therefore, conscious observation represents a tiny sliver of mental life (Gigerenzer, 2007; Norretranders, 1998; Wilson, 2002). So, do we have *unconscious* awareness of split-off versions of ourselves?

When Joan Douglas claimed to see herself, Searles and his associates split into multiple versions of themselves, was this a form of unconscious knowledge seeping into her consciousness? Indeed, could Douglas' visions be evidence supporting the Chalmers/Lockwood Many Minds model? Did my father live with an unconscious realization that, on that bridge in the German village of Zweifall in 1944, he "split in two" as one version of Tom died? I replay that fateful event in my mind.

I imagine Tom seeing a plane dropping from the sky and diving toward him. He slams on the jeep's brakes. He hopes to get beneath the vehicle to protect himself from the plane's cannon fire. The urgently applied brakes cause the jeep to lurch and pull to one side flipping the vehicle over. Hurled from the car, his helmet lifts off his head. Turning in midair Tom realizes, "I'm going to die." Time slows. Looking down at the earth, he sees his helmet land and bounce away just before his forehead crashes against the bridge's surface. He feels his body crumpling behind him, his shoulder bursting into flame. Casually, he realizes he's been hit by the plane's machine gun fire. Bouncing, he comes to rest face-up. Far away, his legs land lifelessly. Indifferent to the Stuka's receding thunder, the world goes quiet. He thinks, "I'm dying." High above a bird flutters before his eyes. The sky darkens.

Tom sinks from consciousness into that gap described by Ching Ling Foo. Gliding between moments in time, he slips into the dream space where I often find him. Foo's brilliant robes swirl before his eyes. Tom finds himself looking down at his body, swirling around it, checking for signs of life. He lifts his hand, trying to rouse himself. He really *is* dead. For being dead he feels fine, literally care-free. Moving effortlessly, he's surprised how easy it is being dead. Glancing back at his body, he feels himself drawn away by a mysterious current. Days later, when Tom regains consciousness aboard the hospital ship "Larkspur," he's surprised to be alive. The other one died. From that time forward Tom never escapes the feeling that life is not his own. He's not its true inhabitant. For years he'll visit physicians complaining there's something wrong inside him, but they find nothing.

Does Frank live with an unconscious awareness that in another dimension of his unconscious mind his son is alive? I imagine Frank's wife, Signe, reaching down and touching the cheek of their sixteen-year-old son. In an afternoon hockey game Anders had been hit in the face by the puck. It struck his right cheek, abrading his flesh and bruising him. As Anders lies down in bed, his mother, who'd cleaned and applied an ointment to the wound, touches his cheek. Her heart skips a beat. She catches her breath. Was that a lump beneath his skin? She ran her finger back across his cheek causing Anders to wince. "Oh, it's nothing," she realizes. Kissing her son's forehead, she says good night.

A graphic novel draped across his chest, Anders slips from consciousness into the gap described by Ching Ling Foo. He steps into a dream space where he sees his father searching anxiously. Foo's brilliant red robes swirl before his eyes, and Anders watches a version of himself and Frank step through his bedroom door into another room in which six years from now he'll be dead, and his father will be sick with grief. Watching them leave, Anders remembers an illustrated book from childhood. He recalls the pleasure he had as a small boy tracing his fingers around the forms in the pictures. He remembers the colors and the surprising black lines heading every which way. He'll grow up loving to draw. In the morning he's surprised to find himself searching under his bed for that tattered book, *Marvin K. Mooney*, hoping to see those swirling lines again.

References

Atmanspacher, H. & Fach, W. (2015). Mind-matter correlations in dual-aspect monism according to Pauli and Jung. In E. F. Kelly, A. Crabtree & P. Marshall (Eds.), *Beyond physicalism: Toward a reconciliation of science and spirituality* (pp.195–226). Lanham, MD: Rowman & Littlefield.

Barbour, J. (1999). *The end of time: The next revolution in physics.* Cambridge: Oxford University Press.

Barrett, J. & Byrne, P. (2012). *The Everett interpretation of quantum mechanics: Collected works 1955–1980 with commentary.* Princeton, NJ: Princeton University Press.

Borges, J. (1998). The garden of the forking paths. *Jorge Luis Borges: Collected fictions* (pp.119–128). New York, NY: Penguin Books. (Original work published 1941)

Byrne, P. (2010). *The many worlds of Hugh Everett III: Multiple universes, mutual assured destruction, and the meltdown of a nuclear family.* Oxford: Oxford University Press.

Chalmers, D. (1996). The interpretation of quantum mechanics. *The conscious mind: In search of a fundamental theory* (pp.333–357). New York, NY: Oxford University Press.

Deutsch, D. (1997). *The fabric of reality.* New York, NY: Penguin Books.

DeWitt, B. (1973). Quantum mechanics and reality. In B. DeWitt & N. Graham (Eds.) *The many-worlds interpretation of quantum mechanics* (pp.155–165). Princeton, NJ: Princeton University Press. (Originally published 1970)

DeWitt, B. & Graham, N. (Eds.) (1973). *The many-worlds interpretation of quantum mechanics.* Princeton, NJ: Princeton University Press.

Everett, H. (1973a). The theory of universal wave function. In B. DeWitt & N. Graham (Eds.) *The many-worlds interpretation of quantum mechanics* (pp. 3–140). Princeton, NJ: Princeton University Press. (Original work 1957)

Everett, H. (1973b). Relative state formulation of quantum mechanics. In B. DeWitt & N. Graham (Eds.) *The many-worlds interpretation of quantum mechanics* (pp.141–149). Princeton, NJ: Princeton University Press. (Original work published 1957)

Everett, H. (2012). Everett to DeWitt, May 31, 1957. In J. Barrett & P. Byrne (Eds.) *The Everett interpretation of quantum mechanics: Collected works with commentary* (pp.252–256). Princeton, NJ: Princeton University Press.

Gigerenzer, G. (2007). *Gut feelings: The intelligence of the unconscious.* London: Penguin Books.

Greene, B. (2011). *The hidden reality: Parallel universes and the deep laws of the cosmos.* New York, NY: Alfred A. Knopf.

Gribbin, J. (2009). *In search of the multiverse: Parallel worlds, hidden dimensions, and the ultimate quest for the frontiers of reality.* Hoboken, NJ: John Wiley and Sons.

Heisenberg, W. (1958). *Physics and philosophy: The revolution in modern science.* New York, NY: Harper and Row Publishers.

Kahn, C. (1979). *The art and thought of Heraclitus: An edition of the fragments with translation and commentary.* Cambridge: Cambridge University Press.

Kaku, M. (2005). *Parallel worlds.* New York, NY: Anchor Books.

Kumar, M. (2008). *Quantum: Einstein, Bohr and the great debate about the nature of reality.* New York, NY: W.W. Norton.

Lockwood, L. (Writer, Producer, Director) (2008). Parallel worlds, parallel lives. [Television series episode]. *Nova.* Boston: PBS/WGBH Educational Foundation.

Lockwood, M. (1996). "Many Minds" interpretations of quantum mechanics. *The British Journal for the Philosophy of Science*, 47, 159–188.

Norretranders, T. (1998). *The user illusion: Cutting consciousness down to size.* New York, NY: Viking.

Robinson, T. (2008). Presocratic theology. In P. Curd & D. Graham (Eds.) *Presocratic Philosophy* (pp.485–498). Oxford: Oxford University Press.

Searles, H. (1979). The function of the patient's realistic perceptions of the analyst in delusional transference. *Countertransference and related subjects: Selected papers* (pp.196–227). New York, NY: International Universities Press. (Original work published 1972)

Tegmark, M. (2007). Many lives in many worlds. *Nature*, vol. 448/5, July, pp.23–24.

Wheeler, J. (1998). *Geons, black holes and quantum foam: A life in physics.* New York, NY: W.W. Norton.

Wilson, T. (2002). *Strangers to ourselves: Discovering the adaptive unconscious.* Cambridge, MA: Harvard University Press.

Chapter 9

The magic of entanglement

At the heart of Hugh Everett's Many Worlds interpretation is his contention that the observer exists in the same quantum reality as the electron. Moreover, the observer has become intimately connected and mathematically correlated with what he's observing. In the language of quantum physics, the observer and the observed have become "entangled." Seeing the observer and particle as members of the same probability wave was fine with Everett (1973) who looked forward to applying his ideas in the context of "unified field theories where there is no question of ever isolating observers and object systems" (p.149). As we've seen, Everett rejected the illusion of the detached observer.

In the early 1930s the phrase "unified field theory" was associated with Albert Einstein who was still living and working in Berlin, so architecture student Max Besessen had heard the expression. A youthful Max would have applauded Everett's conception of observer and object as a unified entity. But Max, with his obsessive philosophical bent, wasn't prepared for the implications of entanglement.

When two or more atomic particles (like an electron) interact, their properties can become "entangled," and these shared qualities continue to exist even if the particles are separated by great distances, even light years apart. Erwin Schrödinger discovered the phenomenon of entanglement in 1926 and gave it its name. He writes,

> When two systems. . .enter into a temporary physical interaction due to known forces between them and when after a time of mutual influence the systems separate again, then they can no longer be described

as before, viz., by endowing each of them with a representative of its own. I would not call that *one* but rather *the* characteristic trait of quantum mechanics.

(Aczel, 2001, p.70)

After separating, the similarity of these two entangled atomic particles is greater than just a few specific attributes acquired when they were previously together. The two particles have joined to form a single, two-particle system having the same probability wave, so they now act in unison (Greene, 2004). Though they are physically independent, and could be separated by a great distance, they've become so intimately linked they now share the same existence.

Subatomic particles become entangled when they're exposed to intense forms of energy. For example, two electrons passing through a superconductor's current can become entangled. Or, when a crystal of calcium is struck by certain forms of light it becomes "excited," absorbing energy from the light. As the calcium returns to its normal state it gives up this extra energy by releasing photons of light, sometimes releasing pairs of entangled photons. At those moments the calcium crystal gives birth to identical twins. Using this technique scientists have created billions of entangled pairs of photons.

Experiments with entangled particles always involve the act of measurement. Like Max, Frank's crazy architect, quantum physicists spend their time obsessively measuring. When studying electrons, the "spin" or angular momentum of the electron is measured. With photons of light scientists measure the angle of polarization, the inclination or "tilt" of the electromagnetic waves. Spin is a property of particles; polarization is a property of electromagnetic waves.

Consider this experiment with pairs of electrons: Two electrons are each sent down a different passageway equipped with a measuring device to detect the electrons' spin. The measuring equipment will be located so that both electrons will be measured simultaneously when they are far enough apart that nothing could pass between them at the speed of light. There is no way to predict an electron's spin. It's an important fact of quantum physics that until the moment of measurement the electron's spin is completely random. So, a succession of electrons passing through the two detectors will demonstrate a random sequence of spin angles. That's true unless the pair of electrons had previously become entangled.

When this experiment is conducted with entangled electrons, we get very different results. Even though, until the moment of measurement, an electron's spin could be any value, once it's measured its entangled partner's spin angle becomes the exact reciprocal. When one electron is measured it appears to instantaneously *create* the other electron's state from a set of random possibilities. Now if you alter the spin of the first electron, the spin of its partner changes instantly, even if its miles away, and even though no force has been applied to it. As researcher Nicolas Gisin (2014) writes, "If we prod one of the two parts, both will quiver" (p.43). Touching one is to touch the other, even though they're miles away. The two entangled electrons move as one quantum system, and as far as we know, they'll remain linked in this way forever (Aczel, 2001; Clegg, 2006; Cramer, 2016; Gilder, 2008; Gisin, 2014; Mauldin, 2011; Musser, 2015; Nadeau & Kafatos, 1999).

In this experiment it appears that information has traveled between the electrons—one has communicated with the other—but this doesn't seem to be the case. The electrons don't behave in this correlated way because of any communication between them. They behave this way because they are "*one.*" Experimentally the correlations between the particles have been shown to remain constant over space and time: they occur "instantly or in 'no-time' in spite of the vast distance between detectors" (Nadeau & Kafatos, 1999, p.79).

While the original experiments with entanglement were conducted with tiny bits of energy and matter, like photons and electrons, in 1997 similar results were achieved using entangled "Bucky balls," molecules made up of sixty to seventy atoms (Aczel, 2001); and in 2015 three thousand atoms were entangled in a single state (Choi, 2015). This may sound big, but it's really tiny when you consider a human cell contains a hundred trillion atoms. The most impressive human-scale experiment occurred in 2011 when entanglement was demonstrated in a pair of small diamonds the size of earring studs (Grossman, 2011). It remains unclear how entanglement affects chunks of matter the size of you and me. But if entanglement can be observed between three-millimeter diamonds, it seems certain this phenomenon affects human beings.

Entanglement is deeply mysterious, and it violates many of our fundamental assumptions about reality. In 1935 Albert Einstein described entanglement as "spooky action at a distance," believing there must be hidden variables that explain it. Einstein declared, "Separated systems cannot directly influence each other—that would be magic" (Maudlin, 2011, p.xiii). Since 1972, several experiments have proven Einstein wrong, simply confirming entanglement's spooky status. As physicist and philosopher Timothy Mauldin (2011) writes, decades of experimental evidence have caused physicists to accept "the magic is real" (p.xiii). Physicists call entanglement "incredible" and "unbelievable." For many scientists encountering entanglement, the experience has been life-altering. Describing an experiment with entangled particles physicist Brian Greene (2004) writes, "This is the kind of result that should take your breath away" (p.113).

Skepticism about mysterious invisible forces acting over great distances is nothing new in physics, where invisible forces have been center stage for centuries. Isaac Newton, a lifelong alchemist and religious scholar, was criticized for dealing in the occult while mathematically describing the force of gravity invisibly affecting the movement of celestial bodies. Equally spiritual and rational, "Newton was not the first of the age of reason, he was the last of the magicians," the Ching Ling Foo of his era (Gleick, 2003, p.188). Newton's contemporary, philosopher Gottfried Leibnitz, appreciated Newton's mathematical calculations describing gravity's effects. But Leibnitz asked Newton to *explain* gravity. Newton acknowledged he didn't understand gravity, writing, "I have not been able to discover the cause of those properties of gravity from phenomena, and I frame no hypotheses" (Christianson, 1984, p.532).

This didn't satisfy Leibnitz who considered Newton's refusal to provide a mechanical explanation of gravity to be an endorsement of magic. In Leibnitz's view, if the cause of gravity wasn't mechanical, it was a "perpetual miracle." In fact, that appears to have been Newton's personal opinion. Newton scholar John Maynard Keynes (1946) writes, "His deepest instincts were occult, esoteric, semantic—with profound shrinking from the world, a paralyzing fear of exposing his thoughts." Sensitive to the reaction he'd received for describing gravity, Newton didn't want to attract more criticism by proposing an immaterial force as the source of gravity's effects. Newton wrote, "Gravity must be caused by an agent acting constantly according to certain laws; but whether this agent be material or immaterial, I have left to the consideration of my readers" (Gleick, 2003, p.148). In the three hundred years since Newton, no one has explained the cause of gravity. It remains deeply mysterious. As George Musser (2015) writes, "If gravity seems magical, that's because it *is* magical" (p.60).

The comfort we derive from living in Leibnitz's world of mechanical certainty depends on us *ignoring* gravity's magical basis.

The problem with entanglement is that it tells us material reality isn't true or isn't the whole truth. The experiments with entangled particles show them violating a principle of "locality," a concept that was very important to Einstein and actually, to all of us. Locality means what happens in one place cannot instantaneously affect what happens in another place. Action takes place locally. For example, if I want to have an effect on someone, I have to travel through space and time until I'm next to him. Then and there I can talk to him, shove or embrace him; or I can send him a text message. In any case, I have to contact him directly, or send a messenger (like a note), and this requires movement through space and time. Belief in "local action" is a bedrock concept for all of us, rooted in a world of space and time. This is the basis for cause-and-effect explanations of reality. This is how we make sense of ourselves in the world.

Almost everything I know about the world is spatial, and the conception of space and time is foundational to my sense of self: My body is spatial, my face has a form. To be alive is temporal and temporary. I know I'll be dead soon, but between now and then, time provides me with a reassuring sense of continuity. My aging face and impending death are irrefutable evidence that I live in a world of space and time. But the instantly coordinated movements of entangled particles across vast distances indicate their independence of space and time. Their coordinated movements make it appear *there is no space*, and *there is no time*. As Nicolas Gisin (2014) writes, "To put it bluntly, these nonlocal correlations seem in some sense to emerge somehow from outside spacetime!" (p. 50). Of course, this is a very different universe than Newton, or Einstein, or any of us imagined. In fact, entanglement eclipses our most basic assumptions about reality making it "a discovery that many regard as the most momentous in the history of science" (Nadeau & Kafatos, 1999, p.3).

But, there's more. Because the entangled particles studied in these experiments have interacted with an enormous number of other particles during the history of the cosmos, with which they've likely also become entangled, scientists infer that nonlocality must be a fundamental aspect of the universe. Robert Nadeau and Menas Kafatos (1999) write, "If nonlocality is a property of the entire universe, then we must also conclude that an undivided wholeness exists on the most primary and basic level of all aspects of physical reality" (p.4). In other words, entanglement is the basis of physical reality.

One is reminded once again of Max Besessen, Frank's crazy architect obsessed with Zeno. Zeno was a student of the ancient Greek philosopher Parmenides. Zeno's paradoxes were meant to support Parmenides' contention that beneath illusory differences there is an undivided wholeness to reality. Quantum entanglement appears to prove such a foundational unity exists. We know Max was consumed by questions posed by Zeno and Parmenides, so we're not surprised to hear him cheering in the background. But this notion of "undivided wholeness" has troubling implications that violate even Max's most basic beliefs.

Einstein insisted on a world filled with objects that have a continuous existence independent of a perceiving observer. Objects are autonomous and independent of each other because they each occupy different areas of space in time. "Locality" is all about spacetime, and this is the problem with entanglement: It demonstrates a reality in which space and time don't exist, or at least the phenomenon of entanglement dramatically alters their meaning. Physicist Amir Aczel (2001) writes, "to understand entanglement, we creatures of reality depend on 'elements of reality,' as Einstein demanded, but. . .the experiments have taught us, these elements of reality simply do not exist" (p.253). Entangled particles "show us, fundamentally, that space is not what we once thought it was" (Greene, 2004, p.123). Time isn't what we think it is, either. Einstein's theory of relativity explains that nothing happens faster than the speed of light, and that time is relative: Time under one set of conditions in one portion of the universe will differ from time in another place, under a different set of conditions. But entanglement indicates events can happen instantaneously (in "no-time"), and there's a single master clock for the universe. So, entanglement is inconsistent with the theory of relativity. This, of course, is why Einstein found it so troubling.

"So, what?" you might be thinking, "Why should I be concerned with what happens between these little bits of energy and matter? Even if entanglement can be demonstrated in tiny diamonds, what do I care?" But entanglement isn't a trivial issue for us nonscientists. Like Einstein, we take it personally, because we're each one of the objects Einstein is describing. Quantum entanglement threatens our sense of self. Entanglement suggests we're not really autonomous after all. If the atoms that comprise my body and mind are invisibly linked to, or the same as, the particles in everyone else, I blend into the fabric of reality like "dust-to-dust." If we aren't each autonomous, who are we? We appear to lose our individual identity. Even Einstein acknowledged, a belief in our separateness is a delusion, "a kind of optical illusion of consciousness" (Nadeau & Kafatos, 1999, p.179). Psychically this loss of individuality feels like death.

Living in the Age of Reason, there is another troubling aspect of entanglement. Science asserts that religion, magic and superstition must be rooted out of our conception of reality. Since the Enlightenment, science made the "disenchantment of the world" its central mission (Wootton, 2015). But entanglement appears to transcend the limits of physical reality. Like gravity, no one can explain entanglement. We can measure it, we know it's real, but we can't explain why it exists. As Gisin (2014) writes, entanglement emerges "somehow from outside spacetime," *outside* material reality (p.50). Gisin continues, "In a certain sense then, reality is something that happens in another space than our own, and what we perceive of it are just shadows" (p.51). That's the essence of nonlocality. Talk about a loss of personal identity! Does that mean I'm a shadow, not a self? Sounds perfectly awful.

Let's look again at those entangled particles. A force is applied to one particle and its entangled partner, potentially light years away, is affected instantly or "in no-time." The physical constraints of time and space are transcended. What caused the entangled partner to change when no force was applied to it? It's mysterious. We can't explain it. Was information or knowledge transferred between the particles "infinitely fast?" We know that no energy was expended transmitting a force between them. Or, was the entangled partner altered by an *immaterial* force applied to it, by a force requiring no energy, occurring in no-time as though space doesn't exist? Well, it looks that way, but there are no immaterial forces in physical theory. So, we're back to the conflict between Newton and Leibnitz about the origin of gravity. Three hundred years ago Newton wrote, "Gravity must be caused by an agent acting constantly according to certain laws; *but whether this agent be material or immaterial,* I have left to the consideration of my readers" (Gleick, 2003, p.148; italics added). We're stuck with the same uncertainty. Newton couldn't explain gravity, and physicists can't explain entanglement. But what words do we use to describe a force appearing to originate outside our space and time that transcends physical laws to alter the energy and matter around us? "Supernatural" or "magical." Entanglement looks like magic, a "perpetual miracle" at the foundation of physical reality.

As noetic researcher Dean Radin (2006) writes, entanglement "looks and feels so much like magic that scientists who haven't thought much about entanglement are either horrified, or they deny there's any problem and vehemently refuse to explain why" (p.238). Although science denies the supernatural, the mysterious nonlocal effects of entanglement are unsettling. Quantum entanglement raises the possibility of an immaterial reality, transcending the constraints of space and time, affecting our material world in fundamental ways. For some people this is reassuring, but most of us find the idea of a mysterious force affecting matter and energy to be "spooky." In Frank's opinion, experiments with entangled particles would lead reasonable people to believe in God. Indeed, one writer, Brian Clegg (2006), describes entanglement as "the God Effect." For some, physics' discovery of entanglement has led to a refreshing re-enchantment of the world. But for many, entanglement is unnerving.

Fear of the metaphysical implications of entanglement, and the spooky universe it reflects, appears to be the reason physics chose to ignore it for thirty years. In American universities a generation of students was discouraged from discussing it. As the twentieth century progressed the culture of quantum physics became increasingly authoritarian and repressive. As we saw in the case of Hugh Everett, "there was no place in physics—no jobs in physics—for anyone who dared to question the Copenhagen Interpretation" (Whitaker, 2016, pp.1–2). Given science's reluctance to lend credibility to spooky or supernatural forces, journals refused to publish anything about entanglement, other than its practical applications. For example, the editor of *Physical Review* formally banned philosophical debate and instructed referees to reject any paper on the topic of entanglement. In response, scientists studying entanglement produced a mimeographed underground newsletter, *Epistemological Letters*, that circulated privately between 1973 and 1984. Professionally speaking, investigating quantum entanglement was a ticket to nowhere.

Following Einstein's objections to entanglement expressed in 1935, one of the first authors courageous enough to publish a paper on nonlocality was John Bell. In 1964 he published his theoretical proof ruling out the possibility of Einstein's hidden variables in the third issue of an offbeat, little-known journal, *Physics Physique Fizika*, that published only four issues before disappearing. Although he was eventually nominated for a Nobel Prize for this paper, Bell waited four years before his work was cited in another publication, and twenty years before his ideas were included in mainstream physics curricula (Musser, 2015). When French researcher Alain Aspect consulted Bell about his design of an experiment to test Bell's theory, Bell's first response was, "Do you have a secure post?" (Whitaker, 2016, p.279). Although Aspect's experiment would definitively prove the existence of entanglement and nonlocality, even conducting such an experiment could bring an end to a promising career in physics. John Clauser, who conducted the first experiments to test Bell's theorem, describes physics' reaction to entanglement as akin to the McCarthy era paranoia (Kaiser, 2011).

The apprehension stimulated by entanglement should be taken seriously. Throughout history, fear of incomprehensible, larger-than-life, forces affecting us is one of humanity's greatest challenges. This fear reverberates throughout this book. We'll see science repeatedly ignoring, suppressing and eliminating frightening evidence. This is what makes Bell's work so courageous.

How does quantum entanglement affect human beings? Could entanglement affect the mind? Do physical laws governing atoms apply to thoughts or feelings? In fact, is a thought physical in any way? No one knows, but after three centuries during which physics deliberately focused on the inanimate, quantum physics has recently turned its attention the study of human consciousness (Atmanspacher, 2015; Penrose, Hamerhoff & Kak, 2009; Stapp, 2011). That's not surprising. The most revolutionary aspect of quantum theory is the movement of consciousness to the center of physical theory. Physicist Henry Stapp (2011) describes this shift as, "A purported theory of matter alone is converted into a theory of the *relationship of matter and mind*" (p.20, italics added). Again, we hear Max applauding from the sideline.

So, does quantum entanglement provide a model that helps us understand the symbiotic mental state that Frank and I appear to have created? The common objection to applying models of quantum reality to everyday life is Bohr's contention made nearly a century ago that we must maintain an invisible wall between the worlds described by Newtonian and quantum physics. For example, psychoanalyst Charles Hanly (1995) insists, "All of us live our lives in a reality governed by the laws of Newtonian mechanics," so it's nonsensical to employ qualities of quantum reality to interpret clinical events (p.239).

But contemporary physicists don't support Hanly's opinion. Michio Kaku (2005) says, "The 'wall' envisioned by Bohr separating large objects from quantum objects is rapidly crumbling" and has been abandoned by most experimental physicists (p.160). Brian Greene (2011) notes that,

> With every passing year, experimenters confirm that Schrödinger's equation works, without modification, for increasingly large collections of particles, and there's every reason to believe that it works for collections as hefty as those making up you and me and everything else
>
> (p.202)

Indeed, if quantum entanglement exists between two three-millimeter diamonds, it must affect human life. Julian Barbour (1999) strongly objects to conservative positions such as Hanley's saying,

> This view must be challenged. It belongs to a mindset that holds the world either to be classical in its entirety, or to have quantum objects within the old classical framework of space and time. How slow are we to move out of old quarters! All the evidence indicates that anything dynamical must obey the rules of quantum mechanics even if it appears classical to our senses.
>
> (p.252)

Efforts to quarantine quantum entanglement appear to be attempts to keep magical reality at bay. Certainly, Hugh Everett rejected the artificial division of quantum and Newtonian worlds in physical science, just as he insisted the conception of "detached observer" was an illusion. We're naturally entangled with the physical reality around us, so we might as well face-up to it.

Could entanglement be the basis of Frank and me dreaming the same dream? We don't know, but the pattern looks the same. After all, with a pair of entangled electrons, to touch one is to touch them both. Though physically different and spatially independent, the two electrons share the same existence. Dreaming the same dream sounds like "sharing the same existence." So, metaphorically speaking, the model of entanglement offers us a way to think about nonlocal telepathic processes (Radin, 2006).

In 2001 Nobel laureate Brian Josephson proposed that quantum physics "may lead to an explanation of processes still not understood within conventional science such as telepathy" (Clegg, 2006, p.226). But could quantum entanglement explain the telepathic processes allowing Frank to write scenes which so parallel my life that he appears to describe an event two months *before* I have it? That means my future would be a cause of Frank's story. Is that possible in the quantum realm? Maybe.

If the mind is an electromagnetic field, like biologist Johnjoe McFadden (2002, 2006) and neurophysiologist Susan Pockett (2000) propose, then advanced electromagnetic waves from the future could combine with retarded waves from the past to create the present (Vannini & Di Corpo, 2011). John Cramer's (2016; Kastner, 2015) transactional interpretation of quantum entanglement depicts an electromagnetic realm where past and future combine to create the present. In Cramer's quantum model of reality, the story of causality is incomplete without the contribution from the future.

But, as far as I know, there isn't any empirical evidence demonstrating entanglement affecting mental life, and we're probably centuries away from such knowledge (Kaku, 2008). Nonetheless, quantum entanglement is certainly real, and the implications of entanglement may cause us to reconsider the nature of our lives. Becoming enchanted by entanglement gives us an opportunity to think in new ways about our subjective experiences.

We employ metaphors of physical reality to interpret mental life. For example, Leibnitz's mechanical metaphor tells us that physical processes in the brain cause thoughts, and that our bodies and brains are sophisticated machines. Our subjective experience corresponds to an exclusively material reality. My problem with the mechanistic metaphor is that it doesn't match my experience. In fact, this materialist paradigm is used to declare thought transference and precognition to be impossible, no matter how much empirical evidence supports their existence, because there's no physical explanation for them. In the materialist model, man is a mindless automaton (James, 1890). In materialism, mind never causes anything. How can psychoanalysis, as a theory of mind, exist in a theoretical model which eliminates mind from consideration?

On the other hand, the model of quantum entanglement describes patterns of physical behavior that closely parallel my experiences with Frank. Dreaming the same dream is a nonlocal event, it's spooky action at a distance. Furthermore, quantum physics introduces the concept of mind affecting physical reality. Physicist Henry Stapp (2011) tells us, in quantum theory *mind is interwoven with matter*. Erwin Schrödinger (1967) writes there is no barrier between thinking observer and physical object, "*this barrier does not exist*" (p.137, italics added). Through the act of observation, mind and matter become entwined. As we'll see in coming chapters, psychoanalysis grows out of a tradition of immaterial mind transforming the physical body. At the origin of psychoanalysis Charcot demonstrated ideas create and alleviate paralysis. So, of these two models of physical reality metaphorically applied to interpret mental life, the quantum entanglement model is more consistent with my subjective experience, with my clinical experience with Frank, and with the therapeutic tradition of psychoanalysis.

Let's apply Nicolas Gisin's statements to Frank's novel. Gisin describes two interrelated realities, one based in space and time which is connected to a larger reality in which space/time doesn't exist. In fact, it's precisely the juncture between these two realities that Frank describes in his novel: It's the juncture between life and death, between this world and the next, between his conscious and unconscious minds. While Gisin is a physicist describing material reality "out there," it sounds like he's describing the immaterial reality of Frank's unconscious. This is like Chalmers and Lockwood who maintain the Many Worlds phenomenon actually occurs within the mind.

While Niels Bohr describes the essential complementarity of matter and energy—they exist as both particle and wave—Frank describes his mind as similarly complementary. His consciousness experience is local; but his unconscious is nonlocal, unbound in space and time, where he exists in an indeterminate state being both alive and dead. Quantum complementarity applied to the mind, embedded in the distinction between consciousness and the unconscious, was proposed in 1954 by Nobel laureate Wolfgang Pauli in a letter to Carl Jung. Pauli writes, "The epistemological situation regarding the concepts of 'consciousness' and the 'unconscious' seem to offer a close analogy to the situation of 'complementarity' in physics" (Atmanspacher & Fach, 2015, p.201). The most curious aspect of Pauli's conception of this complementarity is his declaration that consciousness is inherently subjective while the unconscious is "largely objective reality." This reverses traditional psychoanalytic belief, underscoring the objective aspect of the nonlocal and transpersonal nature of the unconscious. In Pauli's conception, the unconscious is much more deeply connected with external reality than consciousness. But, of course, Frank, has no idea of Pauli. He's just writing stories, making stuff up.

To conclude, let's look at the relationship between entanglement, psychoanalysis and magic. I'll compare physicist Erwin Schrödinger's description of entanglement, psychoanalyst Thomas Ogden's characterization of the analytic third (introduced in the first chapter), and nineteenth-century anthropologist James Frazer's depiction of sympathetic magic.

Here's Schrödinger's description of entanglement: "After a time of mutual influence the systems separate again, then they can no longer be described as before, viz., by endowing each of them with a representative of its own" (Aczel, 2001, p.70). Schrödinger says that in a limited way each quantum particle "becomes the other," and this shared similarity is the basis of their entanglement. Through entanglement the particles come to possess the attribute of "difference in sameness." The different particles begin to function as a single system, and the basic dynamic of entanglement is nonlocal effect: To touch one causes both particles to quiver no matter how spatially separated they are. Schrödinger calls entanglement "*the* characteristic trait of quantum mechanics."

In describing his conception of the analytic third, Ogden (1994) begins by emphasizing the intersubjective nature of psychoanalysis. Ogden writes, "There is no such thing as an analysand apart from the relationship with the analyst, and no such thing as an analyst apart from the relationship with the analysand" (p.63). Like Everett, Ogden has given up the intrapsychic conception of the detached observer. The shared subjectivity of patient and analyst is a defining feature of psychoanalysis. During analytic sessions a simultaneous "dialectic of oneness and twoness, of individual subjectivity and intersubjectivity, [creates] the foundation of the psychoanalytic relationship" (p.74). Through their interactions the patient and analyst create a new "third subjectivity." Ogden (2004) writes,

> The individuals engaged in this form of relatedness unconsciously subjugate themselves to a mutually generated intersubjective third for the purpose of freeing themselves from the limits of whom they had been to that point. . .The new intersubjective entity that is created, the subjugating analytic third, becomes a vehicle through which thoughts may be thought, feelings may be felt, sensations may be experienced, which to that point had existed only as potential experiences for each of the individuals.
>
> (pp.189–190)

Through their interaction patient and analyst come to simultaneously possess "oneness" and "twoness," or "difference in sameness." Through their shared intersubjective state, they each become the other, allowing each to experience new thoughts and feelings. Ogden says the creation of the intersubjective third is "the central clinical phenomenon of psychoanalysis."

Now, let's compare Schrödinger's and Ogden's descriptions with a depiction of contagious magic written at the turn of the last century by anthropologist James Frazer (1922) in his book, *The golden bough: A study of magic and religion.*

> Thus far we have been considering chiefly that branch of sympathetic magic which may be called homoeopathic or imitative. Its leading principle, as we have seen, is that like produces like, or, in other words, that an effect resembles its cause. The other great branch of sympathetic magic, which I have called Contagious Magic, proceeds upon the notion that things that have once been conjoined must remain forever afterwards, even when quite disserved from each other, in such a sympathetic relation that *whatever is done to one must similarly affect the other.*
>
> (p.43, italics added)

Contagious magic is based on the recognition that the sympathetic relationship between two people is so great that, even though separated, what is done to one alters the other. This sounds like the result from an experiment in quantum entanglement! Once again, we encounter spooky action at a distance.

Obviously, there is a similarity between descriptions of traditional beliefs in magic, Ogden's description of the analytic third, and Schrödinger's depiction of quantum entanglement. All three describe a mysterious form of nonlocal connection between discrete forms of matter.

Finally, we should acknowledge that science's elimination of magic was a *political* act, an assertion of its authority over traditional religious institutions. There was no empirical basis for that decision. In fact, after three hundred years the continued absence of physical evidence explaining gravity makes the "perpetual miracle" explanation—originally proposed as an absurdity—seem more compelling. With both gravity and quantum entanglement, science maintains the illusion of mechanistic materialism by ignoring the mystery and magic of nonlocality. Today, following the work of John Bell and his courageous colleagues, the study of entanglement encourages us to open our eyes. As Nobel laureate Ilya Prigogine and philosopher Isabelle Stengers (1984) write, "It is now science that appears to lend credibility to mystical affirmation" (p. 47).

References

Aczel, A. (2001). *Entanglement*. New York, NY: Plume.

Atmanspacher, H. (2015). Quantum approaches to consciousness. *The Stanford Encyclopedia of Philosophy*. http://plato.stanford.edu/archives/sum2015/ entries/qt-consciousness/ (Accessed August 28, 2016)

Atmanspacher, H. & Fach, W. (2015). Mind-matter correlations in duel-aspect monism. In E. Kelly, A. Crabtree, & P. Marshall (Eds.) *Beyond physicalism: Toward reconciliation of science and spirituality* (pp.195–226). Lanham, MD: Rowman & Littlefield.

Barbour, J. (1999). *The end of time: The next revolution in physics*. Cambridge: Oxford University Press.

Choi, C. (2015). Quantum record! 3,000 atoms entangled in bizarre state. www.livescience.com/50280-record-3000-atoms-entangled.html (Accessed September 30, 2016)

Christianson, G. (1984). *In the presence of the creator: Isaac Newton and his times*. New York, NY: The Free Press.

Clegg, B. (2006). *The God effect: Quantum entanglement, science's strangest phenomenon*. New York, NY: St. Martin's Griffin.

Cramer, J. (2016). *The quantum handshake: Entanglement, nonlocality, and transactions*. Heidelberg: Springer.

Everett, H. (1973). Relative state formulation of quantum mechanics. In B. DeWitt & N. Graham (Eds.) *The many-worlds interpretation of quantum mechanics* (pp.141–149). Princeton, NJ: Princeton University Press. (Original work published 1957)

Frazer, J. (1922). *The golden bough: A study of magic and religion*. New York, NY: Macmillan Publishing. (Original work published 1890)

Gilder, L. (2008). *The age of entanglement: When quantum physics was reborn*. New York, NY: Alfred A. Knopf.

Gisin, N. (2014). *Quantum chance: Nonlocality, teleportation, and other quantum marvels*. Heidelberg, Springer.

Gleick, J. (2003). *Isaac Newton*. New York, NY: Random House.

Greene, B. (2004). *The fabric of the cosmos: Space, time, and the texture of reality*. New York, NY: Random House.

Greene, B. (2011). *The hidden reality: Parallel universes and the deep laws of the cosmos*. New York, NY: Alfred A. Knopf.

Grossman, L. (2011). Entangled diamonds blur quantum-classical divide. www.
newscientist.com/article/dn21235-entangled-diamonds-blur-quantum-classical-
divide/ (Accessed September 17, 2016)

Hanly, C. (1995). On facts and ideas in psychoanalysis. *International Journal of
Psychoanalysis*, 76, 901–908.

James, W. (1890). *The principles of psychology*, volume 1. New York, NY: Henry
Holt & Company.

Kaiser, D. (2011). *How the hippies saved physics: Science, counterculture, and
the quantum revival*. New York, NY: W.W. Norton.

Kaku, M. (2005). *Parallel worlds*. New York, NY: Anchor Books.

Kaku, M. (2008). *Physics of the impossible*. New York, NY: Anchor Books.

Kastner, R. (2015). *Understanding our unseen reality: Solving quantum riddles*.
London: Imperial College Press.

Keynes, J. (1946). Newton, the man. http://www-history.mcs.st-and.ac.uk/Extras/
Keynes_Newton.html (Accessed August 28, 2016)

Maudlin, T. (2011). *Quantum non-locality and relativity*. Oxford, UK:
Wiley-Blackwell.

McFadden, J. (2002). The conscious electromagnetic information (Cemi) field
theory: The hard problem made easy? *Journal of Consciousness Studies*, 9,
23–50.

McFadden, J. (2006). The CEMI field theory: Seven clues to the nature of consciousness. In J. Tuszynski (Ed.), *The emerging physics of consciousness*
(pp.385–404). Berlin: Springer.

Musser, G. (2015). *Spooky action at a distance*. New York, NY: Scientific
American/Farrar, Straus and Giroux.

Nadeau, R. & Kafatos, M. (1999). *The non-local universe: The new physics and
matters of the mind*. New York, NY: Oxford University Press.

Ogden, T. (1994). The analytic third: working with intersubjective clinical facts.
Subjects of analysis (pp.61–95). Northvale, NJ: Jason Aronson.

Ogden, T. (2004). The analytic third: implications for psychoanalytic theory and
technique. *Psychoanalytic Quarterly*, 73, 167–195.

Penrose, R., Hamerhoff, S. & Kak, S. (Eds.), (2009). *Consciousness and the
universe: Quantum physics, evolution, brain and mind*. Cambridge, MA:
Cosmology Science Publishers.

Pockett, S. (2000). *The nature of consciousness: A hypothesis*. San Jose, CA:
Writers Club Press.

Prigogine, I. & Stengers, I. (1984). *Order out of chaos: Man's new dialogue with
nature*. New York, NY: Bantam.

Radin, D. (2006). *Entangled minds: Extrasensory experiences in quantum reality*.
New York, NY: Paraview Pocket Books.

Schrodinger, E. (1967). Mind and matter. *What is Life? and Mind and Matter* (pp.97–178). Cambridge: Cambridge University Press. (Original work published 1958)

Stapp, H. (2011). *Mindful universe: Quantum mechanics and the participating observer*. Heidelberg: Springer.

Vannini, A. & Di Corpo, U. (2011). Quantum physics, advanced waves and consciousness. In S. Kak, R. Penrose & S. Hameroff (Eds.), *Quantum physics of consciousness* (pp.177–189). Cambridge, MA: Cosmology Science Publishers.

Whitaker, A. (2016). *John Stewart Bell and twentieth-century physics: Vision and integrity*. Oxford: Oxford University Press.

Wootton, D. (2015). *The invention of science: A new history of the scientific revolution*. New York, NY: HarperCollins.

Chapter 10

Many Worlds, Many Minds, multiple selves

Barbara is in a study group and clinical supervision with me. She tells the following story:

> I was twenty-four-years old in my third year of graduate school. It was the spring term and I had an internship at a local college counseling center. It was after work, late afternoon. I was driving on a campus road, in a line of traffic that came to a stop.
>
> A Payloader was about fifteen feet ahead of me. There wasn't anything unusual about it. There was always a lot of ongoing construction on campus. I was sort of distracted, sitting there in the line of cars. Then I saw the Payloader rolling slowly back toward me. It was backing up. I assumed that a flagman was guiding it so that it would stop before hitting me. But the Payloader didn't stop. I went from being distracted, to watching this Payloader rolling back toward me, to fear and then to panic.
>
> The Payloader was moving slowly. The whole thing happened very slowly. I honked my horn. Then I thought that the front of my car would block it, prevent it from rolling any further back toward me. I was driving a Saab. But the engine of the Payloader was high up off the ground because the wheels are so big, and it protrudes way back while the driver sits in the cab over the wheels. The engine started to slide over the top of my car. I kept honking the horn. I was becoming hysterical. I began screaming. I couldn't believe what was happening. I heard and saw the windshield break, and the engine continued to move through the window frame

toward me. It crashed through the window and stopped just before hitting the steering wheel.

When the Payloader stopped, I stopped shrieking. Shards of glass were everywhere, and all over me. I had some small cuts from the glass. I took a couple of breaths and I realized the event was over. It was when I started to move, to lift my leg to get out of the car, that I thought, "I'm dead."

I kept moving even though I realized I was dead. I thought, "Maybe this is the way it is being dead." I was surprised that nothing changes. People who witnessed the accident got out of their cars and came over to me. They asked me questions. People were responding to me as if I were alive. I'm dead but everything just continues. Everything is the same. Someone called the campus police. The driver of the Payloader came over to talk to me. He may have said he was sorry. There was no flagger because it was after-hours. The driver had been moving the Payloader just to park it for the night. The police were talking to me and they don't realize I'm dead. It didn't occur to me to say anything about being dead. It was just a fact, nothing to report. A dead person would never say they're dead. Life just seemed to move along and I with it. It's like a moving sidewalk in an airport, a conveyer belt. We're all moving. I just happened to be dead and moving.

The police drove me home. I told my boyfriend about the accident, but I didn't tell him how I felt. I didn't tell him I was dead. I was in a cognitive-behavioral program. Have you ever spoken to a real behaviorist? There is no inner experience, there's only behavior. My experience didn't matter, my behavior mattered. It was so obvious to me that I was dead, but death apparently meant nothing changed on the outside. My behavior was the same. Everyone's behavior was the same. It's an indicator of how I was organized emotionally at that time in my life, not connected to my feelings or experience. In my program we only talked about what we could measure, and we couldn't measure being dead.

Then I forgot about it. I don't remember when it happened that I forgot it. It's like I was an anthropologist who'd landed in my life, arrived somewhere new and I was observing what was happening. Only I didn't go anywhere new. I was living the exact life I'd lived before the accident. What was new was that I was dead, nothing else was new. Everything else was the same.

It wasn't until I was thirty, and I was teaching research methods, and a death and dying course. A colleague's wife had a friend who was a psychic. He and his wife were very fond of him, and he did readings at their house, thirty-five dollars per reading. A bunch of us were invited over. I ended up just going along and getting a reading. The psychic's name was Don Cervantes. I mean, I don't know if that was a stage name or his real name. He wanted to hold onto something of mine while I talked, so I gave him a ring to hold in his hand. The reading began with a lot of ridiculous stuff. I was very skeptical. I answered simply "yes" or "no."

Then he said, "I see you died in a car accident." He gave the year and spoke very matter-of-factly about my death. I mean, anyone could guess that a person of a certain age might likely have been in a car accident, but his knowledge of my experience was way beyond that. I began to cry uncontrollably. I thought, "He has some way of knowing this. Somehow he has gotten inside my experience." I hadn't told anyone! I'd been an extremely well-adjusted, high-functioning dead person. How could he know?

I was surprised by how emotional I became. To him dying was no big deal. He said people often died several times in their lifetimes. He was very relaxed about it, very matter-of-fact. I don't know why I cried so when he told me that I *did* die. I guess my answer could be found in my relationship with my father. He disdained women's feelings, their talk of inner experience, and anything mystical. My father would bait women into talking emotionally so he could feel secretly superior. So, along comes Don who nonchalantly accepted what was the craziest experience I'd ever had. I guess it was a feeling of his acceptance and respect that was so different from my father's disdain.

Why else would I become so emotional? I wonder now if my crying emerged from the combination of my two selves, the mutual recognition of 'dead me' and 'me,' bringing together two of me that had been separated in my mind. Perhaps there is something inherently emotional about releasing an "other" state into consciousness, making a fuller more unified me. Anyway, I went from being completely skeptical about Don, really contemptuous, to feeling humbled. From that time forward, I knew some people had a way of *knowing* that I didn't have. I knew mindreading was possible. And I felt less troubled about being dead and alive at the same time.

Barbara believes she felt simultaneously dead and alive as a defensive fantasy to help her cope with mortifying terror. Freudian psychoanalysts reflexively look for defenses, narrowing their field of view. This is the position Barbara adopted, but her explanation didn't make sense to me.

Let's take a look at her psychological defenses as the Payloader event evolved. Her initial defense was disbelief. She denied she was in danger. She couldn't believe the accident was really happening. Looking back at the event, Barbara wonders why she didn't just undo her seatbelt and step out of the car. There was plenty of time to do this. She didn't take this life-preservative step because she was paralyzed by denial.

As the accident continued to slowly unfold, and as she was confronted by imminent death, Barbara wonders if she created her belief that she was *both* dead and alive as a defensive fantasy so that she could remain alive in spite of death. An elaboration of denial, this was her desperate last-ditch attempt to undo death.

Maybe, but I'm not convinced. Frankly, her explanation doesn't make sense to me. First of all, psychological defenses typically facilitate increased feelings of security strengthening one's sense of self. Barbara's proposed defensive fantasy left her in a state of increased confusion with a weakened sense of identity. So, on the face of it, how was she helped psychologically? Second, what is the defensive value of believing you're dead, when all the evidence indicates you're alive? As the accident unfolded Barbara used denial to fend off terror that she would be harmed. It appears at some point, after the Payloader's engine crashed through the automobile's windshield, Barbara unconsciously concluded she was dead. But she had no conscious awareness of this conclusion. Furthermore, when the engine stopped just before striking her, she didn't reverse her assessment and conclude she was alive. Seconds earlier she was alive and denies being in danger, but now she is dead and denies she's alive—or at least struggles to understand how, being dead, she could still be alive. Third, why did Barbara consciously realize she was dead *after* she'd survived the accident? In other words, the apparent defensive fantasy seems to arise *after* the event, when it's no longer needed. In my opinion, these three issues undermine the logic of a psychological defense explanation. I wonder whether her belief had a different origin.

It seems to me that Barbara's belief wasn't a defensive fantasy at all. It was simply an accurate description of her internal reality. Maybe we should take Barbara at her word and accept that, following the accident, in her mind she really was dead and alive simultaneously. As Ferenczi's famous patient, Elizabeth Severn, wrote in 1933, "I find it perfectly possible for a person to be psychically 'killed,' or at least some part of him killed, while he still continues to live in the flesh" (Severn, 2017, pp.108–109). For Severn, being alive and dead is a fact of traumatic life, and certainly this was a traumatic event for Barbara. From this perspective, Barbara looks like Schrödinger's Cat.

Ultimately, Barbara's psychological defense explanation may protect her from a more disturbing reality: Existing in multiple self-states simultaneously. When Barbara offered an explanation for why she became so emotional when the psychic said, "I see you died in a car accident," Barbara notes her gratification at the psychic's acceptance of her crazy secret, something her father would have chastised her for possessing. Then she says,

> I wonder now if my crying emerged from the combination of my two selves, the mutual recognition of "dead me" and "me," a coming together of two of me that had been separated by consciousness. Perhaps there is something inherently emotional about releasing an 'other' state into consciousness; making a fuller more unified me.

Here Barbara suggests that during the accident her identity as a continuous unified self split in two, and thereafter she possessed two selves, a "dead me" and a "me." It was as if she was now an anthropologist who'd entered her life and observed reality occurring around her with detached objectivity. Barbara possessed a new identity but externally her life was the same old life. For weeks after the accident her new "dead me" dominated her conscious mind as she noted the ongoing oddity of being both dead and alive. Because she was unable to reconcile how she could be living in these mutually exclusive states, at some point she partially forgot she was dead. Her dead self slipped into the background, and she became a well-adapted, high-functioning dead person.

Splitting of the personality is believed to be rare and thought to occur in response to traumatic events like those experienced by Barbara. Once a split has occurred, different personalities are usually isolated by dissociative amnesia, a kind of "quantum decoherence." This was not the case for Barbara where her "dead me" was fully aware of her "me" personality which survived the accident.

The splitting of consciousness and personality were first observed in Puysegur's work with Victor Race, a peasant who, when in a somnambulant state, possessed the intellect of a brilliant, well-educated person (Crabtree, 1993). "Double consciousness," "second state" and "multiple personality" were terms applied to the phenomenon in the nineteenth century (Braude, 1995; Crabtree, 1985, 2007; Dell & O'Neil, 2009; Hilgard, 1977; Howell, 2005).

Since the 1880s there's been debate whether multiple personality is pathological. The psychological process of splitting of consciousness was described by Pierre Janet as the "disaggregation" or "dissociation" of mental contents (Haule, 1986). Janet believed dissociative splitting of personality reflected mental weakness: In the face of a powerfully traumatic event the mind wasn't strong enough to fulfill its most basic function, the synthesis of experience and the maintenance of a unified self. Janet and Alfred Binet (1890, 1896) conducted many experiments with multiple personality in hypnotized hysterical patients in Charcot's laboratory.

During the same decade, English poet, classicist and psychical researcher Frederic Myers declared the belief in a unified consciousness to be mistaken. He proposed the unconscious naturally contains a secondary self, or multiple independent centers of intelligent activity dissociated from a primary self. In 1888 Myers writes,

> I hold that we each of us contain the potentialities of many different arrangements of the elements of our personality, each arrangement being distinguishable from the rest by differences in the chain of memories which pertains to it. The arrangement with which we habitually identify ourselves—what we call the normal or primary self—consists, in my view, of the elements selected for us in the struggle for existence with special reference to the maintenance of physical needs, and is not necessarily superior in any other respect to the latent personalities that lie alongside it.
>
> (p.387)

So, Janet and Binet, studying hysterical patients, believed multiple selves to be pathological. Conversely, Myers, observing the same phenomena among everyday people, considered multiple personality to be normal. Freud, more interested in asserting superiority over both Myers and Janet than responding to their research, declared consciousness, *by definition*, must be unitary, rendering multiple personality simply impossible. Freud (1915) writes, "it is questionable whether such a consciousness, lacking as it does, its most important characteristic [unity], deserves any discussion at all. . .The well-known cases of '*double conscience*' (splitting of consciousness) prove nothing against our view" (pp.170–171). Huh? You mean what Puysegur, Janet, Binet, Myers and countless others *observed* could be dismissed as theoretically inconceivable? I'm reminded of Charcot's phrase, "Theory is good, but it doesn't prevent a thing from existing" (Hustvedt, 2011, p.13). Not so for Freud! His position is more bewildering when you realize Breuer's treatment of Bertha Pappenheim, which Freud considered the foundation of psychoanalysis, was a classic case of split consciousness. Breuer (1895) writes, "the patient was split into two personalities of which one was mentally normal and the other insane" (p.45). A positivist at heart, dismissing the evidence, Freud simply side-stepped the phenomenon.

Carl Jung's theory of complexes proposed the self was comprised of numerous personality fragments, some of which are unknown to the primary self. Jung's views tilted in the direction of Myers. And W. D. Fairbairn, pioneer in Object Relations theory, considered dissociative splitting of the self to be a normal part of man's basic schizoid nature. Normalizing dissociative processes, as conceived by Myers and Fairbairn, continues in the work of contemporary American interpersonal psychoanalysts Philip Bromberg (1998), Jody Messler Davies (1998), and Elizabeth Howell (2011) who regard multiple self-states as common, though traumatically conceived. Like Einstein, they may consider the concept of a single unified self to be an optical illusion of consciousness.

In my opinion, it's a mistake to call Barbara's dissociative splitting a psychological defense and looking exclusively for conflict/defense blinds us to other more profitable explanations. If Barbara's splitting wasn't a defense, was it instead an example of a Many Worlds/Many Minds phenomenon? From the Many Minds perspective of David Chalmers (1996) and Michael Lockwood (1996), was Barbara's recognition of a "dead me" simply her realistic awareness of another version of herself who actually died in the accident? Should the Many Minds conception of parallel universes cause us to reconsider dissociative splitting of a unified personality? If the answer is yes, then dissociation as a kind of quantum decoherence could be a fundamental property of the mind. From Hugh Everett's (Byrne, 2010) perspective, splitting the personality isn't the result of psychological weakness or an inability to maintain a unified self. It's a necessary mental outcome of a physical event. If that's true, then Schrödinger's cat lives within us all.

Finally, what are the odds that Frank and I would both dream of waking up dead—that is, experience being alive and dead simultaneously, that he'd make this theme the basis of a novel, *and* that my supervisee would have had a parallel experience in her life? This looks like a meaningful coincidence for the three of us.

References

Binet, A. (1890). *On double consciousness: Experimental psychological studies.* Chicago, IL: Open Court Publishing Company.

Binet, A. (1896). *Alterations of personality.* New York, NY: Springer US.

Braude, S. (1995). *First person plural: Multiple personality and the philosophy of mind.* Lanham, MD: Rowman and Littlefield Publishers.

Breuer, J. (1895). Case 1: Fraulein Anna O. In J. Breuer & S. Freud (Eds.), *Studies on hysteria* (pp.21–47). *Standard Edition.* London: Hogarth Press, 2, 3–309.

Bromberg, P. (1998). *Standing in the spaces: Essays on clinical process, trauma, and dissociation.* Hillsdale, NJ: The Analytic Press.

Byrne, P. (2010). *The many worlds of Hugh Everett III: Multiple universes, mutual assured destruction, and the meltdown of a nuclear family.* Oxford: Oxford University Press.

Chalmers, D. (1996). The interpretation of quantum mechanics. *The conscious mind: In search of a fundamental theory* (pp.333–357). New York, NY: Oxford University Press.

Crabtree, A. (1985). *Multiple man: Explorations in possession and multiple personality.* London: Holt, Rinehart and Winston.

Crabtree, A. (1993). *From Mesmer to Freud: Magnetic sleep and the roots of psychological healing.* New Haven, CT: Yale University Press.

Crabtree, A. (2007). Automatism and secondary centers of consciousness. In E.F. Kelly, E.W. Kelly, A. Crabtree, A. Gauld, M. Grosso & B. Greyson, *Irreducible mind: Toward a psychology for the 21st century* (pp.301–365). Lanham, MD: Rowman & Littlefield Publishers.

Davies, J. (1998). Multiple perspectives on multiplicity. *Psychoanalytic Dialogues, 8,* 195–206.

Dell, P. & O'Neil, J. (Eds.) (2009). *Dissociation and the dissociative disorders: DSM-V and beyond.* New York, NY: Routledge.

Freud, S. (1915). The unconscious. *Standard Edition.* London: Hogarth Press, 14, 159–215.

Haule, J. (1986). Pierre Janet and dissociation: The first transference theory and its origins in hypnosis. *American Journal of Clinical Hypnosis*, 29, 86–94.

Hilgard, E. (1977). *Divided consciousness: Multiple controls in human thought and action*. New York, NY: John Wiley & Sons.

Howell, E. (2005). *The dissociative mind*. Hillsdale, NJ: The Analytic Press.

Howell, E. (2011). *Understanding and treating dissociative identity disorder: A relational approach*. New York, NY: Routledge.

Hustvedt, A. (2011). *Medical muses: Hysteria in nineteenth-century Paris*. New York, NY: W.W. Norton & Company.

Lockwood, M. (1996). "Many Minds" interpretations of quantum mechanics. *The British Journal for the Philosophy of Science*, 47, 159–188.

Myers, F. (1888). French experiments on strata of personality. *Society for Psychical Research, Proceedings*, vol. 5, 1888–1889. https://babel.hathitrust.org/cgi/pt?id=nyp.33433070248665;view=1up;seq=386 (Accessed August 10, 2018)

Severn, E. (2017). *The discovery of the self: A study in psychological cure*. P. Rudnytsky (Ed.). London: Routledge. (Original work published 1933)

Chapter 11

A dream from the future

Pat and I walk to the bay at sunrise. We take this walk every day. It's been a cool spring, and there's a whisper of summer in this beautiful sunny morning. Pat's pleased she's wearing sunglasses because the sunrise is so brilliant. When we reach the bay, I stare into the water looking for the first fish and crabs of the season. My unconscious always looks for something else.

On this Thursday morning there's a large fish lying dead on the bottom in about five feet of water. I show it to Pat. It's unusual to see dead fish lying on the bottom of the bay. My wife thinks the fish has been shot with an arrow just below the gills. Pat says, "It's illegal to spear fish. The Bay Constable should investigate this." I don't say anything. I can't tell if the fish has been speared. But seeing a large dead fish is ominous.

The rest of Thursday is uneventful. I have a normal Friday in New York filled with appointments. I'm back on Long Island and in bed by 10:00. I wake up in the middle of the night to go to the bathroom. I glance at my wristwatch. It's about 1:45. I feel like getting up but tell myself I need more sleep. Each day during the past week I've been writing in the middle of the night, usually getting less than six hours of sleep. I decide to stay in bed and get some rest.

But I can't get back to sleep. I lay in bed thinking about the dream I'd just had. I'd dreamt I was at the college looking at paintings, including mine, hanging on a wall. The wall was covered with pictures, the work of many artists. I was indifferent to my paintings, but I was impressed by how creative my colleague Jim had been. He proudly showed me several pieces. I wasn't sure they were significant paintings, but I was struck by how inventive he'd been. Then he showed me a three-dimensional painting cast in clear Lucite or glass. Seen from the side it had three different levels, like steps. I was proud of Jim and felt enriched by his creativity.

As I lay in bed trying to get back to sleep, on two occasions I look at my watch and it still reads 1:45. I glance over at the battery-operated clock on my nightstand: Ten-to-five. I get up and go downstairs.

As I'm making coffee, I examine my watch. I'm wearing my old wind-up Omega Speedmaster which I received in 1976 as a graduation gift when I completed my master's degree in fine art. The back of the watch is inscribed. It reads, "Flight-qualified by NASA for all manned space missions," announcing it was the first watch worn on the moon. This moonwatch holds a lot of meaning for me. It's a connection to my twenties, a period of painful growth. A few years ago, I spent nine hundred dollars to have it restored. Omega is the last letter in the Greek alphabet and signifies "the end." Presumably, the name was selected by the manufacturer to denote the ultimate in quality. But I figure literally, "when the Omega stops, I should watch."

I'm pretty sure my Omega hadn't wound down. To check, I turn the stem a couple of times and find it's nearly fully wound. So, that wasn't the reason my watch stopped functioning. Given the way my watches work, I wonder if there's something I should be paying attention to. I walk into my office and pick up my cell phone to get the time, so I can reset the watch. Looking at the cell phone's screen I notice I'd received a call in the middle of the night. It's a Long Island area code, but not a number I recognize. I figure I'll listen to the message later after I've had some coffee.

About a half hour later I listen to the message. Last night, at 1:42 am, I received a call from someone named Laura. She said she's living with a woman who has paintings of mine hanging in her home. She knows of my fine reputation at the college, and having looked me up online, she's surprised to see I'm a psychoanalyst. She's considering making an appointment and asks if I accept Medicare.

Saturday was a busy day. I call her back in the afternoon. From her message the night before, I don't expect to work with her. My fee is high, and I don't take insurance. When I speak to Laura, she tells me she's living with and caring for my old friend, Betrice, who is now ninety years old, has kidney cancer and is dying of congestive heart failure in East Hampton. I haven't seen Bette in thirty-five years.

In the 1970s, she owned a home on Castle Street in East Patchogue. When I moved to Long Island fifty years ago, she lived one house away from the small bungalow I rented. She worked as a college administrator in New York, and only came out on weekends. Bette was smart, well read and French. She drove a baby blue Alfa Romeo Giulia sports car, which was exotic during an era when most cars on Eastern Long Island were American made. Bette took a liking to my former wife and me. During the four years we lived on Castle Street, Bette became our best friend.

When I speak to Laura on the phone she says,

> I'm looking at one of your paintings on the wall right now. Bette has two of your paintings. One is a diptych in yellow and blue. The other painting has a circular motif. The circles are sort of floating. It's painted on wood and is three-dimensional.

I recognize the first painting but can't recall making any three-dimensional paintings. I suspect she's confused my work with someone else.

Laura says she attended the college's Eastern Campus where I'd formerly worked. This is how she'd heard of me. I'd spent eighteen years working at this small campus where I was first a teacher and then a dean. When she says this, I think about the parallels between her statements and my dream the night before. She said she was looking at one of my paintings on the wall, and she'd attended the college. In my dream, I'd been looking at paintings, including mine, on the wall at the college. Then I recall my reaction to my colleague Jim's paintings. I wasn't sure they were significant paintings, but I felt proud of Jim and enriched by his creativity. I imagine this is how Betrice felt years ago looking at my paintings. Then I remember in my dream Jim showed me a three-dimensional painting, just as this woman claims I'd made a three-dimensional work. The phrase "three-dimensional painting" is unusual because it describes a unique category: Paintings are typically two-dimensional and anything three-dimensional is usually called sculpture. These several parallels get my attention. How come three elements of my dream match Laura's statements made a half day later?

After speaking to Laura, I think about the ominous dead fish lying in four feet of water that Pat believed had been shot in the lungs, and I consider Bette dying of congestive heart failure. Is this simply coincidental or a form of foreshadowing? It wasn't until after talking to Laura that I realize my watch stopped last night at the time I received her call. I think, "What a strange series of events."

Here's the thing about my wrist watches. I wear an inexpensive battery-operated Timex, and my old mechanical Omega. I use the Timex most of the time and wear the Omega when I dress up. Eight times in the last eight months both watches have malfunctioned during emotionally charged conversations. At first it was the Timex. Last September it sped up, gaining half an hour, during an impassioned conversation with Pat about my concern that she should see her neurologist. Pat had had life-saving neurosurgery three years earlier to repair two aneurysms in her brain, one of which was bleeding. Now, in my opinion, there appeared to be another problem in her brain. In this emotionally wrenching conversation Pat begrudgingly agreed to make an appointment with her doctor.

The second incident with the Timex occurred while I listened to a student who, with tears running down her cheeks, told me about being blamed for the suicide of a high school friend. During that intense experience my Timex gained fifteen minutes. On the third occasion, my Timex stopped completely the morning my son-in-law's father died. After that I replaced the battery in my watch and consciously turned away from thoughts of death.

That worked for four months. Then one night in March I dreamt about seeing a brilliant light that I associated with death. My unconscious mind seemed to be intruding upon my consciously constructed optimism. Hours later both watches malfunctioned in succession. The Timex sped up a half an hour then slowed down. Switching watches, my Omega lost six minutes during the next hour. At first the problem had been my electronic Timex, which I'd hoped to correct with a new battery. Now my entirely reliable, fully restored (flight-qualified by NASA!) mechanical Omega was also misbehaving. A week later my Omega stopped for the fifty-three minutes of Frank's session, though it spontaneously resumed working afterwards. A month later my Omega did the same stopping and restarting during a session with another patient, Mitchell. It seems impossible to relate the watch's functioning to Frank or Mitchell. On the other hand, I chuckle realizing my Omega was conforming to Frank's vignettes where Ching Ling Foo exists "between moments in time." Were my watches being influenced by a "Foo Effect?"

Now my Omega had stopped again. It's possible that I simply have two defective watches, and there's no other meaning to be derived from their malfunctioning. Certainly, reductive materialism declares there can't be any connection between my watches and these interpersonal events, so I must eliminate these experiences from consideration. But I can't.

Sometimes my Timex behaves more mysteriously. On a dozen occasions my Timex watch jumped ahead fifteen to twenty minutes, sometimes bolting ahead fifteen minutes in an instant, and left unattended the watch has returned to the correct time within twenty-four hours. Really, how could this occur? For me, it's deeply perplexing. Entropy works one way. You can see an egg fall from the kitchen counter and break on the floor, but you never see a broken egg fly up from the floor and become a solid egg resting on the counter. So, from my modest understanding of physics, I'm pretty sure the second law of thermodynamics can't be true if this watch experience is a naturally occurring event.

On the other hand, if like Max and Werner Heisenberg, I apply the logic of Heraclitus, and assume these opposite depictions of reality are both necessarily true, then I need to reconceptualize my rational understanding of the world. Anyway, it seems to me there'd have to be two watches within the Timex for it to "reregulate" itself and return to the correct time. This process of "reregulation" suggests an agent, like Foo, affecting my watch.

Anyone hearing this story about my watches would consider it pure madness. Certainly, these experiences can't be true. They must be hallucinations. That's an explanation I've considered, but the swirling hands of my Timex have been observed by a student in one of my drawing classes. When I asked her why my watch was functioning in such a strange way she responded, "Your watch is playing tricks on you."

In addition to her response, there's literature supporting this watch phenomenon in research on people who've survived near-death experiences. Kenneth Ring and Evelyn Valarino (1998) write about hyperesthesia, an unusual sensitivity to environmental stimuli that often occurs following near-death experiences.

> And particularly noteworthy here is a marked increase in electrical sensitivity—Near-Death-Experiencers begin to have many "strange encounters of the electrical kind." A surprisingly large proportion of these persons discover, for instance, that digital wrist watches will no longer work properly for them, or they "short-out" electrical systems in their cars, or computers and appliances malfunction for no apparent reason, and so on.
>
> (p.129)

Another researcher (Atwater, 2007), who has interviewed thirty-three hundred survivors of near-death experiences, writes, "Of the experiencers I interviewed, seventy-three percent fit this profile and give numerous reports of electrical snafus . . . None could wear watches anymore without constantly repairing or replacing them" (p.109). A third researcher, physician Melvin Morse (1992), reports, "One-fourth of a study population that mysteriously stops watches is astonishing, especially compared to other groups we studied" (p.132).

The work of these researchers, combined with the testimony of my student, encourages me to take my watches seriously. I can't explain the mysterious quality of their malfunctioning, but it makes me curious. I take my watches' misbehavior to mean literally "watch," pay attention. What harm can there be in refusing to eliminate these inexplicable phenomena from consideration? I realize I've become like Max the crazy architect in Frank's novel. I question how time is distinguished from the representation of time. Like Max, by focusing on this measurement problem I'm rejecting cultural assumptions about the material world, which raises questions about my reality-testing. If Max is the mad architect of Frank's novel, then I'm the crazy artist/psychoanalyst writing this story.

The next day (Sunday), prompted by my watch malfunctioning, I decide to visit Bette one last time. I think about calling Laura to see if Bette would welcome my visit. After all, I haven't seen her in thirty-five years. Although she described Bette as living in hospice, for some reason I don't feel a need to rush. Because Monday's Memorial Day and a national holiday, I call first thing Tuesday morning. Tuesday afternoon Laura returned my call while I was seeing patients. She left a lengthy message that I listened to between sessions. She said that Betrice would have loved to have seen me, but she'd died Friday night at 9:00. She was with her at her death. I was taken back. I wept. I had to see another patient. Then I ate dinner with Pat and our son Cameron.

After dinner, I thought about how strange it was that Laura described Bette as being alive when I spoke to her on Saturday afternoon when, according to her message, she'd died the night before. Of course, under any circumstance it's unusual to call and leave a message at 1:42 in the morning. Now, for the first time, I connect my watch stopping to Bette's death.

With these thoughts in mind, later Tuesday evening I call Laura and leave a message saying that I want to speak to her again. Ostensibly, I'm calling about funeral arrangements. Wednesday morning Laura calls me back and we have a chance to talk. She describes the last years of Bette's life, and tells me about plans for a memorial service.

Then I ask Laura when Bette died. She repeats, "Friday night at 9:01." I say, "So you called me later that night, Saturday morning about 1:30, about the possibility of an appointment?" Laura responds, "No, I definitely didn't call you later that night, the night Bette died. I spoke to you the first time about a week ago, before she died." I don't question her further. This has to be a very stressful time. She's probably been making a lot of phone calls. In fact, stress might be her reason for wanting a consultation with a psychoanalyst. I figure I can get an obituary online which would give me the day Bette died.

Nonetheless, I consider my brief interactions with Laura to be characterized by a strange inversion of time. First, I appear to dream about the contents of our conversation twelve hours before we have it. Now, perhaps in a parallel fashion, Laura appears to be reversing the sequence of Bette's death and her phone call to me. Bette must have died after our conversation on Saturday afternoon. Maybe she died Saturday or Sunday night.

Then Laura asks me to estimate the value of my two paintings. Bette's furnishings were going to be auctioned. I give her a modest amount of a couple hundred dollars. "They're student works," I say. I ask Laura to describe again the three-dimensional painting on wood, which she does. Now I identify the picture she's talking about. In the mid-1970s I'd made several paintings of what appear to be transparent overlapping circles. The paintings were flat, but the shapes appear to float one over the other, creating an illusion of three-dimensionality. The paintings were studies in color transparency. Then I think again of my dream of Jim's Lucite three-dimensional painting that has three different levels and is "transparent." I realize that our three-dimensional paintings were both transparent. This similarity is simply too unique to be coincidental.

Five days later I dream of Betrice. There is a sense of urgency. There isn't much time and a lot to be done. She's preparing to leave on an important trip. Bette is a whirlwind. That's how she gets at times like this. I've seen it before. She's worked herself into quite a state.

Bette says she wants to take me with her wherever she's going. In the dream, I know she's dead. I agree to go. "Good," she says. "In that case you need to be prepared." There's a special procedure for taking the living. She has instructions for that. It's like I'll have to be embalmed.

But first, there's a party. Bette prepares my face for the party. I need to make an appearance, just my face, that's all that's important at the moment.

After the party, we're in Bette's kitchen in her cottage on Castle Street. Bette is looking down at a paper held in her two hands. She's reading instructions for my preparation. First, I have to be kept cold. She realizes I'm too warm and she has to get me colder. Before the party everything was happening so fast, now everything seems to slow down. Cooling me down will take some time, and I'll have to be kept at a particular temperature for several days. I have a sense of the world around me continuing, but I just stop. Then I slowly re-emerge, like I'm waking up from anesthesia. I realized I'm still standing next to Bette in her kitchen. She's still reading from the sheet of paper held in her two hands. "Okay, good," she says. She looks down and reads some more. It's like a recipe. I remember all those times we were in that kitchen preparing food at the last minute for dinner, sometimes at the edge of panic. I was the novice, the cooperative assistant following Bette's instructions.

Then we walk into her living room. I turn to look at Bette standing a few feet from me. She begins to tremble all over. She's ecstatic, orgasmic. I can tell she's changing. I realize there's no reaching her now. Then she's gone.

I look around the living room for a last time. I look for my favorite chairs though I can't see them. The room is just a mist. Bette had a pair of antique Chippendale armchairs that sat on either side of her fireplace. The carving combined with the joinery in the chairs amazed me. But what I liked more than the woodworking was the upholstery. The upholstered cushions were so worn their threadbare fabric hung from the seats. Bette's respect for the chairs' history, and for their material condition recording their participation in this world, always impressed me.

I woke up. I went downstairs to make coffee. As the coffee brewed, I realize this dream is my last visit with Betrice. What we couldn't accomplish in this world we completed in a dream. In my dream, we met nine days after her death, just before her departure. Talk about waiting until the last minute! Of course, that's the way things are with Bette and I.

Then I remember forty years ago walking through Bette's back door and stepping into her kitchen. I hand her a small shaped painting on Masonite glued to a pine frame: The transparency study. Her hands are dirty, so she wipes them on a cloth before taking the painting from me. She holds my little painting in her two hands. Looking down at it, I describe what I'm trying to accomplish in the picture. She smiles and nods. She's pleased to have it. She thanks me. After looking at it for a moment, she hands it back to me. She asks me to put it in the living room between the Chippendale chairs, by the fireplace. She says, "We'll look at it after dinner."

I think about my two dreams and the direction of time. I wonder if my dreams are gifts from Bette, just as my two paintings had been gifts from me. My first dream of looking at my paintings on the wall at the college appears to be a condensation of Laura's remarks made to me the next day, twelve hours later. For two thousand years people have considered dreams to be composed from the contents of the previous day. Ancient Greek historian Herodotus believed dreams were made from the "thoughts of the day," or what Freud called "day residue." In this case, my dream appears to be made from the residue of a day *not yet experienced*.

Every culture throughout recorded history has regarded dreams as prophetic. Most ancient cultures used the word "divination" to describe premonitions because people believed their origin was divine. For example, an Egyptian divinatory text dating from 1200 BCE interpreted two hundred and thirty prophetic dreams (Hoffman, 2015). Tibetan Buddhism, Sufi Islam and Christianity all recognized the power of visionary dreams (Bulkeley, 2016), and the Bible itself contains fifteen premonitory dreams (Krippner, Bogzaran & de Carvalho, 2002). Plutarch, biographer of the ancient world, wrote, "the dream is the oldest oracle" (Hearne, 1989, p.17), and the largest scientific study of more than ten thousand premonitions, conducted by Louisa Rhine (1967), found that three-quarters occurred in dreams.

Divination was taken seriously by learned members of the ancient world because it was "both hard to understand and a more or less observable fact" (Struck, 2016, p.11). Plato believed divination was a way of knowing the highest truths through insight rather than inference. Divination was considered a form of intuition: "Immediate apprehension by the mind without reasoning" (Sykes, 1964, p.568). Intuition seems nonlocal, spooky action at a distance. It's the product of thinking done somewhere else by an invisible mind.

In *Timaeus* Plato (1961) writes divination arises during altered states of consciousness: "No man, when in his wits, attains prophetic truth and inspiration, but when he receives the inspired word, either his intelligence is enthralled in sleep or he is demented by some distemper or possession" (p.1194). In *On divination during sleep*, Aristotle (1984) associates predictive dreams with divinity permeating nature, noting premonitions occur in the empty-headed unburdened by intellectual activity, or in those experiencing ecstatic states. The earliest medical text, the Hippocratic *On regimen*, contains a chapter on prophetic dreams predicting disease (van der Eijk, 2008).

Since science can't reproduce premonitory dreams in a lab, and the arrow of time makes premonition seem impossible, premonitions defy explanation. But, is it reasonable to dismiss three thousand years of premonitory dreams, emerging across cultures, as primitive superstition? Can we erase three thousand years of cross-cultural evidence just because we can't explain it? Or is this, in the words of philosopher of science, Isabelle Stengers (2003), simply rationalism's "way of disqualifying a phenomenon rather than understanding it" (p.22)? Conversely, does this three-thousand-year body of evidence support my hypothesis that people naturally experience multiple times in the unconscious?

Perhaps within the unconscious a strand of time runs backwards. In that temporal dimension the future is the cause of my present experience, and I remember the future rather than the past. Maybe Paul Dirac's conception of an antimatter universe in which time runs backwards is true, but true within our unconscious mind. Recall that philosophers David Chalmers (1996) and Michael Lockwood (1996) converted Hugh Everett's Many Worlds interpretation of material reality into a Many Minds conception of the unconscious mind. Could we do the same thing with Dirac's conception of time reversal? If so, this temporal dimension could be the basis of premonition and prophecy.

With these questions in mind, I think again about my Omega watch stopping three times in the last two months, first with Frank, then with Mitchell, and now with Bette's death. A possible connection between these three people is the experience of death around Memorial Day. The subject of *Memorial* Day is death, after all. Frank's mother died last year on the Monday after Memorial Day, Mitchell's brother died accidentally three years ago on Memorial Day, and Bette died the day before Memorial Day. But that connection only makes sense looking back from Bette's death. Could my unconscious memory of Bette's *future* death couple with the anniversary memories of Frank and Mitchell to become the cause of my Omega stopping?

But, how could a collection of emotional memories stop a watch? That's *impossible*, isn't it? Can something as immaterial as a thought affect matter? Certainly, in quantum physics human consciousness alters the form matter and energy take. And quantum physicist Henry Stapp (2017) describes conscious intentions creating a bias within quantum-level processes, allowing human intentions to have subtle physical effects. But, can the future effect the present? Well, consider John Cramer's (2016) transactional interpretation of quantum reality where past and future *combine* to create the present. Or, there's physicist John Wheeler's "delayed choice" and "quantum eraser" experiments (Greene, 2004) which demonstrate the future creating the present. These experiments (discussed in the next chapter) reveal a reversal of temporal order and causation.

So, conceptually it *may be possible* for a memory from the future to affect my watch, but it's not something I ordinarily observe. Of course, I see what I expect to see, and probably ninety percent of what I observe merely confirms my view of reality. Who knows? It's a mystery. Such confusing speculations make me realize how much easier it is to conclude I simply have a pair of defective watches.

I think of my second dream in which I visited Betrice after her death. Here the arrow of time is restored. That's what death always proves. The only thing for certain is she's dead and I'm alive. In that dream, after preparing me, Bette leaves without me. She's gone, and I'm left here writing about it. What happened? Did she take an unconscious portion of me, a part I don't consciously miss? Did my preparation fail? Did she change her mind? Or, did she just run out of time? But, of course, it was *just a dream* after all. Perhaps, I shouldn't bother with such questions. I guess time will tell.

A month later, *The East Hampton Star* contained an obituary describing Bette's life and announcing her memorial service. The obituary said Bette died on Saturday evening, not on Friday night as Laura had originally told me. I thought again about my decision on that Sunday to visit Betrice one last time. I remembered feeling then, that even though she was in a hospice, I didn't need to hurry. Now I realize she'd died the night before. In fact, there'd been no need to rush.

References

Aristotle (1984). On divination in sleep. In J. Barnes (Ed.), *The complete works of Aristotle, volume 1* (pp.736–739). Princeton, NJ: Princeton University Press.

Atwater, P. (2007). *The big book of near-death experiences*. Charlottesville, VA: Hampton Roads Publishing.

Bulkeley, K. (2016). *Big dreams: The science of dreaming and the origins of religion*. New York, NY: Oxford University Press.

Chalmers, D. (1996). *The conscious mind: In search of a fundamental theory*. New York, NY: Oxford University Press.

Cramer, J. (2016). *The quantum handshake: Entanglement, nonlocality, and transactions*. Heidelberg: Springer.

Greene, B. (2004). *The fabric of the cosmos: Space, time, and the texture of reality*. New York, NY: Random House.

Hearne, K. (1989). *Visions of the future*. Wellingborough, UK: Aquarian Press.

Hoffman, F. (2015). Ancient Egypt. In D. Collins (Ed.), *The Cambridge history of magic and witchcraft in the west* (pp.52–82). Cambridge: Cambridge University Press.

Krippner, S., Bogzaran, F. & de Carvalho, A. (2002). *Extraordinary dreams and how to work with them*. Albany, NY: State University of New York Press.

Lockwood, M. (1996). "Many Minds" interpretations of quantum mechanics. *The British Journal for the Philosophy of Science*, 47, 159–188.

Morse, M. & Perry, P. (1992). *Transformed by the light*. New York, NY: Villard Books.

Plato. (1961). Timaeus. In E. Hamilton & H. Cairns (Eds.), *The collected dialogues of Plato, including letters* (pp.1151–1211). Princeton, NJ: Princeton University Press.

Rhine, L. (1967). *ESP in life and lab: Tracing hidden channels*. New York, NY: Macmillan.

Ring, K. & Valarino, E. (1998). *Lessons from the light: What we can learn from near-death experience*. New York, NY: Plenum Press.

Stapp, H. (2017). *Quantum theory and free will: How mental intentions translate into bodily actions*. Cham, Switzerland: Springer International Publishing.

Stengers, I. (2003). The doctor and the charlatan. *Cultural Studies Review*, 9, 11–36.

Struck, P. (2016). *Divination and human nature: A cognitive history of intuition in classical antiquity*. Princeton, NJ: Princeton University Press.

Sykes, J. (Ed.) (1964). *The concise Oxford dictionary of current English*. Oxford: Oxford University Press.

Van der Eijk, P. (2008). The role of medicine in the formation of early Greek thought. In P. Curd & D. Graham (Eds.), *The Oxford handbook of Presocratic philosophy* (pp.385–412). Oxford: Oxford University Press.

Chapter 12

Time

Premonitory dreams leave me wondering whether our conscious and unconscious minds each possess a different awareness of time. It's supposed to be impossible to have knowledge of the future. Nonetheless, I can't discount my premonitions as meaningless coincidences. During the past twenty years I've had many precognitive experiences, large and small, with the most elaborate occurring in dreams.

Moments of precognition give me the feeling of my life being lived in two different realities. My unconscious seems to exist within an infinite expanse of space and time, while consciously I move deliberately along a path of successive "presents." Consciously I experience time sequentially. But in my unconscious, my life appears in its entirety "all at once" with no distinction of past, present or future. In the language of quantum physics, consciousness seems local, while the unconscious appears nonlocal, unbound in space and time. My subjective experience is caught between these two realities, between two different truths.

Is there scientific evidence that my conscious and unconscious minds possess different times? Yes. Benjamin Libet's (2004) neurological research proves the conscious mind runs a half-second behind the unconscious, demonstrating actions are initiated in the unconscious prior to conscious awareness. The take home message from Libet's research is that the unconscious is in charge of decision making initiating all actions. So, consciousness is a kind of after-the-fact cognition, double checking the decisions of the unconscious. Unaware of the unconscious, consciousness believes it's in charge (Gigerenzer, 2007; Gilhooley, 2008 Norretranders, 1998; Wilson, 2002), the epitome of self-deception.

Libet's research shows that unconscious and conscious portions of the mind are temporally out of sync, but only by a half-second. At least this is consistent with my impression that different times are experienced in my mind, with my unconscious running ahead into the future. Libet's research distinguishes time from the representation of time in the mind, and again, we're reminded of Max, Frank's crazy architect.

I realize time defines "me" in the world. In my conscious mind I am delineated with hard edges, but in my unconscious I'm a blur. Within the unconscious, awareness of my past, present and future blurs, expanding the edges of me. Rather than being located at a discrete point in space/time as I consciously believe, within my unconscious "I" extends across space and time. Like the electron, the location of "me" in space and time is indeterminate—I'm in there somewhere. In my unconscious I'm nonlocal. Simultaneously possessing past, present and future, this new spatial/temporal shape of "me" shifts from a point to a cloud. Like a photon of light switching from being a particle to being a wave, I shift from being an object and become a *field*. It's a challenge to imagine myself as a "field." I try it on for size.

Certainly, unconscious knowledge of future events would confer evolutionary advantages. But, if I have an unconscious awareness of my future, how much future? Minutes, hours, weeks, months—my whole lifespan? Could I have been born with a nearly instantaneous unconscious awareness of my (eventual) death? Logically, that's what these precognitive experiences imply.

But how could my life have an end at the very beginning before I even live it? Could life be experienced at different rates, with my unconscious experiencing my whole life compressed into an instant while my conscious experience unfolds incrementally over a period of decades? Conceptually, that's how it looks. But what conditions could create this? If in my unconscious I'm a *field* rather than a point in space and time, and if this field is *rotating*, then the outer edges of the field would travel at a faster rate than the center of the field. If the outer edges of the field were traveling really fast, at something approaching the speed of light, then this could be the basis of multiple times being experienced in the unconscious self. At the outer edges of this spinning field an eighty-year lifetime would be lived in a matter of months. So, I'd be alive in the center of the field, but dead along the outer edges. I'd have achieved the status of Schrödinger's Cat, being alive and dead concurrently.

As wacky as this sounds, mathematician Kurt Godel used Einstein's equations for general relativity to prove the universe is actually *rotating*, not expanding (Goldstein, 2005; Holt, 2018). Any resident in Godel's universe could move back and forth in time as easily as he could move spatially in any direction. Who knows, maybe my rotating-self resides in Godel's rotating universe! Anyway, for Godel, the conception of a self as a rotating field may not have been too far out.

Back to premonition. Seven decades of research (Honorton & Ferrari, 1989; Radin, 1997, 2006, 2011, 2013; Bem, 2011; Mossbridge et al., 2014; Palmer, 2015; Cheung & Mossbridge, 2018) provide experimental evidence that people possess knowledge of the future. One of the leading scientists in this field, Julia Mossbridge and her colleague Theresa Cheung (2018) write, "spontaneous precognitive experiences are quite common. . . and the overwhelming evidence is that precognition exists" (p.74). This research remains controversial. Without a theoretical context in which to interpret these results, they contradict our most deeply held beliefs and arouse intense anxiety. As physicist Michio Kaku (2008) writes, proving the existence of precognition "would set off a major shake-up of the very foundations of modern physics" (p.283). If knowledge of the future resides in our unconscious mind, acceptance of that knowledge first requires recognition of the unconscious. For three centuries physical science hasn't even acknowledged the mind, let alone the unconscious! The unconscious mind is the missing theoretical context. Freud was right. Accepting the unconscious has disturbing consequences.

Surprisingly, some of the most compelling empirical evidence of precognition comes from government sponsored remote viewing studies which demonstrate human perceptual abilities extend beyond the constraints of both space and time (May & Marwaha, 2014; Schwartz, 2015; Targ, 2004). In some of these experiments, subjects accurately depict scenes *not yet selected* by a random event generating device. Talk about nonlocal in space and time! More than two hundred remote viewing studies were conducted over two decades in three different laboratories. The likelihood these successful results were produced by chance is one in a billion (Schwartz, 2015).

Consider how this level of statistical evidence is handled in other branches of science. Physicists accept the existence of the Higgs Boson when there is "only" a one in three-hundred-million chance the evidence is coincidental. Comparing precognition research to traditional medical research such as experiments with anti-platelets, the 2016 President of the American Statistical Association, Jessica Utts, points out there's stronger evidence supporting precognition than there are proven health benefits to taking Plavix. Why then, Utts (1999) asks, "are millions of heart-attack and stroke patients consuming anti-platelets on a regular basis, while the results of psi experiments are only marginally known and acknowledged by the scientific community?" (p.48).

And this is in spite of the fact that psi research has a history of leading in the development of methodological rigor in psychological science. A century of intense methodological scrutiny caused psi researchers to develop high standards. In a recent review of psi research Etzel Cardena (2018) writes,

> psi research has initiated or developed rigorous procedural and ana-lytical strategies that mainstream psychology adopted later, and psi research is more rigorous in, for instance, using masked protocols, than psychology in general and other fields.
>
> (p.673)

If psi employs rigorous research methodologies and produces compelling results, why is science blind to its findings? Well, why do any of us close our eyes to facts? Because they're frightening.

Max, Frank's nutty architect, interjects,

> Reminds me of Newton's rejection of Leibnitz's mechanical material-ism. Leibnitz and his colleagues insisted God, the occult and miracles must be dismissed as *absurdities*. They believed in a clockwork uni-verse. Here's what Newton told them: "Must Experimental Philosophy be exploded as *miraculous* and *absurd* because it asserts nothing more than can be proved by experiments, and we cannot yet prove by experiments that all the Phaenomena in Nature can be solved by meer Mechanical Causes? Certainly these things deserve to be better considered."

Max continues,

> Isaac is clearly on the side of Utts and Cardena in this debate. He was all about empirical evidence. He favored the unification of natural and divine knowledge, of material and immaterial forces. Newton is the

quintessential scientific genius. Yet, science ignores the fact that he devoted most of his life to theological research and experimenting in alchemy and the occult. Newton considered his work in physics and math to be irritating distractions. Science doesn't tell us that.

Positivist science considers religion its mortal enemy. People fear immaterial forces affecting their lives. The most obvious immaterial force is the mind. And certainly, the invisible unconscious mind is terrifying. We associate the unconscious mind with madness. While Newton thought his study of religion and alchemy to be just as rational as his work in physics (Iliffe, 2017), science suggests these interests reflect a dark side in Newton's personality, a regrettable streak of madness. In fact, Newton was an unusual, solitary, intensely driven man who at one point suffered a nervous breakdown.

Psychoanalyst Donald Winnicott says the fear of madness is ever present, and reactions to this fear are reflexive and powerful. Winnicott (1989) writes, there's "a split second in which the threat of madness was experienced, but anxiety at this level is unthinkable. Its intensity is beyond description and new defenses are organized immediately" (p.127). In our example, research results which threaten assumptions about reality and the integrity of our minds are immediately dismissed. As psychoanalyst Mikita Brottman (2011) notes, "the very notion of the paranormal—even in its most benign, everyday forms—can generate especially powerful negative reactions and resistances" (p.xviii).

Okay, enough about mind and madness, back to time. What does psychoanalysis have to say about time? Freud (1915) is the origin of the idea that time is experienced differently in the conscious and unconscious minds. Psychoanalyst Andre Green (2002) considers this to be his most important contribution on the subject of time. According to Freud (1915), time serves as the basic organizing property of consciousness, but the unconscious is "timeless," a place where past, present and future can be condensed or reversed; a place where the logic drawn from temporal sequence no longer exists:

The processes of the system Ucs. [the unconscious] are timeless; i.e., they are not ordered temporally, are not altered by the passage of time; they have no reference to time at all. Reference to time is bound up, once again, with the work of the system Cs. [consciousness].

(p.187)

The conscious mind equates temporal continuity with the continuity of self. This is the reason we are each so personally invested in the "flow of time," and why we each respond so aggressively to any idea that violates our sense of temporal order. Undermining our sense of time threatens our feeling of personal continuity stimulating anxiety. Experiences of temporal continuity foster a sense of identity. Donald Winnicott (1965) describes the infant's development of "continuity of being" as the basis of ego integration. A belief in continuous, linear, sequential time creates coherence, unity and a sense of enduring permanence in our lives. Peter Hartocollis (1983) writes, "time in its experiential sense *is* the unifying element of consciousness," providing each of us a unified sense of self in a world of constant change (p.3).

Although Freud proposes neither time nor death is known in the unconscious, the powerful emphasis we place on the temporal continuity of self suggests the opposite must be true. It is the conscious mind that defends against a universal unconscious awareness of death. It seems our unconscious mind possesses a foundational sense of mortality that consciousness continuously fends off.

Freud's contention that the unconscious possesses no awareness of time—is time*less*–appears frankly mistaken in Freud's model. Freud describes the unconscious making various distortions of time through processes of displacement, condensation and time reversals, but this inherently undermines his conclusion that there is no time in the unconscious. After all, if the unconscious distorts time, then time exists to be distorted. Freud's argument, therefore, seems nonsensical. As Freud's confidante Marie Bonaparte (1940) writes:

> Presented in this form the proposition strikes one as unacceptable on *a priori* grounds and certain analysts have accordingly challenged the assumption of a timeless unconscious. For one can scarcely imagine any living thing, or for that matter anything at all, being immune from the effects of time. The unconscious then, the nucleus of our psyche, must itself be subject to them in some way.

> (p.438)

Maybe we should think of Freud's ideas about time in the unconscious as misstated more than mistaken. Perhaps Freud's timelessness isn't an absence of time, but an absence of temporal structure. Maybe his timelessness is a cluster of associated unconscious processes employing representations of experiential moments that can be experienced in any order, and which may be condensed or fused together without logical constraint. This conception is consistent with my experience of "me" in my unconscious as "occurring all at once."

Knowledge of time and its counterpart death seem to be deeply rooted in the body. Psychoanalytic writers (Arlow, 1984; Eissler, 1955; Fenichel, 1945; Hartocollis, 1983; Schiffer, 1978) note that our knowledge of time is rooted in the body's most ancient circadian rhythms. Kurt Eissler (1955) writes the experience of time is among the most primitive and archaic forms of knowledge: Time "is bound to the earliest emotions, to the earliest instinctual processes" (p.265). Like Eissler, linguist George Lakoff and philosopher Mark Johnson (1999) locate the taproot of time in the body. They note that scientists have identified an electrical pulse being sent through the brain forty times a second, suggesting this signal regulates neural firings controlling the body's regular rhythms such as heartbeat and respiration. These somatic rhythms provide a foundation for our subjective awareness of time, supporting Immanuel Kant's (1966) assertion that knowledge of time is not drawn from experience of the world, but rather exists in us *a priori*. Time is a property of the mind and body. Certainly, if time is so deeply somatic, then an awareness of time must exist in the unconscious.

In fact, could it be that Freud's death instinct derives from knowledge of death experienced in the unconscious? When Donald Winnicott (1974) writes in "Fear of breakdown" that the infant has *already experienced* its own disintegration, is it this foreknowledge of death that the infant is unconsciously aware of? My proposal of the "self as a rotating field" allows for knowledge of death in the unconscious. So, when Frank and I both dreamt of waking up dead, were our dreams drawn from memories of our futures? Maybe.

Freud rejected such speculations out of hand. Addressing the concept of prophetic dreams, Freud (1900) wrote, "There is of course no question of that" (p.621). In Freud's linear model, it's impossible to know the future, therefore premonitions don't exist because the future doesn't exist as anything more than a set of possibilities. Ultimately, linear time is the basis of rational explanation, where causes invariably precede effects. For Freud, rationality held the highest priority, therefore he felt wedded to a model of linear time.

Although Freud made little attempt to organize his ideas about time in a coherent manner (Green, 2002), the psychoanalytic theory he developed is rooted in time, emphasizing the past and time's linear nature. For example, Freud's psychoanalytic theory was *developmental* and arrests in normal development become the basis of future pathology. Appropriating Herbert Spencer's (2002; Jackson, 1958) evolutionary concept of *regression*, Freud believed people under stress revert to earlier forms of mental structure. People unwittingly organize their lives so that early conflicts re-emerge across the lifespan, something Freud called the *repetition compulsion. Transference* was a way people brought early patterns into new relationships. Freud's transference interpretations were "genetic," directed back at the historical origin of the relationship pattern. Freud proposed dreams were caused by repressed infantile wishes. Although these wishes appear to seek a better future, Freud (1900) thought "this future, which the dreamer pictures as the present, has been molded by his indestructible wish into a perfect likeness of the past" (p.621). Finally, therapeutic change occurred through a process of *remembering, repeating* and *working through* past emotional conflicts. So, Freud was always looking back, revisiting or recreating the past.

Indeed, there is no future in Freud's model because the future doesn't exist. This gives his theory a cast of implicit hopelessness. Jungian theorist Angeliki Yiassemides (2014) writes, "Freud's theory presents a temporal loophole, a vicious cycle where the past is bound to repeat itself and the future is viewed as a mirror of what has already taken place" (p.20). Although Freud described the unconscious as timeless, this observation is incidental to his theory. Freud kept his focus on consciousness, building a deterministic model based on consciously experienced linear time, moving backward from the present to the past.

Carl Jung's psychoanalytic theory, by contrast, incorporated a conception of time which is relativistic, nonlinear, and multidimensional (Yiassemides, 2014). While Freud's theory was rooted in the Enlightenment science of the eighteenth century, Jung's ideas about time were influenced by Einstein's theory of relativity and later, by quantum physics. Though Jung was only nineteen years younger than Freud, when it came to their conceptions of time, their ideas were informed by scientific eras two centuries apart.

Like Freud, Jung described the unconscious as "timeless." But unlike Freud, Jung placed timelessness at the heart of his theory of mind. Jung (1959) proposed a psychic construct that is independent of individual minds, but which powerfully influences us: A collective unconscious containing archetypal forms. The collective unconscious is an inherited universal human unconscious independent of individual experience. The collective unconscious contains archetypes similar to Plato's ideal forms, or Kant's *a priori* knowledge. These are pre-existing mental structures which become animated by an individual's lived experience. The collective unconscious and its archetypes exist outside of time and space and are therefore eternal. They are literally "timeless." In Jung's model, life emerges from the tension between these eternal and temporal worlds, and this bipolar tension is the psychical equivalent to Freud's biological life and death instincts. An individual's body is strictly time bound, but in his psychical life man lives in the immediate present and also in the eternal realm of a collective unconscious. So, in his mind, man is both time-bound and timeless.

Max, Frank's fictional architect, immersed as he is in Pre-Socratic philosophy, points out this tension between temporal and eternal is embedded within Heraclitus' Doctrine of Flux, where a permanent form like a river exists *because* its waters are continually changing. Max says, "Heraclitus tells us permanence is paradoxically formed from impermanence, and in Jung's model the eternal emerges from the temporal." Max is fascinated by connections between ancient philosophy and modern science.

Eternal archetypes are images, mental structures drawn from the collective past of human existence that give meaning to life. But, when experienced in the present, the archetype propels the individual into the future. Archetypes are *teleological*. This becomes an essential difference between Freud and Jung's conception of time in the mind: Freud emphasizes the past while ignoring the future. By contrast, although Jung's archetypes are ancient forms, like gravity they psychically pull an individual into his or her future.

Teleology is a philosophical concept originating with Aristotle. Aristotle (1984) argues that natural forms develop "for the sake of something," to accomplish a purpose. He writes, "action *for an end* is present in things which come to be and are by nature" (p.339, italics added). Teleology claims nature is organized around final forms, purposes or goals. For example, the purpose of an acorn is to grow into an oak tree, just as the purpose of a child is to grow into an adult. Try as he might, the child can't prevent himself from growing up. There's a relentless natural process propelling the child toward his or her future. Archetypes psychically correspond to this sort of propulsive organic process.

A good example of teleology in the field of infant development comes from empirical research on infants learning to walk (Thelen & Smith, 1994). From analysis of video studies, we discover infants demonstrate walking movements in the first hours and days of life, causing researchers to conclude that walking isn't a discovery learned through a linear succession of experiences. Walking is there from the start. Because the future is there at the beginning, these researchers conceive of human development as nonlinear. For the same teleological reason, Jung's conception of time is also considered nonlinear. In the metaphorical language of Jung, infants are pulled into their futures as walkers by a teleological Walking archetype.

Aristotle, Kant and Hegel are philosophers who made teleological explanation an important part of their philosophies. Teleology fell out of favor when followers of Newton concluded the future could be predicted by examining the present and past. Nonetheless, the teleological aspect of nature is difficult to deny. Nobel laureate and chaos theorist Ilya Prigogine and philosopher Isabelle Stengers (1984) ask, "If the future is already in some way contained in the present, which also contains the past, what is the meaning of the arrow of time?" (p.84). For the purposes of a discussion of time, teleology is a form of retro-causation where the future creates the present, reversing our traditional conception about causation. Also, teleological models require the existence of an objective, eternal, ideal state that transcends an individual's subjective, time bound, lived experience.

Finally, for Jung, Einstein's theory of general relativity and nonlocal phenomena like premonition and telepathy all proved time and space were relativistic. In a lecture in 1933, Jung (2019) declared,

> If time and space are relative dimensions, they cannot have absolute validity. Consequently, we must assume an absolute reality has different properties from our spatial-temporal reality: in other words, there exists a space that is unlike our space, and a time that is unlike our time. That is, it is possible for phenomena to occur that are not subject to the conditions of time and space.
>
> (p.73)

Jung's views are consistent with those of contemporary quantum physicist, Nicolas Gisin (2014) which we encountered earlier in Chapter 9, "The magic of entanglement." Gisin proposes the nonlocal instantaneous effects occurring between entangled particles, which transcend the limits of space and time, demonstrate our universe is connected to a larger universe in which space and time do not exist. So, in Jung's theory time is relativistic and nonlinear, and reality is both temporal and eternal.

This clarifies Freud and Jung's ideas about time in the mind. Freud was committed to an eighteenth-century conception of linear time, where a person's future is nonexistent, and his present continually attempts to recreate his past. Jung conceived of time as nonlinear and relativistic, where eternal teleological archetypes create an individual's present experience and recreate his subjective understanding of the past. But as Prigogine and Stengers ask, if the future already exists, what's the meaning of the arrow of time? Let's take a look at the physics of time.

Time is a prominent feature of our experience of the physical world and the subject of scientific and philosophical inquiry. Time is mysteriously elusive and serious thinkers reach very different conclusions about it. For example, early in the last century Albert Einstein proved time and space are essentially related, and time is relative to an individual's rate of acceleration through space. The faster you're traveling the more rapidly your future arrives. Therefore, there is no universal "now." Einstein said "now" simply doesn't exist within physics: Now is a precious property of mind, but not of the physical world. Furthermore, Einstein proved time can be bent and slowed down by gravity (Muller, 2016). So, if you live in a ground-floor apartment you can take some pleasure knowing you're aging more slowly than your neighbor in the penthouse. In Einstein's theories time is "individualized" (Davies, 1995), and the Newtonian ideal of a master clock governing the universe has to be abandoned.

Meanwhile, Einstein's close friend, logician Kurt Godel, proved mathematically that time doesn't even exist, and instead is another dimension of space (Yourgrau, 2005). As we've seen, using Einstein's equations for general relativity, Godel proved the universe is not expanding but rotating. In this rotating universe time loops back upon itself. Godel wrote:

It turns out that temporal conditions in these [rotating] universes show. . .surprising features, strengthening the idealistic viewpoint (according to which all change is actually an illusion, nonobjective). Namely, by making a roundtrip on a rocket ship in a sufficiently wide curve, it is possible in these worlds to travel into any region of the past, present, and future, and back again.

(Goldstein, 2005, pp.256–257)

In Godel's model, both premonition and time travel are possible. But, Godel reasoned, if the past can be revisited it hasn't really passed. Therefore, logically, time itself doesn't exist (Holt, 2018). So, Godel believed Einstein had gotten time all wrong. Godel presented his proof to Einstein as a gift in honor of Einstein's seventieth birthday. One has to wonder how these close friends—two preeminent geniuses of the last century—could conceive of time so differently.

Time appears to flow like a river toward the future. Physicist Julian Barbour (1999) writes time "seems to move forward relentlessly, through instants strung together continuously on a line" (pp.17–18). But is time moving forward, or are we moving forward through time? Our subjective awareness of time appears to be elaborately and unconsciously constructed by the mind. Neuroscience reveals our perception of time's apparently even flow is illusory. It is an elaborate construction of the brain (Eagleman, 2009), often involving retrospective revision of stimulation to create the illusion of temporal sequence (Eagleman & Holcombe, 2002; Libet, 2004). So, time seems to be a construction of the mind employed to represent reality. We hear Max, Frank's fictional architect, clearing his throat in the background, apparently hoping to draw our attention to the discovery that mind creates illusory representations of reality. As Max likes to say, "Things aren't what they appear to be."

Causality depends on the logic of time's direction. Physicist David Deutsch (1997) writes, "as soon as we say *why* something happened we invoke the flow of time" (p.265). But, Deutsch contends, we don't actually experience time flowing. What we experience are differences between our present perceptions and our memory of past perceptions, from which we infer correctly that these differences mean that things have changed over time. Deutsch notes that "we also interpret them, incorrectly, as evidence that our consciousness, or the present, or something, moves through time" which is simply wrong (p.263). Physicists like Deutsch and Barbour describe time as static. Time doesn't flow.

The subjective experience of time flowing is linked to our feelings about self-continuity. Our need to persistently reassure ourselves of our continued existence causes the mind to create the illusion of time flowing. This existential necessity is so elemental we don't even see it. It's part of the backdrop of our lives and embedded in our conception of time. This is one of several ways we anthropomorphize time. As philosopher of time Huw Price (1996) writes, "We unwittingly project onto the world. . .the idiosyncrasies of own make-up, seeing the world in the colors of the in-built glass through which we view it" (p.20).

It's commonly accepted that time's direction from past to future is propelled by the second law of thermodynamics which declares entropy continually increases in our expanding universe (Hawking, 1988; Penrose, 2010; Zeh, 1992). This explanation for time's arrow proposes that at the moment of the Big Bang our universe was tiny but intensely ordered and in the thirteen billion years since that spark the universe has been expanding and becoming increasingly disordered.

While the second law of thermodynamics may provide an arrow for time, other dynamical physical theories are notably indifferent to time's direction (Greene, 2004; Prigogine, 1996). Newton's laws of motion, Einstein's theory of relativity, and Schrödinger's equation providing the basis for Everett's Many Worlds, all allow for time to run in both directions. Our mathematical conceptions of the foundations of physical reality depict time as symmetric—running in both directions—yet this is inconsistent with our basic experience of time. Life travels inexorably towards death causing Hector Berlioz to quip, "Time is the great teacher, but unfortunately it kills all its pupils" (Davies, 1995, p.214). So, why is there this inconsistency between our mathematical conceptions of the physical world and life's most elemental attribute, the arrow of time?

Apparently, if it weren't for the second law of thermodynamics, physical events would be reversible in time. If time ran backwards the world would still be deterministic, but the future would be the cause of the present, and death would lead inevitably to birth. Such violations of the entropy principle seem extraordinarily improbable—really unbelievable, but in 1933 Nobel Laureate Paul Dirac proposed something similar, universes parallel to our own composed of antimatter. Technically speaking, antimatter is "time-reversed" matter, or matter traveling backwards in time. Positrons were the first form of antimatter discovered in the 1930s, and subsequently many forms of antimatter have been created and studied in the laboratory. Antimatter exists in our universe, but only in very small quantities.

While Dirac's equation calls for matter and antimatter to exist in equal proportions, in our observable universe matter predominates. Physicist Paul Davies (1995) notes "the conclusion we can draw from these observations—and it is a very profound one—is that nature is *not* symmetric between matter and antimatter, so the laws of nature are *not* exactly symmetric in time" (p.207). Here we have a representation of our world where a small amount of time-reversed matter exists within a universe dominated by matter. Phrased a bit differently, this is a physical model where a few instances of time reversal run counter to the dominant direction of time. This is consistent with our quantum conception of nature. As physicist Michio Kaku (2008) writes, in the quantum world "a universe in which left and right are reversed, matter turns into antimatter, and time runs backward is a fully acceptable universe obeying the laws of physics" (p.193).[1]

The arrow of time is the basis of our conception of causation. Yet, on two occasions while driving to the train on the way to see Frank, it looks like my knowledge of the future contributed to my actions in the present. To remind the reader, here are three examples from my work with Frank where knowledge of the future appears to affect behavior in the present:

- Responding to a feeling of danger and a belief that I should change lanes, I move over and avoid being hit a minute later by a mattress flying off a truck.
- Primed by the thought "flat tire," twenty-five minutes later I avoid an accident with a man changing a flat tire.
- Frank's apparent unconscious awareness of my future causes him to write a story of a life-altering event in which a man is killed changing a left rear tire in twilight on a road with no shoulder *two months before* I experience a life-altering event in which I narrowly avoid hitting a man changing a left rear tire in twilight on a road with no shoulder.

Our traditional model of causation relies on the belief that causes precede effects, ruling out backward causation. Nonetheless, in the examples above it appears that memories of both past and future events served as causes for Frank's and my behavior. Can a memory of a future event really become a cause for present action? Is there anything in physical science where awareness of the future alters present behavior? Yes.

You may recall Hugh Everett's dissertation advisor at Princeton was John Wheeler. Wheeler was a brilliant and idiosyncratic thinker who played a significant role in modern physics. Everett described Wheeler as "somebody with such far-out ideas," and this is coming from Everett who claimed reality is comprised of parallel universes (Barrett & Byrne, 2012, p.308)! Along with his work with Everett, Wheeler was also the dissertation advisor of future Nobel laureate Richard Feynman. Working with Feynman, Wheeler researched light traveling backwards in time (Halpern, 2017). Clearly, Wheeler was involved in some curious ideas.

John Wheeler's (1978) "delayed choice" experiment was the first of several related quantum experiments involving backward causation attempting to demonstrate the present is determined by the future (see Greene, 2004, for a popular account). Wheeler's experiment is an updated variation of Thomas Young's famous double slit experiment from 1801 which showed that light exists in the form of waves.

Here's how Wheeler's experiment is designed. Wheeler intends to shoot individual photons of light, one at a time, at a beam splitter, a reflective piece of half-silvered glass that allows about half the photons to pass through it while deflecting the others. As a photon hits the beam splitter it will head in one of two directions: it will either pass through the beam splitter and head along an upper path, or it will be deflected and follow an opposite lower course of identical length. Midway along each path mirrors are used to reflect the photon forward so both paths eventually converge at the same central point on a photoreceptive screen. Along the upper pathway, just before the photographic surface, there is a light detector with an on–off switch that is activated randomly. When the detector is switched on it will be able to detect the presence or absence of a photon, indicating which path the photon traveled.

Under normal test conditions every time a single photon strikes the beam splitter, and heads down one path or the other, it ends up downstream creating an alternating pattern of light and dark stripes rippling across the photographic surface. This characteristic interference pattern indicates that as the photon strikes the beam splitter it is in the form of a wave, and it arrives downstream at the photographic panel having traveled *both* paths. That's right. One photon has simultaneously traversed both paths and arrives *from the two locations* as a wave creating the alternating interference pattern on the screen. One photon being in two locations at once is strange and no one can explain it. Being simultaneously in multiple places at once is an essential feature of quantum physics.

Now the experiment begins. Wheeler shoots one photon which strikes the beam splitter. In its wave form the single photon begins moving down both paths. Then, just before the photon strikes the photographic screen (a matter of nanoseconds after passing the beam splitter) the light detector switches on in the upper pathway and this changes the resulting pattern of light hitting the screen. This time the photon produces only a single patch of light when it strikes the photographic plate—there is no rippling interference pattern. By turning on the light detector Wheeler has determined which path the photon took. At that moment of measurement, the photon assumes the form of a particle, abandoning the wave form it had *previously* assumed at the beam splitter. Wheeler remarks, "We have a strange inversion of the normal order of time" (Jacques et al., 2007, p.2). This appears to be an instance of backward causation where a future event causes the past. Brian Greene (2004) writes,

> It's as if the photons adjust their behavior in the past according to the future choice of whether the new detector is switched on; it's as though the photons have a "premonition" of the experimental situation they will encounter farther downstream, and act accordingly. It's as if a consistent and definite history becomes manifest only after the future to which it leads has been fully settled.
>
> (pp.188–189)

According to Greene, the photon adjusts its behavior at the beam splitter based on an "awareness" if its future. The photon is like me changing lanes to avoid a mattress that in a minute will fly off the roof of a truck! Another interpretation might be that, having passed the beam splitter as it encounters its future, the particle *goes back in time* to alter its past at the splitter. In either interpretation, we have a future event creating the present, or recreating the past. This is backward causation.

It's impossible to write about this phenomenon without attributing mental capabilities to a photon of light. How can a photon have a "premonition," as Greene says? The photon appears to behave in different ways as if it "knows" what the observer knows about it. The photon doesn't switch form from wave to particle because it passes through the detector equipment, it only changes form when the detector is switched on and the observer obtains "which path" information about the particle. In fact, a photon that heads down the path *without the light detector* will still switch form from wave to particle once the detector switches on in the opposite path. In other words, even though the photon itself never encountered the detector, it "knows" the observer will be able to infer that if the photon isn't in the upper path then it must be in the lower path.

Because it's impossible to attribute mental capacities to a photon, the photon, the equipment and the experimenter seem eerily entangled. The "knowledge" the photon appears to possess must be knowledge within the mind of the observer! Michael Lockwood (1996) reminds us "that the effect of measuring an observable is to create an *entanglement* between the states of the system being measured, the measuring apparatus, and the mind of the observer" (p.165). At the moment of observation mind and matter appear to merge. What seems to be happening is the photon, in this entangled state, responds to the experimenter's mental state.

Is this scientific evidence that mind alters matter? It looks that way. For the last seventy years this has been a controversial topic. The science of mind/matter interaction is complex and unresolved, but some physicists like Eugene Wigner, John Wheeler and Max Plank have articulated this viewpoint (Atmanspacher, 2015). For example, Wigner (1967) writes it is "not possible to formulate the laws of quantum mechanics in a fully consistent way, without reference to the consciousness" of the observer (p.169). Wheeler (1978) writes,

> we would seem forced to say that no phenomenon is a phenomenon until—by observation, or some proper combination of theory and observation—it is an observed phenomenon. The universe does not "exist, out there," independent of all acts of observation. Instead, it is in some strange sense a participatory universe.
>
> (p.41)

Of course, Frank's character Max is wholly resonant with this assessment. Where mechanistic materialism of classical physics declares immaterial mind must be excluded from nature, quantum physics reverses this position finding mind and matter to be inescapably entwined. Even more important, where materialism claims mind, if it exists at all, derives from matter, quantum physics again appears to reverse this position. Max Plank (1931), one of the founders of quantum theory, declares, "I regard consciousness as fundamental. I regard matter as derivative from consciousness" (p.17). In 1944 Plank was more definitive:

> As a man who has devoted his whole life to the most clear headed science, to the study of matter, I can tell you as a result of my research about atoms this much: There is no matter as such. All matter originates

and exists only by virtue of a force which brings the particle of an atom to vibration and holds this most minute solar system of the atom together. We must assume behind this force the existence of a conscious and intelligent Mind. This Mind is the matrix of all matter.

(quoted in Braden, 2008, p.212)

This is pure philosophical idealism! Out of the corner of our eyes we see Max joyously pumping his fist.

A more elaborate version of Wheeler's delayed choice design is the "delayed choice quantum eraser" experiment which has been done in several versions. The design of this experiment involves the same principles but is more elaborate producing more complex results. Here's an overview of the simplest example (Greene, 2004). A single photon will be shot at an opaque panel containing two thin vertical slits through which the photon can pass. It's well known that a single photon encountering the double slits will go through *both* as a wave and end up producing the characteristic rippling pattern on a photoreceptive panel placed downstream. In this new experimental design, right in front of each slit is placed a piece of tagging equipment which, if turned on, will adjust any passing photon's angle of spin so that it can be identified later when it hits the photographic screen at the end of the experiment. Each tag is *unique* so that the final location of each photon can be recorded on the screen, and the tag of a photon passing through one slit will always be different from that of a photon passing through the other slit.

From the previous experiment, we can predict that when the tagging equipment is turned on the photon will stop acting like a wave and will behave like a particle. As a particle, it will pass through just one of the two slits and it will end up illuminating a single spot on the photoreceptive screen.

Now, here's the last step in the experiment. After passing through the slits, and just before the photon strikes the screen, the experimenter has the ability to turn on a device that will convert the photon's tag (its previously *unique* spin value) to a *common* value so that whether the photon passed through either slit it will end up having the same value just before it strikes the screen. This piece of equipment is called the "quantum eraser." When the experimenter switches on the eraser, the photon "realizes" the which-path information that had previously identified it has been destroyed, and the photon now functions *as if it had previously passed through the double slits as a wave.*

The photon alters its past behavior not because it interacted with the erasing equipment, or because it has been assigned a spin value, it changes because it's been assigned the *same spin value* as a photon emerging from the other slit. No one knows how a photon is capable of distinguishing spin values, which is a sophisticated bit of thinking. As far as we know, photons don't think. Yet, it appears the photon *understands the intention* of the experimenter. As the photon hits the screen it now produces the characteristic interference pattern of two waves striking a surface, and the "quantum eraser" has erased the past. Brian Greene (2004) writes,

> These experiments are a magnificent affront to our conventional notions of space and time...By any classical—common sense—reckoning, that's, well, *crazy*. Of course, that's the point: classical reckoning is the wrong kind of reckoning to use in a quantum universe.
>
> (p.199, italics added)

Everett, of course, would say that *we live* in a quantum universe, and these delayed choice experiments force us to rethink our Newtonian notions of temporal order and causation.

Alright, let's apply the language of quantum physics to my mind, and to my two precognitive experiences on the way to the train. First of all, my mind appears to function with the same complementarity we see in quantum physics where a photon of light takes the form of either particle or wave. My conscious mind appears to act like a particle being at one point in space and time. My unconscious mind, meanwhile, seems to function like a quantum wave: It's in multiple space/times so both the future and the past affect the present.

Is it *crazy*, as Brian Greene says, to think our unconscious could be in two space/times at once? Only if you're speaking on behalf of our conscious self which considers itself to be a point in space/time. But, if your unconscious self exists as a wave or a field, then a self could be in multiple space/times. Physicist Max Tegmark (2007) agrees, declaring, "Because you are made of atoms, then if atoms can be in two places at once, so can you" (p.23). That's the reality, as Everett would say, of living in a quantum universe.

Max, our architect immersed in Pre-Socratic philosophy, interjects, "Pythagoras was seen in two locations at once! He was thought to be capable of bilocation." I respond, "God help me, Max. Shut up! It's hard enough to wrap my head around these ideas without you interrupting us with this Pre-Socratic nonsense!" Sometimes Max's interruptions are difficult to tolerate. It's just his enthusiasm, really. But, now that I think of it, it is curious how Pythagorean folklore serves as an example—twenty-five-hundred years later—of quantum reality. In response to my rebuke, Max smiles smugly. I have to admit his fictional status affords him a unique perspective.

Okay, if a photon can alter its behavior based on its "knowledge" of its future, is it possible that I can too? Perhaps in my nonlocal unconscious I'd previously seen that mattress coming my way and this time I moved over. Or, maybe as I was leaving my home in Bellport on that Friday morning, I was also simultaneously in Babylon observing a young man changing his tire at the edge of a cloverleaf I'd pass twenty-five minutes later. Perhaps Frank's nonlocal unconscious is entangled in some quantum way with my own allowing him to observe my future and write about it two months before I experience it. Certainly, in the eighteenth-century Newtonian universe none of this is possible. But it all appears to be possible in the quantum world in which Everett insists we live.

Note

1 In 1931 antimatter was theoretically predicted by Paul Dirac. The positron, the mirror image of an electron (or an anti-electron) was experimentally discovered the following year contributing to Dirac being awarded the 1933 Nobel Prize. Though rare, antimatter exists in our world. For example, positrons are used every day in PET scans. As a graduate student Richard Feynman studied light that paradoxically travels backwards from the future to the past. Extending this research, in 1949 he employed Dirac's equation to demonstrate that antimatter is ordinary matter traveling backwards in time (Kaku, 2008).

References

Aristotle (1984). Physics. In J. Barnes (Ed.), *The complete works of Aristotle*, volume 1 (pp.315–446). Princeton, NJ: Princeton University Press.

Arlow, J. (1984). Disturbances of the sense of time—with special reference to the experience of timelessness. *The Psychoanalytic Quarterly*, 53, 13–37.

Atmanspacher, H. (2015). Quantum approaches to consciousness. *The Stanford Encyclopedia of Philosophy*. http://plato.stanford.edu/archives/sum2015/entries/qt-consciousness/ (Accessed August 28, 2016)

Barbour, J. (1999). *The end of time: The next revolution in physics*. Cambridge: Oxford University Press.

Barrett, J. & Byrne, P. (2012). *The Everett interpretation of quantum mechanics: Collected works 1955–1980 with commentary*. Princeton, NJ: Princeton University Press.

Bem, D. (2011). Feeling the future: Experimental evidence of anomalous retroactive influences on cognition and affect. *Journal of Personality and Social Psychology*, 100 (3), 407–425.

Bonaparte, M. (1940). Time and the unconscious. *The International Journal of Psychoanalysis*, 21, 427–468.

Braden, G. (2008). *The spontaneous healing of belief*. Carlsbad, CA: Hay House.

Brottman, M. (2011). *Phantoms of the clinic: From thought-transference to projective identification*. London: Karnac.

Cardena, E. (2018). The experimental evidence for parapsychological phenomena: A review. *American Psychologist*, 73(5), 663–677.

Cheung, T. & Mossbridge, J. (2018). *The premonition code: The science of precognition*. London: Watkins.

Davies, P. (1995). *About time: Einstein's unfinished revolution*. New York, NY: Simon & Schuster.

Deutsch, D. (1997). *The fabric of reality*. New York, NY: Penguin Books.

Eagleman, D. (2009). Brain time. In M. Brockman (Ed.), *What's next? Dispatches on the future of science* (pp.155–169). New York, NY: Vintage.

Eagleman, D. & Holcombe, A. (2002). Causality and the perception of time. *Trends in Cognitive Science*, 6(8), 323–325.

Eissler, K. (1955). *The psychiatrist and the dying patient*. New York, NY: International Universities Press.

Fenichel, O. (1945). *The psychoanalytic theory of the neurosis*. New York, NY: W.W. Norton.

Freud, S. (1900). The interpretation of dreams. *Standard Edition*. London: Hogarth Press, 4, ix–627.

Freud, S. (1915). The unconscious. *Standard Edition*. London: Hogarth Press, 14, 159–215.

Gigerenzer, G. (2007). *Gut feelings: The intelligence of the unconscious*. London: Penguin Books.

Gilhooley, D. (2008). Psychoanalysis and the "cognitive unconscious": Implications for clinical technique. *Modern Psychoanalysis*, 33, 91–127.

Gisin, N. (2014). *Quantum chance: Nonlocality, teleportation, and other quantum marvels*. Heidelberg, Springer.

Goldstein, R. (2005). *Incompleteness: The proof and paradox of Kurt Godel*. New York, NY: W.W. Norton.

Green, A. (2002). *Time in psychoanalysis: Some contradictory aspects*. London: Free Association Books.

Greene, B. (2004). *The fabric of the cosmos: Space, time, and the texture of reality*. New York, NY: Random House.

Halpern, P. (2017). *The quantum labyrinth: How Richard Feynman and John Wheeler revolutionized time and reality*. New York, NY: Basic Books.

Hartocollis, P. (1983). *Time and timelessness*. Madison, CT: International Universities Press.

Hawking, S. (1988). *A brief history of time*. New York, NY: Bantam Books.

Holt, J. (2018). *When Einstein walked with Godel: Excursions to the edge of thought*. New York, NY: Farrar, Straus and Giroux.

Honorton, C. & Ferrari, D. (1989). "Future telling": A meta-analysis of forced choice experiments, 1935–1987. *Journal of Parapsychology*, 53, 281–308.

Iliffe, R. (2017). *Priest of nature: The religious worlds of Isaac Newton*. Oxford: Oxford University Press.

Jackson, J. H. (1958). *Selected writings of John Hughlings Jackson, volume 2, Evolution and dissolution of the nervous system*. New York, NY: Basic Books.

Jacques, V., Wu, E., Grosshans, F., Treussart, F., Grangier, P., Aspect, A. & Roch, J. (2007). Experimental realization of Wheeler's delayed-choice gedanken-experiment. *Science*, American Association for the Advancement of Science, 315 (5814), 966.

Jung, C. (1959). The archetypes and the collective unconscious. *Collected Works of C.G. Jung*, volume 9. Princeton, NJ: Princeton University Press.

Jung, C. (2019). *History of modern psychology: Lectures delivered at ETH Zurich, volume 1, 1933–1934*. E. Falzeder (Ed.). Princeton, NJ: Princeton University Press.

Kaku, M. (2008). *Physics of the Impossible*. New York, NY: Anchor Books.

Kant, I. (1966). *Critique of pure reason*. New York, NY: Doubleday and Company. (Original work published 1781)

Lakoff, G. & Johnson, M. (1999). *Philosophy in the flesh: The embodied mind and its challenge to Western thought*. New York, NY: Basic Books.

Libet, B. (2004). The delay in our conscious sensory awareness. In *Mind time: The temporal factor in consciousness* (pp.33–60). Cambridge, MA: Harvard University Press.

Lockwood, M. (1996). "Many Minds" interpretations of quantum mechanics. *The British Journal for the Philosophy of Science*, 47, 159–188.

May, E. & Marwaha, S. (2014). *Anomalous cognition: Remote viewing research and theory*. Jefferson, NC: McFarland and Company.

Mossbridge, J., Tressoldi, P., Utts, J., Ives, J., Radin, D. & Jonas, W. (2014). Predicting the unpredictable: critical analysis and practical implications of predictive anticipatory activity. *Frontiers of Human Neuroscience*, March 25, 2014; https://doi.org/10.3389/fnhum.2014.00146 (Accessed October 29, 2017)

Muller, R. (2016). *Now: The physics of time*. New York, NY: W.W. Norton.

Norretranders, T. (1998). *The user illusion: Cutting consciousness down to size*. New York, NY: Viking.

Palmer, J. (2015). Implicit anomalous cognition. In E. Cardena, J. Palmer & D. Marcusson-Clavertz (Eds.), *Parapsychology: A handbook for the 21st Century* (pp.215–229). Jefferson, NC: McFarland & Company, Inc.

Penrose, R. (2010). *Cycles of time: An extraordinary new view of the universe*. New York, NY: Alfred A. Knopf.

Plank, M. (1931). Interviews with great scientists, VI: Max Plank, by J. W. Sullivan. *The Observer*, January 25, 1931, p.17.

Price, H. (1996). *Time's arrow and Archimedes' point: New directions for the physics of time*. New York, NY: Oxford University Press.

Prigogine, I. (1996). *The end of certainty: Time, chaos, and the new laws of nature*. New York, NY: The Free Press.

Prigogine, I. & Stengers, I. (1984). *Order out of chaos: Man's new dialogue with nature*. New York, NY: Bantam.

Radin, D. (1997). *The conscious universe: The scientific truth of psychic phenomena*. San Francisco, CA: HarperCollins.

Radin, D. (2006). *Entangled minds: Extrasensory experiences in quantum reality*. New York, NY: Paraview Pocket Books.

Radin, D. (2011). Predicting the unpredictable: 75 years of experimental evidence. In D. Sheehan (Ed.), *Quantum retrocausation: Theory and experiment* (pp.204–217). Melville, NY: American Institute of Physics.

Radin, D. (2013). *Supernormal*. New York, NY: Random House.

Schiffer, I. (1978). *The trauma of time*. New York, NY: International Universities Press.

Schwartz, S. (2015). Through time and space: The evidence for remote viewing. In D. Broderick & B. Goertzel (Eds.), *Evidence for psi: Thirteen empirical research reports* (pp.168–212). Jefferson, NC: McFarland & Company.

Spencer, H. (2002). *First principles*. Honolulu, HI: University Press of the Pacific. (Original work published 1862)

Targ, R. (2004). *Limitless mind: a guide to remote viewing and transformation of consciousness*. Novato, CA: New World Library.

Tegmark, M. (2007). Many lives in many worlds. *Nature*, 448(5), July, 23–24.

Thelen, E. & Smith, L. (1994). *A dynamic systems approach to the development of cognition and action*. Cambridge, MA: MIT Press.

Utts, J. (1999). The significance of statistics in mind-matter research. *Journal of Scientific Exploration*, 13(40), 615–638.

Wheeler, J. (1978). The "past" and the "delayed-choice" double-slit experiment. In A. Marlow (Ed.), *Mathematical foundations of quantum theory* (pp.9–48). New York, NY: Academic Press.

Wigner, E. (1967). *Symmetries and reflections*. Bloomington, IN: Indiana University Press.

Wilson, T. (2002). *Strangers to ourselves: Discovering the adaptive unconscious*. Cambridge, MA: Harvard University Press.

Winnicott, D.W. (1965). Ego integration in child development. In *The maturational processes and the facilitating environment* (pp.56–63). Madison, CT: International Universities Press. (Original work published 1962)

Winnicott, D.W. (1974). Fear of breakdown. *International Review of Psychoanalysis*, 1, 103–107.

Winnicott, D.W. (1989). The psychology of madness. In C. Winnicott, R. Shepherd, & M. Davis (Eds.), *Psycho-analytic explorations* (pp.119–129). Cambridge, MA: Harvard University Press.

Yiassemides, A. (2014). *Time and timelessness: Temporality in the theory of Carl Jung*. London: Routledge.

Yourgrau, P. (2005). *A world without time: The forgotten legacy of Godel and Einstein*. New York, NY: Basic Books.

Zeh, D. (1992). *The physical basis of the direction of time*. Berlin: Springer.

Chapter 13

Falling tree

It's August 8, 2014. We're nearing the end of our annual summer camping trip in the Adirondack. For the past twenty-eight years our family has camped in tents for a week or two in August along Long Lake. Our camping trips began in the 1980s and were organized by my wife's father, Charles. He was born at Long Lake in 1918 and grew up there during the summers in the 1920s and 1930s. His French-Canadian family had traveled south from Montreal to settle on the lake in the 1880s. Many of the men worked as guides leading groups of city dwellers through the wilderness on hunting and fishing expeditions. As a child Charles spent his summers at Uncle Harry's camp about eight miles up the lake. There are no roads up there, and the only way to get to Uncle Harry's camp is by boat or to hike in following the trail to Lake Placid. Harry Sabattis, Charles' uncle by marriage, was the youngest son of Mitchell Sabattis, who was half Abenaki Indian and a famous Adirondack guide.

During the final fifteen years of his life Charles returned each summer to the land of his childhood, bringing his children and grandchildren along. Like Mitchell Sabattis a hundred years earlier, he led his grandchildren through the wilderness introducing them to everything that lived there. Charles died in 1997, but we've continued to make the trip each year without him. In part, we do it to honor his desire that his kin remain connected to this land and lake, learning the ways of the wilderness.

This afternoon my two sons Zach and Cameron, and our ten-year old adopted Ethiopian grandson, Yirdaw, hiked along a creek about a half mile south of our camp. They were hoping to catch snakes, lizards, and toads, and to spot whatever birds and animals they could find. My wife, Pat, and her daughter, Nonnie, went swimming in the lake. I stayed in camp reading a chapter in Roderick Main's (2004) book, *Rupture of time: Synchronicity and Jung's critique of modern Western culture*. As members of my family played at the edge of the lake, I read about Carl Jung's theory about the intersection of mind and matter. Here's a sketch of his idea.

Sometimes two events occurring coincidentally, without an apparent cause, have an important meaning for the person experiencing them. Jung called these meaningful coincidences "synchronicities." Synchronicities are relatively rare and usually appear during periods of transition in a person's life. Synchronicities produce an unusual feeling of resonance. They defy the randomness of life, integrate a person's inner and external experience, and reveal for an instant a deeply unified world. For this reason, synchronicities often possess a spiritual quality. Jung believed synchronicities are created by a force connecting events through shared meaning rather than through physical cause. Jung considered this form of connection to be a basic principle ordering our universe complementing physical causality. Where causality is the product of matter-to-matter interaction, synchronicities are the result of mind-matter interactions. In my reading of Jung's conception, he is really proposing that, like gravity, at these moments mind is an organizing force in nature.

After an hour of heady reading, I looked up and saw Yirdaw running back into camp. Out of breath, in the moments before Zach and Cameron returned, Yirdaw described the creatures they'd captured or seen. There were green and black snakes, a large yellow-bellied lizard, weasels and muskrats. But, he said, there was a really important story he'd promised not to tell until Zach and Cameron were also present. When they walked into camp a few minutes later Zach said, "Okay, Yirdaw, you tell the story."

Minutes earlier the three boys were picking their way through the thick foliage along the creek searching for reptiles. For the past hour the going had been slow and deliberate. They'd captured snakes and lizards. As always, toads were plentiful and easy to catch. Moving slowly, the boys looked mostly at the ground, often crouching down to part the undergrowth. As they searched Cameron asked, "What if we saw a bear at the end of the creek?" Cameron was the only one who'd ever confronted a bear in the woods, a harrowing experience that elevated his status and credibility.

They all lifted their heads and glanced toward the end of the creek. Fifteen feet away, for no apparent reason, a large birch tree fell over and crashed to the earth. The boys were startled, mostly because there was no reason for the tree to fall. It was weird. A perfectly beautiful tree just keeled over. There was no wind. No force of any kind had been applied to the tree, yet at the moment they looked up it fell to the earth right in front of them. Looking for a menacing bear, they were surprised by a falling tree.

Yirdaw lifted his eyes from the fallen birch and turned to his uncles searching for an explanation. They looked at each other dumbly. No one could offer a cause for the tree to fall. Of course, in the wilderness dead trees fall over all the time. But this didn't occur to them because the tree looked completely alive, not dead. The absence of any apparent physical force pushing the tree over made the tree falling seem illogical. Even more irrational, it fell over just as they looked up, making it seem like looking at the tree caused it to keel over. They'd all looked up expecting to see something frightening, and this dramatic development certainly fit the bill. It looked like nature delivered a surprising event to meet their expectations. Their thoughts and physical reality seemed strangely entwined. The boys were spooked.

Zach walked over to the downed birch and saw that, although it looked healthy, its roots were decayed. Cameron stayed put. Half joking, he proposed this had been the work of a spirit. An invisible force had pushed the tree over. Maybe they weren't alone in the woods. If that were the case, Yirdaw said, they should head back to camp immediately, which they did with Yirdaw running ahead.

As the three boys told the story of the falling tree, it had several meanings for me. First of all, it was a remarkable coincidence that at the time the tree fell I was reading about Jung's concept of synchronicity which attempts to explain coincidental connections between events. An apparently healthy tree falling for no apparent reason, at the moment of the boys' anxious expectation, appeared to be an exquisite example of "acausality" and synchronicity. It looked like their mental expectation caused a physical event to occur. It was as if the woods of Long Lake had delivered proof of Jung's theory.

I was reading about synchronicity as research for a final section of the book I'm writing about my patient, Frank, who is grieving his son's death. During the last three years, as a therapeutic response to the loss of his boy, Frank has written a science fiction novel about life after death. Simply put, my book is an analysis of him writing his book. For me, a second meaning of the falling tree is drawn from my interpretation of Frank's work.

As I was working to finish my book, I realized the final scene in Frank's novel contains an image of a healthy tree falling over spontaneously without cause. So, while I listened to the boys tell their tale of the falling tree, this was a second example of synchronicity for me. This image of a falling tree appears in Frank's final vignette when two parallel universes are merging together to create a new world. It is a moment that signals both an ending and a beginning. Here's the scene.

Nigel, the book's protagonist, looks through the window of his country home and sees a large Norwegian pine crash to the earth in complete silence. When Frank first wrote this passage three years ago his son was dead, but his Norwegian wife, Signe, had not yet been diagnosed with metastatic breast cancer. Frank has never spoken of this image as prophetic, but that's how I see it. In Frank's story, after the Norwegian pine falls, Nigel walks from his home into the woods where he's greeted by his son, Anders. They walk through a graffiti filled courtyard and along a river where they find a funeral barge tied to the shore. On the barge Nigel asks his dead son if this is a dream or is he now really dead. His son responds, "Welcome home, Dad. Welcome home." In this final scene, after the Norwegian pine crashes to the earth, Nigel appears to die. Of course, his novel begins with him waking up dead, but now he asks, "Am I *really dead*?" It's a question.

This scene worries me, because it's a question for me too. Will Signe's death kill Frank? If the image of the falling Norwegian pine is prophetic, the events that follow it are prophetic as well. Here's the concluding passage in Frank's novel:

> I let it all go slowly, like letting go a dream when you awake. I felt a cool wind at my face as the barge began to pull away from the pier, drifting toward the setting sun on its journey west.

In this image the reference to awakening and the sensation of a cool breeze touching his face are connected to life. These sentences seem to beautifully capture the essence of life moving toward death: Letting go of dreams, we're sensuously caressed by life as we drift toward a setting sun.

In the closing chapter of Frank's novel, the ambiguous mixture of life and death also occurs in the collision of two parallel universes which Frank describes as an apocalyptic act of creation. Will this cataclysmic event create a new world? Frank suggests the collision of his universe and mine, the therapeutic merger of our personalities, could allow us to create a new universe. But it's unclear.

Frank's novel provides the context for a third meaning I took from the story of the falling tree. Just like Frank, I worry my wife is going to die. Like the boys who responded fearfully to the falling tree, the image frightened me, but for a different reason. Three years ago, Pat had a miraculous surgery to repair two aneurysms in her brain. One was bleeding and almost killed her. Her brain is home to two more. One is peripheral, and one is inoperable.

So, just as Frank writes about a Norwegian pine collapsing to the earth, I wondered if the falling of this flourishing Long Lake birch could be an image of my healthy wife dying. The picture of health, the tree just keeled over. That could be Pat with her aneurysms. In this way, I see Frank's story and mine entwined. We each fear losing our wives, and our lives with them. Perhaps we're secretly certain that we'll die with them. This is how I feel. Our universes destroyed, we wonder whether our therapeutic merger will keep us alive. We awake to feel a dream slipping inexorably through our fingertips. There's nothing to do but let it go. So, as I listened to the boys tell their story of the falling tree, this was a third level of synchronicity for me.

This year, like every year, when we left Long Lake we stopped at the cemetery. The cemetery is simple and neatly kept. The lawn is a field of fragrant purple heather. Braced by a crisp cool breeze, the early morning sunlight was radiant. Each year Pat leaves small beach stones at the graves of many of her thirty relatives buried there. Looking at the headstone of her great-grandmother, Selena St. Onge, Pat said, "I think that I should be buried next to her, don't you?" Although Pat has as many of her mother's family buried at Cooperstown, she doesn't feel as connected to them.

This year Zach and Cameron, like never before, took an interest in the stories about their ancestors. As Pat placed stones at each grave, she described her relative's history. As she spoke Zach photographed each headstone. I placed small American flags at several of the graves. Originally, Pat had hoped to make flags with the St. Onge family crest to place at each grave, but she ran out of time and purchased these American flags instead.

After placing all of her stones, Pat and I climbed into our truck. It was filled with gear and had our canoe tied on top. As we pulled out of the cemetery to head back to Long Island, we talked about our many summers at Long Lake, and silently wondered about the future. This year's trip had been richly satisfying for Pat. She was leaving Long Lake feeling stronger than when she'd arrived. She'd gotten to do everything she'd hoped to, spending time with each of her children and grandchildren, stitching them more tightly into the fabric of her family, and strengthening their enduring tie to the lake and the ways of the woods.

Reference

Main, R. (2004). *The rupture of time: Synchronicity and Jung's critique of Western culture*. New York, NY: Brunner-Routledge.

Part III

History

Chapter 14

Thought transference

On Monday night I had a dream:

> I am driving in a car with my wife sitting next to me. Night, it's raining, and the wipers are sweeping back and forth across the windshield. I look out into the darkness uncertain of where I'm headed. We're going to visit my sister but I'm feeling lost. I think, "She's counting on me, but I don't know where I'm going." My wife receives a phone call. She answers, and I listen as if I'd placed the phone to my ear. It's Jim, my sister's husband. There's been an accident. My sister, who is now much older and has been suffering for some time from a deadly disease, has fallen and hit her head. She is in the hospital and an MRI of her brain shows a fatal problem. The painful struggle of living with a dying person passes through my mind. I recall a friend and his family who agonized for months, prolonging the life of his fatally ill father. I remember what my friend said to me then. I think his words, but I can't say them out loud: "Let her die. You have to let her die." I want to say these words into the phone, but I'm mute.

The next day I describe this dream in analysis and discuss my relationship with my sister. The following day I listen to Lily, someone I've been seeing in weekly therapy for several years. Lily had decades of analysis prior to her work with me. Distressed she says,

> On Monday I got a call from my brother-in-law, Jack, saying my sister had fallen. Laura's in the hospital. She keeled over in the kitchen and hit her head. That's where he found her; he didn't see her fall. She may have had a seizure. They don't know. Jack says a scan shows the cancer's in her brain.

During her long fight with cancer, Lily's older sister had been progressively diminished by disabling surgeries. She was a shell of her former self. Lily continued,

> The doctors say it may not be operable. They're trying to decide what to do. I might need to fly out there, I don't know. God, when I got the call from Jack I just wanted to say, "Let her die, you have to let her die. You can't put her through any more of these surgeries," but I couldn't say it. I really didn't know what to say. How could I say that to him? It's just so awful to see someone you love in pain.

I was stunned. After a moment of reflection, I told Lily about my dream on Monday night. We were both shocked by the striking telepathic quality of my dream and the fact that it occurred on Monday, the day she got the call from her brother-in-law. We wondered how I'd received this expression of her emotional distress about her sister. Was it an anguished cry I'd "overheard?" Was it a message "sent" just to me? I recalled Upton Sinclair's (2008) book from the 1930s, *Mental radio*, in which he described his wife's clairvoyance, and I considered whether on Monday night I'd received an emotional "broadcast" from Lily. If her painful mental state had been broadcast, Lily believed I was the only one who'd received it. Repeatedly Lily came back to the phrase, "Let her die, you have to let her die." It was an awful feeling to wish your sister dead.

"Those were exactly the words I wanted to say but couldn't, those exact words," Lily said. "It really helps me a lot, hearing you say them. I don't know. I'm comforted by you saying those words. I mean, it's an awful thought to have, and I'm glad I'm not having it alone." After her initial surprise, hearing my dream gave Lily the feeling she wasn't alone with a terrible thought. It provided her with a feeling of closeness during a stressful time. Lily talked about loving her sister and not wanting to see her suffer. If another surgery added a few months to her sister's life, would it be worth the pain? But how could she answer that question for her sister? It was her sister's question, not her question. How could she say aloud, "let my sister die?" She felt guilty for even having the thought.

While my dream appeared to comfort Lily, it left me feeling shaken. I was struck by the remarkable parallel between Lily's painful experience and my dream. With Frank, it was never clear whether he and I dreamt the same dream. Beyond the mutually experienced phrase, "I woke up dead," in Frank's case there were only a couple of uncanny parallels between my dream and portions of his story written in consecutive weeks following the dream. Based on those parallels I speculated we might have dreamt the same dream. But in Lily's case my dream was frankly telepathic. In my dream, I've translated Lily's experience to fit the facts of my life. I've aged my sister by more than a decade, given her a serious illness, an accident, and then a brain scan showing a probably fatal condition. During the phone call from her brother-in-law Lily realized, "My sister has brain cancer," and in my dream I received a phone call from my brother-in-law and realize, "My sister has brain cancer." It's as if Lily and I were sharing the same thoughts, though contextualized by our different histories.

In my description of the dream, I've written, "She answered, and I listened as if I'd placed the phone to my ear." Now I considered the "she" I'm referring to might have actually been Lily, not my wife. Perhaps I was in Lily's mind when she received that call from her brother-in-law, and I listened "as if I'd placed the phone to my ear." If that was true, then no information was sent. I was present in her mind at the time she received the call. Particularly compelling was the exact repetition of the phrase, "you have to let her die" which in my dream I felt incapable of saying into the phone, just as Lily had in real life. The prominence of this phrase seemed important. The dream that I seemed to share with Frank also contained a phrase which echoed in my mind: "I woke up dead." Significantly, both dreams dealt with the edge between life and death.

William James (1910) describes feeling shaken when he awoke from a similar dream:

> I began to feel curiously confused and scared. . .Presently cold shivers of dread ran over me: *am I getting into other people's dreams*? Is this a "telepathic" experience?. . .Or is it a thrombus in a cortical artery? and the beginning of a general mental "confusion" and disorientation which is going on to develop who knows how far?
>
> (p.89)

The boundary between me and Lily blurred. I felt like I was losing my mind.

In both dreams, I instantly made conscious interpretations that were reasonable but inaccurate. In the first seconds of consciousness after my

"Waking up Dead" dream I linked my dream to another patient, Ben, who had recently quit treatment. I wondered,

> Why do I have such difficulty accepting the reality of my death in his mind? I'm dead in this case. Get it, I'm dead. It's the part I play. That's part of the transference.

While my statements were partially true in terms of both Ben and Frank, as Frank wrote his story, I began to realize my words made more sense when applied to his case. This caused me to consider that, while my conscious mind was attributing my thoughts and words to Ben, my unconscious was likely speaking about Frank. In my dream about my sister's illness I incorrectly assumed the dream was about me and my sister. It never occurred to me I was dreaming another person's thoughts as if they were my own.

It was this violation of personal integrity that I found so disturbing: The realization that my thoughts were not my own. It now seemed certain a portion of the thoughts and feelings passing through my mind did not originate *in* me, but were passing *through* me, and were being misidentified by my conscious mind as "my own," as representations of me. If that was true, what was really me? If others' thoughts and feelings were passing through me, then my thoughts and feelings were passing through them. If that was true, where did I begin and end? Psychoanalyst Mikita Brottman (2011) writes about the history of thought transference: "Since Freud first established the field, psychoanalysis has been particularly charged with deep anxiety about. . .fears of 'outside' contamination" leading to "ontological uncertainty" (p.42). Right! Who was *I*?

My mind certainly wasn't contained by the physical limits of my body. On this occasion my mind was both in Bellport and Manhattan, sixty miles away. Obviously, I misunderstood mind. Mind isn't "local." Mind is transpersonal without location. Mind is a shared phenomenon I'd misconceived as something uniquely my own, believing it to be housed within my brain. Unlike my body, mind isn't fixed in space and time. Indeed, maybe my unconscious mind exists *outside space and time altogether*.

In the days following this session with Lily these thoughts grew in significance like a silent spreading stain. I felt invaded, and my sense of self felt diffuse and scattered. I realized I was just one voice in a cacophonous crowd of immigrants filling my unconscious mind. I had previously believed all those inner voices were reflections of me, and now I realized

I was simply unable to distinguish my voice from the voices of others. I was led to consider my conception of "me" as a solitary being simply wasn't possible. It was an illusion produced by consciousness. In my unconscious, "me" was really "us." I'd discovered, "I am not myself, I am an other" (Borch-Jacobsen, 1987, p.206). I hated the idea. It filled me with quiet fury.

Although I wasn't consciously aware of feeling frightened, I became increasingly hostile toward Lily and needed to push her away. What had been comforting to Lily upset me deeply.

References

Borch-Jacobsen, M. (1987). Dispute. In L. Chertok (Ed.), *Hypnose et psycho-analyse* (pp.194–217). Paris: Dunod.

Brottman, M. (2011). *Phantoms of the clinic: From thought transference to projective identification*. London: Karnac.

James, W. (1910). A suggestion about mysticism. *The Journal of Philosophy, Psychology and Scientific Methods*, 7, 85–92.

Sinclair, U. (2008). *Mental radio*. Lexington, KY: Forgotten Books. (Original work published 1930)

Chapter 15

Thought transference in psychoanalysis

My "Waking up dead" and "Let her die" dreams reflect forms of thought transference, what appear to be communications directly between me, Frank and Lily across a span of sixty miles, without employing any recognizable channel of communication. Since the 1880s this kind of communication has been called telepathic, but fearing censure, psychoanalysts rarely use that word (Brottman, 2011). For the past century psychoanalysts have described many forms of thought transference, but employ phrases like "induced feelings," "objective countertransference," "projective identification," "narcissistic transference," and "therapeutic symbiosis" to describe this phenomenon. Using these expressions, they disguise the fact they're really talking about telepathy. Under the term "countertransference," since 1950 the emergence of the patient's thoughts and feelings in the mind of the analyst has been one of the most commonly discussed clinical phenomena in psychoanalysis.

In 1919, in a lecture delivered to the British Society of Psychical Research, Carl Jung acknowledges having "repeatedly observed the telepathic effects of unconscious complexes" in his patients (Main, 1997, p.6). Jung considered the receptivity of the unconscious mind far exceeded consciousness. He believed telepathy and precognition were commonplace and derivative of his broader concept of synchronicity. Chafing at popular rejections of telepathy, in a letter to a Protestant pastor in 1933 Jung writes, "the existence of telepathy in time and space is still denied only by positive ignoramuses" (Luckhurst, 2002, p.230).

In 1926, in an essay entitled "Occult processes occurring during psychoanalysis," Freudian disciple Helene Deutsch (1953) describes the telepathic experience where the affective psychic content of the patient, which emerges from his unconscious, becomes transmuted into an inner experience of the analyst, and is recognized as belonging to the patient. . .only in the course of subsequent intellectual work.

(p.136)

The analyst discovers the thoughts and feelings she's having are actually the patient's, not her own. It takes a lot of thoughtful reflection before she comes to this conclusion. Naturally, the analyst begins with the assumption that all her thoughts and feelings originate *in her*. A defining characteristic of being human is the belief that ideas and emotions emerging within us are exclusively our own—in fact, they constitute the bedrock of *me*. It requires a lot of emotional and intellectual effort to relinquish that notion. Deutsch (1953) writes:

> During psychoanalysis the psychic contact between analyst and analysand is so intimate, and the psychic processes which unfold themselves in that situation are so manifold, that the analytic situation may very well include all conditions which especially facilitate the occurrence of such phenomena. Thus very careful observations should enable one to recognize that a given psychic process, which unfolds itself before our very eyes, is "telepathic," and should also help one to reveal its true nature by means of the methodology characteristic of psychoanalytic technique.
>
> (p.134)

Deutsch says telepathic exchanges between patient and therapist are common in psychoanalysis, declaring, "Every analyzed person will recall instants when he felt that his analyst was a 'mindreader'" (pp.138–139).

In 1932 Freud's colleague, Sandor Ferenczi (1988), describes the frequency of telepathic experiences in psychoanalysis.

> Others before me have already drawn attention to the remarkable frequency with which so-called thought-transference phenomena occur between physician and patient, often in a way that goes far beyond the probability of mere chance. Should such things be confirmed someday, we analysts would probably find it plausible that

the transference relationship could quite significantly promote the development of subtler manifestations of receptivity.

(p.85)

Ferenczi's disciple Michael Balint (1955) describes telepathic experiences occurring in sessions as patients' attempt to unmask the emotionally distancing effects of the analyst's professional hypocrisy. It's as if the patient is telling the analyst, "Get real."

> This uncanny talent may occasionally give the impression of, or even amount to, telepathy or clairvoyance. The analyst experiences this phenomenon as if the patient could see inside him, could find out things about him. The things thus found out are always highly personal, in some ways always concerned with the patient, and are in a way absolutely correct and true.
>
> (Balint, 1968, p.19)

Telepathic communications are a way for the patient to inform the analyst, "I see who you really are." Balint's believes patients resort to telepathic communications when the analyst is emotionally detached and are unconsciously intended to shock the analyst into paying attention.

In 1937 Freud's pupil Theodor Reik noted, before the psychoanalyst intellectually comprehends his patient, he discovers the patient's emotions and ideas being aroused within himself. Using a phrase that originates with Ferenczi, Reik writes the analyst becomes *induced* by his patient. Employing a form of inner perception, the analyst sees the patient by looking within himself. Reik (1937) says, "in order to comprehend the unconscious of another person, we must, at least for a moment, change ourselves into and become that person" (p.199).

In 1942 psychoanalyst Robert Fliess (son of Freud's confidante Wilhelm Fliess) writes the analyst steps into the patient's shoes "to obtain in this way an inside knowledge that is almost first-hand" (p.212). Describing a "metabolic" process of empathy, Fliess claims the analyst "introjects the patient's mind. . .convert[ing] the analyst partially into the patient" before he returns a metabolized form of this mental state back to the patient (p.214). In everyday language, Fliess is saying the analyst psychologically absorbs the patient's mind to such an extent the analyst finds himself partially *converted* into the patient. The analyst comes to possess twin identities or "double consciousness": He is simultaneously himself and the patient. This feels risky. It imperils the analyst's sense of identity and his confidence in the integrity of his mind. This unconscious interchange can be so destabilizing for the analyst it "potentially threatens his mental health" (p.216).

Following in the footsteps of Ferenczi and Reik, in a 1949 paper American psychoanalyst Hyman Spotnitz (1987; Spotnitz & Meadow, 1995) described "induced feelings" in which the psychoanalyst experiences a patient's immediate emotional state as if it were his own. Like Deutsch, Spotnitz says the analyst only becomes consciously aware of this phenomenon after a period of emotional confusion leading him to conclude these emotions actually originate in the patient. Like Fliess' conception of a "metabolic" process of empathy, Spotnitz (1987) describes psychoanalytic therapy as a method of the "reciprocal emotional induction" where complex emotional states pass unconsciously between patient and analyst creating a treatment "relationship grounded in genuine emotional understanding" rather than conscious intellectual engagement (p.29).

Spotnitz (1985c) went on to describe complex forms of emotional induction he termed "objective countertransference" in which an analyst experiences a complex configuration of emotions and thoughts uniquely associated with the patient's personality. Again, it is only after a period of conscious reflection that the analyst recognizes he is feeling and thinking in a manner just like his patient. He's adopted aspects of his patient's personality, and to an extent, he's *become* his patient (Geltner, 2013; Madonna, 2017; Marshall & Marshall, 1988; Meadow, 1991). As Marshall and Marshall (1988) write, "The therapist becomes a mirror image for the patient" (p.188). At this moment the analyst has two personalities, two selves.

Beyond providing a window into the patient's mind, objective countertransference feelings "are to Spotnitz a major source of analytic cure" (Sherman, 1983, p.178). Echoing Fliess, Spotnitz (1963–1964) writes, "The analyst has to experience the patient's feelings in order to 'return' them to him" in a detoxified state (p.87).

Several of Spotnitz's contemporaries also described aspects of the patient's personality spontaneously appearing in the mind of the analyst. In the language of psychoanalysis, countertransference is the analyst's emotional reaction to the patient's "transference," i.e., the patient's reaction to the analyst. Theodor Reik's analysand Paula Heimann (1950) proposed the analyst's evenly hovering attention facilitated a "rapport on a deep level" fostering a countertransference that was "the patient's creation. . .part of the patient's personality" emerging in the mind of the analyst (p.83).

In 1957 Argentinian psychoanalyst Heinrich Racker used the expression "concordant identification" as synonymous with Spotnitz's objective countertransference.[1] A concordant identification is the analyst's

> recognition of what belongs to the other as one's own. . .those psychological contents that arise in the analyst by reason of the empathy achieved with the patient and that really reflect and reproduce the [patient's] psychological contents.
>
> (p.312)

The analyst's intimate knowledge of a patient's emotional history can become so richly complex the analyst may identify feelings within himself that relate to members of the patient's family. For example, Deutsch (1953), Margaret Little (1951), Racker (1968) and Spotnitz (1985) all describe forms of countertransference in which the analyst feels the emotions the patient's caregivers originally felt toward the patient. Spotnitz (1983) goes so far as to state the analyst may even experience feelings that were necessary but *missing* in the patient's development. He calls this an "anaclitic countertransference."

Kleinian authors write about a form of countertransference that Melanie Klein (1946) called "projective identification" in which analysts experience what they believe to be their patients' emotions and associated unconscious fantasies *projected into* them. Klein proposed that infants, and by analogy psychoanalytic patients, unconsciously project both good and bad parts of themselves into the other

> to control it and *take possession* of it. In so far as the mother comes to contain the bad parts of the [infant's] self, she is not felt to be a separate individual but is felt to be the bad self.
>
> (p.102)

In an unconscious process, the infant takes *possession* of the mother, and the mother feels *possessed* by the infant. Klein discussed many aims associated with projective identification. Split-off parts of the infant's self might be projected into the mother to rid the infant of the pain associated with them. Or, parts of the self could be projected into others to control them, to make use of their mental capabilities, or to injure them.

While Klein originally associated projective identification with the earliest preverbal phases of development and with pathological states in adults, later Kleinian authors consider it to be a universal form of nonverbal communication. Wilfred Bion (1959) described projective identification as a communicative cycle occurring between patient and analyst, in which the therapist first serves as a container for the patient's projected thoughts and feelings. Then, after a period of transformative reverie, the analyst returns these feelings to the patient in a modified form.

Klein originally conceived of projective identification as a fantasy occurring within the infant's mind, but since 1950 her followers have increasingly portrayed it as an interpersonal process happening between two people. After all, the concept of projective identification depicts an unconscious process through which one individual partially *becomes* the other, or—phrased differently—through which two individuals come to share the same mental contents. For example, Leon Grinberg (1962) notes that under the spell of projective identification "the analyst may have the feeling of being no longer his own self and of unavoidably becoming transformed into the object which the patient, unconsciously, wanted him to be" (p.437). The analyst unwittingly "behaves as if he had *really and concretely* acquired. . .the aspects that were projected onto him" (p.440).

Projective identification represents the interpenetration or fusion of two minds. Robert Hinshelwood (1989) describes it as an individual's unconscious "omnipotent intrusion leading to fusion or confusion with the object," involving an unconscious fantasy of "living inside the object" (p.187). Herbert Rosenfeld (1983) says feelings of fusion "probably involve a regressive phantasy of living happily inside the mother's womb" (p.263). Echoing Grinberg, once inhabited by the patient's mind, Roger Lewin and Clarence Schultz (1992) note that "projective identification may be thought of as a form of psychiatric ventriloquism" in which the therapist unwittingly feels the emotions, thinks the thoughts, and speaks the words of the patient (p.37). Projective identification is really a disguised version of "thought transference." As psychoanalyst Mikita Brottman (2011) remarks, "The term acts as a buffer between the frightening world of thought transference and the secular rationalism of clinical psychiatry" (p.107).

Psychoanalysts use words like "projection," "induction," and "contagion" to metaphorically provide a physical explanation for the movement of feelings and thoughts from one mind into another. "Induction" is a word borrowed from eighteenth-century descriptions of electrical currents that spontaneously jump across space to land in unexpected locations. "Contagion" is a word used since the Renaissance to explain the invisible transmission of disease from one person into another. "Projection" suggests a bundle of feelings propelled like an arrow or a beam of light from person to person.

Analysts also use words like "fusion" or "symbiosis" to describe how analysts' and patients' minds appear to become invisibly linked. Racker (1968) describes "a connexion between the two unconsciouses, a connexion that might be regarded as a 'psychological symbiosis' between two personalities" (p.143). Delineating a process of "therapeutic symbiosis," Harold Searles (1973) writes, "symbiotic relatedness constitutes a necessary phase in psychoanalysis or psychotherapy" (p.247). In endosymbiosis one living form lives *within the body of the other*, and this is certainly the meaning psychoanalysts convey through their use of expressions like induction, contagion, symbiosis and projective identification.

When a patient imagines the analyst's mind is linked to her own—believing the analyst feels her feelings and thinks her thoughts—she is experiencing what Spotnitz (1985b) called "narcissistic transference." In a narcissistic transference

> the patient transfers feelings that he developed for himself as well as others during the first two years of life. He may also confuse the analyst's feelings for his own. In short, a two-way emotional transaction is revived and communicated. . .suggestive of a re-experiencing of the ego in the process of formation.
>
> (p.186)

Spotnitz (1985a), Heinz Kohut (1971) and Harold Searles (1973, 1979) believed the formation of a narcissistic transference was the foundation for psychoanalytic treatment. Narcissistic transference is a state of mental fusion or symbiosis where there is a blurring of boundaries between self and other. Spotnitz (1979) writes, "The patient may experience the therapist as part of the self or like the self. The therapist may feel that he is in the presence of a kindred spirit or experience a strange sense of harmony" a feeling that Spotnitz calls "narcissistic countertransference" (p.548). Spotnitz (1985c) explains that

> it usually becomes clear that some of the feelings experienced with such a patient could have no other source than the patient. Because these feelings are induced by the behavior, communications, and emotions of a patient functioning in a state of narcissistic transference, they are identified in modern psychoanalysis as *narcissistic countertransference*.
>
> (p.230)

When the patient is in a state of narcissistic transference and the analyst enters a corresponding state of countertransference, they are "mutually contaged." This emotional contagion, rather than any form of intellectual insight, becomes for Spotnitz the source of analytic cure. As he and his colleague Phyllis Meadow declare, "The syntonic feeling of oneness is a curative one" (Spotnitz & Meadow, 1995, p.58).

During the first decades of psychoanalysis, experiencing states of symbiosis was considered an indication of mental illness. When patients felt symbiotically related to their analysts it was called a "psychotic transference." But after 1960, as the therapeutic value of countertransference began to be understood, most psychoanalysts stopped describing symbiosis as pathological. For example, psychoanalytic researchers Rachel Blass and Sydney Blatt (1996) write,

> Instead, symbiosis is considered to be an essential component of relatedness to others and as essential to establishing an identity. Ongoing experiences of symbiosis are assumed to be normative throughout the life cycle.
>
> (p.715)

Paradoxically, the experience of fusion states "contributes to a sense of self as separate" (p.738). Such contemporary views of psychological symbiosis support Kohut, Spotnitz and Searles' position that experiences of symbiosis and narcissistic transference are inherently therapeutic and ego strengthening.

While psychoanalysis slowly accepted these fusion states as normal and healthy, American psychiatry (*Diagnostic and statistical manual of mental disorders, fourth edition*, 1994) continues to pathologize them. Interest in paranormal phenomena, a belief in clairvoyance, telepathy, or a "sixth sense," or a feeling that one has "special powers to sense events before they happen or to read others' thoughts" are criteria for a diagnosis of Schizotypal Personality Disorder (p.641). Alternatively, the symbiotic and telepathic experiences analysts write about could merit a diagnosis of Shared Psychotic Disorder (p.306). Psychiatry, as keepers of the community's mental health, is less therapeutic and more punitive than psychoanalysis. Psychiatry stigmatizes people who acknowledge having these experiences and uses its institutional power to suppress acknowledgment of these subjective experiences. Psychiatry is the frontline in the cultural effort to quash frightening evidence of a nonlocal mind.

The centrality of countertransference has caused contemporary psychoanalytic writers to call their work "intersubjective." For example, American psychoanalyst Thomas Ogden describes his and his patient's co-creation of a "third" subjective representation in each of their minds. This "third" is a hybrid form of mental structure mutually created in each mind that contains qualities of both of them. The third is born out of an intersubjective process of projective identification and is used for the purpose of psychological growth. Through this newly created third, both participants are able of experience thoughts, feelings and perceptions that had previously been outside their realm of experience. Ogden (2004a) says, "individuals engaged in this form of relatedness unconsciously subjugate themselves to a mutually generated intersubjective third for the purpose of freeing themselves from the limits of whom they had been to that point" (p.189). Both participants create a form of double consciousness out of "self plus third." Through this shared form of mental structure, the analyst becomes capable of "participating in dreaming the patient's undreamt and interrupted dreams," allowing the patient to ultimately "dream himself more fully into existence" (Ogden, 2004b, p.2). Ogden is articulating the therapeutic symbiosis first described by Racker and Searles.

In summary, for the past ninety years psychoanalysts have written about a clinical phenomenon in which the patient's thoughts and feelings emerge spontaneously in the analyst's mind. Jung, Deutsch, Ferenczi and Balint use the word telepathy to describe this phenomenon, and many others employ metaphors like induction, projection, and contagion to explain how one person's thoughts and feelings pass through space to enter the mind of another. Even contemporary Freudian analysts, among the last to accept the therapeutic value of countertransference, acknowledge "the inner experiences of the analyst spring from, resonate with, and elucidate the inner world of the patient" (Jacobs, 1991, p.220). Analysts describe themselves *becoming* their patients, and they use words like fusion, merger, symbiosis, and the third to describe their shared mental states. Kleinians portray their patients as literally *living within* them.

Since 1950, with wider acceptance and appreciation of countertransference, psychoanalysis has placed greater emphasis on the therapeutic relationship. While the Kleinians made projective identification their defining therapeutic paradigm, Spotnitzians have used induced feelings, narcissistic transference and objective countertransference to guide their form of therapeutic relating. By constructing theories around objective countertransference and projective identification, Spotnitzian and Kleinian analysts have made thought transference their basis for cure.

These authors describe an unconscious therapeutic cycle emerging within the therapeutic relationship: The analyst internalizes portions of the patient's mind, and to a limited extent the analyst begins to possess twin personalities. Using a nineteenth century phrase, they come to possess "double consciousness." Then, for a period of time, the analyst lives the patient's thoughts and feelings as his own. As these ideas and emotions pass through the analyst's psyche they are naturally modified. Thereafter, these feelings, along with the analyst's amendments and modifications, are communicated back to the patient. This almost entirely unconscious process becomes the emotional basis of learning and therapeutic change.

Finally, it is important to recognize that there is no difference between projective identification and traditional notions of spirit possession. This is almost never acknowledged in the psychoanalytic literature. The Kleinian conception of curative action has ancient roots. Psychoanalyst Lawrence Brown (2011) notes that, "In effect, Klein was suggesting a process not unlike the Andean folk doctors" (p.51). Anthropologists and evolutionary psychologists (Bourguignon, 1976; Cohen, 2007; Goldish, 2003; Hayden, 2003; Lewis, 1971; McNamara, 2011; Oesterreich, 1974) describe the concept of spirit possession as widespread historically, believing it to be found in most human cultures. Spirit possession and altered states of consciousness (trance) are linked to ancient healing practices and to the origin of religion. Reviewing hundreds of traditional societies, anthropologist Erika Bourguignon (1976) defines spirit possession as "a total transformation, the apparent substitution of one personality by another" (p.6). In his comprehensive review of possession throughout history, Traugott Oesterreich (1974) describes what spirit possession looks like:

> The patient's organism appears to be invaded by a new personality; it is governed by a strange soul. . .It is as if another soul had entered into the body and thenceforth subsisted there, in place of or side-by-side with the normal subject.
>
> (p.17)

The possessed individual realizes his thoughts, feelings and behavior are being powerfully influenced by a personality other than his own that has taken up residence within him. This is, of course, the same language that characterizes Klein's concept of projective identification and Spotnitz's notion of objective countertransference.

Taking an evolutionary perspective, psychologist Patrick McNamara (2011) describes spirit possession as a natural method of learning in which identity and personality are transformed and enlarged.

> Assimilation of another's identity into one's consciousness entailed considerably greater risks and greater potential payoffs in terms of both intrapsychic and interpersonal interactions. . .Fortunately for us, our forefathers learned how to cultivate and then control these possession experiences so that they enriched the personality or identity or self instead of diminishing it.
>
> (p.5)

This approach to spirit possession is akin to Ogden's description of the third, or Blass and Blatt's conception of symbiotic states being used for psychological growth. It is probable that forms of possession are universally employed unconsciously for learning, development, and adaptation. It appears this unconscious naturally occurring process has been rediscovered by psychoanalysts as they work intimately with their patients.

Of course, consciousness and its powerful advocate, reductive materialism, tenaciously suppress our experience of these unconscious processes. Consciousness naturally attempts to eliminate awareness of the existence of invisible unconscious forces that threaten its integrity and agency.

A century ago, writing in 1909, American psychologist William James (1986) notes,

> The refusal of modern "enlightenment" to treat "possession" as a hypothesis to be spoken of as even possible, in spite of the massive human tradition based on concrete experience in its favor, has always seemed to me a curious example of the power of fashion in things scientific. . .One has to be scientific, indeed, to be blind and ignorant enough to suspect no such possibility.
>
> (p.357)

Our reflexive suppression of awareness of unconscious knowledge keeps us on a perpetual path of fighting to recover truths repeatedly known and forgotten for centuries.

Note

1 When Racker fled Vienna in 1938 and relocated in Buenos Aires, he was initially analyzed by Angel Garma, co-founder of the Argentinian Psychoanalytic Association. Garma, like Paula Heimann, had been analyzed by Theodor Reik in Berlin. Reik's ideas described above—that the analyst understands his patient by looking within himself—had an enduring impact on psychoanalysis in South America (Brown, 2011).

References

Balint, M. (1955). Notes on parapsychology and parapsychological healing. *International Journal of Psycho-Analysis*, 36, 31–35.

Balint, M. (1968). *The basic fault: Therapeutic aspects of regression.* New York, NY: Brunner/Mazel.

Bion, W. (1959). Attacks on linking. *International Journal of Psychoanalysis*, 40, 308–315.

Blass, R. & Blatt, S. (1996). Attachment and separateness in the experience of symbiotic relatedness. *Psychoanalytic Quarterly*, 65, 711–746.

Bourguignon, E. (1976). *Possession.* San Francisco, CA: Chandler and Sharp Publishers.

Brottman, M. (2011). *Phantoms of the clinic: From thought transference to projective identification.* London: Karnac.

Brown, L. (2011). *Intersubjective processes and the unconscious: An integration of Freudian, Kleinian and Bionian perspectives.* London: Routledge.

Cohen, E. (2007). *The mind possessed: The cognition of spirit possession in an Afro-Brazilian religious tradition*. Oxford: Oxford University Press.

Deutsch, H. (1953). Occult processes occurring during psychoanalysis. In G. Devereux (Ed.), *Psychoanalysis and the occult* (pp. 133–146). New York, NY: International Universities Press. (Original work published 1926)

Diagnostic and statistical manual of mental disorders, fourth edition. (1994). Washington, DC: American Psychiatric Association.

Ferenczi, S. (1988). *The clinical diary of Sandor Ferenczi*. J. Dupont (Ed.). Cambridge, MA: Harvard University Press. (Original work 1933)

Fliess, R. (1942). The metapsychology of the analyst. *Psychoanalytic Quarterly*, 11, 211–227.

Geltner, P. (2013). The concept of objective countertransference and its role in a two-person psychology. In *Emotional communication: Countertransference analysis and the use of feelings in psychoanalytic technique* (pp.22–35). London: Routledge.

Goldish, M. (Ed.) (2003). *Spirit possession in Judaism: Cases and contexts from the middle ages to the present*. Detroit, MI: Wayne State University Press.

Grinberg, L. (1962). On a specific aspect of countertransference due to the patient's projective identification. *International Journal of Psychoanalysis*, 43, 437–440.

Hayden, B. (2003). *Shamans, sorcerers and saints*. Washington, DC: Smithsonian Institution.

Heimann, P. (1950). On counter-transference. *International Journal of Psychoanalysis*, 31, 81–84.

Hinshelwood, R. (1989). *A dictionary of Kleinian thought*. Northvale, NJ: Jason Aronson.

Jacobs, T. (1991). *The use of the self: Countertransference and communication in the analytic situation*. Madison, CT: International Universities Press.

James, W. (1986). Report on Mrs. Piper's Hodgson-control. In *The Works of William James, Essays in psychical research*, (pp.253–360). Harvard, MA: Harvard University Press. (Original work published 1909)

Klein, M. (1946). Notes on some schizoid mechanisms. *International Journal of Psychoanalysis*, 27, 99–110.

Kohut, H. (1971). *The analysis of self*. New York, NY: International Universities Press.

Lewin, R. & Schultz, C. (1992). *Losing and fusing: Borderline transitional object and self relations*. Northvale, NJ: Jason Aronson.

Lewis, I. (1971). *Ecstatic religion: An anthropological study of spirit possession and shamanism*. Harmondsworth, England: Penguin Books.

Little, M. (1951). Counter-transference and the patient's response to it. *International Journal of Psychoanalysis*, 32, 32–40.

Luckhurst, R. (2002). *The invention of telepathy: 1870–1901*. Oxford: Oxford University Press.

Madonna, J. (2017). Countertransference issues in treatment of borderline and narcissistic personality disorders. In *Emotional presence in psychoanalysis: Theory and clinical applications* (pp.21–45). London: Routledge.

Main, R. (Ed.) (1997). *Jung on synchronicity and the paranormal*. Princeton, NJ: Princeton University Press.

Marshall, R. & Marshall, S. (1988). *The transference-countertransference matrix: The emotional-cognitive dialogue in psychotherapy, psychoanalysis, and supervision*. New York, NY: Columbia University Press.

McNamara, P. (2011). *Spirit possession and exorcism: History, psychology and neurobiology*. Santa Barbara, CA: Praeger.

Meadow, P. (1991). Resonating with the psychotic patient. *Modern Psychoanalysis*, 16, 87–103.

Oesterreich, T. (1974). *Possession and exorcism among primitive races, in antiquity, the middle ages, and modern times*. New York, NY: Causeway Books. (Original work published 1921)

Ogden, T. (2004a). The analytic third: implications for psychoanalytic theory and technique. *Psychoanalytic Quarterly*, 73,167–195.

Ogden, T. (2004b). This art of psychoanalysis: Dreaming undreamt dreams and interrupted cries. *International Journal of Psychoanalysis*, 85, 857–877.

Racker, H. (1957). The meaning and uses of countertransference. *Psychoanalytic Quarterly*, 26, 303–357.

Racker, H. (1968). The meaning and uses of countertransference. In *Transference and Countertransference*, (pp.127–173). Madison, CT: International Universities Press.

Reik, T. (1937). *Surprise and the psychoanalyst*. New York, NY: Dutton.

Rosenfeld, H. (1983). Primitive object relations and mechanisms. *International Journal of Psychoanalysis*, 64, 261–267.

Searles, H. (1973). Concerning therapeutic symbiosis. *The Annual of Psychoanalysis*, 1, 247–262.

Searles, H. (1979). Concerning therapeutic symbiosis: The patient as symbiotic therapist, the phase of ambivalent symbiosis, and the role of jealousy in the fragmented ego. In *Countertransference and related subjects: Selected papers* (pp.172–191). New York, NY: International Universities Press.

Sherman, M. (1983). Emotional communication in modern psychoanalysis: some Freudian origins and comparisons. *Modern Psychoanalysis*, 8(2), 173–189.

Spotnitz, H. (1963–1964). The toxoid response. *Psychoanalytic Review*, 50D (4), 81–94.

Spotnitz, H. (1979) Narcissistic countertransference. *Contemporary Psychoanalysis*, 15, 545–559.

Spotnitz, H. (1983). Countertransference with the schizophrenic patient: value of the positive anaclitic countertransference. *Modern Psychoanalysis*, 8, 169–172.

Spotnitz, H. (1985a). *Modern psychoanalysis of the schizophrenic patient: Theory of the technique*, second edition. New York, NY: Human Sciences Press. (Original work published 1969)

Spotnitz, H. (1985b). Narcissistic transference. In *Modern psychoanalysis of the schizophrenic patient: Theory of the technique*, second edition (pp.186–217). New York, NY: Human Sciences Press. (Original work published 1969)

Spotnitz, H. (1985c). Countertransference: Resistance and therapeutic leverage. In *Modern psychoanalysis of the schizophrenic patient: Theory of the technique*, second edition (pp.218–248). New York, NY: Human Sciences Press. (Original work published 1969)

Spotnitz, H. (1987). Emotional induction. In *Psychotherapy of preoedipal conditions* (pp.25–30). Northvale, NJ: Jason Aronson. (Original work published 1976)

Spotnitz, H. & Meadow, P. (1995). Toward an understanding of emotional contagion. In *Treatment of the narcissistic neuroses*, revised edition (pp.69–90). Northvale, NJ: Jason Aronson. (Original work published 1976)

Chapter 16

Origins of thought transference in Mesmer and Puysegur

The phrase "thought transference" originates in the 1780s with Amand-Marie-Jacques de Chastenet, the Marquis de Puysegur, and a pupil of the father of contemporary psychotherapy, Franz Mesmer (Chertok & de Saussure, 1979; Crabtree, 1993; Ellenberger, 1970). Living in a world captivated by scientific discoveries of the invisible forces of gravity, magnetism and electricity, Mesmer proposed a superfine magnetic fluid bathed the universe (Darnton, 1968). This fluid penetrated all matter and was "universally distributed. . .of incomparably rarefied nature, and by its nature capable of receiving, propagating, and communicating all impressions of movement" within and between objects (Bloch, 1980, p.67). Mesmer believed the distribution of this magnetic fluid within the body affected emotion, thought and behavior. Illness derived from an obstruction preventing the natural flow of magnetic forces within the body, representing the "chemical imbalance" theory of his day. Mesmer believed there was only one illness emerging in various symptomatic forms, for which there was only one cure, the restoration of magnetic balance.

Mesmer originally applied magnets to his patient's bodies to produce a therapeutic "crisis." This crisis was considered the body's resistance to an invading agent, producing an altered form of consciousness, the first step to restoring a balanced internal magnetic state. Dispensing with magnets, Mesmer concluded his own body possessed a form of "animal magnetism." With his two hands serving as twin magnetic poles, he'd pass his hands over the bodies of patients creating a unique form of *rapport* between the doctor and patient. In a word, he "mesmerized" them.

Using this technique Mesmer was remarkably successful at curing patients of chronic illnesses such as rheumatism and gout, epilepsy, chronic digestive and respiratory ailments, paralysis, blindness and chronic fever. He became a physician of last resort, sought out after traditional medicine had failed.

Mesmer made sensational public demonstrations of his curative technique and tried unsuccessfully to get the scientific community to validate his theory. An envious medical establishment, whose therapeutic measures were leeches, bloodletting, herbs and purgatives, demanded the government do something to protect their interests. Mesmer was contemptuous of ineffective and dangerous medical practices. A government sponsored scientific commission chaired by Ben Franklin and led by Antoine-Laurent Lavoisier (the founder of modern chemistry) investigated his work. They didn't examine his therapeutic success. They questioned whether Mesmer had discovered an invisible magnetic fluid permeating the universe.

The commission was noteworthy for its sophistication and scientific rigor (Chertok & Stengers, 1992; Crabtree, 1993). Considering *rapport* was the basis of Mesmer's therapy, this was the first time the *relationship* between physician and patient had become the subject of scientific study (Chertok & de Saussure, 1979). After careful investigation, the commission determined that many sick people were cured by Mesmer's method. While they couldn't rule out the existence of a magnetic fluid, the commission could find no evidence for it. Instead, these investigators concluded Mesmer's curative results could be explained by the patient and magnetizer's use of imagination, by the palliative effects of physical touch, and by patients' imitation of others' behaviors (Franklin, 1785).

Although the commission made imagination the central therapeutic agent, they never defined imagination nor explained its role in cure. Through their rejection of imagination, the commission inaugurated a powerful form of skepticism: *a deep mistrust of mind and psychological states* (Harrington, 2008). The commissioners claimed imagination was the enemy of rational thought, and a cure—though admittedly real—created through imagination was dismissed as invalid because it defied rational explanation. "In other words," as philosopher Isabelle Stengers (2003) notes, "the cure proves nothing" (p.14).

Mesmer rejected the commission's conclusion that his treatment was based on the patient's imagination noting he successfully treated infants and comatose adults, and that he could magnetize subjects from an adjacent room without their knowledge. This was sufficient evidence, in

Mesmer's view, to prove his technique had a physical basis rather than a mental origin rooted in imagination. He scornfully called the commission's conclusion that he was "healing through the mind" a "miserable objection" (Pattie, 1994, p.2).

Imagination had played a similar role in the sensational cures performed by Mesmer's contemporary, Catholic priest Johann Joseph Gassner, who Henri Ellenberger (1970) describes as "one of the most famous healers of all time" (p.53). Thousands flocked to Gassner's therapeutic performances, where over a period of days he would cure hundreds of people of the widest variety of ailments using his unique form of exorcism. Naturally, Gassner believed his success was religiously based, while Mesmer claimed Gassner was unwittingly curing the sick via animal magnetism. Representatives of the Enlightenment were as incredulous and dismissive of Gassner's success as they were of Mesmer's. They "refused to recognize that in the controversy between religion and reason in the late eighteenth century most of the best empirical evidence lay on the side of the exorcists" (Midelfort, 2005, p.2). Gassner freely admitted imagination was the biggest factor in his therapeutic success, remarking:

> Yes, yes the imagination is according to these philosophers the queen of this world: all luck and misfortune, riches and poverty, victory and defeat consist only in the imagination. So why wouldn't health and sickness also consist of that?
>
> (Midelfort, 2005, p.74)

For Father Gassner, imagination and belief were the basis of cure.

Just as Enlightenment rationalism rejected Gassner's therapeutic success, Mesmer's technique was banned, and he was disgraced. Medical leeches prevailed. According to the commissioners, Mesmer's work was invalid because he proved mind, in the form of imagination, transformed physical conditions in the body. This was unacceptable! The material presence of a leech sucking a patient's blood was an approved basis for therapeutic action. But something as immaterial as imagination wasn't. Only physical explanations were valid, and science *outlawed* empirical evidence proving otherwise. Scientific veneer masked a deep fear of mind and the immaterial. This sort of thing drove Frank's character, Max, crazy. Max felt perpetually marginalized by his neighbors' fears. Max sympathized with Mesmer. Besides, he had a revulsion of leeches.

Mesmer was self-aggrandizing and greedy, but also politically liberal with strong humanitarian values. He was egotistical, mistrusted the powerful, and resented the rich. He was a supporter of the French revolution, and an ardent abolitionist. He was highly moral, but also quarrelsome and litigious (Pattie, 1994). Although he was called a charlatan by some, there's no evidence of dishonesty in his presentation of animal magnetism. He treated people from every social class and, while he demanded high fees from the wealthy, he treated the poor for free. In his later years he accepted no fees for medical treatments. Hoping to bring his medical revolution to the masses, Mesmer taught his therapeutic technique to several hundred people, mostly aristocrats, on the condition they'd treat the poor for free. You can see why the medical establishment hated him.

One of the most prominent of these aristocrats was the Marquis de Puysegur who trained with Mesmer in Paris in 1784, and then returned home to begin his therapeutic practice (Crabtree, 1993; Ellenberger, 1965, 1970; Gauld, 1992). Puysegur's fourth case was Victor Race, his twenty-three-year old servant, who was afflicted with a respiratory illness. Victor would become the Anna O. of animal magnetism, and his case is the first recorded clinical example of thought transference.

When Victor was magnetized by Puysegur he fell into a peculiar trance in which he seemed more expressive, lucid and intelligent than when he was awake. Rather than being a naïve peasant barely able to utter a sentence, he now spoke with the self-assurance, vocabulary and knowledge of a highly educated man. He corrected Puysegur's mistaken conceptions about animal magnetism, diagnosed his own illness, and predicted his process of cure. Victor's altered personality appeared to be more intelligent than Puysegur himself. Most impressively, Victor was able to read Puysegur's thoughts and respond to Puysegur's unspoken commands. At times he allowed Puysegur to take charge of his mind. Puysegur (1784) writes,

> I need not speak to him; I think before him, and he hears me, answers me. Somebody enters his room? He sees him, if so *I want*, speaks to him, tells him the things *that I want* him to say to him, not always such as I *dictate* them to him, but such as truth demands it. When he wants to say more than I believe is safe to be heard, then *I stop his ideas, his sentences* mid-word, and I *change* his *idea* entirely.

(pp.27–28)

When Puysegur (1784) believed Victor's ideas were affecting him disagreeably,

> I stopped them and tried to inspire more pleasant ones. He became calm imagining himself shooting a prize, dancing at a party. . .I nourished these ideas in him and in this way made him move around a lot in his chair, as if dancing to a tune; while mentally singing it I made him repeat it out loud.
>
> (p.28)

To cheer him up, Puysegur (1784) sang a song in his mind causing Victor to sing it aloud. While Victor was impassive in everyday life, when he was in a state of *rapport*, he became emotionally expressive.

> As soon as he is *in a magnetic crisis*, he pours his heart out, he wishes, he says, that one could open him up to see how full of affection and gratitude he is; we cannot hold back tears of admiration and of tenderness hearing the voice of nature expressing itself with such candor.
>
> (p.28)

During *rapport*, Puysegur believed he and Victor had become joined through an invisible connection linking their brains and nervous systems, making them functionally inseparable. Puysegur would later write, "In this state, the ill person enters into a very intimate rapport with the magnetizer, one could almost say becomes part of the magnetizer" (Crabtree, 1993, p.41). Significantly, while entranced Victor was unaware of others and responded only to Puysegur. Upon awakening Victor had no memory of his trance, but his amnesia was peculiar. The next day, when Victor was induced a second time, his memory of the previous trance reappeared. While entranced he remembered everything that had occurred during the previous trance, along with all his other memories. But when he awoke his knowledge of this collection of somnambulant memories disappeared.

Puysegur realized he'd stumbled onto something significant. In contrast to the violent convulsive crises invoked by Mesmer's magnetic technique, Puysegur described this peaceful somnambulance as the "perfect crisis." Spotnitz might have called this intimate *rapport* the perfect narcissistic transference, and Searles would certainly have considered it an exquisite form of therapeutic symbiosis.

Not all of Puysegur's patients fell into a somnambulant state. According to Puysegur's disciple, Joseph Deleuze, only one in twenty patients entered this depth of trance (Gauld, 1992). Puysegur describes Victor's reassuring response to this:

> I have only one regret—not being able to touch [magnetize] everyone. But my man [Victor Race], or perhaps I should say my intelligence, calms me. He is teaching me the conduct I must follow. According to him it is not necessary that I touch everyone. One look, one gesture, one feeling of good will is enough. It is a peasant, the most narrow and limited in this locality, that teaches me this. When he is in crisis, *I know no one as profound, prudent, and clear-sighted.*
>
> (Crabtree, 1993, p.43; italics added)

Puysegur claimed Victor, in his altered state, was the most intelligent person he'd ever encountered.

Puysegur believed his ability to entrance Victor and other patients was based upon the *rapport* they'd established, and each person's capacity for *rapport* was greatest during illness. Puysegur identified five characteristics of "artificial somnambulance": It was a unique form of consciousness, based on a deep *rapport* established between magnetizer and patient, in which they were highly attuned to each other's thoughts and feelings, with the patient often displaying a new personality, and who upon waking had amnesia for the somnambulant experience (Crabtree, 1993). This peculiar form of amnesia caused Puysegur to speculate (in 1784!) that human beings had two separate memory systems, one conscious and one unconscious (Chertok, 1978). Therapeutic outcome was related to this altered state of consciousness, and elimination of illness required the recreation of this somnambulant trance over a period of days, weeks or months.

Puysegur's technique was taught to more than two hundred followers, creating a split in the mesmerist movement. Disciples of Mesmer ("fluidists") continued to emphasize the invisible magnetic fluid believed to be the physical basis of cure, while followers of Puysegur ("animists") highlighted mental states, believing cure arose from the physician's therapeutic intention and affection for the patient, combined with the patient's capacity for *rapport*.

Rapport was a product of the trance. In 1811 Friedrich Hufeland wrote magnetic *rapport* was the most intimate relationship (the ultimate "sympathy") that can exist between human beings. He compared *rapport* to the relationship of a fetus with its mother. *Rapport* was a return to the womb, recreating the generative intrauterine process of somatic regulation. Psychiatric historian Henri Ellenberger (1970) writes, "According to Hufeland, each cure achieved through animal magnetism goes through the same phases as the yet unborn child in its mother's womb" (p.153). "Sympathetic resonance" was an eighteenth-century version of our contemporary phrase "affect attunement." Like the spatial metaphors of projection and induction, the word "resonance" provides a physical metaphor for a mental process.

Charles Richet (1923), a nineteenth-century medical researcher studying animal magnetism, emphasized the telepathic nature of *rapport*:

> Magnetizers gave the name "rapport" to the relation that they supposed to exist between the magnetizer and his patient; this relation being such that the sensations of the former were perceived by the latter, who could also divine the thought of the magnetizer without the utterance of any word.
>
> (p.104)

According to Mesmer's theory, when in *rapport* their minds and bodies had become linked through a process of sympathetic resonance transmitted invisibly through magnetic currents (Deleuze, 1843).

Magnetizers reported being physically affected by patients' symptoms (Darnton, 1968). For example, the Chevalier de Barberin and his colleagues in Lyons noted in 1790 that when they magnetized patients it "produced within themselves a sort of 'doubling' which enabled them to feel in their own bodies the ailments of those they were treating," allowing them to use these feelings to guide the treatment (Gauld, 1992, p.65). This may be the first description in the medical literature (in 1790!) of objective countertransference being used therapeutically.

In fact, magnetizers believed they were susceptible to contracting the patient's illness. Deleuze (1843) writes,

> In magnetic communication there is established a sympathy between the similar organs of the two individuals; whence it follows that a person whose lungs are delicate, cannot without danger, magnetize anyone whose lungs are affected.
>
> (p.172)

Illnesses were thought to be transmitted magnetically between therapist and patient, so mesmerists who were ill were cautioned: "Should one continue for several days to magnetize while in this sickly indisposition, the somnambulist is inoculated with the same illness" (Chertok & de Saussure, 1979, p.29). It would be another sixty years before Robert Koch would propose the germ theory, offering an alternative physical explanation for the transmission of disease.

During their somnambulant state some patients seemed to be capable of what Mesmer called a "sixth sense," a kind of superhuman intelligence allowing them to diagnose illnesses, prescribe treatment, predict the evolution of their illness, and the time of cure. When entranced many patients claimed they could "see" within their bodies, visualizing their organs and diseased tissue. Occasionally autopsies revealed diseased areas corresponding to these visualizations, providing cases of apparent clairvoyance supported by testimony of the attending physician (Gauld, 1992). Finding such accurate "visions" incomprehensible, magnetizers speculated that sensations within the body might be transferred between perceptual organs—reflecting a blending of sensory modalities—to create the subjective experience of visual perception.

Believing patients in a state of somnambulance possessed the ability to diagnose and prescribe curative actions, Puysegur would often magnetize several patients and allow them to work therapeutically with each other's illnesses while he simply observed. When entranced, Puysegur believed his patients possessed an intelligence, wisdom and sensitivity that transcended his own abilities. Where Mesmer tended to dominate his patients and was "little inclined to allow the patient the slightest initiative" (Chertok & de Saussure, 1979, p. 6), Henri Ellenberger (1970) notes that Puysegur's clinical technique "often gave the treatment the aspect of 'patient directed therapy'" (p. 189).

Puysegur was highly respected possessing "the reputation of a thoroughly honest, generous, if somewhat uncritical man" (Ellenberger, 1970, p.74). His approach to patients was characterized by a generosity of spirit. In contrast to Mesmer, he made no physical contact with patients. Doing nothing to provoke the patient, he employed a gentle form of questioning exploring their memories, feelings and beliefs about their illness (Conn, 1982; Pattie, 1994). Puysegur advised,

One must not in the first place overwhelm him with questions, still less try to move him to action in any way. The state in which he finds himself is new to him; one must, as it were, let him become acquainted with it. One's first question must be: *How do you feel?* Then: *Do you feel that I'm doing you good?* After that, tell him what a pleasure it gives you to be able to help him. From there you gradually come to the details of his illness, and your first questions must not extend beyond the subject of his health.

(Chertok & de Saussure, 1979, p.14)

Puysegur made patients' accounts of the manifestation of illness and expectations for cure the focus of his treatment. He spent considerable time working with patients' feelings of hopelessness. Believing patients in a somnambulant trance knew more about their illness than he, he encouraged them to create their own treatments.

Puysegur refused to make clinical demonstrations believing it exploited patients and worsened their condition. He took patients with him on trips so as not to interrupt their treatment, and sometimes he brought patients into his home to improve their care. Once in a somnambulant state he believed the patient experienced complete dependency on the magnetizer, just as an infant would with its mother.

Puysegur achieved remarkable success creating several hundred documented cures ushering in a century where physical illnesses were cured through mental treatment. Over the next three decades he and his followers in France and Germany induced therapeutic trances in thousands of patients. Because somnambulance was combined with other treatments (such as herbs, baths, and bloodletting), it's unclear what role it played in cure. However, because traditional treatments had failed to help these chronically ill patients, it's presumed this altered mental state was a powerful therapeutic agent.

The model of therapeutic action proposed by animal magnetism starts with an interpersonal *rapport* where two individuals begin to function as a single entity. Reports of thought transference were evidence of this invisible connection. But that was only one manifestation of a deeply somatic connection being made between their two bodies. *Rapport* was the somatization of their relationship, a kind of "interpersonal physiology." During *rapport* internal organs developed a sympathetic resonance, allowing the structural characteristics of healthy organs to be transferred to diseased organs. Magnetizers believed these rhythmically vibrating forms constituted a vital life force transmitted between individuals. Through repetitive sessions of *rapport*, typically induced once a day for an hour, this therapeutic process worked incrementally over weeks and months to transform illness into health. Magnetizers considered *rapport*, as a remnant of intrauterine life, to be nature's interpersonal method for restoring health.

Was everyone susceptible to magnetic treatment? No. Writing in 1819 Deleuze, one of animal magnetism's most judicious spokesmen, cautions:

> Not only do I not believe that magnetism cures all ailments, but I am indeed convinced that it cures but a very small number, that most frequently it alleviates without curing, and that it can sometimes prove harmful.
>
> (Chertok & de Saussure, 1979, p.20)

But this conservative estimate isn't consistent with the historical record. Critical reviews of magnetic treatments confirm the mesmerists were successful curing a wide variety of ailments across all segments of society. For example, during a seven-year period (1814–1821) a clinic in Berlin recorded the magnetic treatment of four thousand one hundred and sixty-eight patients who were suffering from fevers and inflammations, paralyzes, wasting diseases, rheumatism and gout, chronic skin conditions, along with eye and hearing complaints. Of these patients, forty-three percent completely recovered, forty-one percent improved, thirteen percent remained unchanged, while three percent became worse or died (Gauld, 1992, p.248). We know little about these patients, and without a comparison group, we can't know how the magnetic treatment contributed to their health. But the fact that eighty-four percent improved is impressive.

Animal magnetism, particularly the clinical work of Puysegur, was centuries ahead of its time. It's little-known today because it was outlawed. Science, supporting the financial interests of the medical community, suppressed evidence of its success. Nonetheless, consider the following: As a "recreation" of intrauterine experience, *rapport* was discovered to be a naturally occurring interpersonal technique used throughout life for physical and mental restoration. *Rapport* was an altered state of consciousness in which the minds and bodies of the therapist and patient begin to function as one, as evidenced by telepathic experience. This intersubjective mental state allowed the physician to experience the patient's illness and use this knowledge to shape therapeutic interventions. During *rapport* the patient's personality changed, displaying new knowledge and abilities, sometimes demonstrating superhuman perception (sixth sense) and knowledge. *Rapport* revealed the mind possessed two memory systems, one conscious and one unconscious. Finally, through *rapport* mind transformed physical states in the body.

In spite of its success, animal magnetism was socially marginalized. Where Gassner's exorcisms were the most successful medical intervention of eighteenth-century Germany, animal magnetism was the most successful form of medicine throughout nineteenth-century Europe. But, as Henri Ellenberger (1970) writes, "curing the sick is not enough; one must cure them with methods accepted by the community" (p.59). If not, Isabelle Stengers (2003) ironically notes, patients successfully treated by animal magnetism were "cured for the wrong reasons" (p.16).

References

Bloch, G. (Trans.) (1980). *Mesmerism: A translation of the original scientific and medical writings of F.A. Mesmer*. Los Altos, CA: William Kaufmann.

Chertok, L. (1978). The unconscious in France before Freud: Premises of a discovery. *Psychoanalytic Quarterly*, 47, 192–208.

Chertok, L. & de Saussure, R. (1979). *The therapeutic revolution: From Mesmer to Freud*. New York, NY: Brunner/Mazel.

Chertok, L. & Stengers, I. (1992). *A critique of psychoanalytic reason: Hypnosis as a scientific problem from Lavoisier to Lacan*. Stanford, CA: Stanford University Press.

Conn, J. (1982). Nature of magnetic treatment. *Journal of the American Society of Psychosomatic Dentistry and Medicine*, 29, 44–53.

Crabtree, A. (1993). *From Mesmer to Freud: Magnetic sleep and the roots of psychological healing*. New Haven, CT: Yale University Press.

Darnton, R. (1968). *Mesmerism and the end of the Enlightenment in France*. Cambridge, MA: Harvard University Press.

Deleuze, J. P. (1843). *Practical instruction in animal magnetism*. New York, NY: D. Appleton & Company. (Original work published 1825)

Ellenberger, H. (1965). Mesmer and Puysegur: From magnetism to hypnotism. *Psychoanalytic Review*, 52B, 137–153.

Ellenberger, H. (1970). *The discovery of the unconscious: The history and evolution of dynamic psychiatry*. New York, NY: Basic Books.

Franklin, B. (1785). *Report of Dr. Benjamin Franklin and other Commissioners charged by the King of France with the examination of the Animal Magnetism as now practiced at Paris*. London: J. Johnson.

Gauld, A. (1992). *A history of hypnotism*. Cambridge: Cambridge University Press.

Harrington, A. (2008). *The cure within: A history of mind-body medicine*. New York, NY: W.W. Norton.

Midelfort, E. (2005). *Exorcism and Enlightenment: Johann Joseph Gassner and the demons of eighteenth-century Germany*. New Haven, CT: Yale University Press.

Pattie, F. (1994). *Mesmer and animal magnetism: A chapter in medical history*. Hamilton, NY: Edmonston Publishing.

Puysegur, A. (1784). *Memoires pour server a l'histoire et a l'etablissement du magnetisme animal*. Paris: Dentu.

Richet, C. (1923). *Thirty years of psychical research: Being a treatise on metaphysics*. London: W. Collins Sons.

Stengers, I. (2003). The doctor and the charlatan. *Cultural Studies Review*, 9, 11–36.

Chapter 17

Somnambulism to hypnotism, Mesmer to Charcot

Mesmerism spread from France to Germany, Scandinavia, England and eventually to America, though always remaining a marginalized medical treatment of last resort. Because it was frequently associated with the occult, it was disparaged and dismissed. "But at the medical grass roots the doctrine was extremely popular" owing to its effectiveness (Shorter, 1992, p.136).

In 1829 the first book length case study of nervous derangement, *The Seeress of Prevorst*, was published in Germany by physician and poet Justinus Kerner (Ellenberger, 1970; Gauld, 1992; Moser, 1967). Kerner's book about his somnambulant patient, Friedericke Hauffe, became a best-seller in Germany fueling popular interest in animal magnetism.

Hauffe was the uneducated daughter of a forester, born in a secluded mountain village where she had a pious but spartan upbringing. From an early age she experienced prophetic dreams and reported seeing apparitions of dead relatives. After the death of her infant daughter she suffered from anorexia, hemorrhages and fever that no physician could treat. Her health worsened after the death of her father, and she retreated into an inner world of somnambulance.

Believing she was possessed her family engaged an exorcist to no avail. After years of serious illness, her exhausted family delivered her into Kerner's care at the age of twenty-five as "a picture of death—wasted to a skeleton" (Kerner, 1845, p.52). Kerner reluctantly took her into his home. A poet as well as the official physician for the city of Weinsberg, Kerner's house was a mecca for intellectuals who witnessed Hauffe's care. Assessing her health to have disintegrated beyond the possibility of full recovery, Kerner's daily magnetic treatment maintained her in a near-death condition for three years until she died.

Though an uneducated peasant who spoke in a rural dialect, once she was entranced Hauffe spoke in high German, and sometimes in verse. Occasionally her speech devolved into an incomprehensible language she claimed was the forgotten mother tongue of mankind. In fact, many of the words she spoke were of ancient Hebrew, Arabic, and Coptic origin. It seems impossible an uneducated girl could have known this. In addition to this unique language, she delivered philosophical teachings resembling the work of Plato who was unknown to her, but familiar to Kerner's associates. Like Victor Race, in her altered state, Hauffe displayed mental abilities far beyond her conscious knowledge and skills.

When entranced Hauffe became clairvoyant. She claimed to be able to see inside bodies, and to envision the future. She made many accurate predictions of peoples' deaths including her own. When encountering a sick person, she instantly manifested the person's physical condition before any symptoms were reported. For an extended period, she slipped back in time, consecutively reliving days from the previous year. Because she was closely observed by Kerner and a group of physicians, philosophers and theologians who attested to the validity of her predictions, her perceptive powers were regarded as mysterious but genuine (Ellenberger, 1970; Gauld, 1992).

Hauffe was a powerful healer and her remarkable skills appear to be associated with her perpetual near-death condition. Her treatment of the Countess von Maldeghem was dramatically successful. At the age of twenty-three the Countess married, and after the birth of her second child she became psychotic. She believed she was dead and didn't recognize her surroundings or family. On the advice of her physician, her husband consulted Hauffe who prescribed a nine-day diet and trance regime. Following Hauffe's directions, the Count magnetized his wife three times each day. At corresponding times Hauffe, one hundred miles away, entered a trance and prayed. On the seventh day Kerner and his associates witnessed Hauffe declaring "the Countess has changed." Apparently, at that same moment the entranced Countess announced she was in a strong *rapport* with Hauffe. The Countess

> felt an invincible necessity to communicate something to her husband, which she had never told any human being whatever. After this revelation, the illusions that had troubled her wholly disappeared; she recognized her husband and children, and also her estate; but felt a great desire to see Mrs. Hauffe.
>
> (Kerner, 1845, p.105)

The Countess visited Friedericke Hauffe and after a week of praying together she declared herself fully cured. Ten years later she remained symptom free.

The Countess' symptoms disappeared at the moment she revealed a secret. Ellenberger (1993b) points out the restoration of health through revealing a pathogenic secret is an ancient conception in medicine and the basis of confession in the Catholic religion, the Countess' faith. One contemporary reader of this case describes it as "the successful psychotherapeutic treatment of an onset of schizophrenia carried out in the form of spiritual healing from a distance" (Moser, 1967, p.165). This nonlocal treatment certainly qualifies as spooky action at a distance.

Reading this chapter, Frank's fictional character, Max, found this history strange but interesting. Throughout his life Max shied away from discussions of insanity because he was sensitive to others' assessment of him as nuts. Now, browsing through Barnes and Noble in Woodstock, Max urged Frank to buy a copy of Michel Foucault's massive *History of madness*—a hard place to start, but that's Max.

As Frank read Foucault, Max felt liberated hearing the voice of a kindred spirit. To his surprise, Foucault's book echoed Max's paper, "The myth of mental illness." Max was unaware of Thomas Szasz's (1974) book of the same title. Like Szasz (1970), Max believed the concept of mental illness was fraudulent. Apart from certain neurological disorders like dementia and epilepsy, there was no evidence that unusual qualities of mental life represented "illness," or that medicine possessed any kind of cure. So, to Max, psychiatry bore no relationship to medicine whatsoever. Instead, psychiatry was an authoritarian institution meant to control mental life. It stood as a cultural guardian protecting society from its deepseated fear of madness. If someone like Max had the courage to let people know what was on his mind, psychiatry slapped him with a stigmatizing diagnosis, gave him a timeout in a hospital, and sedated him chemically so that he wouldn't affect the community at large. Early in the book, Max appreciated Foucault's (2006) description of a Renaissance conception of madness as "inaccessible, fearsome knowledge" revealing truths beyond the capacity of reason to explain. Max concluded this was the kind of intellectual brilliance Friedericke Hauffe possessed.

During the first half of the nineteenth century magnetic sleep was used to anesthetize patients prior to surgery. Major surgeries including amputation were performed on somnambulant patients who experienced no pain and had no memory of the event. James Esdaile (1846), a Scottish surgeon working in India, conducted over a thousand such surgeries. Esdaile believed mesmerized patients had quicker recoveries with fewer side effects than patients receiving ether, a newly discovered anesthesia.

In 1843 another Scottish surgeon, James Braid, renamed somnambulism "hypnotism," separating it from the mesmeric tradition and bringing it into mainstream medicine. Braid proposed hypnotism was the product of brain processes, not a magnetic fluid permeating the universe. Braid recommended hypnotism be employed exclusively by physicians, and he sought to eliminate the interpersonal physiology of *rapport*. As a result, Braid created a hypnotism free from the occult qualities associated with animal magnetism.

Braid had his critics. Comparing hypnotism to animal magnetism's somnambulance, Thomson Jay Hudson (1893) noted the magnetizer "hypnotizes himself by the same act by which he mesmerizes the subject" (p.108). While the magnetizer doesn't enter as deep a trance, he and his patient end up entranced together. Braid, on the other hand, had found a way to hypnotize only the patient while remaining subjectively disengaged. Because therapeutic action in animal magnetism depended on an intersubjective state of mutual entrancement, Hudson claimed Braid's discovery actually "served to retard the progress of hypnotic science" (p.108).

At first there was little interest in Braid's sanitized version of artificial somnambulism. But forty years later, in the midst of a *fin de siècle* rejection of scientific materialism, Braid's re-conception of this trance state emerged in two competing schools of hypnotism in France: Jean-Martin Charcot's clinic at the Salpetriere Hospital for women in Paris, and Hippolyte Bernheim's school in Nancy. Psychoanalysis was born within the walls of these two institutions.

Charcot was interested in using hypnotism experimentally to study hysteria, while Bernheim was continuing the tradition of Puysegur, employing hypnotic suggestion to restore health. At the beginning of his career Sigmund Freud visited both schools, first studying with Charcot, and three years later working with Bernheim to improve his technique as a hypnotist. Freud's enthusiastic interest in hypnotism led him to translate the works of both Charcot and Bernheim into German.

In 1885 a twenty-nine-year old Freud, having completed his medical studies with a specialization in neurology, received a postgraduate travel scholarship to spend five months visiting Salpetriere Hospital to learn about hypnotism and hysteria. Freud was professionally transformed by his trip to Paris where he was captivated by Charcot (Jones, 1953; Chertok, 1970; Chertok & de Saussure, 1979; Ellenberger, 1993a; Sulloway, 1979). After his first month in Paris, Freud wrote to his fiancée describing his reaction to the eminent neurologist:

> I think that I am changing a great deal. I will tell you in detail what is affecting me. Charcot, who is one of the greatest of physicians and a man whose common sense borders on genius, is simply wrecking all my aims and opinions. I sometimes come out of his lectures as from out of Notre Dame. . .Whether the seed will bear any fruit, I don't know; but what I do know is that no other human being has ever affected me in the same way.
>
> (Freud, 1960, pp.184–185)

Charcot was charismatic and authoritarian, a spellbinding teacher who was "at the zenith of his fame. No one before or since has so dominated the world of neurology" (Jones, 1953, p.207). Freud idolized his teacher, savoring the precious hours he spent in the magic of a great personality (Freud, 1892–1894).

Charcot was a consulting physician to kings. Patients and students came from around the world to work with him. Salpetriere Hospital, a sprawling institution comprised of more than forty buildings and five thousand patients, was the world's center for the treatment of nervous illness. Charcot's medical career evolved from careful anatomical studies of neuropathology to his mature conception of neurology based on a dynamic interplay of physiological and psychological elements (Ellenberger, 1993a; Micale, 1995a, 1995b). Charcot began his career by making important discoveries about multiple sclerosis and ended it trying to explain miracle cures at Lourdes.

Charcot was an imaginative free thinker who focused on clinical evidence that pushed the edges of theory, causing him to be eclectic rather than doctrinaire. Retracing Mesmer's footsteps, in 1876 Charcot began his foray into hypnotism through an examination of the therapeutic use of magnets (Goetz, Bonduelle & Gelfand, 1995; Owen, 1971). Charcot was charged with scientifically investigating claims made by a Parisian physician that metals applied to the bodies of hysterical patients could temporarily reverse paralysis and associated anesthesia. Although initially skeptical, Charcot's team of researchers conducted experiments demonstrating such effects, though they couldn't determine if the results were produced by the metals.

Following these experiments, and under the influence of Charles Richet who was a physiological researcher interested in somnambulism, Charcot began to employ hypnotism to study hysterical patients at the Salpetriere. To obtain training in hypnotic technique, he employed an animal magnetist, the Marquis de Puyfontaine. Through this choice Charcot linked his work directly with the tradition of Puysegur and separated himself from Braid's positivist orientation.

Using hypnotism was a courageous act since somnambulism had been held in disrepute for most of the previous century. After four years of studying hypnotism, in 1882 Charcot delivered a paper endorsing it to the French Academy of Sciences. Pierre Janet, who was in attendance, called Charcot's performance a *tour de force* completely reversing the Academy's century-long rejection of animal magnetism. After a hundred years in the shadows, trance was back on center stage.

Charcot approached hypnotism with caution. He considered hypnotism to be a hysterical phenomenon, and he regarded hypnotism and hysteria to be equally pathological. Charcot used hypnotism experimentally, but unlike Bernheim he was skeptical about its therapeutic use. Regarding hypnosis as dangerous, Charcot agreed with Freud's teacher Theodor Meynert who considered hypnosis to be "induced psychosis" (Sulloway, 1979). Freud's visit to the Salpetriere coincided with Charcot's research on the psychical basis of hysterical paralysis. Charcot proposed hysterical paralyzes were not caused by physical lesions in the brain but rather by *ideas, memories* and *fears* associated with previous traumatic events. To prove his thesis, Charcot hypnotized hysterical patients, and through posthypnotic suggestion, caused paralyzes to spontaneously emerge in the patients' bodies once they awoke from their trance. Then he reversed the process, hypnotized the patients a second time, and returned them to their original state.

Freud was profoundly affected by Charcot's lectures. Freud became aware of the mysterious leap from idea to paralysis, revealing a mental element within physical illness (Chertok, 1970). Freud (1924) notes through hypnosis "one was given convincing proof that striking somatic changes could after all be brought about solely by mental influence" (p.192). Just as Mesmer and Gassner had successfully demonstrated, mind transformed physical conditions within the body.

Listening to Charcot's lectures, Freud developed an appreciation of a dynamic unconscious where memory and knowledge exist outside the control of consciousness. Freud (1924) found, "now for the first time in the phenomena of hypnotism, [the unconscious] became something actual, tangible and subject to experiment" (p.192). Through Charcot's hypnotic experiments Freud further realized the role of trauma in the psychogenesis of hysteria. Looking back at this visit to Paris, Freud writes,

> It is not easy to over-estimate the importance of the part played by hypnotism in the history of the origin of psycho-analysis. From a theoretical as well as from a therapeutic point of view, psycho-analysis has at its command a legacy which it inherited from hypnotism.
>
> (1924, p.192)

The trance Puysegur discovered in 1784 laid the foundation for psychoanalysis a century later.

References

Chertok, L. (1970). Freud in Paris: A crucial stage. *International Journal of Psychoanalysis*, 51, 511–520.

Chertok, L. & de Saussure, R. (1979). *The therapeutic revolution: From Mesmer to Freud*. New York, NY: Brunner/Mazel.

Ellenberger, H. (1970). *The discovery of the unconscious: The history and evolution of dynamic psychiatry*. New York, NY: Basic Books.

Ellenberger, H. (1993a). Charcot and the Salpetriere School. In M. Micale (Ed.), *Beyond the unconscious: Essays of Henri F. Ellenberger in the history of psychiatry* (pp. 139–154). Princeton, NJ: Princeton University Press. (Original work published 1965)

Ellenberger, H. (1993b). The pathogenic secret and its therapeutics. In M. Micale (Ed.), *Beyond the unconscious: Essays of Henri F. Ellenberger in the history of psychiatry* (pp. 341–359). Princeton, NJ: Princeton University Press. (Original work published 1966)

Esdaile, J. (1846). *Mesmerism in India, and its practical applications in surgery and medicine*. London: Hartford: Silas, Andrus and Son.

Foucault, M. (2006). *History of madness*. London: Routledge. (Original work published 1961)

Freud, E. (1960). *Letters of Sigmund Freud*. New York, NY: Basic Books.

Freud, S. (1892–1894). Preface and footnotes to the translation of Charcot's "Tuesday Lectures." *Standard Edition*. London: Hogarth Press, 1, 131–143.

Freud, S. (1924). A short account of psychoanalysis. *Standard Edition*. London: Hogarth Press, 19, 190–209.

Gauld, A. (1992). *A history of hypnotism*. Cambridge: Cambridge University Press.

Goetz, C., Bonduelle, M. & Gelfand, T. (1995). *Charcot: Constructing neurology*. New York, NY: Oxford University Press.

Hudson, T. (1893). *The law of psychic phenomena: A working hypothesis for the systematic study of hypnotism, spiritism, mental therapeutics, etc.* Chicago, IL: A.C. McClurg.

Jones, E. (1953). *The life and work of Sigmund Freud*, volume 1. New York, NY: Basic Books.

Kerner, J. (1845). *The Seeress of Prevorst: Revelations concerning the inner-life of man, and the inter-diffusion of a world of spirits in the one we inhabit*. London: J.C. Moore. (Original work published 1829)

Micale, M. (1995a). Charcot and *les nervroses traumatiques*: Scientific and historical reflections. *Journal of the History of Neuroscience*, 4, 101–119.

Micale, M. (1995b). Charcot and the history of hysteria. In *Approaching hysteria: Disease and its interpretations* (pp.88–97). Princeton, NJ: Princeton University Press.

Moser, L. (1967). Dr. Justinus Kerner and the Seeress of Prevorst. In E. Dingwall (Ed.), *Abnormal hypnotic phenomena: A survey of nineteenth-century cases*, volume 2, Belgium and the Netherlands, Germany and Scandinavia (pp.161–173). London: J. & A. Churchill.

Owen, A. (1971). *Hysteria, hypnosis and healing: The work of J.-M. Charcot*. New York, NY: Garrett Publications.

Shorter, E. (1992). *From paralysis to fatigue: A history of psychosomatic illness in the modern era*. New York, NY: Free Press.

Sulloway, F. (1979). *Freud, biologist of the mind*. London: Burnett Books.

Szasz, T. (1970). *Ideology and insanity: Essays on the psychiatric dehumanization of man*. Syracuse, NY: Syracuse University Press.

Szasz, T. (1974). *The myth of mental illness: Foundations of a theory of personal conduct*. New York, NY: Harper Perennial.

Chapter 18

The birth of psychoanalysis
From trance to transference

Freud arrived at Charcot's clinic in 1885 with a story to tell. Three years earlier a respected Viennese family physician, Joseph Breuer, told the young Freud about a hysterical patient named Bertha Pappenheim whom he'd treated with hypnosis. Freud (1925) was captivated by Breuer's account and he wrote enthusiastically, "I determined to inform Charcot of these discoveries when I reached Paris, and I actually did so. But the great man showed no interest" (p.19). This wasn't surprising since Charcot disapproved of hypnosis being used therapeutically.

When the fledgling Freud returned to Vienna his enthusiasm for Charcot created conflicts which diminished his professional prospects. Julius Wagner-Jauregg, a fellow medical student, describes Freud:

> After returning to Vienna he gave a lecture [on hysteria] before the Society of Physicians in which he spoke only of Charcot and praised him in the highest terms. But the Viennese authorities reacted badly to this. In the discussion which followed, Bamberger and Meynert harshly rejected Freud; and with that he fell into disgrace, as it were, with the faculty. Thus he was a practitioner in neurology but without any patients. But now there took pity on him a man whom I myself esteemed more than any other colleague. . .Josef Breuer. . .He now kept Freud in work by referring hysterical patients to him for treatment.
>
> (Swales, 1986, p.4)

Fourteen years older than Freud, Breuer had an established practice as an internist. He was a respected scientific researcher having authored several publications in physiology. Physician to many prominent families in Vienna, including what Peter Swales (1986) calls "the whole Viennese Jewish aristocracy," he participated in the most sophisticated intellectual circles (p.24). Breuer helped Freud launch his career, frequently giving him money and sending him wealthy patients whose treatments he supervised. When Freud published his German translation of Charcot's lectures, he gave a copy to Breuer with this inscription: "To [my] most highly esteemed friend, Dr. Josef Breuer, secret master of hysteria" (Skues, 2006, p.163). Freud believed Breuer's knowledge of hysteria, demonstrated through his treatment of Pappenheim, exceeded that of Charcot.

Bertha Pappenheim was born in Vienna in 1859 into a wealthy Orthodox Jewish family (Borch-Jacobsen, 1996; Breger, 2009; Freeman, 1990; Guttmann, 2001; Skues, 2006).[1] Up the age of sixteen she received a private education emphasizing languages, literature and music. She became fluent in five languages. She was bright with an excellent memory, a penetrating intuition and a powerful imagination. But her life was constrained by her rigidly conservative family. Owing to the deaths of two sisters, her parents were very protective. Because she was female, a university education wasn't considered. Bertha responded to her limited prospects for mental stimulation by frequent daydreaming, creating a "private theater" for her personal entertainment. Her father spoiled her while her mother was harshly critical, resulting in Bertha being maintained in an immature and oppositional state.

At the age of twenty-one her father, who she adored, fell ill with an abscessed lung. Breuer tells us one evening, while Bertha was waiting at her father's bed for the arrival of a surgeon, she

> gradually fell into a state of absence. In the course of the absence she hallucinated black snakes crawling out of the walls, and one which crawled up to her father to kill him. Her right arm had become anesthetized owing to its position, and her fingers were transformed into small snakes with death's heads [for fingernails]. She probably tried to drive the snakes off with her immobilized right arm. When the hallucinations had passed she had an anxious desire to pray, but speech failed her.
>
> (Hirschmuller, 1978, p.278)

This hallucination marked the beginning of her illness. For the next five months Bertha devoted herself to her father's care while her own health disintegrated.

She began to display physical symptoms. She stopped eating, developed a facial neuralgia, a cough, and a variety of visual disorders beginning with double vision and extending to an inability to recognize faces of family members. She experienced paralysis in the right and left sides of her body followed by a loss of feeling in her arms, and finally a paralysis of her neck muscles that prevented her from lifting her head from her chest. Most of her symptoms emerged during her states of *absence* or "clouds," somnambulant trance states occurring in the evening. Bertha called these dissociative periods "time-missing" because she was amnesiac about their contents. At this point, four and a half months after her first hallucination, Breuer was consulted.

The Breuer and Pappenheim families had been closely connected for generations. Breuer was probably the Pappenheim family physician, in which case he would have been involved with Bertha's father's care. Breuer's initial diagnostic impression was hysterical psychosis, though for a time he considered meningitis as a possible organic cause. To confirm his diagnosis, he had Bertha evaluated by psychiatrist Richard von Krafft-Ebing, who'd just proposed hysterical psychosis as a diagnostic category (Libbrecht, 1995).

No longer able to care for her father, Bertha took to bed for three months. Her somatic symptoms were now accompanied by more dramatic changes. She developed two different forms of consciousness: One that was normal but melancholy and a second state, associated with her *absences*, filled with hallucinations and accompanied by destructive behavior. Bertha complained of having two selves, her normal self and an evil twin. She saw her black hair turning into a cluster of snakes, and declared she was going insane. Her speech disintegrated into a word salad drawn from four languages. She became mute for two weeks. Then for several months she spoke only in English while believing she was conversing in German, causing her to feel persistently misunderstood.

It was Breuer's reaction to Bertha's aphasia that set the direction of her treatment. Breuer knew that Bertha had been offended by her father, and in an act of retaliation she'd decided not to talk about him. Breuer guessed this wish for revenge was related to her aphasia. When, in one of her somnambulant states he compelled her to speak of her father, she did so in English. Her aphasia partially subsided and the paralysis in her right arm disappeared. At that moment Breuer concluded many of her symptoms were based on emotionally charged memories and had no organic cause.

Even more significantly, thereafter Breuer decided to work with Bertha each evening in her autohypnotic (what he called "hypnoid") state to help her talk about the origin of each of her symptoms. In this somnambulant state Bertha had access to unconscious traumatic memories that were ordinarily blocked from awareness, and her stories built around these troubling memories became what Bertha called her "talking cure."

Breuer believed Bertha was actually suffering from two illnesses: An initial underlying physical sickness (possibly tubercular and related to her father's lung condition), and a group of psychologically based hysterical symptoms. He saw these illnesses having two different trajectories. He estimated the somatic sickness peaked a month after his initial consultation when Bertha first took to her bed. Symptoms associated with this condition slowly melted away on their own.

Breuer was left to treat the psychological symptoms, and Bertha's talking cure accomplished just that. As she talked about the emotionally troubling memories associated with the origin of each symptom, one by one they disappeared. Significantly, all this occurred in her self-induced trance of which she was amnesiac. As Breuer writes, "She never had any recollection whatsoever of her 'English' evening sessions" (Hirschmuller, 1978, p.283). Breuer believed her improved condition derived from catharsis, the releasing of suppressed emotion through imaginative narratives made while somnambulant.

After three months Bertha was improved and able to get out of bed. She had not seen her father during her confinement, and her family had not informed her of his fragile condition. Four days later he died. Her father's death threw Bertha into a psychotic and suicidal state. She was enraged at her mother for not allowing her to see her beloved father before he died. After two months of increasingly suicidal behavior Bertha was moved against her will to a private villa on the grounds of a sanitarium.

Now she spent most of her time in a hypnoid state in which she recognized only Breuer who alone was able to feed her. When he arrived for a session, Breuer notes, "She never began without first touching my hands to make sure it was really me" (Hirschmuller, 1978, p.287).

Bertha became increasingly dependent on him, and her condition deteriorated in his absence when she wouldn't eat or drink anything until his return. Then angry at him for abandoning her, she'd refuse to participate in her talking cure.

The treatment intensified. Breuer doubled down, coming twice daily, spending hours with her each morning and night. Breuer's devotion to Bertha was truly remarkable, but it came at a price. One researcher (Schweighofer cited in Borch-Jacobsen, 1996) estimates Breuer put one thousand hours into her care over the twenty months of treatment. But Breuer also felt angry and burdened by Bertha's dependency, coerciveness and oppositional behavior. Breuer described Bertha's treatment as an "ordeal," and years later he would write "it is impossible for a general practitioner to treat such a case without having his practice and private life completely ruined by it" (Breger, 2009, p.43). Obviously, Breuer had intense feelings for Bertha. His biographer Albrecht Hirschmuller (1978) writes,

> in taking on the case of [Bertha] Breuer had let himself in for something the consequences of which he could not foresee at the outset. As the treatment progressed it must have become increasingly clear to him how close the attachment of the patient to himself—and of him to her—had become. It seems to me beyond dispute that there was a conflict between his personal and medical interest in the case and a certain fear of the consequences of such a deep relationship.
>
> (p.130)

After a year of treatment, Breuer privately contacted a sanitarium about the possibility of transferring her care, but then abandoned the idea. Instead, he took a different approach.

Under pressure to increase the pace of treatment, he started hypnotizing Bertha in the mornings to augment her evening autohypnotic states. This strategy paid off. Breuer writes,

> Her afternoons continued to be somnolent, at sunset she experienced the "cloud" [in English], and told her stories in the evening. . .we always saw in the daytime what she would have to recount in the evening because she lived through these things and to some extent acted them out. . .The change in her was remarkable when she had

given her account of these matters; she came out of her absence, was at ease, cheerful, set herself to work, spent all night drawing or writing, perfectly rational, went to bed at 4 o'clock. . .The contrast between the irresponsible invalid by day, beset with hallucinations, and the perfectly lucid person at night was most remarkable.

(Hirschmuller, 1978, p.285)

Now her treatment entered an unusual final phase that mentally returned her to periods of intensified physical and psychological symptoms of the preceding year. Christmas was the one-year anniversary of her taking to bed, her last contact with her father, and what Breuer considered to have been the peak of her somatic illness. In December, 1881, during her evening autohypnotic trances, Bertha began to vividly reexperience the traumatic events of the same day from the previous year. During the morning hours she lived in December, 1881, but in the evening when she entered her autohypnotic trance she lived the corresponding December day of 1880. Transported back in time, she lost all awareness of the events of 1881.

These evening sessions were conducted in a state of sustained hallucination: "she was carried back to the previous year with such intensity that in the new house she hallucinated her old room" (Breuer, 1895, p.33). This pattern of "temporal dissociation" continued for the next six months, and her hallucinatory narratives through which she relived her traumatic past brought her considerable relief. Once again, imagination—in this case in the form of sustained hallucination—could be identified as the therapeutic agent.

Importantly, *active reliving* played an important part in the elimination of Bertha's symptoms. For example, when failing to remember a terrifying hallucination experienced in a relative's home during the previous year, Breuer took Bertha to that residence. He (1895) writes, "In order to get over the obstruction to our progress she visited the same place again, and on entering the room, again fell to the ground unconscious. During her subsequent evening hypnosis the obstacle was surmounted" (p.37).

During this period Bertha would sometimes waken in the middle of the night and become frightened because her surroundings differed from those of the previous year. Breuer describes how he protected her from these disorienting experiences by "shutting her eyes in the evening and giving her the suggestion that she would not be able to open them till I did so myself the following morning" (Breuer, 1895, p.38). This phrase gives us a feeling for the intimacy of their relationship. Like the mother of an infant, he put her to bed at night and was the first to welcome her each morning.

Bertha determined her treatment would end on June 7, the anniversary of being forcibly moved to a sanatorium after her successive suicide attempts. Breuer considered this period to have been the most intensely disabling of her psychological illness. He writes,

> On the last day—by the help of re-arranging the room so as to resemble her father's sickroom—she reproduced the terrifying hallucination which I have described above and which constituted the root of her whole illness. During the original scene she had only been able to think and pray in English; but immediately after its reproduction she was able to speak German. She was moreover free from the innumerable disturbances which she had previously exhibited.
>
> (Breuer, 1895, p.40)

Remarkably, Bertha chose to structure the final phase of her treatment as a daily hallucinatory reliving, in Breuer's presence, of her life between the two most traumatic periods of her emotional crisis, the twenty-four weeks between her December convalescence and her June hospitalization. The final phase of her recovery was accomplished through her creative, imaginative and regenerative use of this psychotic dissociative process. On that last day Bertha transported herself even further back in time to her original hallucination during the first days of her father's illness. Creating a perfect symmetry, she ended at the beginning.[2]

From a historical perspective, what's surprising about Breuer's reaction to Bertha's dizzying set of symptoms is that he didn't apply any of the conventional treatments for hysteria which a general practitioner would have naturally considered in 1880: Anti-hysteria drugs, electrotherapy, hydrotherapy, metallotherapy with magnets, exercise/massage, or a diet regime (Hirschmuller, 1978). These were the recommended treatments, and he ignored them all. Instead, capitalizing on her autohypnotic abilities, he chose to work within her trance state, and in the final phase of treatment to employ hypnotherapy.

It's remarkable an esteemed general practitioner like Breuer would have considered using hypnotism to treat hysteria in Vienna in 1880.

Theodor Meynart's view that hypnosis induced psychosis was powerfully influential. And though much of Bertha's therapeutic work would be accomplished through her creative use of psychosis, Breuer couldn't have anticipated that. Hirschmuller (1978) writes, "between 1860 and 1880 there was hardly a physician who could offer a course of hypnotherapy if he did not wish to be regarded as a charlatan" (p.91). In 1880 Danish stage hypnotist Dane Hanson gave several public demonstrations of hypnosis in Vienna (one of which was attended by Freud) only to be banned by the Faculty of Medicine. Charcot's famous paper on hypnosis which would win over the French Academy in the more liberal city of Paris was two years away. So, what caused Breuer to use a hypnotic treatment?

Breuer went to the source of Bertha's symptoms, her *absences*, and looked there for the solution to her illness. Breuer reasoned: If symptoms were created in Bertha's autohypnotic trance, then this was where they could also be eliminated. So, he gave up the security of administering an approved therapy, and uncertainly entered her world of trance "which may well be likened to a dream in view of its wealth of imaginative products and hallucinations" (Breuer, 1895, p.45). This was a courageous step. After all, like Dr. Meynart, few people willingly enter an unconscious world of dreams and madness.

Ellenberger (1970) says Bertha's treatment,

> radically differs from other cases of hysteria at that time, but is analogous to the great exemplary cases of magnetic illness in the first half of the nineteenth century. . .To the older magnetizers, [Bertha's] story would not have seemed as extraordinary as it did to Breuer.
>
> (p.484)

For example, Bertha's treatment followed the typical course of a magnetic cure: It occurred entirely in a hypnotic state in which she recognized only Breuer upon whom she became solely dependent. She created her own therapeutic process (her talking cure), and she predetermined the date of her cure. Breuer's therapeutic technique perfectly paralleled Puysegur. Breuer approached his patient with affection and generosity of spirit. He worked with Bertha in her hypnoid state in which he gently interrogated her about the origin of her symptoms, and when she identified her therapeutic process of "chimney sweeping," he willingly complied. Breuer's indulgent response to Bertha's demands for attention parallels Puysegur's treatment of Alexandre Hebert, a violently psychotic young man whom Puysegur took into his home, maintained in a nearly continuous somnambulant state, and from whom he was nearly inseparable for six months until his cure (Conn, 1982; Crabtree, 1993).

Hirschmuller (1978) observes, "It is in fact remarkable how many similarities we find between the case of [Bertha] and Justinus Kerner's 'Seeress of Prevorst'" (p.129). Both young women were brought up in pious puritanical families. Both women retreated from an external world of stunted opportunity into an inner world of daydream. Both responded to traumatic life events such as the deaths of their fathers with intensified somnambulance and serious psychosomatic illness, beginning with anorexia and double vision. Each spoke in a disorganized and incomprehensible language. Both spent an extended period sequentially reliving days of the previous year. And perhaps, most importantly, both had unusually intimate relationships with their doctors. Hirschmuller (1978) notes, "It is true that the practitioners of mesmerism had formed relationships similar to that between Breuer and Bertha Pappenheim. . .But it was an exceptional relationship for Breuer's time" when physicians adopted an authoritarian and emotionally distant attitude toward patients (p.129).

So, although we think of Bertha's treatment as original, it was nothing new. Breuer and Bertha both behaved in accordance with a typical magnetic case. Breuer's treatment continued a tradition of animal magnetism that had simply been forgotten. Furthermore, Ellenberger (1970, 1993) and Macmillan (1991) point out the notion of catharsis and the therapeutic value of revealing pathogenic secrets were prominently featured in the history of medicine and religion. Nonetheless, Freud described Breuer's treatment of Bertha as the birth of psychoanalysis. In his lecture at Clark University in 1909 he declares, "If it is a merit to have brought psychoanalysis into being, that merit is not mine. . .another Viennese physician, Dr. Josef Breuer, first (in 1880–1882) made use of this procedure on a girl who was suffering from hysteria" (Freud, 1910, p.9). Clearly, what Freud described as the origin of psychoanalysis was actually his "rebranding" of animal magnetism.

In fact, Bertha's case has been consistently misrepresented beginning with Breuer himself (Gilhooley, 2002). Rather than being cured, at the end of her treatment Breuer hospitalized Bertha for addiction to morphine and chloral hydrate he'd been administering at high doses because he couldn't tolerate her emotional outbursts.

More importantly for the future of psychoanalysis, Freud's appropriation of Bertha's case as the beginning of psychoanalysis is misleading. As we've seen, the form of Bertha's treatment was typical of animal magnetism, and Breuer's technique (perhaps unknowingly) was identical to Puysegur's. Furthermore, the case bears little relation to the psychoanalysis Freud would develop. Freud's psychoanalysis would be conducted in a state of wakeful consciousness and emphasize rational reflective thinking. Freud believed cure derived from unconscious thoughts and emotions being brought under conscious control. But Bertha's treatment occurred in a trance of which she had no conscious recollection. There was no conscious memory, no rational reflection, no insight. Most importantly, in the last stage of treatment, Bertha's cure resulted from one hundred-sixty sessions of hallucination. She cured herself through consecutive doses of insanity. This doesn't look like psychoanalysis to me. In the rational world of psychoanalysis, the therapeutic role of psychosis in the case has never been acknowledged or discussed. This omission—the collective negative hallucination of psychoanalysis—is the most significant misrepresentation of Bertha's treatment.

And this is the essential point. If mind transforms physical conditions in the body—and that's what Mesmer, Charcot and Bertha's case demonstrate—then what form of mentation accomplishes this feat? The scientific commissioners investigating Mesmer concluded he cured patients through *imagination*. Father Gassner, the eighteenth-century exorcist who Ellenberger (1970) identifies as "one of the most famous healers of all time," freely admitted imagination was the basis of his cures (p.53). Certainly, Bertha's hallucinations were irrational imaginative actions, not rational reflection. Bertha's imagination took the form of "*emotional embodied action*" not cognition (Asma, 2017, p.4). Her treatment couldn't be further from the passive, conscious, rational, insight-oriented thinking Freud fostered. Using mind as the therapeutic agent, Freud hoped to substitute conscious rational reflection for imaginative embodied action occurring in a trance. He was wrong, and Freud would never achieve a clinical success equal to Breuer's work with Bertha.

Notes

1 Bertha Pappenheim was given the pseudonym "Anna O." in Breuer and Freud's (1895) monograph, *Studies on hysteria*. The sources for my description of Bertha's treatment are Breuer's (1895) published case study and his original case notes prepared in 1882 when Breuer transferred her to Bellevue

Sanatorium; these notes were discovered by Ellenberger (1972) and can be found in Hirschmuller (1978).

2   At the conclusion of his case study Breuer (1895) describes Bertha as fully recovered from her hysterical symptoms, though noting "it was a considerable time before she regained her mental balance entirely" (p.41). Subsequent research by Ellenberger (1970, 1972) and Hirschmuller (1978) reveal that five weeks later Breuer transferred Bertha to a sanatorium in Switzerland where she stayed for four months, primarily to be weaned off the morphine and chloral hydrate he'd been administering. She would be hospitalized three more times between 1883 and 1887, exhibiting some of the same hysterical symptoms, and on each occasion receiving a diagnosis of hysteria. In light of this research, scholars are divided when assessing the success of Breuer's treatment. I believe Bertha's cathartic talking cure was broadly successful and faithfully reported in his case study. However, Breuer exaggerated the permanent elimination of symptoms, concealed the way drugs may have affected her condition, and misrepresented the treatment's conclusion (Gilhooley, 2002).

References

Asma, S. (2017). *The evolution of imagination*. Chicago, IL: University of Chicago Press.

Borch-Jacobsen, M. (1996). *Remembering Anna O.: A century of mystification*. New York, NY: Routledge.

Breger, L. (2009). *A dream of undying fame: How Freud betrayed his mentor and invented psychoanalysis*. New York, NY: Basic Books.

Breuer, J. (1895). Case 1: Fraulein Anna O. In J. Breuer & S. Freud, Studies on hysteria (pp.21–47). *Standard Edition*. London: Hogarth Press, 2, 3–309.

Breuer, J. & Freud, S. (1895). Studies on hysteria. *Standard Edition*. London: Hogarth Press, 2, 3–309.

Conn, J. (1982). Nature of magnetic treatment. *Journal of the American Society of Psychosomatic Dentistry and Medicine*, 29, 44–53.

Crabtree, A. (1993). *From Mesmer to Freud: Magnetic sleep and the roots of psychological healing*. New Haven, CT: Yale University Press.

Ellenberger, H. (1970). *The discovery of the unconscious: The history and evolution of dynamic psychiatry*. New York, NY: Basic Books.

Ellenberger, H. (1972). The story of Anna O.: A critical review with new data. *Journal of the History of the Behavioral Sciences*, 8, 267–279.

Ellenberger, H. (1993). The pathogenic secret and its therapeutics. In M. Micale (Ed.), *Beyond the unconscious: Essays of Henri F. Ellenberger in the history of psychiatry* (pp. 341–359). Princeton, NJ: Princeton University Press. (Original work published 1966)

Freeman, L. (1990). *The Story of Anna O.* New York, NY: Paragon House.

Freud, S. (1910). Five lectures on psychoanalysis. *Standard Edition.* London: Hogarth Press, 11, 9–55.

Freud, S. (1925). An autobiographical study. *Standard Edition.* London: Hogarth Press, 20, 2–74.

Gilhooley, D. (2002). Misrepresentation and misreading in the case of Anna O. *Modern Psychoanalysis*, 27, 75–100.

Guttmann, M. (2001). *The enigma of Anna O.: A biography of Bertha Pappenheim.* Wickford, RI: Moyer Bell.

Hirschmuller, A. (1978). *The life and work of Josef Breuer: physiology and psychoanalysis.* New York, NY: New York University Press.

Libbrecht, K. (1995). *Hysterical psychosis: A historical survey.* New Brunswick, NJ: Transaction Publishers.

Macmillan, M. (1991). Anna O. and the origins of Freud's personality theory. In *Freud evaluated: The completed arc* (pp.3–24). Cambridge, MA: MIT Press.

Skues, R. (2006). *Sigmund Freud and the history of Anna O.* New York, NY: Palgrave Macmillan.

Swales, P. J. (1986). Freud, his teacher, and the birth of psychoanalysis. In P. Stepansky (Ed.), *Freud appraisals and reappraisals: Contributions to Freud studies*, volume 1 (pp.3–82). Hillsdale, NJ: Analytic Press.

Chapter 19

Love

While Freud believed in the fundamental value of Bertha's cathartic talking cure, he privately circulated the view that Breuer had actually ended the treatment abruptly in response to Bertha's emerging erotic transference creating a "cure with a defect" (Forrester & Cameron, 1999, p.930).[1] Freud claimed, if Breuer had had the courage to confront Bertha's erotic transference, her cure might have been complete. Of course, Freud had a vested interest in demonstrating the sexual origin of mental illness. He dismissed Breuer's (1895) insistence that

> the element of sexuality was astonishingly undeveloped in [Bertha]. . . in all the enormous number of hallucinations which occurred during her illness that element of mental life never emerged.
>
> (pp.21–22)

Freud insinuated Breuer was just hiding this dimension of the treatment, which may be true. But it is hard to know why he would.

Sexual feelings emerging in a medical case were commonplace. In fact, seven years before he authored the Anna O. case, Breuer documented these emotions emerging in his treatment of a hysterical female patient when he referred her to a colleague (Hirschmuller, 1978, p.140). Since the time of Mesmer, patients had fallen in love with their hypnotists leading a secret commission to recommend animal magnetism be outlawed simply on moral grounds.[2] Although Mesmer worked in an emotionally intimate way, he was reputed to be highly moral and no charge of sexual impropriety was ever levied against him. Nonetheless, within the Viennese medical community "warnings were continuously being issued which told of the occasional openly sexual relationship, and the possibility of seduction. . .Breuer and Freud must have been singularly familiar with these arguments" (Hirschmuller, 1978, p.182). So, what we call erotic transference wasn't unusual.

The problem for Breuer was bigger than that. He loved Bertha. Indeed, they loved each other, and maybe that was worth hiding. Certainly, Breuer's love for Bertha led to a degree of devotion that created problems for him personally and professionally. But *his* problem of loving Bertha couldn't have been addressed by confronting *her* erotic transference. It's obvious that Bertha's talking cure was accomplished in an emotional context of love. So, an accurate description of her treatment would be: *The cathartic communication of imaginatively re-experienced trauma to a listener with whom there is a mutual feeling of love.*

If Bertha's case was effectively a magnetic treatment, was love an ingredient in animal magnetism? Yes. Whether taking the form of simple affection or intense sexual desire, love was always a part of animal magnetism. For example, Deleuze (1843) writes "to act efficaciously, [the magnetizer] should feel himself drawn towards the person who requires his care, take an interest in him, and have the desire and hope of curing, or at least relieving him" (p.27). Jean-Jacques Virey goes quite a bit further. In an 1818 medical dictionary description of animal magnetism Virey says magnetism takes its power from emotions produced naturally "by the imagination, or by the affection between different individuals, and principally that which arises from sexual relations" (Chertok, 1968, p.561). For magnetizers, and for Bertha and Breuer, love was the basis of cure. But what would be the role of love in the psychoanalysis Freud was developing?

Following the examples of Breuer and Charcot, Freud used hypnotism with modest success over a five-year period from 1887–1892. He began cautiously. Having gotten himself into trouble over his enthusiasm for Charcot, he probably considered hypnotism too risky. After opening his practice in 1886 he employed electrotherapy for the first twenty-one months before trying hypnosis, and then waited another eighteen months before attempting a cathartic treatment like Breuer's (Chertok, 1968, 1984). So, while he was deeply impressed by Breuer's work with Pappenheim, it took him three years before attempting something similar with "Emmy von N." reported in *Studies on hysteria.*[3]

Considering Freud's tentativeness, it may be the trance simply frightened him. Freud was able to hypnotize only a fraction of his hysterical patients and he typically used hypnotism to suggest the posthypnotic elimination of symptoms. He probably never attempted Breuer's cathartic method because this required a deep trance which he was unable to achieve with patients (Aron, 1996). Remember, Bertha's therapeutic sessions were conducted in an autohypnotic trance which Breuer simply witnessed. Frustrated with his inability to emulate Breuer's work, Freud traveled with his patient Anna von Lieben to visit Bernheim in Nancy. Von Lieben's "hypnosis had never reached the stage of somnambulism with amnesia," and Freud hoped Bernheim could show him how to achieve a deeper trance (Freud, 1925, p.18). Instead, Bernheim suggested ways Freud might try to accomplish similar results working with conscious patients (Swales, 1986).

Then, early in the 1890s, Freud (1925) had an experience that must have brought Breuer's case to mind, and which affected Freud's future use of hypnosis and his ideas about transference:

> One day I had an experience which showed me in the crudest light what I had long suspected. It related to one of my most acquiescent patients, with whom hypnotism had enabled me to bring about the most marvelous results. . .As she woke up on one occasion, she threw her arms around my neck. The unexpected entrance of a servant relieved us from a painful discussion, but from that time onwards there was a tacit understanding between us that the hypnotic treatment should be discontinued. I was modest enough not to attribute the event to my irresistible personal attraction, and I felt that I now grasped the nature of the mysterious element that was at work behind hypnotism. In order to exclude it, or in all events isolate it, it was necessary to abandon hypnotism.
>
> (p.27)

Love was the mysterious element at work behind hypnotism, and Freud's reaction was to exclude or isolate it.

Love was the natural product of *rapport. Rapport* was considered the most intimate form of human relatedness. What else could be expected from a therapeutic dyad conceived of as a fetus/mother relationship? Indeed, Freud (1905) notes, "rapport in the case of hypnosis, finds a parallel in. . .a mother who is nursing a baby" (p.295), "or in certain love-relationships where there is extreme devotion" (p.296). Hypnosis was "a state of being in love with the directly sexual trends excluded" (Freud, 1921, p.115). For Freud, love and hypnosis were inextricably entwined. He writes,

> From being in love to hypnosis is evidently only a short step. The respects in which the two agree are obvious. There is the same humble subjection, the same compliance, the same absence of criticism, towards the hypnotist as towards the loved object. . .no one can doubt that the hypnotist has stepped into the place of the ego ideal. It is only that everything is even clearer and more intense in hypnosis so that it would be more to the point to explain *being in love by means of hypnosis* than the other way around.
>
> (1921, p.114, italics added)

For Freud, being in love was being hypnotically entranced.

Freud experienced his patient's love in mature interpersonal terms, expecting these feelings to lead inevitably to sexual contact. So, love frightened him, and he struggled to keep from being swept away by his emotions. But the emergence of love in the treatment could be related to a much earlier period of development, as the patient's creation of a purely narcissistic ego ideal which is inherently nurturing (Benjamin, 1994). This is how a fetus or infant conceives of its mother's love, and it's in this sense that being in love reflects a mutually dependent symbiosis (Hedges, 2011) or a state of narcissistic transference (Spotnitz, 1985). When one combines the mental merger of *rapport* with the narcissistic nature of being in love, and the qualities of lucid sleep where the subject is solely aware of the hypnotist, it's easy to equate "being in love" with the mental state of a fetus in a mother's womb, just as Hufeland had proposed in 1811. Had Freud conceived of love in these narcissistic, intrauterine and preoedipal terms he may have felt more secure.

Instead, to control his emotions Freud believed he had to fend off *rapport* and the psychic infection of love. Freud's fearful reaction to love, and his development of clinical techniques to manage his fears, was uniquely his own. Pierre Janet had more experience with hypnosis than Freud, and never stopped using it. Janet considered "somnambulistic passion" to be a natural expression of attachment like that of a child for its mother, rooted in the need for guidance (Ellenberger, 1970). These emotions develop naturally in treatment and may need to be moderated, but they didn't frighten Janet and he didn't regard them as dangerous (Chertok & Stengers, 1992). On the contrary, Janet believed a "perfect *rapport*" rooted in these loving feelings were the basis of cure (Haule, 1986, 1996).

Love emerged in telepathic *rapport*, and in this sense, love is a dimension of the occult or, vice versa. As Adam Phillips (1997) notes, "in psychoanalysis the supernatural returns as the erotic" (p.19). Early psychical researcher, Frederic Myers (1903), found telepathy to be inextricably linked with love. He writes, "Love is a kind of exalted, but unspecialized telepathy" (p.282). Perhaps it was this telepathic aspect of love that frightened Freud. Maybe he sensed his entranced patients were able to read his thoughts. Mesmerist Alphonse Teste observed in 1840 that the somnambulist "penetrates your most secret desires, associates her soul with all the emotions of your soul, and without perceiving that she only obeys your will, anticipates even your most secret intentions" (Crabtree, 1993, p.103). Freud may have realized his hypnotized female patients had access to his unconscious wishes, even before he did.

By abandoning hypnotism Freud believed he'd be insulating himself from the dangers of *rapport*. But Freud took a second step to further protect himself from loving feelings emerging in treatment. He discovered transference, and within it found "a means of defense against the potential erotic demands of his female patients, and perhaps against his own temptations" (Chertok, 1968, p.568). As Guy Thompson (1998) writes, "Freud's views about transference were rooted almost entirely in his observations about the nature of love" (p.544).

When Freud introduces the idea of transference at the end of *Studies on hysteria* he notes the patient may be frightened to find herself

> transferring on to the figure of the physician the distressing ideas which arise from the content of the analysis. This is a frequent, and indeed in some analyses a regular, occurrence. Transference on to the physician takes place through a *false connection*. I must give an example of this. In one of my patients the origin of a particular hysterical symptom lay in a wish she had had many years earlier and had at once relegated to the unconscious, that the man she was talking to at the time might boldly take the initiative and give her a kiss. On one occasion, at the end of a session, a similar wish came up in her about me.
>
> (Breuer and Freud, 1895, pp.302–303)

For Freud, the idea of a *false connection* was a second insulating barrier allowing him to experience the patient's feelings as "impersonal." Freud explained to his patient: You don't really want to kiss me. You wanted to kiss this earlier gentleman and felt ashamed of that emotion, so you repressed it thereby creating a neurotic symptom. This feeling is now reemerging in relation to me as your neurosis entering treatment.

By abandoning hypnotism and defining transference as a "false connection" Freud believed he was securely protected from the possibility of *rapport* and sexual seduction. As George Makari (1992) writes, transference

> served to free Freud from swirling accusations of *psychic infection* or *sexual seduction.* Freud's innocence from such nefarious manipulations was guaranteed, for any embarrassing statements or acts by patients could be conceptualized as strictly intrapsychic.
>
> (p.429, italics added)

Focusing on his patient's transference, Freud transferred both his and his patient's loving feelings onto the *false connection*, imaginatively transporting the feelings out of the consultation room and into the past. By relocating the emotion in space and time one could say Freud "transfers the transference." He metaphorically moved a troubling feeling from his mind onto a remote object.

In Freud's view, the appearance of his patient's sexuality was an expression of pathology. Freud (1914) saw "the emergence of the transference in its crudely sexual form. . .in every treatment of neurosis. . .to be the most irrefragable proof that the source of the driving forces of neurosis lies in sexual life" (p.12). But what Freud defined as the sexual source of mental illness was actually an expression of the narcissistic transference the patient had unconsciously achieved in her natural attempt at cure. After all, erotic transference is based on an implicit belief that *"we're in love,"* reflecting unconscious recognition of the mental merger associated with *rapport*. Mikkel Borch-Jacobsen (1992) writes,

> the phenomenon of transference is, as Freud himself admitted, nothing other than the reemergence, within analysis, of the characteristic relationship ("rapport") of hypnosis.
>
> (p.53)

By construing the emergence of sexual feelings as evidence of the patient's illness, Freud pathologized *rapport*. By explaining to the patient her feelings weren't real but rather a remnant of her past, Freud injured the patient and damaged the *rapport* emerging between them. By construing sexuality as the source of illness, Freud misunderstood that sexuality was a natural expression of the narcissistic merger that was itself the source of cure. This was a profound misunderstanding.

Seen from this perspective, Freud's discovery of transference was really a renaming and derealization of *rapport*, and Freud's transference interpretations represent his defense against the experience of *rapport*, the merger of narcissistic transference. Psychoanalyst Glen Gabbard (1994), an authority on erotic transference/countertransference, describes the hostility analysts feel in response to the threatened merger with their patients. He writes,

> The anxiety thus generated by concerns about the loss of one's identity as a separate person may cause analysts to regard their patients with contempt as a way of exaggerating the differences between themselves and their patients, to preserve their separateness.
>
> (p.1089)

This hostility may be the basis of Freud's interpretations of erotic transference.

The true irony is that Freud developed a theory of therapeutic action based on transference interpretation, which may have been nothing more than his persistent defense against the experience of *rapport*, the actual basis of cure. Freud *completely misunderstood love in treatment.* That's a powerful claim. I'm proposing Freud's misunderstanding of love in the therapeutic setting blinded him to the role of *rapport* in cure. Let's think about that.

Erotic transference is a subset of a broader category of transference interpretation. If transference interpretation is the heart of therapeutic action as Freud proposed, is there scientific research supporting its use? Not much. In the realm of psychotherapy research five studies (Piper et al., 1991; Hoglend, 1993; Connolly et al., 1999; Hoglend et al., 2006, 2007) find increases in the frequency of transference interpretations to be associated with poor treatment outcomes. The leading transference interpretation researcher, psychoanalyst Per Hoglend (2004), reports that of eight naturalistic empirical studies of transference interpretation, five found an increase of interpretation to be related with poor outcome, and only one associated interpretation with improvement. In other words, in these studies the more transference interpretations were given, the worse patients got. Some studies show self-critical, depressed patients (Blatt, 1992), and borderline patients with a history of poor relationships (Kernberg et al., 2008) benefiting from transference interpretations. Nonetheless, the majority of research links transference interpretation with bad treatment. This is consistent with my suggestion that transference interpretations are counter-therapeutic. In the case of erotic transference, they are implicitly hostile, defending analysts from experiences of symbiotic merger. If transference interpretation was the basis of cure, one would expect to see opposite research results.

So, where does this leave psychoanalysis? The love Freud needed to eliminate from treatment was the natural expression of *rapport*, the mental and physical merger that was the source of cure in animal magnetism. Love is the basis of telepathic *rapport*. Indeed, in the view of Frederic Myers, the telepathic love is the primary passion binding life-to-life and is the foundation of spirituality itself. Myers (1903) writes,

> That primary passion, I repeat, which binds life-to-life. . .is no mere organic, no mere planetary impulse, but the inward aspect of the telepathic law. Love and religion are thus continuous. . .At one end of its scale love is based upon an instinct as primitive as the need for nutrition; even at the other end it becomes, as Plato has it, "the Interpreter and Mediator between God and Man."
>
> (p.112)

Clinically, love is the source of therapeutic change (Baur, 1997; Mann, 1997). Psychiatrist Ethel Person (2006) calls love the fundamental "agent of change." She writes, love is "the primary vehicle for self-realization, transformation, and transcendence" (p.330).

But the power of love was simply too frightening for Freud. By eliminating *rapport* Freud was behaving like James Braid the Scottish surgeon who coined the term hypnosis. Braid was able to strip Puysegur's artificial somnambulance of its occult characteristics by inducing a trance while remaining subjectively disengaged. Freud did exactly the same thing. By adopting a posture of emotional coldness, by eliminating the trance, by pathologizing sexuality, and by employing transference interpretation to distance himself from his patient's emotional attachment, Freud protected himself from the telepathic nature of *rapport*.

Nineteenth century theorist Thomson Jay Hudson's (1893) criticism of Braid applies equally well to Freud. By eliminating the intersubjective quality of mutual entrancement, Hudson claimed Braid retarded the development of hypnotic science. Similarly, by the elimination of the intersubjective nature of *rapport*, that is, *by eliminating love*, Freud retarded the development of psychological treatments begun by Mesmer and Puysegur. As a result, while psychoanalysis has a dedicated following (including me), it never displayed the pattern of therapeutic success enjoyed by animal magnetism.

Notes

1 Fifty years after the conclusion of the case of Anna O, Freud privately offered his personal reconstruction proposing the treatment ended abruptly with Bertha in the throes of a hysterical childbirth prompting a horrified Breuer to abandon his patient. This reconstruction was embellished by Jones in his 1953 biography of Freud and resulted in the story becoming accepted as the secret true account of the treatment's end. There is, however, no evidence to support Freud's conception, and a considerable amount of evidence suggests that it never occurred. Today, prominent scholars (Ellenberger, 1970, 1972; Hirschmuller, 1978; Borch-Jacobsen, 1996; Skues, 2006) reject Freud's reconstructed ending.

2 In 1784 J. S. Bailly authored a secret report for King Louis XVI describing orgasmic female patients in a state of rapport who are experiencing a crisis: "The continence becomes gradually inflamed, the eye brightens, and this is the sign of natural desire. . .the eyelids become moist, the respiration is short and interrupted, the chest heaves rapidly, convulsions set in, and either the limbs or the whole body is agitated by sudden movements. In lively and sensitive women this last stage, which terminates the sweetest emotion, is often a convulsion; to this condition there succeed languor, prostration, and a slumber of the senses" (Bailly, 2002, p.365). The political split between Puysegur and Mesmer was based, in part, on Puysegur's creation of the somnambulant "perfect crisis" that distanced his practice from these overtly sexual convulsions.

3 While Freud employed hypnotism in his treatment of Frau Emmy von N., his clinical technique bears little resemblance to Breuer's treatment of Anna O., and appears to have been inspired primarily by the work of Bernheim, and possibly by Janet or Delboeuf (Macmillan, 1979).

References

Aron, L. (1996). From hypnotic suggestion to free association: Freud as a psycho-therapist, circa 1892–93. *Contemporary Psychoanalysis*, 32, 99–114.

Bailly, J.-S. (2002). Secret report on mesmerism, or animal magnetism. *International Journal of Clinical and Experimental Hypnosis*, 50, 364–368. (Original work published 1784)

Baur, S. (1997). The active ingredients of the intimate hour. *The intimate hour: Love and sex in psychotherapy* (pp.245–275). Boston, MA: Houghton Mifflin Company.

Benjamin, J. (1994). What angel would hear me?: The erotics of transference. *Psychoanalytic Inquiry*, 14, 535–557.

Blatt, S. (1992). The differential effect of psychotherapy and psychoanalysis with anaclitic and introjective patients: The Menninger Psychotherapy Research Project revisited. *Journal of the American Psychoanalytic Association*, 40, 691–724.

Borch-Jacobsen, M. (1992). *The emotional tie: Psychoanalysis, mimesis, and affect*. Stanford, CA: Stanford University Press.

Borch-Jacobsen, M. (1996). *Remembering Anna O.: A century of mystification*. New York, NY: Routledge.

Breuer, J. (1895). Case 1: Fraulein Anna O. J. Breuer & S. Freud, Studies on hysteria (pp.21–47). *Standard Edition*. London: Hogarth Press, 2, 3–309.

Breuer, J. & Freud, S. (1895). Studies on hysteria. *Standard Edition*. London: Hogarth Press, 2, 3–309.

Chertok, L. (1968). The discovery of transference—towards an epistemological interpretation. *International Journal of Psychoanalysis*, 49, 560–576.

Chertok, L. (1984). Hypnosis and suggestion in a century of psychotherapy: An epistemological assessment. *Journal of American Academy of Psychoanalysis*, 12, 211–232.

Chertok, L. & Stengers, I. (1992). *A critique of psychoanalytic reason: Hypnosis as a scientific problem from Lavoisier to Lacan*. Stanford, CA: Stanford University Press.

Connolly, M., Crits-Christoph, P., Shappell, S., Barber, J., Luborsky, L. & Shaffer, C. (1999). Relation of transference interpretations to outcome in the early sessions of brief supportive-expressive therapy. *Psychotherapy Research*, 9, 485–495.

Crabtree, A. (1993). *From Mesmer to Freud: Magnetic sleep and the roots of psychological healing*. New Haven, CT: Yale University Press.

Deleuze, J. P. (1843). *Practical instruction in animal magnetism*. New York, NY: D. Appleton & Company. (Original work published 1825)

Ellenberger, H. (1970). *The discovery of the unconscious: The history and evolution of dynamic psychiatry.* New York, NY: Basic Books.

Ellenberger, H. (1972). The story of Anna O.: A critical review with new data. *Journal of the History of the Behavioral Sciences*, 8, 267–279.

Forrester, J. & Cameron, L. (1999). "A cure with a defect": A previously unpublished letter by Freud concerning "Anna O." *International Journal of Psychoanalysis*, 80, 929–942.

Freud, S. (1905). Psychical (or mental) treatment. *Standard Edition*. London: Hogarth Press, 7, 283–302.

Freud, S. (1914). Observations on transference-love. *Standard Edition*. London: Hogarth Press, 12, 159–171.

Freud, S. (1921). Psychoanalysis and telepathy. *Standard Edition*. London: Hogarth Press, 18, 175–193.

Freud, S. (1925). An autobiographical study. *Standard Edition*. London: Hogarth Press, 20, 2–74.

Gabbard, G. (1994). Sexual excitement and countertransference love in the analyst. *Journal of the American Psychoanalytic Association*, 42, 1083–1106.

Haule, J. (1986). Pierre Janet and dissociation: The first transference theory and its origins in hypnosis. *American Journal of Clinical Hypnosis*, 29, 86–94.

Haule, J. (1996). *The love cure: Therapy erotic and sexual.* Woodstock, CT: Spring Publications.

Hedges, L. (2011). Symbiosis and separation: Mutually dependent relatedness. In *Sex and psychotherapy: Sexuality, passion, love, and desire in the therapeutic encounter* (pp.81–96). New York, NY: Routledge.

Hirschmuller, A. (1978). *The life and work of Josef Breuer: Physiology and psychoanalysis.* New York, NY: New York University Press.

Hoglend, P. (1993). Transference interpretations and long-term change after dynamic psychotherapy of brief to moderate length. *American Journal of Psychotherapy*, 47, 494–507.

Hoglend, P. (2004). Analysis of transference in psychodynamic psychotherapy: a review of empirical research. *Canadian Journal of Psychoanalysis*, 12, 279–300.

Hoglend, P., Amio, S., Marble, A., Bogwald, K., Sorbye, O., Sjaastad, M. & Heyerdahl, O. (2006). Analysis of patient-therapist relationship in dynamic psychotherapy: An experimental study of transference interpretations. *American Journal of Psychiatry*, 163, 1739–1746.

Hoglend, P., Johansson, P., Marble, A., Bogwald, K., & Amio, S. (2007). Moderators of the effects of transference interpretations in brief dynamic psychotherapy. *Psychotherapy Research*, 17, 160–171.

Hudson, T. (1893). *The law of psychic phenomena: A working hypothesis for the systematic study of hypnotism, spiritism, mental therapeutics, etc.* Chicago, IL: A.C. McClurg.

Jones, E. (1953). *The life and work of Sigmund Freud*, volume 1. New York, NY: Basic Books.

Kernberg, O., Yeomans, F., Clarkin, J. & Levy, K. (2008). Transference focused psychotherapy: Overview and update. *International Journal of Psychoanalysis*, 89(3), 601–620.

Macmillan, M. (1979). Delboeuf and Janet as influences in Freud's treatment of Emmy von N. *Journal of the History of the Behavioral Sciences*, 15, 299–309.

Mann, D. (1997). *Psychotherapy: An erotic relationship: Transference and countertransference passions*. London: Routledge.

Makari, G. (1992). A history of Freud's first concept of transference. *International Review of Psychoanalysis*, 19, 415–432.

Myers, F. (1903). *Human personality and its survival of bodily death*, volumes 1–2. London: Longmans, Green, and Company.

Person, E. (2006). *Dreams of love and fateful encounters: The power of romantic passion*. Arlington, VA: American Psychiatric Publishing.

Phillips, A. (1997). *Terrors and experts*. Cambridge, MA: Harvard University Press.

Piper, W., Azim, H., Joyce, A. & McCallum, M. (1991). Transference interpretations, therapeutic alliance, and outcome in short-term individual psychotherapy. *Archives of General Psychiatry*, 48, 946–953.

Skues, R. (2006). *Sigmund Freud and the history of Anna O.: Reopening a closed case*. London: Palgrave Macmillan.

Spotnitz, H. (1985). Narcissistic transference. In *Modern psychoanalysis of the schizophrenic patient: Theory of the technique*, second edition (pp.186–217). New York, NY: Human Sciences Press. (Original work published 1969)

Swales, P. J. (1986). Freud, his teacher, and the birth of psychoanalysis. In P. Stepansky, (Ed.) *Freud appraisals and reappraisals: Contributions to Freud studies*, volume 1 (pp.3–82). Hillsdale, NJ: Analytic Press.

Thompson, M. (1998). Manifestations of transference: Love, friendship, rapport. *Contemporary Psychoanalysis*, 34, 543–561.

Chapter 20

Telepathy and Freud

Where mesmerism was always a marginalized medical phenomenon, hypnotism fueled by Charcot's research briefly emerged as a respectable branch of medical science during the last two decades of the nineteenth century in France. Then, after this brief ascendance, it swiftly returned to the margins (Ellenberger, 1970; Gauld, 1992). Following in the footsteps of Mesmer, by the turn of the century Charcot's reputation had been tarnished by his sensational hypnotic demonstrations. At a centennial celebration of his birth his contributions to the study of hysteria, which Freud believed to have been profound, were described as "a slight lapse" in an otherwise brilliant career (Micale, 1995, p.102). Hysteria had blossomed in France and Germany during Charcot's prominence, and then vanished ten years after his death (Shorter, 1992; Micale, 1993). Neurology at the Salpetriere returned to the organic focus of Charcot's early years, and the study of hypnotism was abandoned. As Ellenberger (1970) notes, "the reaction against Charcot went so far as to promote a rigidly organicist, antipsychological spirit among French neurologists" (p.408).

The world once again turned its back on somnambulance, and Freud's rejection of hypnotism was consistent with this trend. In fact, this is typical of trance throughout its two-hundred-year history, where its prominence in therapy repetitively reappears only to be dismissed and forgotten. Why? Altered states of consciousness are frighteningly inexplicable. They produce experiences such as telepathy and premonition which are difficult to integrate into our understanding of the world. These experiences appear to defy rational explanation so, like the commissioners investigating Mesmer, we invalidate, disparage and pathologize them. Then, we forget about them.

A classic case of selective forgetting is *sommeil a distance* or "telepathic hypnotism"; a trance induced at a distance. Obviously, an effect occurring at a distance lies at the heart of telepathy, and my two telepathic dreams appeared to connect my mind with patients sixty miles away. Telepathy is the mental version of spooky action at a distance. The model of quantum entanglement is, metaphorically, a good way to think about telepathy (Radin, 2006). Telepathy is as upsetting as entanglement was to the physicists who first studied it. Like entanglement, telepathic hypnotism is nonlocal. It suggests an immaterial force alters the mental and physical state of person in a remote location.

Mesmer began the practice of hypnotic induction at a distance in 1775 by magnetizing a patient from an adjacent room without her knowledge (Gauld, 1992). Several of Puysegur's colleagues reported inducing trances in patients from a distance, a practice Puysegur reported as common but one he disapproved of as irresponsible. For example, Barberin and his followers in Lyons claimed to have induced trances in patients in distant villages, some as far away as ten miles (Crabtree, 1993). In 1820 physicians witnessed the Baron Jules du Potet repeatedly induce a state of magnetic sleep in his patient from a concealed closet or from an adjacent hospital room (Dingwall, 1967).

The first detailed description of experiments with *sommeil a distance* is reported in 1885 by the twenty-two-year old Pierre Janet (1968a, 1968b; Kopell, 1968), who figures prominently in the history of hysteria and the origins of psychoanalysis (Ellenberger, 1970). Janet had an academic orientation. He earned two doctoral degrees, first in philosophy and then in medicine, and he taught philosophy in schools for twelve years early in his career (Ellenberger, 1993a). Janet's experiments with *sommeil a distance* were conducted for his doctoral dissertation in philosophy.

The results of Janet's first group of experiments were presented at a meeting of the Society of Physiological Psychology in Paris on November 30, 1885. The meeting was chaired by Charcot, and it's likely Freud attended (Eisenbud, 1953). Janet's two published papers describing these experiments created a sensation and were highly regarded in scientific circles. Based on these papers, Janet went on to become a student of Charcot at the Salpetriere. Charcot supervised his medical dissertation and in 1890 appointed him director of the new psychology lab at the hospital.

In 1885 and 1886 Janet conducted a series of experiments over several days with Mrs. Leonie Boulanger. Boulanger was an uneducated fifty-year old peasant described as honest, timid, and intelligent (Dingwall, 1967; Ochorowicz, 1891; Owen, 1971). She was married and the mother of several children. From childhood, she'd been subject to natural somnambulism, and as a young woman she'd been hypnotized by du Potet and one of his disciples.

In this series of experiments Mrs. Boulanger was repeatedly hypnotized by Janet or her regular physician while they were separated from her by more than a half mile. Janet (1968b) describes one experimental result:

> On the 25th of February, without telling anyone, I again started my experiment. Under the same condition, at about five o'clock in the evening, I *thought* of putting her to sleep. I *thought* about it as strongly as I could for about eight minutes. Then I immediately went to her place [about a half mile away]. She was stretched out on a sofa in a very deep sleep. Shaking could not awaken her, but if I squeezed her fingers or if I lightly touched the skin of her arm, the adjacent muscles would strongly contract. . .She was truly in a state of hypnotic sleep which began by the strangest of coincidence just before my arrival. She quickly became agitated and began to speak in a state of somnambulistic lucidity. She showed a great amount of joy in sensing me near her and knew very well that it was I who had put her to sleep at five o'clock.
>
> (p.260, italics added)

In the first experimental cycle, in which Janet or her physician *willed her* into a hypnotic trance from a distance, Boulanger fell into a trance during eighteen of the twenty-five experimental trials, without a false positive result. Several months later, during their second set of experiments, Janet and his colleague successfully willed her into a trance from a distance on sixteen of twenty-two attempts. During these experiments she spontaneously entered a trance independent of the experimenter on two occasions.

Janet conducted experiments at random times (times were selected by a third party, or by lot) and he tried to prevent forms of suggestion from affecting the results. The frequent coincidence of the experimenter willing

Leonie into somnambulance and her falling into a trance, coupled with the fact that she rarely entered a trance independently, makes it improbable the results were due to chance.

Here's the most remarkable part of the experiments. On two occasions Leonie was willed by her hypnotist to walk over a half mile from her residence to the physician's office. She was observed making these trips in a somnambulant trance walking hesitantly with her eyes closed appearing to other pedestrians to be blind (Janet, 1968b). Two of Janet's colleagues who witnessed these events, Julian Ochorowicz (1891) and Frederic Myers (Gurney, Myers & Podmore, 1886), published their own accounts.

Janet (1968a) describes Leonie's telepathic abilities when in a somnambulant trance:

> These facts show that in the case of Mrs. B. there is a sort of faculty, I don't know what sort, by which she is able to perceive the thoughts of others, and it seems that this is truly one of the principal characteristics that one observes during her somnambulistic state. Mrs. B. seems to be able to experience most of the sensations that are felt by the person who is putting her to sleep. She believes that she is drinking and one sees the motions of the deglutations in her throat when this person drinks. She is always exactly aware of the substance that I put in my mouth and can perfectly distinguish if I am tasting salt, pepper, or sugar.
>
> (pp.130–131)

Janet depicts Leonie in her somnambulant state just as Puysegur described Victor Race, and as Justinus Kerner had described Friedericke Hauffe. Puysegur would think a melody and Victor would sing it aloud. Hauffe instantly experienced the symptoms of sick people she encountered. What quality of mind facilitates such a duplication of experience? We're reminded of quantum physicist Nicholas Gisin (2014) who writes, "If we prod one of the two parts, both will quiver" (p.43). The entranced mind appears to function like a transpersonal network of entangled photons.

Two years later, Charles Richet tried to replicate Janet's experiments with Boulanger. Richet was a free-thinking professor of physiology in the Paris Faculty of Medicine. He was a prolific researcher with an avocational interest in somnambulism. Recipient of the Prix de Moscow, in

1913 he would win a Nobel Prize in Medicine for his discoveries related to anaphylactic shock and the human immune system. He'd end his career as President of the French Academy of Science (Wolf, 1993).

In Richet's experiments the date and time of each trial was selected at random. He reported nine attempts to will Leonie into a hypnotic trance from a distance of fifteen-hundred meters. He recorded a successful attempt if she fell into a trance within twenty-one minutes of his effort. Richet claimed to have been successful in six of the nine attempts and calculated the probability of this occurring by chance to be one in two million (Kopell, 1968).

While these experiments with Leonie Boulanger were remarkable, it's even more extraordinary that Janet never followed up on them. At the very beginning of his career "he hit the jackpot but walked away without picking up his winnings" (Eisenbud, 1953, p.5). It appears his discoveries with Leonie were too frightening to continue. Rather than conducting further experiments, while working at the Salpetriere Janet began to research animal magnetism. To his surprise he discovered that *sommeil a distance* had an extensive history among animal magnetizers of previous generations. Ellenberger (1970) writes,

> Everything taught by Charcot and Bernheim as amazing novelties had already been known to these obscure men. It was a world of forgotten knowledge that Janet rediscovered and, going back into the past from generation to generation, he found that even the earliest magnetizers, Puysegur and Bertrand, had already known most of what the moderns believed they discovered.
>
> (p.339)

Uncomfortable with the notoriety associated with his experiments with Boulanger, and concerned with their effect on his emerging career, Janet directed his attention elsewhere. Later, working in the antipsychological culture of post Charcot neurology, Janet expressed reservations about this early research. Like the work of Puysegur, Janet's experiments in telepathic hypnotism, which had created a sensation, were forgotten.

In 1882 Puysegur's "thought transference" was renamed "telepathy" by British psychical researcher Frederic Myers to describe the experience of feeling another's emotional state (*pathos*) from a distance (*tele*) (Luckhurst, 2002). Along with Richet in France, Myers was one of the first to study telepathy scientifically. Myers emphasized *feeling* at a distance. Religious historian Jeffrey Kripal (2010) writes, "telepathic communications often emerge from highly charged events involving people who care about one another deeply, that is, they often involve the two greatest themes in human emotional experience: love and death" (p.81).

In 1882 Myers and his colleagues created the British Society for Psychical Research, and between 1883 and 1900 membership grew from one hundred and fifty to nine hundred and forty-six including such eminent figures as scientists Alfred Russell Wallace and Pierre Curie, philosopher Henri Bergson, authors Alfred Lord Tennyson and Henry James, psychologist William James, and future prime minister Arthur Balfour (Luckhurst, 2002). In 1886 Edmund Gurney, Frederic Myers and Frank Podmore published an epic thirteen-hundred-page compendium of research entitled *Phantasms of the living* containing over seven hundred case studies of telepathy and related phenomena. All cases were first person accounts with participants and witnesses interrogated by one of the three authors. Publication of this research presented a strong public case that the human mind is nonlocal, transcending the limits of space and time.

By the end of the Victorian era, telepathy captured the professional interest of Sigmund Freud. In 1911 Freud became a corresponding member of the Society for Psychical Research.[1] With his associates Carl Jung and Sandor Ferenczi, Freud explored telepathy, conducted casual experiments, and visited psychics. Telepathy intrigued Freud because it provided evidence the unconscious of one human being could invisibly influence the unconscious of another, without passing through either consciousness or traditional communication channels.

Ferenczi, who was intuitively gifted, called himself a "great soothsayer. . . a reader of thoughts" (Brabant, Falzeder & Giampieri-Deutsch, 1993, p.235). In 1915 Ferenczi (1950) conceived of psychoanalytic treatment as "dialogues of the unconscious" mind of the patient and the analyst (p.109). Beginning his career as an ardent hypnotist, his first publication in 1899 was "Spiritismus" which examined trance states in mediums, identified spiritualism's roots in the unconscious, and recommended further scientific investigation of somnambulism (Casonato, 1993; Meszaros, 1993).

Jung's interest in the occult was inherited from his mother and other relatives who reported visions (Bair, 2003; Gyimesi, 2010). His medical dissertation, "On the psychology and pathology of occult phenomena," examined a young medium, Helene Preiswerk, who was his cousin (Ellenberger, 1993b). During Jung's experiments, her visions, altered speech and clairvoyant predictions of a birth and two deaths resembled Friedericke Hauffe. In 1911 Freud wrote to Jung, "I am aware that you are driven by innermost inclination to the study of the occult and I am sure that you will return home richly laden" (McGuire, 1974, p.422).

While Ferenczi and Jung both began their professional careers studying mediums, and often reported clairvoyant or telepathic intuitions, Freud wasn't as sensitive. Freud (1921) writes, "My own life. . .has been particularly poor in the occult sense" (p.193). Freud claimed to never experience a telepathic dream nor hear one from a patient. Freud responded to Jung and Ferenczi's enthusiastic research in thought transference with a mixture of excited interest and anxious caution. He wrote that Ferenczi's observations shattered any "doubts about the existence of thought transference" and he believed Ferenczi was onto something really big (Brabant, Falzeder & Giampieri-Deutsch, 1993, p.211). But a year later he called Ferenczi and Jung's experiments "dangerous expeditions," adding "I can't go along there" (Brabant, Falzeder & Giampieri-Deutsch, 1993, p.274). Freud's expressions of excited interest in telepathy were always followed by nervous denial. Indeed, an historian studying telepathy during the Victorian era calls Freud's behavior "a perfect instance of disavowal," noting that "Freud knows not to know" (Luckhurst, 2002, p.270). For Freud, it seemed too dangerous to accept the reality of telepathy.

Although Freud claimed to live a life "particularly poor in the occult sense," that may not be true. Luckily, Frank's novel contains a character who was part of Freud's inner circle who can provide a first-hand account. The reader may recall Frank's chapter about parallel universes. There a young mathematician named Watson Page meets his double from another universe named Graf.

Graf lives several parallel existences simultaneously, and in one of these he is Max Graf, a musicologist and associate of Freud. Graf was the father of a four-year old called "Little Hans," the subject in one of Freud's case studies. In 1908 Freud supervised Graf's interactions with his son. Graf was a devoted disciple of Freud. He participated in the Wednesday evening meetings of the Vienna Psychoanalytic Society, sometimes serving as recording secretary. Graf has a story to tell us about Freud and telepathy.

While he was helping Graf with his son, Freud was also discussing his most successful case, Rat Man, in the Wednesday evening group. Rat Man is the name given to Freud's twenty-nine-year old obsessional patient, Ernst Lanzer. A young attorney, Lanzer believed others could read his mind. He possessed a gift for prophetic dreams, and he worried about the power of his thoughts. For example, in his third session Lanzer told Freud he wished a rival would drop dead. Then he dreamt of a corpse and awoke to discover the man had had a stroke. Many would consider Lanzer's dream telepathic or precognitive. Apparently, Freud didn't hear it that way.

Freud discussed Lanzer on four occasions with the Wednesday evening group. The last time was April 8, 1908. Here's Graf's account of that meeting (Nunberg & Federn, 1962). After perfunctory reports by members, Graf described two telepathic experiences, one which is salient: A day after his marriage he thought with great intensity about his former sweetheart living in Trieste, believing he'd seen her several times on the streets of Vienna. Later that day his mother mentioned his first love was actually in town visiting. Then Freud addressed the group describing details of his treatment of Lanzer.

Lanzer is dubbed Rat Man because he had an obsessional fantasy about a rat torture. The torture was described to Lanzer by a military officer, Captain Novick. In this Chinese form of torture, a ravenous rat in a jar is affixed to the buttock of the victim. The rat burrows up the victim's anus.

While Captain Novick is describing this, Lanzer finds himself fantasizing about the rat torture being applied to his girlfriend, Gisela Adler. Suddenly Lanzer is struck with terror, fearing the Captain will be able to read his thoughts. Indeed, Novick next says he'd like the torture performed on "Gisela Fluss." Hearing the name "Gisela," Lanzer gasps. This confirms Lanzer's fear the Captain is reading his mind! As Lanzer tells this story to Freud, upon hearing the name "Gisela Fluss," Freud gasps. Gisela Fluss was Freud's childhood sweetheart! At that moment, both Lanzer and Freud are imagining the rat torture being applied to their first loves. Graf, meanwhile, is considering the coincidence of having just given a report of his telepathic experience with his first love.

Captain Novick continued, declaring the rectal punishment should be applied to a member of Parliament, "Gerald Adler." Hearing Gisela's surname, "Adler," Lanzer is doubly certain the Captain has read his mind. Now he feels the walls are closing in on him. Coincidentally, Gerald Adler was Freud's friend and the former occupant of Freud's apartment at Berggasse nineteen. So, the walls surrounding Lanzer at that very moment had previously belonged to Adler.

Graf considered this extraordinary confluence of events. How could life unfold in such a remarkable way? Could this be a life "particularly poor in the occult sense?" Hardly! Fifty years later Carl Jung (1960) and Wolfgang Pauli will call this symphony of meaningful coincidences "synchronicity," better explained by the occult than by reason or chance. It's reasonable to question the veracity of a fictional source, but Graf's account is consistent with the *Minutes of the Vienna psychoanalytic society* (Nunberg & Federn, 1962) and Patrick Mahony's (1986) authoritative *Freud and the rat man*. So, what does this tell us about Freud? Graf claims, "Freud isn't telling you the whole truth when it comes to telepathy."

Freud's (1921, 1922, 1925a, 1933) professional writing on the subject of telepathy disguises his enthusiasm and stresses his ambivalence to insulate himself and psychoanalysis from ridicule (Jones, 1957b). As we've seen, hypnotism and telepathy were certain to be met with derision by the scientific community, and when Freud broke off relations with Jung and Ferenczi he'd use their interest in the occult as a way of discrediting them. Freud's papers on telepathy are more studies in tortured resistance than thoughtful treatments of the topic. As he acknowledges, "I discuss the subject of occultism under the pressure of the greatest resistance" (Freud, 1921, p.190). His 1922 paper "Dreams and telepathy" ends with Freud saying he hopes the reader hasn't gotten the impression he supports the existence of telepathy, "since I have no opinion on the matter and know nothing about it" (p.220); causing his biographer Peter Gay (1988) to quip, "One wonders why Freud published the paper at all" (p.444). Freud's evasive behavior is consistent with Graf's assessment.

In 1925, fearful of arousing public criticism that would endanger psychoanalysis, Freud cautioned Ferenczi not to present a paper on thought transference: "Don't do it. . .With it you are throwing a bomb into the psychoanalytic edifice, which will certainly not fail to explode" (Falzeder & Brabant, 2000, p.209). Beyond simply discrediting psychoanalysis through its association with the occult, Freud believed the real problem with telepathy was that it was true.

In his paper, "Psychoanalysis and telepathy," Freud (1921) writes, "There is little doubt that if attention is directed to occult phenomena the outcome will very soon be that the occurrence of a number of them will be confirmed" (p.179). In the absence of any scientific theory to explain these phenomena, "there may follow a fearful collapse of critical thought, of deterministic standards and of mechanistic science. Will it be possible for scientific method. . .to prevent this collapse?" (p.180). The eighteenth-century model of mechanistic materialism which Freud subscribed to didn't allow for immaterial causes like imagination, let alone telepathy. For Freud, the validity of scientific determinism hung in the balance.

Max, Frank's crazy architect, passionately interrupts this historical discussion with the following clarification:

> Mechanistic materialism is associated with Newton's descriptions of gravity, but Newton *refused* to declare a material origin for gravity! What Newton *actually* said was, "Gravity must be caused by an agent acting constantly according to certain laws; but whether this agent be *material or immaterial*, I have left to the consideration of my readers."

Max is irrepressible. He urgently continues,

> Scientists studying gravity knew it was nonlocal and there was no physical explanation for it. Three hundred years later, there's still no physical explanation for gravity. So, the dogmatic belief in a clockwork universe was *always an illusion* based on the omission of this *scientific fact*! Besides, Newton makes his personal opinion clear: God is the origin of gravity. He says the universe "could only proceed by the counsel and domination of an intelligent and powerful Being." Gravity was the result of God's "continuing intervention." He says God "endures forever, and is everywhere, he *constitutes duration and space*" for Christ's sake! Read his *Principia*. Newton was a Puritan, a radical Protestant, a true believer! He never believed in a material explanation for gravity. And he considered mechanistic materialism to be the false god of Leibnitz and his Cartesian buddies.

This is a sore subject for Max. It's bad enough to falsely connect mechanistic materialism with Newton's genius. But dogmatic illusions based on the elimination of empirical evidence has literally driven Max nuts. In his opinion, scientists paper over troubling aspects of reality creating theories based on what they find acceptable. Case in point, the elimination of mind as a subject in physical science. Wolfgang Pauli called this the biggest blunder made in physics in the last three hundred years! Then, these "mindless" distortions become the definition of reality imposed on everyone and enforced by medical science.

It was Freud's combined relationship to science and medicine that upset Max. In Max's opinion, Freud endorsed what he knew to be a false conception of reality, then exploited his scientific position to amplify the mystifying power of the physician, giving himself quasi-divine status. (By now, Max was deep into Frank's reading of Foucault.) "Freud was gutless and corrupt!" A ruthless assessment. For Max, feeling ostracized is deeply threatening. Then his paranoia gets the best of him, and he goes over the top.

"Oh Max, that's *much too* harsh!" I respond trying to recover my narrative voice.

Max, Freud was ostracized for his exploration of the unconscious, and he was publicly humiliated for his ideas about sexuality, particularly infantile sexuality. Freud earned his own scars developing psychoanalysis. And mechanistic materialism was the dominant intellectual paradigm of his time. You expect him to buck that? Come on. He would have gotten nowhere! That would have destroyed his whole project. Besides, Freud was bewildered. He was boxed-in by materialism. He didn't know what to do. Freud was a courageous investigator. Developing psychoanalysis cost him a lot, personally and professionally. Come on. Cut him some slack.

"Bullshit!" Max responds. I'm not sure if this phrase is meant for Freud, positivist science, or me—maybe all three! But I have a sense of what Max means. In a previous conversation, Max referenced moral philosopher Harry Frankfurt's (2005) essay, *On bullshit*. Frankfurt contends the bullshitter misrepresents his intentions and beliefs. He's "bluffing," pretending to be what he's not. On that basis, Max regarded Freud's four papers on telepathy to be bullshit. More insidious, Frankfurt writes, "Bullshit is disconnected from a concern with truth" (p.40). Through its indifference to truth, "bullshit is a greater enemy of the truth than lies are" (p.61). This was Max's moral complaint with materialist dogma, its disregard for truth.

Max's startling interjections are difficult to recover from. Regaining control of my narrative, I continue.

Freud's fears about telepathy were personal as well as professional (Massicotte, 2014). In a letter to Jones, Freud confesses his true feelings, finally revealing both his acceptance of, and his anxiety about, telepathy.

> When anyone adduces my fall into sin, just answer him calmly that conversion to telepathy is my private affair like my Jewishness, my passion for smoking and many other things, and that the theme of telepathy is in essence *alien* to psychoanalysis.
> (Jones, 1957a, pp.395–396; italics added)

At last, Freud professes his belief in telepathy. But what does Freud mean, "telepathy is in essence *alien* to psychoanalysis?" Is he again sheltering psychoanalysis from his sinful interest in telepathy?

Anyway, how could Freud think communication from one unconscious mind to another is unrelated to psychoanalysis? After all, Ferenczi believed this was the basis of psychoanalytic treatment, and Freud himself had recommended the analyst "turn his own unconscious like a receptive organ towards the transmitting unconscious of the patient" (Freud, 1912, p.115). Ferenczi (1988) noted "the remarkable frequency with which so-called thought-transference (telepathic) phenomena occur between physician and patient" (p.85). But telepathy wouldn't play a part in Freud's idea of therapeutic action. Freud's therapy centered on consciousness. He believed psychological benefit derived from *consciously* motivated use of *conscious* knowledge of unconscious conflict. In Freud's model, unconscious communication bypassing consciousness, though interesting, had no therapeutic value.

But "alien in its essence" is different. "Alien" sounds dangerous. Throughout the *Standard Edition* Freud uses the word alien sixty-one times, usually to describe the shock experienced by the conscious ego when encountering evidence of the unconscious. For example, Freud (1915) writes the unconscious possesses "characteristics and peculiarities which seem *alien*. . .to the attributes of consciousness" (p.170). Dreams are commonly seen as "something *alien*, arising from another world and contrasting with the remaining contents of the mind" (1900, p.4). Or, in his paper on "Negation" Freud declares, "What is bad, what is *alien*, and what is external are in the beginning identical" (1925b, p.237). For Freud, instances of telepathy are proof *the unconscious is alien*, "external," and therefore dangerous. By using the word "alien" Freud appears to respond in a paranoid way to the idea of a telepathic intrusion of a "foreign body" into his mind. Like my reaction to the telepathic dream I shared with Lily, Freud found the idea of such invasions threatening to his sense of personal integrity.

But it's worse than that. In an ironic twist, Jacques Derrida (2007) writes if one accepts the reality of telepathy then, "The truth, what I always have difficulty getting used to: [is] that non-telepathy is possible" (pp.236–237). If telepathy is real, is it possible to think of something as an isolated mind? Can there be such a thing as a thought that is uniquely one's own (Forrester, 1990)? No. This is the ultimate affront to consciousness, revealing the simplistic conception of a "unique identity" as nothing more than a tenaciously maintained illusion. If telepathy is real, a self could be, at most, a unique amalgam of associated selves populating the unconscious. Derrida (2007) continues: it's "difficult to imagine a theory of what they still call the unconscious without a theory of telepathy" (p.237). If telepathy is real, then the unconscious must inevitably involve "others," and can never be simply "me."

In 1932 Freud writes to his colleague Eduardo Weiss, "I am, it is true, prepared to believe that behind all so-called occult phenomena lies something new and very important: the fact of thought-transference, i.e., the transferring of psychical processes through space to other people" (Jones, 1957a, pp.453–454). But was Freud prepared to believe the consequences of thought transference? Because telepathy changes everything. Freud conceived of thoughts and feelings as intrapsychic, occurring in a hermetically sealed mind. Telepathy proves such a conception is false, and that mind is both transpersonal and nonlocal.

Consider my telepathic dream in which I appear to be dreaming Lily's anxious thoughts about her sister's medical condition. We both seem to have responded to the news of our sister's prognosis with the phrase, "You need to let her die." In my dream, as I hear about my sister's condition, I recall a close friend's comment in a similar situation. His comment was literally, "you need to let her die" and I *import* his thought into my dream. In fact, I'm aware of the appropriation of his phrase as it occurs to me in my dream. Lily, having her own history of living with her sister's medical condition, forms the identical phrase in her mind. So, whose thought was it? Was it my thought transferred to Lily? Was it Lily's thought transferred to me? Was it my friend's thought transferred *through me* to Lily? Or, was it *our* thought formed in a shared unconscious mind? Ultimately, if one accepts the reality of telepathy, there is only one answer to that question: It's *our* thought, the product of *our* unconscious. Once you admit the possibility of telepathy the boundary separating our unconscious minds disappears. We relinquish ownership of "our" unconscious mind. As Mikita Brottman (2011) writes, "then we are not—as we have always assumed ourselves to be—the masters of our own homes" (p.43).

Note

1 Richet, Janet, Freud, Jung and Ferenczi were members of the British Society for Psychical Research (Gyimesi, 2010). Richet would become president of the organization in 1905 (Wolf, 1993). In 1912 Freud published a paper "Note on the Unconscious in Psychoanalysis" in the SPR's *Proceedings*. Myers introduced and promoted Freud's theories in England where Freud's conception of the unconscious was often considered derivative of his rival, Janet (Keeley, 2001). Janet's second series of experiments with Leonie Boulanger were overseen by Myers and three other representatives from the SPR.

References

Bair, D. (2003). *Jung: A biography*. Boston, MA: Little, Brown and Company.

Brabant, E., Falzeder, E. & Giampieri-Deutsch, P. (1993). *The correspondence of Sigmund Freud and Sandor Ferenczi, volume 1, 1908–1914*. Cambridge, MA: Harvard University Press.

Brottman, M. (2011). *Phantoms of the clinic: From thought-transference to projective identification*. London: Karnac.

Casonato, M. (1993). Ferenczi's preanalytic writings (1899–1908). *Contemporary Psychoanalysis*, 29, 736–745.

Crabtree, A. (1993). *From Mesmer to Freud: Magnetic sleep and the roots of psychological healing*. New Haven, CT: Yale University Press.

Derrida, J. (2007). Telepathy. In *Psyche: Inventions of the other*, volume 1 (pp.226–261). Stanford, CA: Stanford University Press. (Original work published 1981)

Dingwall, E. (1967). *Abnormal hypnotic phenomena: A survey of nineteenth-century cases, volume 1, France*. London: J. & A. Churchill.

Eisenbud, J. (1953). Psychiatric contributions to parapsychology: A review. In G. Devereux (Ed.), *Psychoanalysis and the occult* (pp.3–15). New York, NY: International Universities Press.

Ellenberger, H. (1970). *The discovery of the unconscious: The history and evolution of dynamic psychiatry*. New York, NY: Basic Books.

Ellenberger, H. (1993a). Pierre Janet, philosopher. In M. Micale (Ed.), *Beyond the unconscious: Essays of Henri F. Ellenberger in the history of psychiatry* (pp.155–175). Princeton, NJ: Princeton University Press. (Original work published 1973)

Ellenberger, H. (1993b). C.G. Jung and the story of Helene Preiswerk: a critical study with new documents. In M. Micale (Ed.), *Beyond the unconscious: Essays of Henri F. Ellenberger in the history of psychiatry* (pp.291–305). Princeton, NJ: Princeton University Press. (Original work published 1991)

Falzeder, E. & Brabant, E. (2000). *The correspondence of Sigmund Freud and Sandor Ferenczi, volume 3, 1920–1933*. Cambridge, MA: Harvard University Press.

Ferenczi, S. (1950). Psychogenic anomalies of voice production. In *Further contributions to the theory and technique of psycho-analysis* (pp.105–109). London: Hogarth Press. (Original work published 1915)

Ferenczi, S. (1988). *The clinical diary of Sandor Ferenczi*. J. Dupont (Ed.). Cambridge, MA: Harvard University Press. (Original work 1933)

Forrester, J. (1990). Psychoanalysis: gossip, telepathy and/or science. In *The seductions of psychoanalysis: Freud, Lacan and Derrida* (pp. 243–259). Cambridge: Cambridge University Press.

Frankfurt, H. (2005). *On bullshit*. Princeton, NJ: Princeton University Press.

Freud, S. (1900). The interpretation of dreams. *Standard Edition*. London: Hogarth Press, 4, ix–627.

Freud, S. (1912). Recommendations to physicians practicing psychoanalysis. *Standard Edition*. London: Hogarth Press, 12, 109–120.

Freud, S. (1915). The unconscious. *Standard Edition*. London: Hogarth Press, 14, 159–215.

Freud, S. (1921). Psychoanalysis and telepathy. *Standard Edition*. London: Hogarth Press, 18, 175–193.

Freud, S. (1922). Dreams and telepathy. *Standard Edition*. London: Hogarth Press, 18, 195–220.

Freud, S. (1925a). The occult significance of dreams. *Standard Edition*. London: Hogarth Press, 19, 135–138.

Freud, S. (1925b). Negation. *Standard Edition*. London: Hogarth Press, 19, 233–240.

Freud, S. (1933). Dreams and occultism. *Standard Edition*. London: Hogarth Press, 22, 31–56.

Gauld, A. (1992). *A history of hypnotism*. Cambridge: Cambridge University Press.

Gay, P. (1988). *Freud: A life for our time*. New York, NY: W.W. Norton.

Gisin, N. (2014). *Quantum chance: Nonlocality, teleportation, and other quantum marvels*. Heidelberg: Springer.

Gurney, E., Myers, F. & Podmore, F. (1886). *Phantasms of the living*, volumes 1–2. London: Rooms of the Society for Psychical Research, Trubner and Company.

Gyimesi, J. (2010). The problem of demarcation: Psychoanalysis and the occult. *American Imago*, 66, 457–470.

Janet, M. P. (1968a). Report on some phenomena of somnambulism. (B. Kopell, Trans.) *Journal of the History of the Behavioral Sciences*, 4, 124–131. (Original work published 1885)

Janet, M. P. (1968b). Second observation of sleep provoked from a distance and the mental suggestion during the somnambulistic state. (B. Kopell, Trans.) *Journal of the History of the Behavioral Sciences*, 4, 258–267. (Original work published 1886)

Jones, E. (1957a). *The life and work of Sigmund Freud*, volume 3. New York, NY: Basic Books.

Jones, E. (1957b). Occultism. In *The life and work of Sigmund Freud*, volume 3 (pp.375–407). New York, NY: Basic Books.

Jung, C. (1960). Synchronicity: An acausal connecting principle. *Collected Works of C.G. Jung*, volume 8. Princeton, NJ: Princeton University Press.

Keeley, J. (2001). Subliminal promptings: Psychoanalytic theory and the Society for Psychical Research. *American Imago*, 58(4), 767–791.

Kopell, B. (1968). Pierre Janet's description of hypnotic sleep provoked from a distance. *Journal of the History of the Behavioral Sciences*, 4, 119–123.

Kripal, J. (2010). The book as seance: Frederic Myers and the London Society for Psychical Research. In *Authors of the impossible: The paranormal and the sacred* (pp.36–91). Chicago, IL: University of Chicago Press.

Luckhurst, R. (2002). *The invention of telepathy: 1870–1901*. Oxford: Oxford University Press.

Mahony, P. (1986). *Freud and the Rat Man*. New Haven, CT: Yale University Press.

Massicotte, C. (2014). Psychical transmissions: Freud, spiritualism, and the occult. *Psychoanalytic Dialogues*, 24(1), 88–102.

McGuire, W. (Ed.) (1974), *The Freud/Jung Letters: The correspondence between Sigmund Freud and C. C. Jung*. Princeton, NJ: Princeton University Press.

Meszaros, J. (1993). Ferenczi's pre-analytic period embedded in the cultural streams of the fin-de-siecle. In L. Aron & A. Harris (Eds.), *The legacy of Sandor Ferenczi* (pp.41–51). Hillsdale, NJ: Analytic Press.

Micale, M. (1993). On the "disappearance" of hysteria: A study of the clinical deconstruction of a diagnosis. *Isis*, 84, 496–526.

Micale, M. (1995). Charcot and *les nervroses traumatiques*: Scientific and historical reflections. *Journal of the History of Neuroscience*, 4, 101–119.

Nunberg, H. & Federn, E. (Eds.) (1962). *Minutes of the Vienna psychoanalytic society, volume 1: 1906–1908*. New York, NY: International Universities Press.

Ochorowicz, J. (1891). *Mental suggestion.* New York, NY: Humboldt Publishing.

Owen, A. R. (1971). *Hysteria, hypnosis and healing: The work of J.-M. Charcot.* New York, NY: Garrett Publications.

Radin, D. (2006). *Entangled minds: Extrasensory experiences in quantum reality.* New York, NY: Paraview Pocket Books.

Shorter, E. (1992). *From paralysis to fatigue: A history of psychosomatic illness in the modern era.* New York, NY: Free Press.

Wolf, S. (1993). *Brain, mind, and medicine: Charles Richet and the origins of physiological psychology.* New Brunswick, NJ: Transaction Publishers.

Chapter 21

Telepathy

Coda

It started with a dream of waking up dead in which I hovered over my body disbelieving my death. Frank, my patient in mourning, told me he too dreamt of waking up dead. Then I had a second dream in which I was driving to see my sister when I got a call saying that she'd fallen, and was stricken with brain cancer. That same evening my patient Lily received a call about her sister's deadly brain cancer. Again, someone was at the edge between life and death.

Both dreams demonstrate telepathic *rapport*. Arriving unbidden, telepathic experiences reveal an unconscious mind whose capacities exceed our conscious ability to understand or control it. Telepathic experiences are often frightening. When telepathic moments occur, they're usually pathologized, suppressed and forgotten. Until they happen again, and the process is repeated.

Derrida (2007) tells us the consequences of telepathy are profound. Telepathy reveals dimensions of unconscious awareness that transcend space and time. Telepathy destroys beliefs about boundaries between self and other. Therefore, each time telepathy emerges it must be invalidated. Derrida says, "Everything, in our concept of knowledge, is constructed so that telepathy be impossible, unthinkable, unknown" (p.244). Our conscious minds can't tolerate the unconscious, particularly if our unconscious contains the minds of others. This unconscious is literally "alien," to use Freud's expression. Our awareness of it needs to be extinguished and forgotten. Knowledge of trance and telepathic *rapport* can be temporarily suppressed but these phenomena continuously reoccur.

In the middle of the nineteenth century James Braid converted Puysegur's artificial somnambulance into hypnotism. Braid was a physician concerned with cerebral processes, and he successfully created a hypnotism free of *rapport* and thought transference. Forty years later the hypnosis employed by Charcot and Breuer side-stepped Braid's sanitized version of somnambulance. In fact, their work was a continuation of the outlawed treatment of animal magnetism. Hypnotism in the hands of Charcot was nothing less than miraculous: Charcot demonstrated *ideas produce paralysis*. In Bertha Pappenheim's talking cure, words spoken during an autohypnotic trance caused such paralyzes to disappear. Bertha proved ordinary *words could work magic*. Even more important in Bertha's case, successive doses of embodied hallucination—or *unreason*—cured her. It was the power of mind to alter physical conditions in the body that caused animal magnetism to be banished. The power of the mind exceeded reason. It was too frightening to behold.

By abandoning trance and attempting to recreate Bertha's talking cure in a conscious state, Freud followed the same path as Braid. Freud fought off the psychic infection of *rapport*, while hoping to retain the magical effect of ideas and words altering physical states. In his therapeutic equation Freud substituted rationalism for somnambulism. He developed a clinical technique in which imagination and *rapport* were suppressed in favor of thoughtful reflection. Everything in Freud's construction of psychoanalysis—his emotionally cold, nonrelational, neutral, interpretive, one-person intrapsychic model—was meant to defend against telepathic *rapport*. As Derrida (2007) would say, Freud created a theory which makes telepathy impossible.

In addition to quieting his personal fears, Freud was professionally compelled to create a theory which alleviated the fears of the scientific community. For example, empiricist Charles Bernard writes in his influential 1865 *Introduction to the study of experimental medicine,*

> Our reason scientifically includes the determinate and the indeterminate but it cannot admit the indeterminable, because that would be nothing but accepting the marvelous, occult or supernatural which should be absolutely banished from all experimental science.
>
> (Bernard, 1927, p.178)

Science *required* Freud to exclude the possibility of telepathy. This is where Max is wrong: To be taken seriously, Freud had no choice but to adopt a positivist perspective and deny telepathy.

In his memoir, *Memories, dreams, reflections*, Jung (1961) describes a conversation he had with Freud in 1910.

> I can still recall vividly how Freud said to me, "My dear Jung, promise me never to abandon the sexual theory. That is the most essential thing of all. You see, we must make a dogma of it, an unshakable bulwark." . . . In some astonishment I asked him, "A bulwark—against what?" To which he replied, "Against the black tide of mud"—and here he hesitated for a moment, then added—"of occultism."
>
> (p.150)

For Freud, a conception of mental illness based on a sexual instinct rooted in the physical body stood as a defense against a theory like Puysegur's based on immaterial thoughts and feelings, on thought transference and *rapport*.

Materialism demanded a physical explanation of every event (Stoljar, 2017). Mind didn't exist in the world of science, so it couldn't be used scientifically to explain anything. Look what happened to Mesmer. Science concluded his patients were cured by the mental act of imagination. Therefore, his cures—though real—were declared invalid, his medical practice was outlawed, and he was professionally disgraced. Materialism places mind *off-limits*. Mind is dangerous. Imagination is one step from madness. And telepathy is the essence of the uncanny which Freud (1919) says, "arouses dread and horror" leading us back to our most ancient and "long familiar" fears (p.219).

Did the existence of telepathy mean mental illness could derive from what Puyseger called "troubled *rapport*?" Similar to Freud's concept of transference, Puysegur proposed individuals lived in states of troubled *rapport* with caregivers long gone, even deceased. If telepathy is nonlocal, representing a mind outside of space and time, then it's possible the dead are still alive within us. That's a frightening idea. Describing the dangers telepathy posed for Ferenczi and Freud, Pamela Thurschwell (1999) writes, "What if [the dead] invade our very selves? What if they speak through us? What if other living minds are closer to us than we like to think, what if they too invade us?" (p.153). Anxiety stimulated by such possibilities were alleviated by a materialistic and intrapsychic conception of mental life.

But Freud couldn't escape the natural process of altered consciousness. Trance and transference are inescapably entwined. Freud's transference was a renaming of *rapport*. His erotic transference reflected a psychic merger facilitated by a mild autohypnotic trance occurring naturally in the treatment. Though suppressed and a shadow of its former self, a silent somnambulance of mutual entrancement emerges through the patient's free association and the analyst's evenly hovering attention.

Throughout the last century psychoanalysts have consistently moved to return *rapport* and psychic infection to the center of our work. Growing awareness of countertransference, emotional induction, narcissistic transference, projective identification, and intersubjectivity has fostered a psychoanalytic theory of "symbiotic relatedness" (Blass & Blatt, 1996), "therapeutic symbiosis" (Searles, 1979) and "corrective symbiotic experience" (Mahler, 1967; Mahler & Furer, 1960) moving it ever closer to Hufeland's 1811 conception of an intrauterine treatment based on the mother/fetus dyad. For the past two hundred years, whether as the origin of hysteria or as the source of therapeutic regeneration, the womb has served as a central motif in our conception of illness and cure. By 1932 the mutual entrancement Hudson claimed to be the basis of magnetic cures evolved into Ferenczi's (1988) mutual analysis where he declares, "two halves. . .combined to form a whole soul" (p.14).

While Freud constructed his one-person psychoanalytic theory as a defense against the experience of telepathic *rapport*, Spotnitz's (1985, 1987; Spotnitz & Meadow, 1995) therapeutic model relying on emotional induction, narcissistic transference and objective countertransference made the psychic infection of *rapport* the foundation of his work. In this sense, Spotnitz bears greater resemblance to Puysegur than Freud. Spotnitz's use of psychic infection is likely the reason his work has been so widely ignored by Freudians. Larry Epstein (2008) suggests Spotnitz's commitment to the talking cure is pre-Freudian. By utilizing the model of Bertha's talking cure and emphasizing ego supportive techniques, narcissistic merger and emotional communication over interpretation—that is by emphasizing *rapport* over rationality—Spotnitz offers an alternative path from Puysegur and to the present.

In telling this story I've focused on four important clinical cases, the first three of which contain occult phenomena: Puysegur/Race, Kerner/Hauffe, Janet/Boulanger, and Breuer/Pappenheim. In the past century, there has been a slowly emerging acceptance of the occult in psychoanalysis, though nothing approaching the fearless curiosity of psychologists and philosophers, scientists and writers in the second half of the nineteenth century when the seeds of psychoanalysis were being sown.[1]

Grappling with epistemological questions associated with telepathy and clairvoyance, in 1851 Arthur Schopenhauer writes, "Whoever at the present time doubts the facts of animal magnetism and its clairvoyance should not be called a skeptic but an ignoramus" (1974, p.229). Forty years later the popularity of *fin de siècle* occultism was part of a broader critique of positivist rationality that many believed failed to provide a meaningful account of reality (Owen, 2004). In France in 1895 there was a dynamic debate about the moral "bankruptcy of science" which was believed to be incapable of legitimately addressing the transcendental dimensions of life (Paul, 1968). Occultism attacked these epistemological shortcomings of positivism while championing the importance of unconscious mental processes. Occultism asserted knowledge derived naturally from intuition and imagination as well as from critical reflection (Monroe, 2008). This criticism of positivism—which throughout the Enlightenment had gained political leverage by fostering a vision of technological progress—is truer today than it was in 1895.

In several of the clinical cases I've presented, psychosis has played a prominent therapeutic role. A classic example for psychoanalysts is the one hundred-sixty consecutive sessions of hallucinatory temporal dissociation used by Bertha Pappenheim to eliminate her hysterical symptoms. Bertha's highly structured hallucinations were embodied emotional acts of creative imagination therapeutically expressed. Simply put, her insanity cured her. What would Mesmer's scientific commissioners, or Freud's followers, say about that? *Nothing at all.*

The irony of the phrase, "her insanity cured her," captures the limitations of rationalism that so frustrated psychical researchers at the end of the nineteenth century. If insanity is conceived of as an unfortunate byproduct of illness, how can it be understood as an imaginative, creative, and curative agent? This is a good example of "an instrumental reason that can only disavow that which does not accord with its own conceptual dictates" (Owen, 2004, p.242). At these moments, rationalism becomes "just a way of disqualifying a phenomenon rather than understanding it" (Stengers, 2003, p.22). The scientific commissioners investigating animal magnetism correctly identified the patient's and therapist's imagination as the foundation of curative action, but on that very basis dismissed these cures as invalid. They concluded imagination was the enemy of rationalism. In parallel fashion, in his embrace of Enlightenment science, Freud made reason his basis for cure. Therefore, psychosis or "anti-reason" couldn't possibly be curative. Yet, for Bertha Pappenheim, the constraints of rationalism appear to have been the source of her illness, while imaginative insanity restored her health.

After appropriating Bertha Pappenheim's successful treatment and calling it the "origin of psychoanalysis," Freud created a model of therapy that eclipsed Bertha's embodied imaginative hallucinations, replacing them with conscious rational reflection. What a reversal!

For Freud, like Mesmer's commissioners, imagination was akin to madness. But looking back at our conceptions of illness and cure, it's clear that creative imagination, with its origins in the unconscious, has always been at the center of physical and mental health. Indeed, mind's most generative force is imagination.

Note

1 Jung (1960) studied paranormal phenomena and, with Wolfgang Pauli, developed the concept of synchronicity. Devereux's (1953) edited volume *Psychoanalysis and the occult* includes contributions during the first half of the century. The principal American psychoanalysts interested in paranormal phenomena since mid-century are Ehrenwald (1948), Eisenbud (1970, 1982, 1983), and Meerloo (1964). Lazar (2001), Mayer (2007), Rosenbaum (2011), Massicotte (2014), de Peyer (2016) and Farber (2017) have discussed the integration of psychoanalysis with the scientific study of telepathy and precognition. Totton (2003) provides a contemporary edited collection. Ullman, Krippner and Vaughan (1973) conducted extensive laboratory research on dream telepathy. Eshel (2001) and Stoller (Mayer, 2001) are two psychoanalysts who report telepathic dreams in their clinical practice. Nelson (1965), Silverman (1988), Bass (2001) and Tennes (2007) are analysts who write about everyday telepathic experiences in their practices. Brottman (2011) claims projective identification is a disguise for processes analysts are too frightened to acknowledge as telepathic. Strean and Nelson (1962) describe thought transference in psychoanalytic supervision.

References

Bass, A. (2001). It takes one to know one; or, whose unconscious is it anyway? *Psychoanalytic Dialogues*, 11, 683–702.

Bernard, C. (1927). *Introduction to the study of experimental medicine.* New York, NY: Macmillan and Company. (Original work published 1865)

Blass, R. & Blatt, S. (1996). Attachment and separateness in the experience of symbiotic relatedness. *Psychoanalytic Quarterly*, 65, 711–746.

Brottman, M. (2011). *Phantoms of the clinic: From thought-transference to projective identification*. London: Karnac.

de Peyer, J. (2016). Uncanny communication and the porous mind. *Psychoanalytic Dialogues*, 26(2), 156–174.

Derrida, J. (2007). Telepathy. In *Psyche: Inventions of the other*, volume 1 (pp. 226–261). Stanford, CA: Stanford University Press. (Original work published 1981)

Devereux, G. (Ed.) (1953). *Psychoanalysis and the occult*. New York, NY: International Universities Press.

Ehrenwald, J. (1948). *Telepathy and medical psychology*. New York, NY: W.W. Norton.

Eisenbud, J. (1970). *Psi and psychoanalysis*. New York, NY: Grune and Stratton.

Eisenbud, J. (1982). *Paranormal foreknowledge: Problems and perplexities*. New York, NY: Human Sciences Press.

Eisenbud, J. (1983). *Parapsychology and the unconscious*. Berkeley, CA: North Atlantic Books.

Epstein, L. (2008). Some implications of conducting psychoanalysis as a talking cure. *Contemporary Psychoanalysis*, 44, 377–399.

Eshel, O. (2001). Where are you, my beloved?: On absence, loss, and the enigma of telepathic dreams. *International Journal of Psychoanalysis*, 87, 1603–1627.

Farber, S. (2017). Becoming a telepathic tuning fork: Anomalous experience and the relational mind. *Psychoanalytic Dialogues*, 27, 6, 719–734.

Ferenczi, S. (1988). *The clinical diary of Sandor Ferenczi*. J. Dupont (Ed.). Cambridge, MA: Harvard University Press.

Freud, S. (1919). The uncanny. *Standard Edition*. London: Hogarth Press, 18, 218–252.

Jung, C. (1960). Synchronicity: An acausal connecting principle. *Collected Works of C.G. Jung*, volume 8. Princeton, NJ: Princeton University Press.

Jung, C. (1961). *Memories, dreams, reflections*. New York, NY: Vintage Books.

Lazar, S. (2001). Knowing, influencing, and healing: paranormal phenomena and implications for psychoanalysis and psychotherapy. *Psychoanalytic Inquiry*, 21, 113–131.

Mahler, M. (1967). On human symbiosis and the vicissitudes of individuation. *Journal of the American Psychoanalytic Association*, 15, 740–763.

Mahler, M. & Furer, M. (1960). Observations on research regarding the "symbiotic syndrome" in infantile psychosis. *Psychoanalytic Quarterly*, 29, 317–327.

Massicotte, C. (2014). Psychical transmissions: Freud, spiritualism, and the occult. *Psychoanalytic Dialogues*, 24(1), 88–102.

Mayer, E. (2001). On "telepathic dreams?": an unpublished paper by Robert Stoller. *Journal of the American Psychoanalytic Association*, 49, 629–657.

Mayer, E. (2007). *Extraordinary knowing: Science, skepticism, and the inexplicable powers of the human mind.* New York, NY: Bantam Books.

Meerloo, J. (1964). *Hidden communication: Communication theory of telepathy.* New York, NY: Helix Press.

Monroe, J. (2008). *Laboratories of faith: Mesmerism, spiritism, and occultism in modern France.* Ithaca, NY: Cornell University Press.

Nelson, M.C. (1965). Birds of a feather. . .psychoanalytic observations on parapsychological phenomena. *Israel Annals of Psychiatry and Related Disciplines,* 3, 73–88.

Owen, A. (2004). *The place of enchantment: British occultism and the culture of the modern.* Chicago, IL: University of Chicago Press.

Paul, H. (1968). The debate over the bankruptcy of science in 1895. *French Historical Studies,* 5, 299–327.

Rosenbaum, R. (2011). Exploring the *other* dark continent: Parallels between psi phenomena and the psychotherapeutic process. *Psychoanalytic Review,* 98, 57–90.

Schopenhauer, A. (1974). Essay on spirit-seeing. E. Payne (Trans.), *Parerga and paralipomena,* volume 1 (pp.225–309). Oxford: Clarendon Press. (Original work published 1851)

Searles, H. (1979). Concerning therapeutic symbiosis: The patient as symbiotic therapist, the phase of ambivalent symbiosis, and the role of jealousy in the fragmented ego. *Countertransference and related subjects: Selected papers* (pp.172–191). New York, NY: International Universities Press.

Silverman, S. (1988). Correspondences and thought-transference during psychoanalysis. *Journal of American Academy of Psychoanalysis and Dynamic Psychiatry,* 16, 269–294.

Spotnitz, H. (1985). *Modern psychoanalysis of the schizophrenic patient: Theory of the technique,* second edition. New York, NY: Human Sciences Press. (Original work published 1969)

Spotnitz, H. (1987). Emotional induction. *Psychotherapy of preoedipal conditions* (pp.25–30). Northvale, NJ: Jason Aronson. (Original work published1976)

Spotnitz, H. & Meadow, P. (1995). Toward an understanding of emotional contagion. *Treatment of the narcissistic neuroses,* revised edition (pp.69–90). Northvale, NJ: Jason Aronson. (Original work published 1976)

Stengers, I. (2003). The doctor and the charlatan. *Cultural Studies Review,* 9, 11–36.

Stoljar, D. (2017). Physicalism. *Stanford Encyclopedia of Philosophy* (Winter 2017 Edition). https://plato.stanford.edu/archives/win2017/entries/physicalism/ (Accessed December 31, 2018)

Strean, H. & Nelson, M.C. (1962). A further clinical illustration of the paranormal triangle hypothesis. *Psychoanalytic Review,* 49, 61–73.

Tennes, M. (2007). Beyond intersubjectivity: The transpersonal dimension of the psychoanalytic encounter. *Contemporary Psychoanalysis*, 43, 505–525.

Thurschwell, P. (1999). Ferenczi's dangerous proximities: telepathy, psychosis, and the real event. *Differences: A Journal of Feminist Cultural Studies*, 11, 150–178.

Totton, N. (Ed.) (2003). *Psychoanalysis and the paranormal*. London: Karnac.

Ullman, M., Krippner, S. & Vaughan, A. (1973). *Dream telepathy: Experiments in nocturnal extrasensory perception*. Charlottesville, VA: Hampton Roads Publishing.

Chapter 22

Drawing

Agnes and Melissa applied for my independent study course at the college. Every summer for the past decade I've helped small groups of students prepare portfolios of thematically based drawings. Students work at home and we meet for an hour each week to critique their work. A couple of years ago, Agnes had done a summer project mourning the death of her mother from Alzheimer's. This year she returned with a related project entitled "Hauntings" which depicted hallucinatory experiences of her mother pestering her. Agnes described how she'd feel her mother's presence above and behind her, and how she'd hear her mother's voice giving her advice. These visitations were unwelcome intrusions. Her mother was often critical of Agnes. She was a difficult person before and after death.

As proof of the reality of these events, Agnes offered the following detail. One of her mother's favorite songs was "Pennies from heaven," and whenever she felt her mother's presence, collections of pennies would mysteriously appear. For example, one time her mother appeared as Agnes stepped out of the shower and looked into her cloudy bathroom mirror. On that occasion, documented by a captivating pencil drawing, there was a pile of pennies on the bottom of the shower. "How could those pennies have gotten there?" Agnes asked. "I don't have pennies lying around my bathtub."

Agnes hoped, through her drawings, to be able to exorcize the presence of her mother, and she used our critique sessions to obtain reassurance she wasn't crazy. For Agnes, having a teacher who was both an artist and psychoanalyst was a unique opportunity. I told Agnes she was functioning in the world at a high level, demonstrating effective reality-testing (the measure of craziness), and she should consider these unusual experiences with her mother to be a normal part of mourning. On the other hand, I felt uneasy about Agnes' efforts to kick her mother out. During critique sessions I asked Agnes how her mother was responding to these attempted exorcisms. I wondered aloud whether Agnes and her mother would each be happier if they were more accepting of one another. I, for one, would enjoy meeting her mother, even though I realized she was a pain in the neck. While looking at drawings pinned to a wall, we did family therapy with a ghost.

Melissa's proposal was to illustrate a children's book, authored by her mother, in which Melissa is the central character. The story takes place in the enchanted woods along Abet's Creek. Melissa's family owns several acres of land along this creek, and she played there as a child. In the story Melissa wanders with her sketchbook into the woods surrounding her home. She falls, hits her head, and loses consciousness. When she awakes, she's greeted by a fairy and her personal journey begins. In the story, every time Melissa leaves the forest a new drawing of a fairy appears in her sketch pad. These mysterious images become the basis for Melissa's illustrations.

When Melissa applied for the independent study, she had to provide an email address. Her email address used a last name that differed from my class roster. During the first critique session, when Melissa mentioned Abet's Creek, I told her I remembered someone with that last name who lived on a property abutting the creek. Surprised, she said, "That's my father." Although I acknowledged knowing where Abet's Creek was, I didn't mention that when I first moved to Long Island in 1970, I lived for several years just three houses away from her father's home on Abet's Creek. The creek runs through the woods to the Great South Bay. I liked to walk along the edge of the creek down to the bay. I must have taken that walk thirty times a year. I didn't tell this to Melissa at the time. I didn't mention it until months later.

During that first critique session, as Melissa spoke about Abet's Creek, I realized I'd often walked through the enchanted area depicted in her drawings. Of course, that was over forty years ago, and six years before she was born. I recalled her father shouting at me as I walked across the corner of his property to enter the woods along the creek. After that, I entered the wooded area at the edge of the creek several hundred feet south of his cottage.

It's strange how my life on Castle Street was reemerging. Bette's death made me think about that short street dead-ending at Abet's Creek. In fact, when I heard of her death, I drove down Castle Street to look at Bette's former home. Not much had changed. Her cottage was equidistant between the bungalow I rented and Melissa's father's house. Thinking back, I remembered in 1970 I'd decided to be an artist full time. I was trying to paint forty hours a week in addition to attending school in New York. Frequently I went for walks along the creek to clear my head after painting for several hours. So, I entered Melissa's enchanted playground in a dreamy state of mind. In fact, as Melissa spoke about Abet's Creek, it felt like I was waking from a forty-year old dream.

During the next critique session Melissa brought in photographs of the woods along Abet's Creek which she was incorporating into her illustrations. These images stirred more memories. I recalled the creek's dark water flowing around stones and fallen branches, creating eddies and pools with patches of bright sky reflected on its surface. When I walked along the creek, I was often depressed. I was a thousand miles away from my home in Wisconsin, and still reeling from my father's suicide four years earlier. His violent death wrecked that place for me. I had to get away. Of course, I couldn't escape entirely. Sometimes when I took those walks, I thought of killing myself, just as my father had. An effect of his suicide was my deep assurance I'd shoot myself too. It was just a matter of time.

On the fifth week Melissa brought in a painting she'd done of her younger brother, Cliff, who'd died six years earlier of a heroin overdose in the cabin at Abet's Creek. Her painting was extraordinarily somber. Melissa had been deeply affected by his death. Two years later she became depressed, stopped working and withdrew from life. I wondered if her current interest in artmaking was part of her recovery. Cliff had been addicted to heroin. She saw it coming but couldn't prevent it. When we discussed Cliff's death, I automatically called it a suicide. Melissa corrected me. "It was an accident," she said.

Six months later in January, Melissa and Carlita were two of twenty-four students enrolled in my Drawing II course. Each had taken a previous course with me. During the initial class session, I gave the first homework assignment. Students were to begin drawing their hands from observation at life size scale in graphite. They were instructed to select an emotionally expressive pose for their hand, and then spend several hours beginning a detailed rendering, recording as much textural and tonal difference as possible.

As I drove to the college for our second session, I found myself thinking again about my solitary walks along Abet's Creek, this time in the context of Bette's death. My experience of her death led me to consider time running both ways in my unconscious. Now I wondered when I walked along that creek forty years ago, could I have unconsciously experienced past and future events occurring there? Could I have been aware of a child *not yet born* who'd be playing there years later? Cliff died at Abet's Creek thirty-eight years *after* I first walked along that trail. But, if in my unconscious past and future coexist, could I have witnessed Cliff's death, like seeing a car accident occurring right next to me?

I wondered what Frank would say about this. My ruminations were consistent with his presentation of time in his novel, *The journey west*. As I pulled into the college parking lot, I chuckled to myself, "I'm thinking just like Frank."

I began teaching. Students drew their hands while the Rolling Stones played on a stereo. Melissa's drawing contained some proportional errors. To demonstrate this, I took hold of her hand and placed it on top of her drawing. I traced around the edge of her hand to leave this outline superimposed on her drawing. Lifting up her hand I looked down at our two edges, one echoing the other. Taking hold of her hand and forcefully placing it on top of her drawing was abrupt and aggressive. As I released her hand Melissa stuck me with the sharp point of her pencil. I yelped, she laughed. I made a joke about her stabbing me with her pencil.

I moved on to help Emily Finch, a tall blonde student from Vinton, Iowa. Emily had recently moved to Long Island to work as a nanny. During our first encounter I sensed a budding *rapport*. After helping Emily with her drawing, I moved on to work with another student. Perhaps to measure our *rapport*, I told the class I'd heard al Qaeda was recruiting tall blond women from the Midwest to serve as suicide bombers. "Ms. Finch is more dangerous than she looks. Don't be fooled," I told the class. "Note the large backpack," I said raising my eyebrows and glancing down at the black backpack resting at her feet. I suspected Finch didn't know a single student in the room; maybe only a few people in New York State. A few minutes later, when I finished helping another student, Emily raised her hand and asked that I return to help her.

"I just helped you," I said. "You're monopolizing my time. These other students need my help, too." Finch looked at me coldly. She was silent for a moment. All eyes turned to Ms. Finch. How would she handle this rejection? Emily leaned over and grasped the handle of her backpack. Looking up she said dispassionately, "If you don't help me right now, I'm blowing you up, along with this entire class." Everyone laughed. I said, "Notice how quickly we've all been taken hostage by the ruthless Ms. Finch. Just as I suspected." I had no choice but to help her. I knew then that Finch and I were on the same wavelength.

About ten minutes later I began helping another student, Carlita. Carlita had taken Drawing I with me last term. She began talking about karma. Carlita believed I'd developed bad karma by teasing a student during the previous semester. At the beginning of that course I'd discovered a student named Gerald had a puppy which I suggested was being mistreated by his parents, both physicians at the local university hospital. As a joke, I told Gerald I was going to report his parents to the ASPCA. As the semester progressed, I'd frequently poke fun at this student.

Carlita said,

You have to be careful what you say to people. For all you know, Gerald may snatch up his little dog and leap to his death from the roof of this building. Then you'd have that on your soul. That would be some bad karma.

Carlita continued, "It was probably karma that caused Melissa to stab you with her pencil."

"Really, karma?" I said. I was sure Carlita and Melissa had never even seen each other before this class.

Carlita responded, "In a previous life you probably did something to her that caused her to stab you."

I said,

Karma? I can think of plenty of reasons in our current life for Melissa to stab me. We don't need to go back to a previous lifetime to find an explanation for this. Melissa, do you think we were related in a previous life?

"Undoubtedly," Melissa said, playing along.

I was struck by the parallels between my thoughts while driving to school and Carlita's remarks an hour later. Carlita mentioned Melissa and I related in another space and time. This seemed uncanny, as though

Carlita had been unconsciously aware of what I was thinking while driving to work. Then there were the issues of me behaving in a way that could cause a suicide, and of a karmic force propelling events. A few moments earlier I'd identified Emily Finch as a dangerous suicide bomber, and we'd humorously conspired to create the fantasy of me causing her to blow herself up, killing us all.

As I moved on to help another student, I wondered again about Cliff's death. Certainly, as I walked along Abet's Creek in the early 1970s my thoughts of suicide had a karmic quality. My father's death propelled me toward suicide. Now I wondered if, as I walked along that creek, I'd been carrying a propulsive karmic force that contributed to Cliff's death decades later. Maybe I wasn't the neutral observer I'd imagined while driving to work. Maybe my father's suicide infected me with Death that I brought to Abet's Creek in the hair on my head and left lingering among the pine needles. Maybe I wasn't a witness but a harbinger, or worse, a curse. Her father was right to keep me out. Melissa called those woods enchanted. Now I wondered if I'd begun haunting those woods a few years before she was born. Did I still carry my father's disease, forty years later, infecting a student like Gerald?

There was another uncanny aspect of this interchange I didn't realize until later. Melissa had drawn her hand in the shape of a pistol. Her index and middle fingers were pointing straight ahead to form the barrel, her ring and pinky fingers curled around to make the pistol's handle, and her thumb was cocked like the hammer at the back of a gun. Later after class, when I realized this, I got a chill. I didn't think either Carlita or Melissa were aware my father had shot himself. Neither could have been aware of my memories of those walks along Abet's Creek. But maybe unconsciously I was predisposing them to express a self-destructive theme. Maybe it was my father's infection again.

One reason I felt a chill was because I realized that I *hadn't seen* a pistol in plain sight. For fifty years, in the middle of every night, I've woken up saying, "Get the gun." Now I wondered if, before my father's suicide, the pistol was there in plain sight, but I hadn't seen it. Was not-seeing the result of some karmic force? Maybe it was my part to be haunted by the thing only my unconscious sees.

But there was another reason I got a chill. Two weeks later Carlita's cousin, Adam, shot himself with a handgun. I was stunned. Carlita had been talking about a young man's suicide two weeks earlier. Were her statements and Melissa's pistol pose simply coincidental, or were they both premonitions of Adam's death? If these were premonitions, what does it mean if two people, completely unrelated, simultaneously behave in a premonitory way? As I drove to work the morning of our second class, were memories of my suicidal thoughts as a young man also premonitory? Were all three of us simply articulating versions of the same suicidal theme two weeks before this tragic event? That's the way it looked. If that was true, then our individual actions were responses to a common source of unconscious knowledge originating in the world around us, like reading a cosmic newspaper.

I considered the remarkable connections around suicide. There was my father's suicide; my identification with my father contributing to me walking in the woods ruminating over killing myself; Melissa's brother's overdose that I called a suicide; and Carlita's cousin's death. By the end of the week I learned from Emily Finch that suicide also figured significantly in her past. Emily had fled Iowa after being unfairly blamed for the suicide of a fellow student. So, when I announced to the class that she was dangerous and could be the death of us all, I realized now that this was her unspoken fear. When Carlita was saying I could behave in a way that would lead to Gerald's suicide, she was also echoing Emily's agonizing experience. Carlita and I appeared to be speaking directly to Emily.

The way this story was emerging among us, it looked like there was a larger pattern: Four suicides, four survivors, each of us concerned about contributing to another's death. I wondered whether Emily, Carlita, Melissa and I had been drawn together by a force outside ourselves. We seemed to be swimming in the same stream, like being swept along in the eddies of Abet's Creek. This current didn't seem to be affecting others in the class, but I seemed to be on the edge of an invisible whirlpool watching suicide survivors swirling my way.

Two months later, I met with my supervisee, Raul. He's a social worker and a graduate of the psychoanalytic institute where I teach. I've supervised his clinical work for the past fourteen years. Raul told me the following story.

A couple of months ago he'd received an application in the mail, unsolicited, asking him to participate in New Jersey's Hurricane Sandy Relief Project. He joined the project and began meeting referrals in his Hoboken office. In addition to his private practice, Raul works part-time in the emergency room of a community hospital covering a couple of weekends a month. When he arrived this Sunday morning at seven, the emergency room was filled with activity. Hospital administrators were milling about—unusual for a Sunday morning. Raul heard one nurse ask another, "Do you think we'll be on the news?" Another nurse asked, "Did we overlook anything?"

When Raul met the social worker coming off-duty she told him a young man had shot himself in the heart in the parking lot around midnight. He was discovered by security. Surgeons tried to save him, and he'd received several transfusions. But he died. Everyone in the emergency room was upset, even now six hours later. The social worker pointed to his dead body lying on a table in the next room. Raul turned and looked at the undraped body of the dead man. The young man's family, who'd come to identify him, had just left the room. Raul realized he'd walked past the family on his way into the ER.

A month later, Raul received another referral from the Sandy Relief Project, requesting the client be seen urgently. Raul met with the young woman two days later. When she arrived, Raul asked how she'd been affected by the storm. She said her apartment had been damaged. She'd lost everything, but mostly she was struggling to recover from her brother's death four weeks earlier. As she told her story, Raul realized she was speaking about the young man who'd shot himself in the hospital parking lot—a remarkable coincidence.

A tension emerged inside Raul. He wanted to tell her he'd been there, he'd been in the emergency room, he'd seen her brother. In fact, he'd walked right past her as he entered the hospital that morning. Could he tell her this? He'd talked to this woman for fifteen minutes and she was obviously very distressed. Could he predict the impact hearing this would have on her? How fragile was she? Would it harm her?

The young woman told Raul she'd felt very close to her brother. They were soulmates, like twins. She loved him so much. And she felt terrible she'd had an argument with her brother on the morning of his suicide. She felt guilty that those were the last words she'd spoken to him. She visited his grave every day. She'd lie down next to him and talk to him. She'd read to him. She was attending college and was studying for her finals right there at his grave. She couldn't leave him, and she didn't want him to leave her.

The tension continued to build inside of Raul. The feeling was now becoming urgent. He could barely control his urge to speak. He'd never experienced anything like this. He finally lost the ability to contain his thoughts and feelings. Raul told me, "It was *involuntary.*"

He spoke to the young woman, "I don't know if telling you this is the right thing to do, but I was there at the hospital. I was there that morning. I saw your brother's body." The young woman burst into tears. "In fact, I walked right past you and your family as you were leaving the emergency room that morning. I think your brother wants me to tell you this. I think he's the reason you're here." Raul explained to me that he'd concluded her brother was the source of the tension inside him. Raul felt her brother was inside him. He felt possessed.

"Oh, thank you for telling me," the young woman said. "It makes me feel so much better." She believed her brother's spirit was in the room. In fact, her mother had gone to a local Santero, a priest in the Santeria religion, to ask whether her brother was still in this earthly realm. The priest told her mother he remained on earth to make sure his family was alright. Santeria is a Caribbean mixture of Christian and African traditions which includes communication with the dead. Raul's family had been involved with Santeria when he was growing up in Cuba. He told the young woman his sister often saw the same priest. The young woman never visited the Santero because she was too apprehensive, and Raul acknowledged he felt the same way, even though he has a relative in Cuba who is a priestess.

Raul said to me,

> You know, I've never had a case like this, where someone is in such pain. I'm overwhelmed by her pain. Maybe it's strange, but I've been practicing for twenty-five years and I've never worked with someone so powerfully grieving the death of a loved one, or a suicide.

This seemed inconceivable. "Really?" I said. "I experience a lot of this in my practice and in my life. I started early with death, and I've been recovering ever since. I work with a lot of people struggling with death. It's sort of a specialty." I didn't mean it to be, it was inevitable. Death is the essential pain of life, and everyone experiences it multiple times. How could the agony of death have missed Raul? On the other hand, why was Raul encountering his first survivor of suicide now, coincident with my experience with Emily, Carlita and Melissa? Was Raul swimming in our stream? Was he adrift in the creek like the rest of us? It looked that way.

As I listened to Raul, the synchronicities of the last few months played through my mind. All of these experiences occurred at the edge of life where death is imminent or has just occurred. Five years ago, in the wake of Anders' death, Frank and I seemed drawn together by what I'd called the "magnetism of loss." Now more of us appeared to be swimming in a similar magnetic current. What drew Carlita, Emily, Melissa and me together, and what drew Raul's young patient to him?

Carlita said karmic forces form our futures. In the story emerging between Raul and his young patient, they believed the girl's dead brother brought them together. Agnes, Raul and the young girl feel certain the dead are living within or around them. The dead are described as vital agents affecting our lives.

In the months following these events several more survivors of family suicide contacted Raul. By the end of the year he was working with nine survivors, a third of his practice. This development seemed improbable. Raul attributed this phenomenon to me. I was the common denominator. Using the language of chaos theory, he claimed I was a strange attractor. *I was the whirlpool* sucking survivors my way. From his perspective, I'd drawn Emily, Carlita and Melissa to my side. Now I was pulling patients toward me through him. But how could survival of my father's suicide cause people to be drawn toward me? Was the phrase "magnetism of loss" more than a metaphor? Could my mind influence the behavior of nine strangers hundreds of miles away? "Impossible," I thought.

It turns out, in Raul's family he's just a generation away from several suicides. Four aunts and uncles had taken their lives. His maternal grandfather tried but failed. "There're probably more," he said, "if I look further back." When he was an adolescent, he'd come close to killing himself, too. So, Raul simply wasn't seeing himself born into the current. "And, oh," he remembered, "When I was four my babysitter set herself on fire." Did his family's pattern of suicides suck her into its wake?

Do our unconscious emotional states invisibly affect others at a distance? These stories suggest they do. My telepathic experiences are nonlocal. Certainly Mesmer, Barberin, du Potet, Janet and Richet's examples of hypnosis at a distance provide evidence of nonlocal effects. Friedericke Hauffe's treatment of Countess von Maldeghem was a nonlocal cure. There are decades of research supporting telepathy (Radin, 2013). However, research on intercessory prayer, where a group prays for someone's recovery, is inconclusive (Baruss & Mossbridge, 2017). Researcher Russell Targ (2012a) writes,

> Taken as a group, laboratory and hospital results are quite variable. Consequently, most researchers agree that there is strong evidence for various kinds of distant and spiritual healing, but the results depend strongly on who is doing it.

> (p.153)

Okay, but could a dead brother orchestrate a series of events leading his sister to Raul's office? Agnes, Raul and his young patient believe it's possible, and they may not be alone. According to the Pew Research Center (Lipka, 2015), twenty percent of Americans report having seen a ghost and a third claim they've had contact with the dead, views supported by earlier research (Fox, 1992).

Could I be a strange attractor drawing people unwittingly toward me? Maybe. But it's difficult to accept. Could Carlita, Raul, Emily, Melissa and me together contribute to a *field of emotional energy* causing nine strangers to gravitate toward Raul? Who knows?

If our emotions are affecting others at a distance, then their emotions are affecting us. Does that mean we're all being influenced by a global field of mental/emotional currents swirling through us like psychic weather? This feels subjectively true, but how could it happen? Let's face it, if we're being influenced by fields of mental forces, we're a thousand years from explaining the phenomenon. Of course, Newton couldn't explain gravity, he only described it. In the last three hundred years no one has explained the origin of nonlocal effects. But, even if we can't explain it, can we at least *imagine* a model of psychic weather? Let's give it a try.

First, there's a basic condition that's fundamental to creating a model: Locality, the topic we considered when discussing "action at a distance" in quantum entanglement. The mind appears to deal with locality by splitting in two, producing a conscious and an unconscious mind. Our conscious mind focuses on local effects while our unconscious is nonlocal, and the tension between these two realities creates the fabric of mental life. This split between local consciousness and a nonlocal unconscious lies at the heart of the mind/body problem.

For the past fifty years cognitive science has studied the unconscious mind. Here's what we've learned about the relationship between our conscious and unconscious minds (Gigerenzer, 2007; Gilhooley, 2008; Libet, 2004; Norretranders, 1998; Wegner, 2002; Westen, 1998, 1999; Wilson, 2002). The unconscious is vast but invisible and can only be examined indirectly, therefore we build our knowledge of it inferentially. It's assumed the unconscious is the original form of mentation and consciousness is a more recent evolutionary development. That may be the reason the unconscious appears to be aware of both itself and consciousness, while the conscious mind sees only itself.

The unconscious is the source of consciousness. All sensory information is processed in our unconscious and only a tiny fraction of that information filters into consciousness. For example, researchers estimate our unconscious mind processes ten million bits of visual information per second, of which less than twenty can be consciously manipulated. Consciousness is the product of extensive filtering of sensory input, memories, and unconscious knowledge creating a highly reductive version of reality.

The unconscious is the origin of thought and emotion. Drawing from an enormous reservoir of unconscious memory, the unconscious mind makes decisions and initiates action with consciousness following along a half-second behind (Libet, 2004). Being unaware of the unconscious mind, consciousness believes it's the beginning and end of mental life. It assumes it's in charge of our minds and bodies, which is an illusion (Norretranders, 1998; Wilson, 2002; Wegner, 2002). We know consciousness is an observer, not an initiator, of action. Consciousness doesn't make decisions. It creates after the fact explanations for the behavior it's witnessing. We know this empirically, but consciousness tenaciously rejects awareness of this fact.

The unconscious is the origin of intuition, creativity and exceptional mental experiences. Altering our state of consciousness to temporarily bypass its filtering function allows unconscious knowledge to slip into consciousness (Baruss, 2003; Cardena & Winkelman, 2011). Dreaming is a universally experienced altered state of consciousness. Researchers find we're more creative after "believing the impossible" in our dreams (Kahn & Gover, 2010), and it appears that all invention originates in the unconscious. The unconscious is believed to possess extraordinary knowledge, to be the origin of genius, and the source of exceptional experiences such as telepathy and precognition (Grotstein, 2000; Kelly & Grosso, 2007; Simmonds-Moore, 2012; Atmanspacher & Fachs, 2015). Meditation and prayer are methods of altering consciousness to gain access to religious or spiritual experience (James, 1982; Kripal, 2010; Marshall, 2005; Winkelman & Baker, 2010).

Empirical research has overturned a two thousand-year-old belief that consciousness *is* mental life. It radically reduces the significance of consciousness, shifts agency and authority to the unconscious, thereby altering our understanding of mind. Given its auxiliary status, the purpose of our conscious mind is unknown. One researcher aptly calls consciousness an "afterthought" (Harnad, 1982). One purpose of consciousness appears to be the maintenance of the illusions of an autonomous self, local agency, and free will.

"What a relief, that helps a lot!" Max, Frank's fictional architect, blurts out. Max is upset. Who wants to accept our conscious mind, the only mind we directly observe, exists to support an illusion? Even worse, cognitive science shows us empirically (even more conclusively than Freud) that we're driven by invisible unconscious forces over which we have no conscious control. This is not welcome news for any of us. Max doesn't doubt the truth of it. But it makes him angry. Again, things aren't what they appear! The gap between the conscious and unconscious mind is just as frustrating as the epistemological gap between mental representations and reality itself. Max is trapped in these gaps! Indeed, in *Mind and matter* Erwin Schrödinger (1967) confirms, "No complete gapless description of any physical object is ever possible. . .it flies in the face of the principle of understandability of nature" (p.135). It's difficult to accept this reality. "Thanks a lot," Max snaps sarcastically.

I find this a lot more exciting than Max does. Let's take a look at what we've learned about the unconscious mind. The most important feature of the unconscious is that it's nonlocal (Baruss & Mossbridge, 2017; Kelly, Crabtree & Marshall, 2015). My precognitive and telepathic experiences tell me my unconscious mind isn't located in a specific space and time, as my body and conscious mind appear to be. For example, in my precognitive "flat-tire" experience I was in both the present and the future, *and* I was in Bellport and Babylon simultaneously. In my telepathic dream with Lily I dreamt her thoughts as if they were my own. At that moment, I existed in a transpersonal place where my individual identity merged with hers sixty miles away.

A hundred and thirty years of scientific research demonstrates telepathy and precognition are real (Broderick & Goertzel, 2015; Cardena, 2018;

Cardena, Lynn & Krippner, 2000; Cardena, Palmer & Marcusson-Clavertz, 2015; May & Marwaha, 2015; Radin, 2006, 2013). Leading experimentalist Etzel Cardena (2018) writes,

> The evidence provides cumulative support for the reality of psi, which cannot be readily explained away by the quality of the studies, fraud, selective reporting, experimental or analytical incompetence, or other frequent criticisms. The evidence for psi is comparable to that for established phenomena in psychology and other disciplines, although there is no consensual understanding of them.
>
> (p.663)

Here's an example of this research. Cornell psychologist Daryl Bem (2011) recently published "Feeling the future: Experimental evidence for anomalous retroactive influences of cognition and affect" in the premier *Journal of Personality and Social Psychology*. Bem showed statistically significant evidence of precognition in eight of his nine studies. Across all nine experiments, with over a thousand participants, the combined odds that his positive results were produced by chance were seventy-three billion to one. Evidence in favor of telepathy is similarly compelling. A meta-analytic study of forty-two-hundred telepathy trials conducted between 1974 and 2010 showed a combine "hit rate" of thirty-one percent when chance (meaning "no telepathy") would produce a twenty-five percent response (Radin, 2013, p.190). The overall odds this positive result is the product of chance is thirteen billion trillion to one, causing researcher Dean Radin (2013) to declare, "The likelihood that telepathy exists is as close to 'proven' as contemporary science can establish" (p.199). People have difficulty accepting these results because the consequences are frightening, threatening the integrity of their minds. So, they suppress the evidence calling it pseudoscience. But every year the proof grows stronger (Utts, 1999), and cowardice gets us nowhere.

So, if we take recent scientific evidence about the unconscious mind and combine it with the empirical research supporting telepathy and precognition, what do we get? A nonlocal unconscious that invisibly determines our futures. Using a little imagination, what can be inferred from the nonlocal quality of the unconscious mind to inform a model of psychic weather? From the perspective of consciousness, this is where things get weird. But here goes.

If, within our unconscious, we're unbound by space and time, and if we're capable of knowing the future, then we're alive and dead simultaneously. This isn't a statistical anomaly emerging from the basic equation of quantum physics, it's a fundamental reality of mental life. If we're already dead, that means we've already lived our lives, which means our futures are predetermined. It may be we experience an Everettian multiverse of optional futures, but all options are determined, and in all of them we're already dead. Of course, this isn't how we consciously experience our lives. But it's a necessary consequence of the nonlocal nature of the unconscious.

Furthermore, if the unconscious is transpersonal as William James and his colleagues Edmund Gurney, Frederic Myers and Frank Podmore (1886) demonstrated a hundred years ago in *Phantasms of the living*, my predetermined future is entwined with the past and futures of everyone else creating what Carl Jung called a collective unconscious. As Erwin Schrödinger (1967) concludes, "In truth there is only one mind" (p.139). It's this transpersonal quality of the unconscious that makes psychic weather inevitable.

So, within the nonlocal unconscious, psychic weather emerges from the collective thoughts and emotions of the dead, the living, and the unborn formed by a dynamic process of "binding" and "associating." Binding is a basic feature of mental life (Cleeremans, 2003). For our purposes, I'll propose binding employs an immaterial force to link mental products together. Binding is the "hallucinatory adhesive" Frank's character, Max, claims is holding together time and our perceptions. Binding is the glue that builds gestalts, the mental structures which preoccupy Frank's character, Dr. Distanziert. Freud (1938) considered "binding" to be the function of the life instinct, Eros. Binding forces are probably small within an individual mind but could be amplified at a collective level. Next, I presume commonalities and differences among thoughts and emotions would cause them to coalesce and separate. Associated thoughts bind together to create stable enduring structures like Jung's archetypes and Plato's ideal forms. The quintessential eternal structure could be what people call the divine, or what psychoanalyst Wilfred Bion (1965) describes as O, absolute truth and ultimate reality. Truth binds together.

While binding would twist past and future thoughts and emotions into permanent structures, binding would similarly produce transitory forms from emotional thoughts being experienced locally in the present. This is where the forces of the past and future residing within the nonlocal unconscious connect with emotions in the present and with local consciousness. Here permanent and transitory psychic forms interact to produce local patterns of emotional thoughts swirling through our transpersonal unconscious. This is psychic weather.

Responding to these emotional currents, our unconscious would initiate action which would then appear in our conscious minds. In our example, Melissa, Carlita and Emily each unwittingly register for my drawing course; Carlita's cousin Adam secretly obtains a pistol; and Raul applies to become a provider for the Sandy Relief Project. Each individual creates his or her own conscious explanation for their behavior. They are unaware their actions are motivated by emotional forces originating in their nonlocal transpersonal unconscious. They've been pushed into action by the emotional currents of psychic weather.

What we experience as synchronicities likely occur at the intersection of a powerful eternal structure involving Bion's O and an emergent local form (Jung, 1960). In our example, an enduring structure like "Survivor" binds together the traumatic experiences of fourteen survivors to create a group. Perhaps the binding force itself, amplified within the collective unconscious, is powerful enough to draw my mind, and the minds of Carlita, Melissa, Emily, Raul and his nine survivors together. But, why are these fourteen people linked together, and not fourteen others? Who knows? Maybe it's the magnitude of commonality, or perhaps a complementary dissociative counterforce exists that is "nonbinding," something like quantum decoherence, which prevents other structures from forming.

As a complement of synchronicity, creative and imaginative thinking, or artmaking, also links powerful eternal structures of O with a local emergent form. But artmaking occurs in an altered state of consciousness, a dissociative trance, and in this sense it's similar to automatic writing and dreaming (Cardena & Winkelman, 2011). Traditional conceptions of artmaking find the origin of creativity in "inspiration" which is transpersonal (Kelly & Grosso, 2007). For example, Frederic Myers (1903) writes, "inspiration of genius" is one's manipulation of ideas "which he has not consciously originated, but which have shaped themselves beyond his will, in profounder regions of his being" (p.71). "That's right," Nigel's pal, Fritz Nietzsche, says, "Everything occurs quite without volition, as if in an eruption of freedom, independence, power and divinity."

Because synchronicities are O-inspired meaningful coincidences, they represent a correlation between local consciousness and O, though they occur outside local agency (they are "acausal"). Artmaking, on the other hand, represents a disconnection between local awareness and O. In other words, art works are O-inspired, but they originate in a nonlocal transpersonal unconscious, outside individual consciousness and local agency. That's why Frank can declare "the story writes itself." This is how he can write about my experiences before I have them, and how he can "create" a character like Watson Page who is a clear rendering of Hugh Everett, while never having heard of Hugh Everett.

What's the role of the divine in the creation of psychic weather? Perhaps all enduring structures in the mind, collectively, are what we think of as the divine. Maybe mind is the divine. So, whenever we personally encounter an enduring mental form like love, the hope of birth, or death's despair there is a spiritual dimension to the experience. In addition, if lives are predetermined then human actions are guided by both the inertial power of their pasts and teleological forces originating in their futures. These inertial and teleological forces are likely influenced by permanent mental structures. This may be where karma fits in. Finally, it's likely that "O," or the divine, is dynamically evolving. Like Heraclitus' river where the everchanging flow of water paradoxically creates the permanent form of the river, the reverse is also probably true: The enduring form of O is paradoxically everchanging. In that sense, God is a work in progress. God, as mind, is continuously evolving.

Okay, there's an imaginary model of psychic weather. It's a model that explains how Carlita, Melissa, Emily, Raul, and I were drawn together, and how nine patients were pulled toward Raul. As weird and mystical as it sounds, it's a logical elaboration of the limited scientific evidence we have. A consciousness-centric world would find it impossible to accept because it shifts agency outside of the conscious mind, and even worse, it appears to shift agency outside the Self altogether. It suggests enduring structures in the mind, ultimately even the divine, play a part in shaping our lives, a heretical thought in an individualistic and secular world.

Max boldly interrupts,

This is the worst model of mind I've ever heard of! This is precisely why Newton warned us about the dangers of imagination—it leads us into wild and destructive fantasy! You're telling me I'm controlled by external immaterial forces I don't recognize or understand, my future is predetermined, I'm actually dead, and my consciousness is an illusion of free will?

"Well, something like that," I respond.

"And you expect me to go along with that?" Max asks incredulously.

"No, actually I don't expect anyone will go along with it. That's what consciousness is for. To protect people from this kind of thinking."

"Who would even want to be alive under those circumstances?"

"Exactly," I agree, "it's very undesirable."

"Have you given any thought to what you're saying here? This is complete rubbish!" Max closes his copy of the book and hurls it across the room. I duck.

Luckily, he doesn't hit me with it. I chuckle, but I understand Max's point. These are upsetting ideas and he's unusually sensitive. This isn't the first time my imagination has gotten me into trouble. Maybe Newton was right. On the other hand, psychic weather is a form of idealism, a philosophical position Max subscribes to. So, maybe he'll come around.

Actually, this imaginary model of psychic weather redefines what a Self is. Psychoanalysis has been revising its notion of the Self from the beginning. Freud thought the Self resided within a hermetically sealed mind, and motivated action was an intrapsychic process driven by conflicts born from an individual's instinctual endowment combined with his or her past. Around the same time, Pierre Janet and Frederic Myers were discovering multiple personalities existing within a single person, expanding our understanding of Self. Freud ignored this research, probably considering it a messy complication. The next generation of Freudian analysts included others and the environment as influences on an individual's motivated action, and the Self began to be understood within a social and interpersonal matrix.

I'm proposing something similar within the context of a nonlocal and transpersonal unconscious producing an immaterial environmental matrix of psychic weather. This is psychoanalytic field theory cubed (Baranger & Baranger, 2009; Ferro & Civitarese, 2015; Katz, 2017)! This is where *bi-personal* field theories meet *transpersonal* "theories of global consciousness" (Braud, 2003; McTaggart, 2002; Radin, 2013; Targ, 2012b). This psychic weather model redefines the intrapsychic process of motivated action to include organizational forces from one's past *and future* mediated by dynamic forces emerging from a *transpersonal* unconscious. Add to this the teleological influence of psychic forces emanating from *eternal mental forms* such as Jung's archetypes, and even from the quint-essential eternal form, O. This Self is a lot more complicated than Freud or relational analysts envisioned! In this imaginary model, every individual breath and heartbeat are linked to an eternal beating heart of humanity itself. This, in fact, is the basis of the model. I glance over at Max looking for a reaction. His eyes are closed.

I think back to my walks along Abet's Creek. I remember light reflecting off those dark currents flowing around stones and fallen branches out to the Great South Bay. Those fluid movements forming calm pools, rippling eddies and little whirlpools serve as a model for the emotional currents of psychic weather.

So much has changed in the years since I walked along that creek. I think again about what I'd inherited from my father, the contagion of Death. Fifty-five years ago, I was caught in the storm of my father's life. I was living in the emotional wake of his landing on Omaha Beach. When my father leaped into the waters along that French coast, he waded ashore through water darkened by the deaths of three thousand men who came before him. Nearly a thousand died in water rendered sacred through their sacrifice. This was Tom's baptism. The storm of that deadly invasion was too powerful for my father's mind to contain. Through his suicide the murderous violence of Normandy hit me.

But Tom's suicide transformed the Death that flowed through him to me. My father's mind filtered that destructive current, so what passed to me didn't take my life. It seems I was actually immunized by that dose of Death, and what became contagious in me was the *transformation of Death*, not Death itself.

Shamanic traditions using ecstatic trance to cure physical illness appeared throughout the world during the Neolithic period (Eliade, 1964; Hayden, 2003; Kakar, 1982; Winkelman, 2010). Using a mental state to transform the body, Mesmerism and psychoanalysis are modern incarnations of this ancient tradition. The novice shamanic healer was initiated through an ordeal of sickness, followed by a symbolic death and resurrection. In an ecstatic trance, the novice faced Death in its many forms. The initiation was meant to kill him. In most traditions the novice passes through Death and is reborn a healer. His initiation cures the young shaman of sickness, and this becomes the source of his therapeutic power.

Walking through the woods along Abet's Creek, I traveled the shaman's path. My suicidal thoughts were the voice of violence inherited from my father. As psychic weather, Normandy was speaking through him. Normandy ignited a murderer within me, and Normandy meant to kill me. At Omaha Beach it was kill or be killed. But the murderer animated inside me was transformed. Through my initiation, I was cured of Normandy's addiction to Death.

In the model of psychic weather, contagion is a current. If Raul is right, if I'm a strange attractor, it's because of my initiatory process passing through Death. But I wonder if there's something more. Is there a teleological force originating in an archetype, an eternal verb "Survive?" Does this archetype draw out of me this transformative power, mixing it into the emotional currents swirling through and around me? Drawing from my past *and my future*, this might be my contribution to psychic weather.

References

Atmanspacher, H. & Fach, W. (2015). Mind-matter correlations in duel-aspect monism. In E. Kelly, A. Crabtree, & P. Marshall, (Eds.) *Beyond physicalism: Toward reconciliation of science and spirituality* (pp.195–226). Lanham, MD: Rowman & Littlefield.

Baranger, M. & Baranger, W. (2009). *The work of confluence: Listening and interpreting in the psychoanalytic field.* London: Karnac.

Baruss, I. (2003). *Alterations of consciousness: An empirical analysis for social scientists.* Washington, DC: American Psychological association.

Baruss, I. & Mossbridge, J. (2017). *Transcendent mind: Rethinking the science of consciousness.* Washington, DC: American Psychological Association.

Bem, D. (2011). Feeling the future: Experimental evidence for anomalous retroactive influences on cognition and affect. *Journal of Personality and Social Psychology*, 100(3), 407–425.

Bion, W. (1965). Transformations. London: Maresfield Library.

Braud, W. (2003). *Distant mental influence: Its contributions to science, healing, and human interactions.* Charlottesville, VA: Hampton Roads Publishing.

Broderick, D. & Goertzel, B. (Eds.) (2015). *Evidence for psi: Thirteen empirical research reports.* Jefferson, NC: McFarland & Company.

Cardena, E. (2018). The experimental evidence for parapsychological phenomena: A review. *American Psychologist*, 73(5), 663–677.

Cardena, E., Lynn, S. & Krippner, S. (Eds.) (2000). *Varieties of anomalous experience: Examining the scientific evidence.* Washington, D.C.: American Psychological Association.

Cardena, E., Palmer, J. & Marcusson-Clavertz, D. (Eds.) (2015). Parapsychology: A handbook for the 21st century. Jefferson, NC: McFarland & Company.

Cardena, E. & Winkelman, M. (Eds.) (2011). *Altering consciousness: Multi-disciplinary perspectives*. Santa Barbara, CA: Praeger.

Cleeremans, A. (Ed.) (2003). *The unity of consciousness: Binding, integration, and dissociation*. Oxford: Oxford University Press.

Eliade, M. (1964). *Shamanism: Archaic techniques of ecstasy*. Princeton, NJ: Princeton University Press.

Ferro, A. & Civitarese, G. (2015). *The analytic field and its transformations*. London: Karnac.

Fox, J. (1992). The structure, stability, and social antecedents of reported paranormal experiences. *Sociological Analysis*, 53, 417–431.

Freud, S. (1938). An outline of psycho-analysis. *Standard Edition*. London: Hogarth Press, 23, 141–207.

Gigerenzer, G. (2007). *Gut feelings: The intelligence of the unconscious*. London: Penguin Books.

Gilhooley, D. (2008). Psychoanalysis and the "cognitive unconscious": Implications for clinical technique. *Modern Psychoanalysis*, 33, 91–127.

Grotstein, J. (2000). *Who is the dreamer who dreams the dream?* Hillsdale, NJ: The Analytic Press.

Gurney, E., Myers, F. & Podmore, F. (1886). *Phantasms of the living*, volumes 1–2. London: Rooms of the Society for Psychical Research, Trubner and Company.

Harnad, S. (1982). Consciousness: An afterthought. *Cognition and Brain Theory*, 5, 29–47.

Hayden, B. (2003). *Shamans, sorcerers and saints*. Washington, DC: Smithsonian Institution.

James, W. (1982). *The varieties of religious experience: A study in human nature*. New York, NY: Penguin Books. (Original work published 1902).

Jung, C. (1960). Synchronicity: An acausal connecting principle. *Collected Works of C.G. Jung*, volume 8. Princeton, NJ: Princeton University Press.

Kahn, D. & Gover, T. (2010). Consciousness in dreams. *International Review of Neurobiology*, 92, 181–195.

Kakar, S. (1982). *Shamans, mystics, and doctors: A psychological inquiry into India and its healing traditions*. Chicago, IL: University of Chicago Press.

Katz, S. (2017). *Contemporary psychoanalytic field theory: Stories, dreams, and metaphor*. London: Routledge.

Kelly, E. F. & Grosso, M. (2007). Genius. In E. F. Kelly, E. W. Kelly, A., Crabtree, A. Gauld, M. Grosso & B. Greyson (Eds.). *Irreducible mind: Toward a psychology for the 21st century* (pp.423–494). Lanham, MD: Rowman & Littlefield.

Kelly, E.F., Crabtree, A. & Marshall, P. (Eds.) (2015). *Beyond physicalism: Toward a reconciliation of science and spirituality*. Lanham, MD: Rowman & Littlefield.

Kripal, J. (2010). *Authors of the impossible: The paranormal and the sacred*. Chicago, IL: University of Chicago Press.

Libet, B. (2004). The delay in our conscious sensory awareness. In *Mind time: The temporal factor in consciousness* (pp.33–60). Cambridge, MA: Harvard University Press.

Lipka, M. (2015). 18% of Americans say they've seen a ghost. *Fact Tank*, October 30, 2015 http://www.pewresearch.org/fact-tank/2015/10/30/18-of-americans-say-theyve-seen-a-ghost/ (Accessed August 1, 2017)

Marshall, P. (2005). *Mystical encounters with the natural world: Experiences and explanations*. Oxford: Oxford University Press.

May, E. & Marwaha, S. (2015). *Anomalous cognition: Remote viewing research and theory*. Jefferson, NC: McFarland and Company.

McTaggart, L. (2002). *The field: The quest for the secret force of the universe*. New York, NY: HarperCollins.

Myers, F. (1903). Genius. In *Human personality and its survival of bodily death*, volume 1 (pp.70–120). London: Longmans, Green, and Company.

Norretranders, T. (1998). *The user illusion: Cutting consciousness down to size*. New York, NY: Viking.

Radin, D. (2006). *Entangled minds: Extrasensory experiences in quantum reality*. New York, NY: Paraview Pocket Books.

Radin, D. (2013). *Supernormal*. New York, NY: Random House.

Schrödinger, E. (1967). Mind and matter. In *What is life? and Mind and matter* (pp. 97–178). Cambridge: Cambridge University Press. (Original work published 1958)

Simmonds-Moore, C. (Ed.) (2012). *Exceptional experience and health: Essays on mind, body and human potential*. Jefferson, NC: McFarland & Company.

Targ, R. (2012a). Mental influence and healing from a distance. In *The reality of ESP: A physicist's proof of psychic abilities* (pp.151–172). Wheaton, IL: Theosophical Publishing House.

Targ, R. (2012b). *The reality of ESP: A physicist's proof of psychic abilities*. Wheaton, IL: Theosophical Publishing House.

Utts, J. (1999). The significance of statistics in mind-matter research. *Journal of Scientific Exploration*, 13(4), 615–638.

Wegner, D. (2002). *The illusion of conscious will*. Cambridge, MA: MIT Press.

Westen, D. (1998), Unconscious thought, feeling, and motivation: End of a century-long debate. In R. Bornstein & J. Masling (Eds.), *Empirical perspectives on the psychoanalytic unconscious* (pp.1–43). Washington, DC: American Psychological Association.

Westen, D. (1999). The scientific status of unconscious processes: Is Freud really dead? *Journal of the American Psychoanalytic Association, 47,* 1061–1106.

Wilson, T. (2002). *Strangers to ourselves: Discovering the adaptive unconscious.* Cambridge, MA: Harvard University Press.

Winkelman, M. (2010). *Shamanism: A biopsychosocial paradigm of consciousness and healing.* Santa Barbara, CA: Praeger.

Winkelman, M. & Baker, J. (2010). *Supernatural as natural: A biocultural approach to religion.* Upper Saddle River, NJ: Pearson Prentice Hall.

Part IV

Collaboration

Chapter 23

Nigel, Mekes and Distanziert

At the conclusion of Frank's novel his protagonist, Nigel, and his twin Raymond join "to meet their fate as one." Their fictional relationship served as a model for the therapeutic and literary collaboration Frank and I would develop. Our creative work together grew naturally from Frank's imagination. So, an account of our collaboration begins with a descriptive interpretation of Frank's fiction.

Frank's novel begins with Nigel declaring, "I woke up dead." Having discovered he's dead, Nigel hopes to escape rebirth and another round of human suffering. Life after death is a spiritual quest through a netherworld where Nigel encounters a succession of tests on his way to judgment. Combining the Egyptian *Book of the dead* with Buddhist, Hindu and Christian iconography, Frank's novel is rooted in various religious traditions. He similarly bases his story in ancient Greek philosophy as well as contemporary science. Looking desperately for a way to survive the death of his son, Frank searches for answers in the expanse of human knowledge and spiritual practice.

The first thing to know about Nigel is that he's nameless. Having died, he's lost his identity. When asked who he is, he can't say so he gives the name of his cat, Nigel. Nigel is worn down by a life that out maneuvered and overpowered over him. Defeated and angry, he wants out. Looking to escape rebirth, Nigel is putting everything he's got into his quest for eternal life. So, even though he's dead, he's relentlessly inquisitive. The search for knowledge is his remaining passion. But finding the path to eternal life isn't easy and the cards seem stacked against him. Like Schrödinger's electron, Nigel exists in a hazy state of indeterminacy. He's never sure if he's dreaming or awake. Only a few facts are illuminated momentarily before him, and he moves from clue to clue through a mist of uncertainty. Like a detective in the tradition of Philip Marlowe, Nigel navigates a dangerous underworld.

Throughout the book Nigel is in pursuit of Dr. Mekes. Nigel hopes Mekes can clarify a translation of the Egyptian *Book of the dead*. Mekes is a brilliant but elusive leader of a cult. Mekes closely resembles the ancient Greek philosopher Pythagoras who is believed to have traveled to Egypt and Persia, studied the Egyptian *Book of the dead*, and appropriated Egyptian religious beliefs on the transmigration of the soul (Barnes, 1979; Burkert, 1972; Huffman, 2014; Kahn, 2001). Pythagoras left no writing, so we can't be certain of his views. We learn about him from his contemporaries and followers. Pythagoras was considered the most learned man of ancient Greece, and like Isaac Newton he was part magician, part mathematician. Frank, who earned degrees in mathematics, appears to place the father of Western mathematics at the center of his story. Frank's interest in past lives, shamanism and the combination of mathematics and the divine is embodied in Mekes.

"Mekes" in Hebrew means "computation," and Pythagoras believed the essence of all things derived from number, proportional relationships, and repetitive cycles. Number is the foundation of natural processes and provides the basis for reason. Pythagoras dedicated his life to the service of the divine, and his central concern was the human soul. Pythagoras is said to have made frequent trips to the netherworld where Nigel now finds himself. Just as we only know about Pythagoras through the words of others, in Frank's novel we only learn about Mekes through Max, his next-door neighbor. Considering Mekes means computation, and Max is obsessed with the epistemology of measurement, it makes sense they're neighbors.

The oldest biography of Pythagoras says he journeyed among the Assyrians and Magi. Who were the Magi? Traditional scholarship considered the Magi to be Persian Zoroastrians, but more recent research (Landau, 2011; Mair, 1990) suggests the Magi were a cult of Chinese mystics who traveled the silk routes connecting China and Persia. This link between Pythagoras and Chinese shamanism is deeply satisfying to Frank, who suspects he was Chinese in another lifetime.

In Frank's novel, Dr. Mekes works with a Chinese Magi, Ching Ling Foo, to create the holographic lives we each experience. Ching Ling Foo was an actual turn-of-the-century magician and colleague of Houdini. Foo appears throughout Frank's book as either an elderly associate of

Mekes, or as a stage magician. Although he goes unrecognized in this world, Foo is actually Yeng-wang-yeh, the Chinese god of death who determines the fate of each soul. Nigel believes Mekes and Foo together hold the key to eternal life. Nigel has several encounters with Foo and deals repeatedly with two of Mekes' assistants: A beautiful Chinese woman named Ba (to whom Nigel is briefly married), and Ba's bodyguard, Khu. According to the *Book of the dead*, if a soul wandering the netherworld dies, it's curtains. On two occasions Khu saves Nigel's soul from eternal death. Where Mekes is elusive, Foo is gently instructive, guiding Nigel on journeys to acquire wisdom.

In Frank's novel, Max Besessen and Dr. Distanziert share an apartment, and as the reader may recall from the first chapter, Max routinely hurls Distanziert out the window to his death only to have the analyst reappear in the next scene. Max, Nigel, Raymond and Watson Page are all patients of Dr. Distanziert. Nigel thinks of Distanziert as his tormenting inquisitor. On several occasions Distanziert holds Nigel captive in his private sanitarium and interrogates him under forms of hypnotic sedation in which Nigel remembers past, or dissociated, lives. In the 1960s American psychiatrists employed this technique while treating patients suffering from multiple personality disorder, a condition apparently afflicting Nigel. Other than relentless inquisition, it's never clear what Dr. Distanziert is after.

Nigel also has several encounters with a friend from his college days, Fritz Nietzsche. Sometimes Fritz and Nigel appear to be roommates, which of course they could be since they're both dead. Although they share a deep emotional bond, they argue continually about the nature of reality and life's choices. Fritz tries unsuccessfully to discourage Nigel from his spiritual quest for eternal life, while Nigel considers a pursuit of the divine to be the essence of life.

Throughout the novel, by shifting states of consciousness, Nigel slips through space and time. He becomes an eighteenth-century Chinese warrior, a merchant transporting Chinese silk across India, a detective in turn-of-the century New York City, a Buddhist fighting in the Boxer Rebellion, a marine fighting in the Pacific, and a Nazi killing Polish Jews in World War II. In Frank's novel, these vignettes are presented as past or parallel lives that Nigel is experiencing. Throughout these journeys, Nigel brushes shoulders with a cast of historical characters such as Nietzsche and Ching Ling Foo, Bauhaus architect Walter Gropius, fashion designer Elsa Schiaparelli, Chinese mobster Big-Eared Du, and authors Christopher Isherwood and William Burroughs.

Just as his old friend, Max, is obsessed with Parmenides and Zeno, Nigel's character is shaped by Pre-Socratic conceptions of Pythagoras and Heraclitus who both believed in the immortality of the soul. Nigel continually slips back into past lives just like Pythagoras who claimed to remember four previous lifetimes. In Western philosophy Pythagoras is the origin of the concept of Eternal Recurrence (Eliade, 1954), Frank's model for the cyclical structure of Nigel's experience. Nigel's shape-shifting emerges out of the Unity of Opposites Heraclitus (Kahn, 1979) describes: Nigel is simultaneously alive and dead; he's conscious and unconscious, asleep and awake; he's sane and insane; he's creative and destructive. Nigel embodies the opposites of good and evil. For example, he fights for both the Allies and Axis powers in WWII. Nigel's state of hazy indeterminacy and pursuit of eternal life can be seen as a version of Heraclitus' Doctrine of Flux, where perpetually changing states paradoxically produce permanent forms. In Heraclitus' example, the everchanging flow of water creates the permanent contour of the river. Similarly, Nigel's indeterminacy leads paradoxically to eternal life.

At the conclusion of most chapters in Frank's novel, Nigel encounters a boy spray painting graffiti on the walls of a rundown courtyard. The boy is Frank's teenage son Anders who was a graffiti artist in the counterculture world of New York City. The most recurrent theme of Frank's work is being reunited with his dead son. In these scenes, the painter proudly invites Nigel to appreciate his work. The young man says, "I am your Ka. Come, your journey is almost at its end." Nigel has found his one true guide. The detective and the boy walk up the gangplank onto a large barge filled with excited travelers. The barge departs on its journey west, presumably floating into eternal life.

References

Barnes, J. (1979). *The Presocratic philosophers*. London: Routledge.

Burkert, W. (1972). *Lore and science in ancient Pythagoreanism*. Cambridge, MA: Harvard University Press.

Eliade, M. (1954). *The myth of the eternal return: Cosmos and history*. Princeton, NJ: Princeton University

Huffman, C. (2014). *A history of Pythagoreanism*. Cambridge: Cambridge University Press.

Kahn, C. (1979). *The art and thought of Heraclitus: An edition of the fragments with translation and commentary.* Cambridge: Cambridge University Press.

Kahn, C. (2001). *Pythagoras and the Pythagoreans: A brief history.* Indianapolis, IN: Hackett Publishing Company.

Landau, B. (2011). Lost Syriac text gives Magi's view of the Christmas story. *Biblical Archaeology Review*, Nov/Dec.

Mair, V. (1990). Old Sinitic myag, Old Persia magus, English magician. *Early China*, 15, 27–47. https://www.jstor.org/stable/23351579 (Accessed August 6, 2018)

Chapter 24

Raymond, the Hand of God and Ching Ling Foo

Frank devotes three chapters to Raymond who becomes his most complexly rendered and controversial character. In Frank's novel, the journeys of Nigel and Raymond become entwined. Here's an interpretive sketch of Raymond drawn from bits of information offered in these chapters.

Raymond's parents met as students at Stanford University. In the 1960s Raymond attends a small religious college where he improbably studies art. He's fascinated by the Baroque painter Caravaggio whose work he emulates. Caravaggio created dramatic religious pictures while pursuing a life of murderous violence. The combination of spirituality and murder will emerge as Raymond's lifelong passions. After college Raymond travels to Tibet to join a Buddhist monastery only to be expelled after killing three Maoist soldiers who assault him in a barroom brawl (paralleling Caravaggio's life). This violent act sets the course of his life. Returning to the United States, Raymond enlists in the army to fight in Vietnam.

In 1968 Raymond serves in Project Delta's covert operation 5-68 (Alamo). On a mission he's grievously wounded and loses an eye when his team is ambushed. He's the only American survivor of the firefight, and half blind it takes him eight days to crawl out of the jungle, even though he only has rations and water for five. Near-death, people think it's a miracle he survived, and it literally was.

Raymond's life is permanently altered by his years fighting in Vietnam. He returns home but is haunted by flashbacks and appears to suffer from the same dissociative episodes as Nigel. A brief marriage ends in divorce. His experience in covert military operations is natural preparation for the CIA where he works undercover for many years, occasionally as an assassin.

He's involved in covert actions in South America and Iraq. Disillusioned and world weary after a couple of decades of service in the CIA, he begins a career as a private investigator in New York City. Like Nigel, he works the streets in the tradition of Philip Marlowe.

Having concluded his official relationship with the CIA, after entering private life Raymond joins a group of disaffected retired agents who work directly for the Lord. Now, guided by angels, Raymond serves periodically as God's assassin. But professional killing is literally a dead-end job, and depression is the natural sequel to being so intimately involved in death. Through the act of murder, Raymond becomes inextricably entangled with each of his victims. For Raymond, it's tragically ironic that killing for the Lord is leading him straight to hell. Working at a high professional standard, Raymond tries to manage the emotional aspects of killing by obsessively focusing on the details of his profession. But the deaths weigh on him, and each murder is experienced repeatedly in his mind. So, Raymond becomes a patient of Dr. Distanziert who is both understanding of Raymond's burden and accepting of angels.

The character of Raymond prompts strong reactions among Frank's readers. Because he's the most complex and fully developed of Frank's characters, and perhaps because he's the most crazy and violent, Raymond is a favorite. On the other hand, the sympathetic portrayal of a serial killer guided by angels appears to be Frank's endorsement of madness. This led Frank's editor to recommend a revision to the plot of one of Raymond's murders, which Frank reluctantly made. In other chapters of Frank's book, in addition to his role as professional killer, Raymond serves in the WWII German Third SS Panzer Division Totenkopf which committed numerous war crimes. During the 1944 Warsaw Uprising, Division Totenkopf fought off several Red Army attacks in Warsaw's eastern suburbs. *The journey west* depicts a scene in one of these suburbs where Raymond impassively shoots a young Jewish girl in the back. In these situations, Frank associates Raymond with genocide, living in a primitive realm at the edge of humanity, leaving morality and civilization behind.

Because I see Frank's book as a therapeutic act, I have a sympathetic response to Raymond. I think about Raymond's evilness as a personification of what Frank experienced happening to him. Frank suffered a genocidal act. A random murderous force killed his son. There was no rational or moral basis for it. So, in my reading, Raymond is the face of cancer, a true serial killer guided by God.

One of the ways people respond to trauma is to identify with the force attacking them in an attempt to adapt. This psychological defense is called "identification with the aggressor." Perhaps one of Frank's responses to cancer was to create Raymond. Cancer is vigorous, devoid of emotional conflict, and relentless in the execution of its destructive intent. This is the character Raymond tries to be.

Frank doesn't agree with this interpretation of Raymond. He angrily rejects my suggestion that Raymond represents the cancer that killed Anders. Frank clarifies, "Cancer appears nowhere in my novel!" Frank claims Raymond is simply a longstanding part his personality. Frank is, in part, a genocidal maniac, and in Frank's view, I can't accept this. In his opinion, my difficulty accepting this murderous part of his nature causes me to come up with bullshit concepts like identification with the aggressor. I should grow a set of balls and accept him for who he is. Frank's probably right.

Raymond's principle role in Frank's novel is private investigator. This is how he encounters Ching Ling Foo, and how he becomes involved with Mekes and Nigel. The beautiful Ba, and the elderly Foo, meet with Raymond. They represent Dr. Mekes who wants Raymond to find a dead man named Nigel. Nigel is subtly affecting Mekes' technical work. Of course, Raymond is incredulous. "A dead man disrupting your project? What is this, a ghost story?" he asks dismissively. "Yes," Ba explains, "as impossible as it seems, this is a real life ghost story."

Ba shows Raymond an old photograph of a Nazi taken during the second World War. This is a picture of Nigel, last known as a German SS officer who was killed on the Eastern front in 1944. Ba says Nigel has taken a different face. He's currently living alone in New York in an apartment with his cat, and he's been nosing around the edges of Mekes Technical Services, subtly affecting the gravitational and electromagnetic fields that form the basis of Mekes' work.

Raymond is flabbergasted. His first inclination is to simply dismiss Ba as beautiful but nuts. But then Ba's story gets even weirder. Ching Ling Foo demonstrates to Raymond that some of the wartime flashbacks he's been suffering from have nothing to do with Vietnam. The images in these flashbacks actually come from a different war, WWII. In these scenes Raymond and Nigel are serving together as German soldiers, and they're living through the same traumatic events. Now Raymond is truly incredulous because he realizes the flashbacks Foo describes *have actually been in his mind* for years. The face of the Nazi in the faded photograph *is actually* the comrade of his dreams. This is impossible!

How could Foo even know what's inside his head? How could Foo see his dreams, his visions? Even weirder, how could he have flashbacks of a war he never fought in? "I was *born* in 1944. I couldn't be killing Jews in '44."

Raymond realizes for years he's been having flashbacks of events which occurred before his birth. This is by far the craziest experience of his life. Foo explains:

> Mr. Raymond, it is no mistake that we have contacted you and requested your services. I will be frank with you. You and the man we are interested in are intertwined. Your lives have intersected many times. It is almost as if you are the same person, your Qui are so similar as to be almost indistinguishable. You are our best hope to obtain the information we require.
>
> Yes, Mr. Raymond you are drawn together across time, you have been drawn together in this time. You are the perfect operative; you will come to know all his moves, his thoughts. Always in concert, always in harmony.

Raymond, an experienced assassin, tells Foo, "I will not kill this man for you." Foo just laughs.

> Kill, Mr. Raymond? Why this man is already dead. There is no escaping. It is foretold. I have flipped the coin, rolled the dice, picked the card. . . Mr. Raymond, simply find out what Nigel wants.

Chapter 25

Nigel and Raymond meet their fate as one

Raymond takes the case and Ba gives him his first lead. Nigel has recently contacted an underworld mobster, Fat Man, trying to obtain a translation of an old version of the Egyptian *Book of the dead*. Fat Man is a Manhattan criminal specializing in the sale of stolen Egyptian antiquities. Hot on Nigel's trail, Raymond visits Fat Man who introduces him to Khu, an associate of Mekes. Khu tells Raymond he can lead him to Nigel. But Raymond will need to go with him to the netherworld—a dangerous land—on a quest like no other. It will be the final journey. They'll travel to a place where all things begin and end, the Alpha and the Omega, where everything converges to a singularity. Looking Raymond in the eye, Khu asks, "Mr. Raymond, what have you got to lose?"

In fact, Raymond has nothing to lose. His marriage ended decades ago. He lives alone with a cat. What's he got? Debts, regrets, a bottle of gin and some painkillers. He'd taken the same bet fifty years ago in Vietnam. This is Project Omega all over again, another mission of long-range recon. He'd developed some special skills in Vietnam. Maybe he's the man for the job. Raymond rolls the dice and takes the bet.

Raymond closes his one eye and when he opens it, he's in a dimly lit warehouse. Ching Ling Foo stands before him. Foo says, "I've taken my magic on the road, the wonders of the Orient revealed to Western eyes." With a snap of his fingers he pulls a dove out of the air and releases it. Foo says,

> You have powerful allies and many demons. Your light is bright, but you degrade yourself. You fight the Tao. Here I am Ching Ling Foo, but everywhere I am Yeng-Wang-Yeh. I judge, I judge you. Pass through the door behind me. The tide is high. It is not time to

dwell with the immortals nor is it time for the tenth court, the hell of rebirth. Through the door tests await. Look for the one true guide.

Raymond opens the door and steps into a courtyard. He's surrounded by members of the Chinese Society of Righteous and Harmonious Fists who are practicing Yi He magic boxing. He is dressed like the others in a loose-fitting shirt and a pair of trousers. Men around him are performing ritual forms of martial arts while chanting sacred mantras.

A man approaches him. Bowing at the waist, with his hands forming the symbol of brotherhood, he says, "Welcome master." Raymond responds intuitively. He points his thumb up and the man responds by pointing his little finger down. Raymond counters by tilting his head. Realizing he's performed a ritual greeting without a moment's hesitation, Raymond concludes he must be an insider. He belongs. Raising both fists to the sky, he thinks, "I am a Boxer, a Magic Boxer. I will kill many yang guizi."

The year is 1900 and Raymond is standing on the northern coastal plains of China. He's a member of a White Lotus Buddhist sect which will participate in the Boxer Rebellion. The Boxers are homegrown Chinese nationalists opposed to foreign imperialism and Christian evangelism. They want to purify China by purging it of corrupting foreign influence. Buddhism teaches them their spirits transcend the limitations of material reality. Through spiritual training they will be able to perform extraordinary physical feats. Mind will triumph over matter. In battle Boxers will be invincible to foreign weapons, and at the moment of rebellion a million Spirit Boxers will descend from heaven to join them in repulsing the foreign invaders.

The Boxers disperse, and Raymond walks slowly to his tent. Lying down he wonders why he's a Buddhist Boxer living in China in the last century when he's actually a detective pursuing a man named Nigel in New York City in 2012. Raymond falls asleep. In a dream someone is shaking him awake. Raymond slowly opens his eyes and sees a man kneeling beside him. It's Nigel, the German officer in the photo. "Wake up. You have to get going," Nigel says urgently. Raymond looks at him groggily. Nigel continues,

I came through the door. It's Ching Ling Foo, he's manipulating this dream. You are me but one door behind. I came back to warn you. This iteration is ending. All things will be no more. There is a door, but it's closing. If we stay here, we'll be in a loop of infinite length. Time will have no meaning.

Raymond wakes from his slumber to the sounds of Boxers assembling for battle. It's mid-August and ten-thousand Boxers have laid siege to the foreign legations. But they're no match for the modern weaponry and war making skills of their British, French and German opponents. In the early morning hours, the Buddhist shamans are called together. They collectively chant the sacred mantras to summon the spirit army. The time has come for their collective soul to triumph over matter, for ancient religious tradition to prevail over modern materialism. As dawn breaks the earth shakes and the sky darkens. Perhaps this is a sign.

With renewed faith the Boxers make a final assault. Raymond races forward into battle. An explosion knocks him off his feet, killing many around him. Raymond momentarily loses consciousness. Suddenly Nigel appears kneeling beside him. Nigel pours water over Raymond's face and bald head. Raymond looks up into Nigel's eyes. Is he alive or dead, awake or unconscious? Is this reality or a dream, now or eternity? Is he's waking up dead? Even if he's awake, why is he waking up in a previous century?

Nigel pulls Raymond to his feet saying, "The path is this way, Mr. Raymond. We have done all we can. We'll meet our fate as one." Nigel and Raymond rush forward into battle. There is an enormous crash of thunder and the heavens open. A million Spirit Boxers rain down from heaven to join the battle. Reversing certain defeat, the army of Magic Boxers is victorious. The sky fills with brilliant light and the figure of Ching Ling Foo floats above the earth. With a broad brush he paints the sky with the graffiti of eternity. Raymond and Nigel bow their heads in devotion. The Boxer Rebellion—which in August, 1900, was crushed by a group of European nations—is now victorious. Like a quantum eraser, the course of history is reversed.

Or, was it just a dream?

Chapter 26

Eternal Recurrence

Frank's final chapter, "Heaven and earth," completes his rumination on life after death. The chapter is composed around a spiral motif in which events unfold in a circular fashion always looping back, repeating with subtle variation. Frank's design is influenced by Kurt Godel, Friedrich Nietzsche and Pythagoras. In Godel's rotating universe, time continually loops back upon itself (Goldstein, 2005). Godel created a mathematical model of the age-old conception of Eternal Recurrence which in the Western world is thought to have originated with Pythagoras and was revivified by Nietzsche (Eliade, 1954). The reader recalls in college Nigel developed an enduring friendship with Fritz Nietzsche who we hear saying, "All that's straight lies, all truth is crooked, and time itself is circular." We each eternally return.

At the beginning of the chapter Frank opens a small window into his life, offering a real-life example of recurrence. The chapter begins with Nigel asleep. He briefly wakes to find Ching Ling Foo standing next to his bed. Foo smiles and says, "Mr. Nigel, this has been a pleasant interlude. How long has it lasted, one year, ten years, ten-thousand years?" Nigel wonders why he's seeing Foo. Foo is about transformation. But Nigel is done with that. He's come to the end of time. He's found eternal life. Hasn't he?

Then an uneasy feeling descends upon him. Nigel realizes his world is still changing. There's more to be done. There's no way out. He falls back asleep and briefly dreams of a young boy whispering, "Mom will be alright." This phrase, placed at the beginning of the final chapter, has profound meaning.

A terrible feeling descends upon Frank. Like Nigel, he sees no way out. Frank's wife, Signe, is diagnosed with breast cancer. Next year it will become metastatic. Frank is besieged again: First his son, then his mother, and now his wife. Cancer comes for all three. This is the chapter's first example of recurrence. As Frank writes this chapter, he reads Shakespeare to me, "Once more unto the breach, dear friends, once more." Frank gathers up his strength to face one more cancer, one more death. He summons me to stand with him. I think, "God help Frank," and with these words I encourage our readers to stand with him, too.

Nigel wakes up and feeds his cat. Walking through the living room he notices Raymond sitting on the couch. Raymond asks, "Well, here we are. I'm wondering if you have any ideas."

Nigel responds, "Ideas? I just woke up. I'm still trying to get my hands around what's just slipped through my fingers."

Raymond says,

> Come on, neither one of us are awake. The question is, how do we break out of this timeline, this loop? I, for one, would love to go back to the last iteration. I had money, power and women. I was living the good life. We were Magic Boxers. Now we're back to being a small time private dick, and a tortured soul looking for a way out.

Nigel walks to the door of the apartment and opens it. He sees a few feet of hallway and then a swirling gray mist, nothing more. Nigel returns to the living room, sits down in his armchair and closes his eyes. When he opens them Raymond is gone, replaced by Graf.

Graf is the doppelganger from Frank's chapter about parallel universes. Graf is unknown to Nigel. This is their first acquaintance. Graf explains that instruments used in recent experiments have produced anomalous results traced back to Nigel who is apparently disturbing the electromagnetic field. Like Mekes, Graf senses Nigel is a disruption.

Graf tells Nigel they're witnessing the collision of two universes. Graf explains his continuum is closing down. There are electromagnetic fluctuations moving backwards in time. Graf says, "Mr. Nigel, we are in a closed temporal curve. What is past is present, what is future is past, what is present is future." Nigel is confused. Time has skipped a beat and shifted out of phase. Okay, but what are "fluctuations moving backwards in time?" Sounds like Richard Feynman talking about electrodynamics. Or, John Wheeler's quantum eraser experiments where the future alters the present and the present alters the past. Sounds like a successful Boxer Rebellion reversing history.

Nigel responds with irritation, "What the hell are you talking about? I'm not alive. I'm dead. I'm moving from east to west. Whatever you call it, I want out." Graf invites Nigel to travel with him to a "threshold" where they can move back and forth in time. Graf says, "Causality is a little unstable that close to the event horizon, but it's a good place to confer." Graf and Nigel are instantly transported to the living room of a house in Woodstock where they stand before Dr. Distanziert.

Distanziert, in a three-piece gray flannel suit, sits comfortably in a black Le Corbusier chair. Distanziert says to Nigel, "Sit back and relax. We're here to talk about the delusions of time. And as it works out, we have all the time in the world."

Nigel sees Graf and Watson Page in an adjacent room sitting in front of a bank of monitors displaying a white mist. After keying in a series of instructions Watson turns to Graf and says,

> The probe has been modified and is now moving toward the event. We're witnessing the birth of a new universe. All mathematical bending will never sidestep the impossibility of singularity. There never was a point of zero volume and infinite energy. The second law of thermodynamics is preserved. Quantum gravity effects are giving rise to a new universe expanding and contracting in Eternal Recurrence.

Nigel doesn't understand the mathematical mumbo jumbo. But he figures something must be happening on those monitors. This is weird science.

Dr. Distanziert explains to Nigel that he's a patient in his private sanatorium. Nigel's journeys are facilitated by Distanziert's pharmacological treatment. The doctor says, "You had a breakdown after accidentally killing a young man changing a tire on the side of the road. We've been administering a drug allowing dream states to coexist with reality, bringing you to this point." In a previous chapter it was Watson Page who'd entered Distanziert's sanatorium after killing a young man changing a tire. Now it's Nigel who has killed the boy. Another form of recurrence. Has one person's history slipped into another's life? Or, are Nigel and Watson Page the same person: A multiple personality?

Nigel asks Dr. Distanziert, "What about Raymond, Ba, Khu, Ching Ling Foo, Mekes and the Spirit Boxers?"

Distanziert explains, "Most of them are patients here, some are staff. The man you call Ching Ling Foo is our janitor. You've had conversations with most of them."

Nigel asks about Ba, an alluring source of romantic interest, "Is she crazy?"

Distanziert responds, "She thinks she represents a form of Egyptian afterlife. She believes she's one of the souls that departs a dead body. In reality she murdered her husband. He was abusing her in many ways."

There's a short rap at the door. Three men enter the living room. The first shoots Distanziert in the chest with a tranquilizer dart. He'll be out for several hours and have no memory of this event: A little "time-missing" as Bertha Pappenheim would say.

The three men begin interrogating Nigel about his combat experiences in Special Forces in Vietnam in 1969. Nigel has no memory of these events. The reader realizes it was Raymond, not Nigel, who served in Vietnam. One of the interrogators shows Nigel a photograph of a disheveled Asian man with his hands tied behind his back. He asks, "Do you recognize this man in the photo? His name is Thai Khac Chuyen. Does that name mean anything to you?"

Nigel said, "No."

"Do you recall he was a Project Gamma operative? You took him for a boat ride in the South China Sea and killed him for giving intel to the North Vietnamese."

Nigel seems to remember the eyes of the Asian man in the photo. Was it a dream, or some movie? He remembered standing in the rain in a small boat rocking gently up and down. This Asian man, in a drugged stupor with his hands tied behind his back, was brought out from the cabin below. In the mist, their eyes met. The Asian man's eyes were glassy but filled of terror. He remembers that look of terror. Nigel stares into his milky-brown eye, then shoots him in the forehead.

Nigel opens his eyes. His interrogators are gone but there's a man sitting across from him dressed in a suit under his white lab coat. Nigel recognizes him as Ching Ling Foo. The man introduces himself, "Hello, Mr. Nigel, I'm the assistant director of this facility, Dr. Chin." Foo is playing him. Dr. Chin says, "Let's start this session with something that interests you. It says here you've read a great deal about American baseball in the early twentieth century."

"Cut the crap, Foo," Nigel says aggressively. "What the hell is this about? I was told by Distanziert that you're the janitor."

The man responds,

> Foo? My name is Dr. Chin and I'm here to bring you back, Mr. Nigel. We've been working with you for a while and have made some significant breakthroughs. Focus, Mr. Nigel. There is no Distanziert. He only exists as your tormentor, your interrogator. Just relax and focus on baseball. Tell me something about baseball.

Nigel closes his eyes and experiences an elaborately detailed dream in which he's playing baseball with Ty Cobb and Dutch Leonard in 1925. When he opens his eyes, he's sitting in Mekes' office. Ching Ling Foo is sitting across from him in a gold brocade chair. Foo says,

> Mr. Nigel, it's no mistake that we've contacted you and requested your services. I'll be frank. You and the man we're interested in are intertwined. Your lives have intersected many times. It is almost as if you are the same person, your Qui are so similar as to be indistinguishable. You're our best hope to obtain the information we require.

Nigel screams, "You're the god damn janitor! This is a dream, a delusion." Foo looks calmly into Nigel's eyes. Nigel feels himself sliding down a velvet chute—fade to black.

By this time the reader's mind, like Nigel's, is likely spinning out of control. The reader may be ready to scream. Our grasp of reality is lost, and we're adrift in psychosis. Life is a relentless unfolding of one recursive dream after another, dreams within dreams. Time shifts out of phase, the boundaries of space and time dissolve, and one character's history slides into another's life. At this point my supervisee, Barbara, a dedicated reader of Frank's work, declares with exasperation, "There's nowhere to stand! There's no vantage point from which to interpret these events. What part of this could be real?"

Max, of all people—a fictional creation of Frank—responds:

> Barbara, you sound like Hugh Everett claiming the idea of an 'outside observer' is an illusion. You're right. Frank's questioning the context we use to interpret reality. There's really no outside from which to peer inside. Instead, *we're all inside one unconscious mind*. Now what?

Max turns to me and explains,

> Barbara is in the same quantum soup as Nigel. All Frank's characters are riding Schrödinger's wave, and Barbara's surfing right alongside us. Frank's saying within the unconscious the structure of time and space dissolve, and the boundaries separating him, his characters and the reader are blurry. Frank's asking a serious question, "In the unconscious, where does my imagination end and your reality begin?" The answer is elusive and is the meaning of life itself.

Leaning back, Max says, "Nigel's confusion is a reflection of Frank's anguished uncertainty." It's ironic when any writer, let alone a novice like Frank, is critiqued by his own character. But then, surfing in the curl of Schrödinger's wave gives Max a unique perspective.

Nigel opens his eyes and sees the sensuous figure of Ba approaching. Her alluring beauty makes her an attractive guide. Nigel is a silk merchant delivering products to a wealthy client living in a villa by the sea. Nigel has made this trip across India many times, sometimes accompanied by Ba who is now his wife. On this trip, he's joined by fellow travelers who'll separate from the group at various points along the way. Nigel is disoriented. He has no memory of any of this. Apart from Ba, he's never seen any of these people before in his life. He thinks, "This can't be real." Ba explains,

> Sorry. Mekes recorded this months ago along with a number of other scenes. Yeng-wang-yeh just picked this one. It's your move. Relax. There's safety in numbers and you have all the numbers in the world.

Nigel considers this paradox. If he's living a scene recorded months ago, what choice does he have? There are no choices, no free will. On the other hand, "having all the numbers in the world" sounds like a spectrum of possibilities: Schrödinger all over again. Which is it? Maybe both.

Nigel asks the guide leading the troupe of travelers, "How far to the sea?"

"The sea, sahib?" The guide looks puzzled. "Oh, the distance never changes. The sea is just a thought. You should know that by now."

Nigel tries a different tack. "How long is the trip, how many days and nights?"

"No, no time. No time at all," the guide says smiling. Nigel asks Ba, "What's this guy talking about? He told me the sea is just a thought." Ba responds,

> The sea *is* just a thought. We're all thinking about the sea. The sea is where it all began, and the sea is where we're headed. The sea. You'll lie comfortably and watch the waves roll into shore and you'll doze in the midday heat and I'll make you lunch. It will be a pleasant time and then we'll start the trip again. It'll all be new: the road, the people, the smells, the sounds, the sun, the moon. It will all continue.

Ba touches his arm and Nigel relaxes. Is this destiny? No time, no distance, heading to the sea where life begins, to the sea that's just a thought?

Then Nigel feels the familiar fury stirring in his belly. Anger is his defining characteristic. He's on a quest for eternal life grasping at the ghost of a chance. Can he leave his anger behind? If eternity depends on it, can he accept a temperate life traveling back and forth to an idea?

Looking up Nigel notices leaves falling from trees that don't exist on the Indian subcontinent. A flaw in the set. Should he be concerned? Could this imperfection jeopardize his opportunity for eternal life? Nigel wonders, "Is Mekes asleep at the switch?"

Nigel lays down along the side of the road and falls asleep. He has a familiar dream in which he and Raymond are Nazis, members of the Waffen-SS Division Totenkopf rounding up Polish Jews in a Warsaw suburb. Nigel and Raymond have versions of this dream throughout the novel. Raymond shoots a Jewish girl in the back. Walking over her dead body, Nigel turns her over with his boot. He looks down into her face covered with tangled hair. Nigel briefly opens his eyes and looks up at Ba peering down at him, her dark hair falling around her face. For an instant Ba and the dead Jewish girl are one and the same. He begins to speak but Ba puts a finger to her lips.

Nigel awakes to the red sky of a setting sun. Campfires are lit, and a meal is being prepared. Nigel overhears two men talking. One says, "All is ready. The graves are dug." Nigel is frozen in fear. He tells Ba about this strange conversation. She explains, "These men practice Thuggee and worship the Hindu goddess Kali." Kali is the goddess of time and death. Her followers have created a secret cult to quietly engage in murder. Thugs work in teams infiltrating groups of travelers, usually killing them in their sleep. Nigel asks, "Should I be worried?" Ba responds, "They should hold no power over you." As she speaks, he notices that she's wearing a small death's head amulet around her neck—SS Division Totenkopf. Ba is the embodiment of genocide. Nigel is shaken by feelings of affiliation and betrayal.

Within a minute Nigel is strangled: A cloth slips over his head, a garrote slides around his neck, and a knee shoves into his back. Then, in a world of pure chaos, the pressure around his neck ceases. He falls forward face first gasping for air. He looks up to see Khu subduing the last of the thugs, saving Nigel from eternal death. Nigel calls out to Ba as she evaporates into the twilight. The tables have turned—another recurrence. The Nazi Nigel is himself the victim of genocide.

Nigel hears a small sigh and looks up to see Dr. Distanziert seated next to him. Nigel eases himself up on the black Le Corbusier couch and asks, "How long?" Distanziert looks at him impassively. Nigel thinks, "Silence. Typical psychoanalyst bullshit." Nigel says, "I've had another treatment. I experienced several dreams representing past lives, past events. I'm tired doctor. All this technology, all this pharmacology, what's the purpose?" Distanziert leans forward in his chair, "Do you want a clinical explanation?" Nigel nods.

Dissociative identity disorder manifesting in frequent fugue behavior. You reject who and what you are and continually take on new identities, maintaining your name is the name of a cat you once had as a pet.

Nigel hears a short rap at the door. Three men enter the room. The first shoots Distanziert in the chest with a tranquilizer dart. He'll be out for several hours and have no memory of this event: A little "time-missing" as Bertha would say.

This begins a second recursive interrogation about Nigel's service in Project Omega during the Vietnam War. At first the reader is disoriented, thinking this must be a misprint—believing the pages of Frank's novel have gotten mixed up. Then the reader realizes this iteration is slightly different than the first.

Nigel opens his eyes and looks around. An angel is sitting beside him on the bed. This angel was last seen in Caravaggio's "Saint Matthew and the angel," a painting destroyed in the 1945 bombing of Berlin. Sitting at a table Nigel starts reading a confidential dossier beginning with a report on Project Omega's Special Forces operations in Cambodia in 1970. What's up with this angel? The reader remembers Raymond served in Special Forces and now hangs out with angels.

Nigel believes his life was enlarged and enriched by the Vietnam War. It's the car wreck years later that destroyed him. His son was killed one evening on a highway changing the left rear tire on his Toyota. He was sideswiped. Visibility was bad and the driver who hit him never saw him. Nigel actually met the driver, a college professor. From what Nigel could tell, their lives had followed parallel trajectories. Originally Nigel had wanted to kill him. But the professor was so broken by the accident that murdering him would have been meaningless.

The reader recognizes that, in real life, Dan is the college professor who nearly killed a young man in twilight changing the left rear tire of his broken-down car on the side of the road. Although Frank has no conscious knowledge of this event, he's making another uncanny reference to it. The reader also sees that Watson Page, Nigel, and now Dan, have all been identified as being responsible for the young man's death, a reference to Frank's son, Anders.

Nigel glances back at the bed. The angel's gone. Nigel continues reading. The report describes sightings of angels, and two pages are devoted to a shooter who claimed to see them before and after an assassination. Nigel had worked with this guy in South America and knew him only by his code name, Raymond. Now this shooter has mysteriously disappeared.

The dossier describes a world unraveling. Things just stop working, bits go missing, food spoils, and angels begin appearing everywhere. Nigel wonders if this depiction is accurate or deeply paranoiac. Can he trust this apocalyptic vision of reality, or does the dossier represent the ultimate conspiracy theory? But, there's the angel. This is Nigel's first encounter with an angel. Was the angle real or an apparition? If he can believe in angels, then an angel may lend credibility to this report. The whole thing is unsettling. Nigel needs to get some sleep. He takes two Ativan with juice, lays down and waits for the drug to take effect.

Nigel finds himself standing in a rundown courtyard with walls covered in graffiti. As Nigel scans the walls he's stunned by the luminosity, the shimmering beauty of the colors and forms. He turns toward the hiss of gas and paint caressing the wall. A figure in the shadows is putting the final touches on a piece of spray-painted calligraphy. The painter steps into the light and pulls the breather mask off his face. It's Nigel's son. Smiling radiantly, with a sweeping gesture the young man proudly displays his work for his father's adoring eyes.

Nigel sits up in a bed. He often dreams of his son, but now he wonders if there's a connection between this dream of his dead son and the angel who'd just visited him in waking life. Startled, Nigel realizes someone is sitting in a chair next to his bed. Nigel shouts, "Christ! How'd you get in here?"

It's Graf who Nigel is encountering for the first time. The reader remembers that Nigel had actually met Graf earlier in the chapter—this is another recursive loop. Graf tells Nigel that Watson Page has sent him. Page wants Nigel to be aware of certain scientific measurements. Nigel is in no mood for this. He is angry at Graf for scaring him. Graf ignores Nigel's distress, and calmly explains that he knows why the angels appear and what they mean.

Nigel finds himself back in Woodstock standing before Dr. Distanziert who is sitting in a leather and chrome Le Corbusier armchair, and wearing a gray flannel suit. (By the way, Dan owns eight gray suits.) Distanziert says, "Hello, Mr. Nigel. I'm Dr. Distanziert. Please sit back and relax. We're here to talk about the delusions of time, and as it works out, we have all the time in the world."

Nigel stares at a large villa perched on a sandy cliff overlooking the ocean. Waves rhythmically lap the shore. This is the destination Ba described, a villa by the sea. Next to the villa is a small bungalow in a grove of black bamboo. Nigel walks down stone steps to the bungalow's entrance encased in purple bougainvillea. An ancient Ching Ling Foo opens the door. Nigel enters and meets Ba, her old weathered face as beautiful as ever. Not a word is spoken, yet Nigel is filled with relief. The relentless agitation in his soul disappears. Sitting on a gold davenport, Ba hands him an antique porcelain opium pipe. Nigel takes a pull on the pipe and drifts off.

Nigel's in Venezuela. He and Raymond are working undercover for the Department of Defense, there to assassinate two Venezuelan officials who are spies. This dream is filled with elaborate technical detail. Nigel lures the Venezuelans to Angels Falls for the promised sale of Russian shoulder fired surface-to-air missiles, irresistible bait. SAMs are credited with starting the Rwandan Genocide when one was used to kill its president by shooting down his airliner. From an extremist's perspective, the spectacular result was eight hundred thousand deaths in a hundred days. Talk about national renewal! Nigel and Raymond, working seamlessly, orchestrate a chaotic execution. The killing is easy; getting out alive is the real trick. Using members of an indigenous tribe for cover, Nigel and Raymond perform a perfect escape.

This combat drama ushers in the concluding portion of Frank's final chapter, a kaleidoscopic presentation of six swirling dreams leading to the final scene of the book. While the reader is already aware of the spiral motion of the chapter, now the narrative picks up speed, and the reader's mind begins spinning like a top. The first four dreams have the novel's leading characters climbing aboard a barge to travel presumably across the Nile. In the fifth dream Raymond re-experiences the pleasure of intuitively realizing he's an insider, a member of the Magic Boxers. In the final dream Nigel, Ching Ling Foo and Ba are together again in the bungalow by the sea. They're joined by Dr. Distanziert who brings an end to the dream by announcing, "That's all the time we have for today." These six dreams are a prelude to the novel's final scene.

Nigel awakes with a start in Woodstock. The late afternoon light in the great room seems perfect. He must be mistaken. Something is holding this moment together, something independent of all the equations defining his life.

Something's different. A mist is rolling in off the tree line. Nigel walks into the war room and checks the monitors—a milky mist. Nothing new. The same screens had previously displayed the birth of a new universe. He walks back into the great room and gazes again out the windows. A large Norwegian pine leans and then crashes to the earth in complete silence. He looks down at his cat, Nigel, curled up on the black leather Le Corbusier couch. The cat is unperturbed, almost like he's read the script already.

Nigel looks out the window a third time. Halfway up the hill stands his young son beckoning him. Nigel picks up his cat and together they walk out the door and up the hill. When he reaches his son, they smile radiantly at each other. The young man takes Nigel's arm and leads him away from the house. Nigel's cat jumps from his grasp and runs ahead. Father and son walk through a rundown courtyard and stop to admire the graffiti painted on the walls. Now the infinite sequences of shapes and colors converge making perfect sense. All the despair of life falls away.

Nigel and his son walk down a winding path to a river where a barge awaits. They climb a gangplank flanked by two large cats. When they reach the deck, they're greeted by all the cats Nigel had ever known. His son picks up his best buddy, Steve, a gray and white shorthair. Nigel asks, "Is this another dream? Will I wake up dead?" His son smiles that sweat smile and says, "Welcome home, Dad, welcome home."

Nigel lets it all go slowly, like letting go of a dream when you awake. Feeling a cool breeze gently caress his face, the barge pulls away from the pier drifting toward the setting sun on its journey west.

References

Eliade, M. (1954). *The myth of the eternal return: Cosmos and history*. Princeton, NJ: Princeton University Press.

Goldstein, R. (2005). *Incompleteness: The proof and paradox of Kurt Godel*. New York, NY: W.W. Norton.

Chapter 27

Contemplating convergence

We both dreamt of waking up dead. Frank called the dream a turning point and started writing a story. I began writing about Frank's writing. Frank's first chapter continued our subjective entanglement. The connection between Frank's stories and my life seemed unbelievable, so I wrote to document these uncanny parallels. From the beginning of Frank's novel there are two writers of the same text. In his first chapter, completed before I'd written a word, Max and Distanziert both claim to have written "The myth of mental illness." In his second chapter, Page and Graf are both authors of an article entitled "Conversations with Schrödinger's Cat." We were writing twins.

In the fall of 2012 Frank finished his book, *The journey west*. Through his imaginative act of fiction, I believed Frank described a journey through his unconscious as he struggled to recover from the death of his son. Frank's creative writing played an important role in his therapy. The entangled relationship of his characters, Nigel and Raymond, appeared to represent our therapeutic relationship, and by the end of his novel they'd joined forces to meet their fate as one.

By the summer of 2013, I assembled my writing into what I hoped could become a book about Frank's book. I had about one hundred and twenty pages that I began to organize into chapters. Some of these chapters were fairly complete, but others were unfinished. I figured I'd produced half a book. I'd spent a year studying the quantum physics origins of Frank's stories, and another year researching Mesmer, hypnosis and the development of psychoanalysis. I'd reached a tipping point. Creating a book began to feel real.

Now I was confronted with the reality that I was writing an in-depth study of Frank's novel without his knowledge or consent. This was a problem. My analysis of his novel wasn't clinical writing in the sense of describing sessions. I was writing an analysis of a book Frank was trying to publish. On the other hand, I was interpreting Frank's novel as an inter-subjective therapeutic event and, of course, that's not how he presented it. His therapy was entirely private. So, writing about the therapeutic aspects of his story was an ethical problem.

At the very beginning, I spoke to Frank about my desire to present his case in a lecture. I said his struggle to recover from the death of Anders was valuable for others to learn about. Recovery from death was a universal aspect of human suffering, and his experience was an important story to tell. Frank agreed.

I asked how he'd like his and his son's identities to be disguised, and I made several suggestions which he rejected. He wanted his story told straight. He wanted people to know how much Anders had endured in his struggle to stay alive. Frank said,

> Listen, I understand in your profession this is an issue for you. But what are people going to learn about me? That my son died, that I'm depressed and sometimes I want to kill myself. Wouldn't anyone feel that way? I should be worried about that?

Months later I again talked to Frank about the possibility of presenting his case at a conference on psychoanalysis and creativity. I wanted to present a paper on the role his writing had played in his mourning. Frank believed his creativity had been therapeutic, and he agreed that sharing his story would be valuable. In fact, there was a particular aspect of his writing he wanted me to highlight.

In the final months of Anders' life, his son had been in a neighborhood bar with a couple of friends. At this stage of his illness Anders' face was disfigured by a large tumor and the loss of one eye. A drunk at the bar made an insulting statement about Anders' appearance. The bartender, who knew both Frank and Anders, escorted the drunk out. Later, when Frank heard this story, he was so angry he wanted to kill this man. For weeks Frank was obsessed with a fantasy of finding and killing him. Then Frank wove his fantasy into a story he was writing. He described in brief but vivid detail the act of stabbing the man to death. Frank murdered him in his imagination. Mysteriously his obsession disappeared, and he never thought of this man again. This change was so remarkable Frank thought others should know about the transformative power of imagination.

As I worked privately on my analysis of Frank's novel, I felt increasingly dishonest. The deeper I got into interpreting the details of his story the more deceptive it felt to be writing behind Frank's back. I worried about how this deception was affecting Frank's therapy. This is a universal problem in writing psychoanalytic case reports. Writing and presenting case reports, almost always without the patient's knowledge, is the foundation of psychoanalytic education. Indeed, the case report is the centerpiece of all psychoanalytic literature from Freud forward. Traditionally, the patient is disguised to protect his or her identity, but of course this is fundamentally deceptive. In fact, in a psychoanalytic case study "no details given should be assumed to be factually accurate" (Kantrowitz, 2006, p.33). This lack of veracity means this clinical literature can't be used in scientific research, undermining psychoanalysis' claim to be scientific. This double deception, in which the patient and reader are both deceived, is embedded in psychoanalytic history and is accepted as normal.

Nonetheless, the more I wrote the more this deception seemed to be a betrayal of Frank and of our therapeutic work together. More specifically troubling, as I wrote each day, I felt I was engaging in a form of artistic dishonesty. I knew my writing would hold a reader's interest because Frank's stories were so intriguing. His creative invention was the compelling basis of my writing. So, in this sense, I was stealing his creation which seemed exploitative.

Having concluded I actually intended to write a book about Frank's novel, these were the problems writing such a book created:

1 Writing an in-depth study of Frank's writing, without his knowledge, was deceptive and left me wondering what effect this was having on him and our work together. Working this way didn't seem good for either of us.
2 It was impossible to engage in a detailed analysis of Frank's novel while disguising it to protect Frank's identity. Disguise, the traditional psychoanalytic device, wasn't a possibility.
3 To describe Frank's novel as a therapeutic event, without his permission, was unethical. I needed to obtain his consent, and therefore I needed to involve Frank in my writing.

4 But, I was uncertain what effect reading my writing would have on Frank. During the past century, there are many examples of patients being injured by the experience of reading their psychoanalysts' descriptions of them. The origin case of psychoanalysis is a perfect example.

Breuer's patient, Bertha Pappenheim, went on to become a prominent social figure advocating for women's rights. She was the founder and president of the League of Jewish Women which grew to a membership of fifty thousand, and she ran an orphanage for unwed mothers and their children. Her relative and first biographer, Dora Edinger, believed Bertha had read Breuer's account of her in *Studies on hysteria* (Freeman, 1990). According to Edinger, Bertha publicly disparaged psychoanalysis. She "violently opposed any suggestion of psychoanalytic therapy for someone she was in charge of," and destroyed records of her life during the period of her illness (Borch-Jacobsen, 1996, pp.27–28). When someone suggested one of her wards would benefit from psychoanalysis, she exclaimed vehemently, "As long as I live, psychoanalysis will never penetrate my establishment" (Guttmann, 2001, p.120). In 1953, when Ernest Jones identified Bertha as Anna O., her family accused him of defamation.

Bertha's negative attitude toward psychoanalysis suggests she doubted the contribution Breuer's treatment made to her recovery, and that she felt exploited by the publication of her case. What was a triumphant publication for Sigmund Freud, used to launch his psychoanalytic enterprise, came at the cost of injuring Bertha Pappenheim. With this in mind, I felt it was important to mitigate any damage my writing would have on Frank.

5 Before I began writing about Frank, I'd been studying the psychoanalytic literature on the topic of writing about patients. For years I'd been supervising students writing single case research papers in a psychoanalytic institute. These experiences contributed to my belief that my writing should have a therapeutic effect on my patient (Gerson, 2000). A paper written by psychoanalytic researcher, Robert Stoller, deeply affected the way I thought about this issue. Stoller studied gender and sexuality and some of his research was based on extensive analyses of his patients. Over time, Stoller (1988) developed the position that "we would do better ethically and scientifically if throughout the process of writing and publication, we let our patients review our reports of them" (p.371).

Stoller made his writing and research part of his patient's psychotherapy. As Stoller would write about his patients he would give them his analyses and ask them to edit and revise them. He asked patients to delete or change whatever they wished, and some patients excised entire chapters of books to protect themselves, their family and friends. Stoller wouldn't submit anything for publication that hadn't been approved by his patient. Significantly, Stoller recommended making this review process a part of ongoing therapy so that any injurious aspect of his writing could be handled immediately as it arose.

Once the case was published there was a continued need to respond therapeutically to the patient's reaction to the publication. What might have seemed like a great idea before publication could look very different to the patient once his or her case was actually in print. Stoller believed that only by involving patients in the entire writing and publication process, and by working with them therapeutically throughout, could patients be protected from harm. I decided, if I moved ahead with my writing about Frank, I'd attempt a similar approach.

6 Taking the step to involve Frank in my writing was contrary to my approach to psychoanalysis. Basically, I'd be altering our therapeutic contract by inserting myself into his treatment. If I took this step, I'd be shifting attention from him to me. I'd be forcing Frank to respond to my desires and interests. Even bringing up the subject of my writing would force Frank to make a decision, to take an action. Frank could decide not to grant his permission to write about him and his novel, but then he'd have to deal with the emotional consequences of that decision. Even to put Frank into this position seemed unfair to him. It seemed like I'd be bullying him into complying with my request, which felt exploitative. Should he sacrifice some quality of his treatment to help me out?

I felt guilty about forcing my interests upon him. This internal conflict made me reluctant to talk to Frank about my writing. I was also uncomfortable with practicing psychoanalysis in a way that diverged from beliefs I'd accumulated over thirty years. By collaborating on this writing project, I'd be departing from a longstanding, empirically proven psychological treatment. Frank's therapy would become experimental.

7 Was it ethical to encourage Frank to participate in a therapeutic experiment to accommodate my wish to write about our work together? Why should he take the risk? Was it right for me to expose him to risks that may emerge during such an experiment? I liked to experiment. It felt exciting and alive. In fact, my approach to psychoanalysis was to see it as an ongoing experiment. But this was an experiment with significant consequences.

If I involved Frank in my writing, I'd be crossing several professional boundaries, and psychoanalysts take a dim view of boundary violations. In my ruminations over this problem I was helped by Emanuel Berman's (1997) assessment of the value of clinical experiments involving professional boundaries: "To keep psychoanalytic treatment alive, and to render it more effective, we need innovative experiments. *Such experiments may require attempts to reassess our conception of boundaries. Defining innovative approaches as boundary violations may delegitimize them and support barren conservatism*" (p.570).

8 Involving Frank in this writing project would have a negative impact on my future as a psychoanalyst. To work with Frank in a collaborative writing project like Stoller recommended would subject me to criticism by many of my colleagues. In their view, such an act would so fracture the traditional psychoanalytic frame, they'd be justified in subjecting me to a fierce negative reaction. I'd be ostracized, kicked to the fringes of the psychoanalytic community.

Nonetheless, I recognized that a large part of the negative reaction I'd encounter was the product of the deadening conservatism Berman described. While I didn't know how to approach this issue with Frank, I knew doing nothing to conform to these conservative views was a mistake.

9 The therapeutic aspects of Frank's novel dealt with how his mind and mine became entangled. To demonstrate this entanglement meant I'd be disclosing intimate details of my life. This is a serious issue for psychoanalysts where protecting their anonymity is as important as protecting the patient's confidentiality. My disclosures would restrict Frank's freedom to say whatever came to mind. Of course, Frank was

already engaging in self-censorship based on his own interests and what he concluded my interests to be. So, it was unclear how my self-disclosures would affect his freedom as a patient. But this was a consideration.

10 How would involving Frank in my writing project affect his transference? What would be the effect of revealing our remarkable unconscious connection? While Freud believed bringing the unconscious into consciousness was a goal of treatment, I was less certain. I worried that revealing the uncanny nature of our therapeutic relationship might ruin it. On the other hand, I concluded that not disclosing the mysterious telepathic nature of our relationship would be part of the broader social resistance to acknowledging the reality of these events. Just as writing behind Frank's back felt like an unhealthy act of deception, not acknowledging the telepathic nature of our relationship was part of an equally unhealthy act of denial.

Certainly, the effect of making Frank aware of these unconscious qualities of our relationship couldn't be predicted. Should I remain silent if I couldn't predict the effect this would have upon him? Or, was a belief in the ability to make such a prediction really an illusion, and the best I could do was to proceed on faith? Overall, I believed my writing would have a positive effect on him. But I wrestled with the realization that this could be a self-serving delusion.

11 While I focused almost exclusively on the negative consequences of involving Frank in my writing, I also recognized there would be benefits for his treatment. I expected Frank would respond favorably to our work as a team. I envisioned Frank and me as real life versions of his characters Nigel and Raymond, Page and Graf, Max and Distanziert, and I fantasized about publishing both our books together in a single volume.

Most obviously, Frank would be deeply affected by my serious involvement in him and his creation. This would be therapeutic for Frank. In fact, I believed involving Frank in my writing—in essence to write the story together—could be an exquisite therapeutic achievement. I recognized the source of criticism I'd encounter derived from Freud's one-person therapeutic model. In its original form, this treatment model called for the psychoanalyst to function like a surgeon; to remain an aloof, unemotional, fully objective interpreter of the patient's experience. For Freud, emotional involvement with a patient was dangerous and contaminating. If the analyst had a significant emotional reaction to the patient, Freud believed it was the result of continuing pathology in the analyst's personality. This treatment model viewed the patient and analyst as independent, solitary individuals and the therapeutic encounter as dialectic and hierarchical.

If, however, we adopted the therapeutic model proposed by Frank's novel, that is, if we considered Frank and me to be a single therapeutic unit possessing "one mind," then writing the story together could be seen as confirmation of that reality. In fact, this would be a true expression of a "one-person" model. On the other hand, was this simply an elaboration of my self-serving delusion? Was I constructing a theoretical rationale to help me do what I want, to write the book?

I struggled with these issues for a year. Although I was uncertain, I concluded I had to discuss my writing with Frank, sooner rather than later. If I actually wanted to write this book, I felt that I had to make it a collaborative effort. To do otherwise seemed unethical and damaging to Frank's therapy. I felt that I had to discuss this with Frank, but I didn't know where it would take us.

References

Berman, E. (1997). Mutual analysis: Boundary violation or failed experiment? *Journal of the American Psychoanalytic Association*, 45, 569–571.

Borch-Jacobsen, M. (1996). *Remembering Anna O.: A century of mystification*. New York, NY: Routledge.

Freeman, L. (1990). *The story of Anna O.* New York, NY: Paragon House.

Gerson, S. (2000). The therapeutic action of writing about patients: Commentary on papers by Lewis Aron and Stuart A. Pizer. *Psychoanalytic Dialogues*, 10(2), 261–266.

Guttmann, M. (2001). *The enigma of Anna O.: A biography of Bertha Pappenheim*. Wickford, RI: Moyer Bell.

Kantrowitz, J. (2006). *Writing about patients: Responsibilities, risks, and ramifications*. New York, NY: Other Press.

Stoller, R. (1988). Patients' responses to their own case reports. *Journal of the American Psychoanalytic Association*, 36, 371–391.

Chapter 28

Talking to Frank

I decided to tell Frank about my writing and request his participation. During a session Frank described collaborating with a friend on a musical composition. I used this as a segue to bring up our possible collaboration. I told Frank I had been writing about his novel as his therapeutic response to his son's death. Now I was thinking of organizing what I'd written into a book. I wanted to work on this book with him, but to do so would alter his therapy. Frank said he was interested in discussing the project.

I told Frank I expected such a collaboration would affect his therapy in many ways. I was uncertain about benefits which might emerge, but I was sure about some negative effects for him. My anticipation of these made me uncomfortable. I believed I had to explain to him what I considered to be the therapeutic losses for Frank to make a fair decision about whether to proceed.

I told Frank he'd discover things about me that would likely cause him to censor himself. He'd have less freedom to say whatever came to mind. Time would be taken during sessions to discuss this project which would deprive him of therapy he'd otherwise receive. I'd be introducing ideas and feelings into his treatment that were completely unbidden by him. I would be imposing these upon him, and he'd feel compelled to respond. To an unknown extent, this project would alter the direction of his treatment. I pointed out that this collaboration would be unorthodox. We'd be departing from a traditional form of psychoanalytic psychotherapy. This would be an experiment with unknown risks to both of us. It would be like Raymond and Nigel traveling through the netherworld together. Connecting my writing project with Frank's characters, Nigel and Raymond, appeared to affect how Frank responded. I presented my writing as a natural extension of his novel, and I appealed to his desire to be part of a team.

Frank's only reservation involved money. Frank wondered whether he should pay for this sort of treatment. I said this was an excellent question. It was unclear how the project would unfold, but my goal was to incorporate the project into his therapy. For this reason, I believed he should pay for it. However, it was an open question that we could continue to discuss because we didn't know what would happen. An alternative was to try to separate the writing project from the therapy. We could meet separately at no charge to discuss only the writing, but this wasn't my first choice. I told Frank I hoped to incorporate my writing into his therapy in small bits just as he had done with his writing. I'd follow the model he'd introduced.

As we discussed the ways Frank's treatment might be affected by this project, it became apparent how uncertain it was. How would learning more about me might affect his therapy? Frank couldn't say. How would knowing about me alter his freedom to speak in the sessions? For example, if he discovered I held particular religious views, would that alter what he felt comfortable saying about religion? Frank didn't think this was significant. He cited examples of two close friends who held political views he considered ridiculous, but this didn't affect the deep connection felt between them. How would his participation in this project affect his therapy? In general, because it would involve rereading or reinterpreting his story, it seemed like a good idea. He expected to benefit from it.

What about the unorthodox nature of this undertaking? Was he concerned that his therapy would take an uncertain experimental path, one which many therapists wouldn't recommend? Frank said that he felt psychiatry needed a wake-up call. Psychiatry had blindly allied itself with a pharmaceutical industry driven by for-profit science producing suspect results. Psychiatry had lost sight of the fact that psychological healing is based on meaningful human interaction. Frank thought of his writing as a spiritual undertaking. But the dehumanizing materialism of psychiatry denied the role of spirituality in health. Frank suggested our project could become an example of a healthier form of therapy. Frank said actions I considered "experimental" only seemed unusual because of the misguided therapeutic community in which I worked.

Frank asked whether our two stories would be published together in one book. I said that that would be ideal, but we were a long way from having a finished product, and ultimately it would depend on the publisher. Really, who knew if we'd even get to that point? I said, no matter what, we would be co-authors of whatever I was writing. Furthermore, if there were ever any financial profit from this project, we should split it equally. Frank liked the idea of collaboration but said jokingly that I'd have to do the Charlie Rose interview alone. I told him no way, fifty-fifty meant I expected he'd be doing half the talking.

I told Frank the most important thing about this project was its effect on him and his therapy. It was uncertain what impact this project would have on him, and we'd have to make that a continual focus in his therapy. If the process seemed to affect him negatively, we could stop at any time. But if we decided to start this journey together there was no returning to where we were today. Frank likened our position to the many figures in his story who find themselves standing at a door, knowing that passing through this portal will alter the course of their lives. We were at the same point of deliberation. Stepping through this door was a one-way ticket. There'd be no turning back. Just like every character in Frank's novel, we stepped forward into an uncertain future.

Chapter 29

The Project begins

I gave Frank a copy of my first chapter, "I woke up dead." Frank said
he'd read it and email me his response prior to our next session. Frank
wanted his reactions recorded before any discussion colored his views.
He wanted an honest account of his experience. This sparked the idea
that a portion of the book should be documentation of our collaboration.
Perhaps our book should weave together three layers: His story, my historical accounts of psychoanalysis and quantum physics as a basis for
analyzing his story, and our collaboration. While I liked the idea of having Frank's written comments to document our partnership, I didn't like
Frank feeling obliged to write anything. Frank, on the other hand, was
excited about participating in what he called "The Project."

I eagerly awaited Frank's written reaction to "I woke up dead." It
arrived the day before our next appointment.

> I have read through the chapter three times.
> First Read:
> I did not connect with the ideas expressed in the chapter. As I
> often do, I focused on the little things first, like the name Al, which
> I do not like and the character of Al next, seeming to miss most of
> what was transpiring in the rest of the chapter. [In the original draft
> of the chapter I named Frank "Al" to disguise his identity.] I
> thought Al came off as smug, an asshole, a pathetic man adrift with
> childlike beliefs. I did not empathize with him and was embar-
> rassed that this was the persona I project. Unconsciously, I then
> proceeded to minimize the growing symbiosis that is described. I
> felt confused and shocked.

There is a strong element of The cabinet of Dr. Caligari *that weaves through my perception of the patient/analyst relationship. In the film, Francis goes to Holstenwall's local insane asylum to ask if there has ever been a patient there named Caligari, only to be shocked to discover that Caligari is the asylum's director. Understand my reaction when, in my case, the situation is reversed. I went to the local insane asylum to see if Max's psychoanalyst is the director only to find out that he is a patient. So, I shared Francis' shock, thereby rejecting almost all of the subsequent discussion. The very fact that the analyst was revealed to be symptomatic, as unsure and living with guilt, added to my shock. It was an image of Caligari in a straitjacket, and it was an iteration of reality that was frightening.*

Second Read:

Before I began reading, the discussion I had with the analyst the week before comes into focus. Some of the analytical quotes from the chapter play out before me, drifting forward from my unconscious. The veil has been lifted. The analyst stands before me: Ecce Homo. I remember seeing pictures posted on his Facebook account, showing him in a group setting dressed as I imagine he does each weekend. He had a little leather holster attached to his belt. I had a peak.

In light of the tragedy revealed from the analyst's childhood, how can my fascination with fire arms be expressed? I have begun to regret the endless talk about weapons and the feel of a gun in my hands. I begin to project my shame onto Al, whom I hate already.

As I read, I ignore the frailty of Al and step through to a new reality. I cannot associate myself with Al. Am I another figure, partially drawn? Is Al the reality, the sum total of who I am? I reject the notion. Yet Al represents the patient's face, the mask worn in the analyst's office. I finish the chapter once again. The analyst appears now seated across from me as I lay on the chesterfield with unlaced wingtips.

Third Read:

I focus on the end of page three: "I wondered about the coincidence of Al ending up with me as a therapist." Much of the rest of the chapter is devoted to the subsequent "dream of waking up dead." There are several interpretations of the dream. Coincidence: It started with the first step through the front door of the analyst's office. Coincidence: Through a friend, a recommendation is made. Then it starts with the first step through the front door of the analyst's office.

Jung believed that many experiences that are coincidental in terms of causality suggest the manifestation of parallel events or circumstances in terms of meaning, reflecting this governing dynamic. The idea of the first event, the choosing of a therapist, and the second, the dream, cannot be explained in terms of causality. The concept that covers these events is true to Jung's idea of synchronicity. As the story unfolds in time, time and space are bent, distorted. So, the two events do not, by nature, need to be simultaneous in time. It is not in a brief psychosis that the analyst observed a patient Ben as a young boy beside him, but in a brief convergence of another space/time. The equations have all been calculated and verified well before Graf meets Watson. It is quite possible that Watson remembers it as an event yet to occur.

The doctor and I are exploring new avenues of treatment. So much is happening on the quantum level. The facts that these events appear in some logical time flow is misleading. They have happened before and at the same time have yet to happen. Our relationship is forever changed. It was as the analyst predicted. I was fearful, angry and confused at first. Just maybe he has seen these events before.

I was shaken by Frank's words. I read his *First Read* twice and then his *Second Read*. I was upset by Frank's negative reaction to how I had depicted him. Strangely, I laughed broadly. I thought, "It couldn't have been worse." We'd begun The Project in the worst possible way. Why would this cause me to laugh? Though I had a knot in my stomach, I also felt calm and self-assured. My laugh seemed to erupt from the juncture of these divergent feelings.

I read Frank's *Third Read*, and then got up from my computer and walked away. I busied myself with something trivial. This was a lot to take in. About ten minutes later I came back and read through Frank's response again, focusing more on his second and third reading. I liked the way Frank rejected my depiction of him "as the sum total of who I am." Frank had concluded what I had written might be an accurate description of how I saw him in the office, but this wasn't who he really was. This seemed perfectly true, certainly more completely true than what I had written. This confirmed the value of adding Frank's voice to the book, making this project a true collaboration.

I noted that with each successive reading, Frank's reaction relaxed and expanded. In his *Second Read* Frank seemed to recover from the disorienting image of me as symptomatic, and from the narcissistic injury caused by my description of him. Frank concluded his *Second Read* with the playful image of the analyst sitting across from him as he "lay on the chesterfield with unlaced wingtips." The straitjacket image of *First Read* evolved into unlaced wingtips of his *Second Read*. This image of unlaced relaxation was excerpted from his novel and placed into the middle of his response to my writing. Frank was mixing his writing with my own. Our stories were playfully intertwined. This was just what I'd hoped for.

Frank's *Third Read*, which focused on synchronicity, causality and distortions of space and time, was deeply reassuring to me. Frank concluded this section with the sentence, "It is quite possible that Watson remembers an event yet to occur." Frank could have no conscious awareness that the next bit of writing I intended to share with him were my two chapters "Convergence" and "Local time." In "Local time" I struggle with the idea that I remembered a future event, and the even more impossible idea that Frank telepathically acquired my unconscious memory of that event and wrote about it two months before I experienced it. So, when Frank concludes *Third Read* with the phrase, "Watson remembers an event yet to occur," I was convinced he was "all-in." Frank's unconscious fully endorsed this writing project and eagerly anticipated receiving the next installment. Or, perhaps he'd already read it!

I was certain we were doing the right thing. I'd reacted to Frank's *First Read* with the feeling "it couldn't be worse." Now I believed we were on the right path. As my confidence expanded, I was reminded of my hearty laugh which appeared to erupt from the intersection of fear and self-assurance. My attention shifted to the last sentence of Frank's *Third Read*. He wrote, "Just maybe he has seen these events before." Was this the basis of my self-assurance? Had I seen the future?

When we met the next morning, I asked Frank about his negative reaction to my portrayal of him. Frank said that he hated the character "Al," starting with the name. He also hated the name, "Robert," which I had given to his son Anders. I asked if there were specific qualities about Al he'd like me to change. Frank couldn't think of anything. He didn't like the overall sense of the character who represented him. Frank didn't feel sympathetically disposed to Al. I asked Frank if he'd rewrite the character to create a more accurate version of himself. Frank said he'd change nothing. He thought it was important to have two different views of his character. As long as his hatred of Al was noted, that was fine with him.

Frank believed a realistic depiction would only be achieved by presenting multiple perspectives. Besides, his problem with Al could be an expression of his negative view of himself. Frank talked about shameful things he'd done. These memories pained him. He punished himself internally when recollecting them.

Frank concluded there were two Franks. There was the full-bodied Frank he knew himself to be. Then there was the abbreviated Al I'd described. Although this persona was my creation, Frank suggested this character might actually be the person he brought to our sessions. I asked Frank again if he'd like to change anything in my description of him. He was opposed to that. It was important that both Franks were accounted for.

Frank said he now regretted his talk about guns. He suspected guns must be an upsetting topic for me. I told him suicide was troubling, but guns didn't bother me. If he *had* a gun I'd be upset.

Then there was the issue of me being a person with a disturbing past. This came as a shock to him. He felt he'd reversed positions with me. Usually the analyst is a shadowy figure, barely visible. In fact, that is how I'd appeared. But now, I was in clear view and he was shadowy. Because he rejected the persona of Al, the real Frank had slipped into the shadows.

At the end of the session I gave Frank a copy of my chapters "Conversations with Schrödinger's Cat" and "Local time." He said he'd follow the same procedure of emailing me his response prior to our next session. On the day before our session Frank's email arrived. It began:

Quantum entanglement on a macro level? "The quanta of our thoughts"—is it possible to speak in these terms?

There is a debate among neuroscientists about theories of consciousness. A number of theories are electromagnetic in nature. One of the explanations of how consciousness arises is Quantum Brain Dynamics. We now know that electrical synapses are more common in the central nervous system than previously thought. Neurons firing create an electromagnetic field, and it is this electromagnetic field that creates a representation of the information contained in the neurons (McFadden, 2002). The physicist, Herbert Frolich, postulated that since the brain is 70% water, the electric dipoles of the water molecules constitute a quantum field. This quantum field interacts with quantum coherent waves generated by the biomolecules to form

*consciousness. The cognitive process, the neural process, and infor-
mation transmission all become items to consider in the story
Conversations with Schrodinger's Cat.*

I was impressed by Frank's interest in the intersection of quantum physics
and consciousness. I knew nothing about this literature. I looked up the
McFadden paper online and read it. The paper is complex and disorienting, and I struggled to understand it. Here's a synopsis:

Johnjoe McFadden (2002) proposes a model of quantum consciousness based on the electromagnetic field surrounding the brain. The
human brain contains one hundred billion electrically active neurons
which together generate an electromagnetic field. McFadden argues that,
instead of focusing on the neuron as the basis for information creation
and transmission, we should pay attention to the electromagnetic radiation that neuronal activity creates. McFadden urges us to see the conceptual advantages of an electromagnetic field theory of consciousness. In
McFadden's model of mind, perceptions, thoughts and feelings exist as
waves of electromagnetic radiation, and the distinction between brain
and mind is based on this distinction between neurons and the electromagnetic field surrounding them. McFadden's paper was filled with
complicated science supporting his claim, evidence I'm unable to evalu-
ate. Nonetheless, I realized this was familiar territory. Television and
radio are based on information encoded, transmitted and received via
electromagnetic radiation. Vision—as an artist my most treasured form of
perception—is based on my eyes' reception of electromagnetic radiation
called light.

It's at this electromagnetic level that quantum effects might influence
mental life. What a conception: Thoughts, feelings, and memories are patterns of electromagnetic radiation. Okay, but does the mental entanglement Frank and I seem to experience become more comprehensible if we
think of our thoughts as intersecting waves of radiation? Can this model
of mind as electromagnetic radiation explain how I could be in two places
at once—how I could be in Babylon when I step onto my porch in
Bellport? Maybe. In McFadden's model, *mind is like light.* When a photon
of light exists in a wave form, it can be in two places at once, so maybe
my mind can be too. Would an electromagnetic field theory of mind offer
an explanation for the strange way time appears in Frank's stories? If
space and time are two unified aspects of reality, and if my mind could be

in two places at once, then I could also be simultaneously in two times, for example, the present and the future. Okay, this model of mind seems to make such things possible.

Finishing McFadden's paper, I was struck by the similarity of his argument with the views of Mesmer two hundred years earlier. Mesmer conceived of a vital life force being rhythmically transmitted as waves through an invisible magnetic field surrounding and permeating each of us. By analogy, just as McFadden shifts our attention from the neuron to the field of radiation it produces, Mesmer tried to shift our attention from our bodies to the magnetic radiation we produce, transmit and receive.

Frank continued:

Who cares about the times our consciousness warns of danger and it does not come to pass? I scatter a thousand seeds, statistically speaking, to watch a few flowers grow.

Unconscious perception? We are postulating the quantum wave moves backwards as well. There can be a reversal in the direction of information transmission. Future events are past events that become present events. "If I'd only known what I know now." Is this a self-fulfilling prophecy?

"I woke up dead." The fact that an incident involving the changing of a tire plays out in two different states, is one state influencing another? Two minds, one thought? Did the consciousness of the coherent waves created by the information contained in one set of neurons influence the consciousness of the other? In a thought experiment (Ma et al., 2012) the decision whether two particles were in an entangled or an inseparable quantum state can be made even after these particles have been measured and may no longer exist. The future has affected the past. Maybe all of this is too far-fetched, too fantastical, or possibly a total misunderstanding of quantum physics. Maybe not.

"I don't understand you," Alice said. "It's dreadfully confusing."

"That's the effect of living backwards," the Queen said kindly. "It always makes one a little giddy at first—"

"Living backwards!" Alice repeated in great astonishment. "I never heard of such a thing!"

"—but there's one great advantage in it, that's one's memory works both ways."

> *"I'm sure* mine *only works one way,"* Alice remarked. *"I ca'nt [sic] remember things before they happen."*
>
> *"It's a poor sort of memory that only works backwards,"* the Queen remarked.

I was surprised and delighted by Frank's references to quantum theories of consciousness, to quantum eraser experiments, and to *Alice in wonderland*. The way I appeared to "remember things before they happened" such as my flat-tire experience on my drive to the train station, and the way Frank's story seemed to record this experience months before it occurred, had had an enduring effect on me. This experience had completely undermined my confidence in knowing my place in the world. It was dreadfully confusing. Perhaps, as the Queen said, this was the effect of living backwards. Frank's concluding reference to Lewis Carroll's (2000) *Alice in wonderland* gave me the feeling of being deeply understood. Actually, I did feel a little giddy, lighter, and a little less burdened by uncertainty.

When Frank arrived for his appointment the next morning, I was very happy to see him. I felt like Raymond to his Nigel. We were doubles, kindred spirits. During the session Frank described two events from the previous week which affected on how he thought about The Project. First of all, Frank's wife (a physician) and a longtime friend both thought working on The Project would be good for him. His friend George called it an ideal form of therapy: Frank and his writing were taken so seriously that he and his therapist were working on a book about it! What could be more validating and supportive? Frank said, "As far as George is concerned, this is the best thing since sliced bread."

Then Frank described a disturbing dinner conversation with a family friend who was an attorney. When Frank's wife described his working together with his therapist on a book about Frank's story, the attorney was outraged. In the view of the attorney, this was completely unethical. At the very least, Frank's therapist was violating standards of professional conduct. Not wanting to get into an argument that might spoil dinner, Frank didn't say much. But the attorney's harsh reaction affected him. As far as he could see, working on The Project seemed good for him. His wife and friend concurred. So why did this attorney, who Frank liked and had known for years to be a very nice person, have such a critical reaction?

I reminded Frank that what we were doing was unorthodox, and that many people would be critical. "This will upset a lot of people for many reasons," I said. Like Frank, I was shaken by the attorney's assessment. Frank said,

> Sitting there thinking about it, I realized this guy is risking a lot by working on this project with me. He's really taking a chance. He could damage his career. And I thought, this guy has always had my back. He's been with me through the worst. He has my back, so I've got his.

Frank said to me, "It takes a lot of guts for you to do this. I admire your courage." The attorney's negative reaction caused Frank to come to my defense and deepen his commitment to The Project.

References

Carroll, L. (2000). *The annotated Alice: Alice's adventures in wonderland & Through the looking glass by Lewis Carroll*. New York, NY: W.W. Norton. (Original works published in 1865 and 1871)

Ma, X., Herbst, T., Scheidl, T., Wang, D., Kropatschek, S., Naylor, B., Mech, A., Kofler, J., Anisimova, E., Makarov, V., Jennewein, T., Ursin, R. & Zelinger, A. (2012). Quantum teleportation over 143 kilometers using active feed-forward. *Nature*, 489 (7415), 269–273.

McFadden, J. (2002). The conscious electromagnetic information (Cemi) field theory: The hard problem made easy? *Journal of Consciousness Studies*, 9, 23–50.

Chapter 30

Pentimento

Frank and I worked together on The Project for a year. I introduced my writing into the treatment just as Frank had, bit at a time. During this period Frank began to work on a second novel. It was set in Chinatown at the beginning of the twentieth century. A detective named Giuseppe Finnegan was its main protagonist. The first scene introduces a shadowy figure named Gilhooley.

Frank was an advocate for the effect of creative writing in his therapy. In his opinion, its value derived from his freedom to write whatever came to mind. He let his mind wander in the freest of free association. Frank thought his writing and our work together on The Project constituted a new therapeutic paradigm. His enthusiasm caused us to talk about taking our show on the road.

Jointly publishing our work would inevitably lead to some public presentation. We considered making a presentation at a national conference. As we discussed this possibility, I realized I'd be exposing Frank to a lot of stress and an uncertain public reaction. Such an experience could harm him. I needed to consider any presentation from a therapeutic perspective: How would it affect Frank and his therapy? Using The Project to expand Frank's therapeutic experience *within* our sessions was one thing. But how could I use the public presentation of The Project to extend Frank's therapeutic experience into the world? That seemed complex and potentially dangerous.

I thought about using The Project as the basis of a ten-week course given to a local psychoanalytic study group. For the past decade I'd developed courses on a variety of topics for this group. They were friendly and supportive. This seemed like a safe place to bring The Project into the world.

We attracted five participants, four of whom I knew well. They were: Barbara and Lois, psychologists in private practice; David, a psychologist working in a hospital psychiatry department; Jennie, a social worker and director of a psychotherapy clinic; and Margo, a social worker, actress and student in a psychoanalytic training program. David and Jennie were long-time participants I knew well. Barbara and Lois were in supervision with me. I was meeting Margo for the first time.

I discussed the design of the course with Frank and selected weekly readings from both our work. From the beginning, Frank and I talked about him participating in the course near the end of the ten-week session. Frank wanted the opportunity to speak personally about his experience. Along with writing, for the past several years Frank had been creating electronic music. He had no previous experience making music. Frank composed about fifty pieces and produced several CDs. Frank and I selected pieces of his music for a CD he produced to accompany the course. Frank wanted readers of his fiction to also hear his music.

On a Saturday morning in mid-December I arrived to meet the group carrying five Anders Larson-Toich Foundation tote bags. Each bag contained a syllabus with a link to the Foundation's website where participants could learn more about Anders, the first week's readings, the CD of Frank's music (with an album cover containing two images of Anders), and a photograph selected by Frank. This picture was a curious way for Frank to introduce himself to the group.

The grainy photo showed the haggard face of a guy in camouflaged fatigues with a shaved head and weary dark eyes. He appeared to be saluting the viewer with his left hand. In the US military, a proper salute requires the fingers of the right hand to touch the temple above the eye. Frank's fingers extended across his forehead, partially covering his left eye, making it appear he was both saluting and holding his head. A salute indicates mutual respect. This gesture, combined with the downward tilt of his face and sleepless eyes, expressed dedication and preoccupation. Saluting with his left hand plus the murky image made me think the photograph was taken of a reflection in a mirror.

The photograph looked like Frank, but I wasn't sure it was him. It was so blurry I couldn't tell. Frank would only say the photo was "an intel shot of someone purported to be the author." I recalled Frank thought of himself as a shadowy figure in my writing: My representation of Frank looks a little like him, but so much is missing you can't really tell it's him. This image, included with a package of documents at the beginning of the course, cast our study group into the position of Captain Willard assigned to find Colonel Kurtz at the beginning of *Apocalypse now*. Readers were embarking on a dangerous journey upriver looking for an officer who'd gone around the bend. Frank was letting us know we were heading into a heart of darkness.

We were locked out of the building. Although I had a key which I'd used for several years, they'd obviously changed the lock. Our fledgling group adjourned to a local coffee shop. It seemed oddly appropriate that we were locked out. I told the group this was the nature of The Project. We'd have to make our own way. We needed to be inventive and resilient. I introduced the course and explained the background leading up to Frank and me embarking on The Project. Participants seemed excited to experience this clinical experiment first-hand.

Then I explained that by participating in a "live experiment" they'd be developing a relationship with Frank through his work. By participating in the course, they'd inevitably be accepting therapeutic responsibility for Frank. This was the nature of human relationships. This way of thinking was new for them. How could the subject of a case study they'd read about, actually become someone they'd care for?

Then I told the group I expected Frank would join us for a class at the end of the term. They'd have the opportunity to meet and interact with Frank. Where in the history of psychoanalytic case studies do readers of a case actually have the opportunity to interact with the subject? When has the patient ever had a voice? How would the history of psychoanalysis have differed if Anna O. had been an active participant in authoring her case history? Throughout the past century, what would we have learned about the unconscious and the therapeutic process if we'd collaborated with our patients?

Certainly, this wouldn't be a traditional course. It required an unexpected level of intimate involvement. The magnitude of this hit home for David after class. He emailed me his reaction to our first meeting:

I was scared and angry at you, Dan; scared and angry because I felt pulled into something I didn't expect and wasn't sure that I wanted to be a part of. I didn't ask to be part of "The Project." And this is separate from whether I'm willing to be a part of the project. I am willing. I'm intrigued by what we may learn and look forward to seeing if I can help in any way. I'd like to help. But you didn't ask if we wanted to be involved and I felt imposed on. I felt scared; worried that I would get lost in this world you and your patient have created and lose my sense of who I am. And I was scared for you; worried about the professional consequences to you for engaging in this project.

David was anxious and angry about the idea of actually meeting Frank. "*It's enough that he's in our class through his writing. I don't want him literally in our class!*" On the other hand, he wrote, "*I do thank you, though, for giving me the opportunity to have this experience; it's not easy or comfortable, but it is life-affirming.*" Then David included a poem he'd written about listening to a patient's voice. Thereafter, every week David sent me pieces of writing that we folded into the course. David became a writer just like Frank and me, and the group discussed the work of all three of us.

Each week during our session Frank and I would talk about the group's reaction to his chapters. From Frank's perspective, this course was like having a focus group read and respond to his work. He enjoyed the feedback. He was the center of attention. Everyone thought of Frank as a natural storyteller. They were intrigued by his unusual cast of characters, his evocative imagery and the dreamlike quality of his writing. They enjoyed the unexpected form his stories took. After reading Frank's chapter, "The path," Barbara said,

I love his style, how his narrator moves the reader's eye around, the dance-like and trance-like feel, how people keep reappearing, the funny word play with people's names, Dr. Morpheus' enchanting encounters with exotic characters, the hysterical image of Willy's beastly mother chewing her bratwurst. I'm so happy for Willy when his father reappears. But maybe what sticks the most—Willy "could not overcome the feeling of a lengthy tragedy being played out, of which he was only a spectator." Then, where does personal agency fit in? Is this an illusion?

Barbara was onto something. Frank's stories were sometimes playful but always posed serious philosophical questions. The group seemed to identify most with the characters of Willy Herold and Raymond: Willy because he was a sympathetically rendered outsider, and Raymond because everyone felt like a born killer. Being murdered by a madman is an everyday occurrence in America.

On the other hand, group members found Frank's writing disorienting, where the shift from dream to reality, sometimes jumping across continents and centuries in the space of a paragraph, left them feeling there was "nowhere to stand." Barbara called this disorienting place "Frankland." At the beginning of each sentence you were uncertain where you'd be at its end. Barbara said once she gave up requiring continuity of time, space, or personality and accepted the fluidity of the story, she loved going along for the ride. Other readers agreed. They became less anxious the more they read. But readers' distress over disorienting jumps of space or time underscored how sensitive people are to symbolic threats to their psychological security. Everyone's sense of their place in space and time seemed to be affected by the weekly readings. For example, Margo said, "Class for me has thoroughly negated the linear sense of time, space, weight, life. . .forever."

After a couple of weeks, with David's permission, I gave his writing to Frank to read. Most of David's pieces were poetry, a genre unfamiliar to Frank. Nonetheless, Frank wrote up his response to David's poems, which then became part of the course. For many weeks, there was a running exchange between them about David's poetry. For example, Frank said one of David's poems contained a feeling of "controlled anguish." For a decade I'd worked with groups of psychoanalytically sophisticated people who knew David well, and no one had ever expressed an interest in his "controlled anguish." It was Frank, who'd never met him and had only read his poetry, who extended himself to David in this intimate way. Frank said, through their writing they had "met each other with open hearts."

As the term progressed Margo and Jennie often used the course to discuss their own experiences of the death of family or friends. After all, the theme of Frank's novel was life after death. Margo's husband, Don, had died a year earlier of cancer. Before his death, Margo asked Don—if possible—to return to assure her of his continued existence. After his death, there were a number of occasions when she sensed his presence. There were inexplicable rapping sounds that seemed to confirm her husband's continued existence. Margo said,

Don continues to let me know he is somewhere. I often wonder how difficult this must be for him, but he is surely persistent. The latest occurrence: The morning of the anniversary of his death, I woke at the

moment I discovered he was not breathing next to me, stayed awake for next three hours until a picture of him crashed to the floor with absolutely no physical provocation.

Margo was comforted by the group's acceptance of her experience. This was a class where mysterious events were welcomed.

Jennie related Frank's ordeal to her friend Jan's parallel experience of losing her daughter. Jan's daughter, Anna, died in an automobile accident. Six months after Anna's death, Jan discovered she had cancer. Jan told Jennie she was distressed by her diagnosis, but strangely it brought her back to life after the loss of Anna. Later that summer, Jennie found herself surrounded by butterflies wherever she went. She talked to Jan about it. Jan encouraged her to get a butterfly tattoo. Spending a weekend in Woodstock, Jennie and her husband passed a tattoo parlor. Sixty minutes later Jennie left the shop with a blue butterfly on her back.

Jan fought cancer for three years. Then she too died. The deaths of Anna and Jan affected Jennie deeply. On the one-year anniversary of Jan's death, Jennie was sitting in a hammock in her backyard. Suddenly twenty butterflies swarmed around her. Several landed on her feet and legs. Jennie was amazed and felt certain Jan was present. She wanted to retain that certainty, but when the butterflies departed so did her belief in Jan's presence. Jennie couldn't suspend her disbelief. Skepticism washed away her feeling of connection. A week later, at the beach, Jennie asked Jan to send her a message. Instantly, out of the ocean a butterfly flew toward her. Jennie thought, "*I know this is Jan. But I also know that after it flies away, I won't believe it. I'll try to retain the certainty of this moment.*"

Unexpectedly, the course became an experiment in "writing cure." Barbara wrote a religious essay about Israelites leaving Egypt, being lost in the wilderness, and longing for an elusive Promised Land. The group talked about constrictions pushing each of us to leave our Egypt. Then we're lost in a personal wilderness. From this perspective, the Promised Land looks like a mirage. We called Egypt "*the constraints of consciousness*" and the Promised Land "*glimpses of deep unconscious awareness revealing our human essence.*" We naturally long to know our essence— to find our true selves—but we're prevented by a barren consciousness. The wilderness is the confusion of being stuck between our conscious and unconscious minds. When Frank read Barbara's piece, he described her as an ancient soul.

Halfway through the course, one of Lois' patients attempted suicide. As we discussed the case in class, I wondered about suicide bursting into the middle of our course with Frank. What was the meaning of Lois' case in terms of Frank and me? Frank had spent years trying to harness and transform his enormous rage. In part, the course was a form of suicide prevention, giving Frank another reason to live.

Frank and I finalized our plan for him to visit the class during the ninth week. The group would have read his entire novel by then, and that would give us a concluding class session to process the experience. For four weeks, we all planned his visit. Because Frank was coming down from Woodstock for our Saturday morning class, we decided to put him up Friday night at an inn in Stony Brook. We considered different restaurants for a Friday evening dinner. We were fortunate to get our own private dining room at the Pentimento Restaurant. For weeks leading up to the event Frank and the class separately wondered what we'd talk about. Everyone was nervous about actually meeting face-to-face. Barbara thought,

We're hosting him. It's our job to make him comfortable. But how? He appeared ghostly, menacing, ephemeral in the photo "purported to be him." Like his skin was molting. Not someone with whom I could make small talk.

Frank originally planned to drive from Woodstock, but at the last minute he decided to take Amtrak into the city. We planned to meet at Penn Station and together we'd take the Long Island Railroad out to Babylon. From there I'd drive him to the inn in Stony Brook. I wondered what it would be like to be with Frank in this social way. We sat side-by-side on the train. This seemed completely normal except when sitting down, Frank was taller than me. I'm actually taller than Frank, but when seated it was disconcerting to find Frank looking down at me. On the train, Frank said he'd considered cancelling several times. The whole thing filled him with anxiety.

We drove into Stony Brook, a quaint eighteenth-century village. I checked him into the inn and left him there. In about an hour Barbara, who lives in Stony Brook, would escort him to the restaurant half a block away. I drove a couple miles to my college office where I did paperwork before returning to the restaurant. Our group was escorted into a private room separated from the main dining room by a velvet curtain. We each took seats around the table and waited for Barbara and Frank. They were late. "Where are they?" I thought, "Something must be wrong."

A few minutes later they arrived. Frank explained he'd cut his head shaving. He'd bled a lot and had a small bandage behind his left ear. He hoped no one from the inn would enter his room. *"They'd call the cops,"* he said. *"There's so much blood it looks like a murder scene."* What a way to start! Barbara recalls,

> *All my worries melted away upon meeting him. He made it easy. I knew there was something about his needing a band-aid because he called the front desk about it while I was waiting for him in the lobby. A band-aid? Did he slit his wrists? So, I recognized him when he appeared in the lobby, both taller and shorter than I expected. He had a half-chagrined smile and opened his arms out wide to the side. He looked sweet. He quickly explained about needing the band-aid and showed me the wound on the back of his head. He said he'd cut his scalp shaving. He was more anxious than he'd realized. I said, "We're all anxious!" Could he make this any easier? The gash wasn't bleeding, but it was quite a gash. It seemed natural for me to offer to place the band-aid on his head. No way he could see to do it for himself. He seemed so apologetic. What an ice breaker! Band-aid in place, and anxiety mutually acknowledged, I felt quite comfortable with him.*

Frank sat at the head of the table and the waitress took our drink order. For a group of people previously anxious about meeting, everything flowed comfortably. Frank's a natural storyteller, and he regaled the group with one tale after another. By all accounts, this was an extraordinary evening.

The next morning Barbara picked up Frank at the inn and drove him to our group session. The warm feeling from the night before was rekindled, though on this occasion the group asked many more questions about Frank's novel and his writing process. Some of Frank's stories are based on visions and dreams he had while working in trance with a shaman. And Frank talked about his earlier work with a Jungian analyst. As the class ended, everyone lingered in the parking lot not wanting leave, not wanting to sever the bond we'd created.

After the class I drove Frank to Babylon to catch a train back to New York. We ate lunch in a diner. Waiting for his train, we walked through the village window shopping. Frank purchased a gift for his wife, Signe, and one for himself. Then I put him on a train to New York.

Frank's visit had been richer and more satisfying than I could have expected. Later that day Jennie sent me an email.

Wow! What an amazing and emotionally packed experience. The love in the room was an invisible cushion surrounding us: ALIVE, ALIVE, ALIVE. It was an incredibly moving, touching experience. It was evocative of my emotions around my losses of my dear friend Jan and her daughter Anna. I felt such love and admiration for Frank. I also felt a strong loving connection to you and our group. It was a healing experience for me.

Although Frank's book focused on death, Jennie found Frank to be so alive. That view was shared by others in the group.

During the week Barbara also wrote to me describing her experience of the dinner and class.

I felt like an older sister to a younger brother who didn't need protection—happy he seemed to open up so quickly, a little worried about what kind of drinker he was after listening to his exchange with the waitress about whether the bartender could make a drink I'd never heard of. Does the type of gin really matter? I don't know one from another. At times, he seemed like the host, regaling us with stories, easy to be with, containing mountains of rage. Hockey/guns/guns/ hockey. I felt close to the group, like we'd all taken up the task of connecting to him. Strange to look around the table: So many years sitting in class with them, and then seeing everybody through a new lens. The whole thing seemed unreal and yet very real. Eating, drinking, telling stories, laughing, making a new friend. Such a natural feeling to have him in class, a member of the family. I miss him.

At dinner David seemed distracted. We were all aware his mother had had surgery for cancer a few days before. David had spent the previous week in New Jersey with his parents. After dinner and our class with Frank he wrote to me.

I'm feeling so frazzled with all that I'm doing these days and my worry about my mother. At the same time, I'm feeling alive and connected with others. Ironically, my most recent poem is in part about my ambivalence about both connection and solitude. But these days I mostly want connection and I'm welcoming that feeling.

David supplied a final poem entitled, "What the Smith Corona saw." Throughout the course David and Frank had had—through me—a continuous email conversation about David's poetry. This was David's final interaction with Frank, and the poem was a response to a comment made previously by Frank.

One of David's poems made a reference to William Faulkner. When Frank read the poem, he remarked he'd never read Faulkner and knew only one thing about him. Frank then told the story of Faulkner working with Howard Hawks on the screenplay for Raymond Chandler's *The big sleep*. Faulkner and Hawks were confused about details in the book's plot. So, Hawks asked Faulkner to send Chandler a telegram to ask the author, "Who killed Sherwood's chauffer?" Chandler cabled back, "No idea." Frank was delighted that Chandler was unable to explain his own story. This supported Frank's view that his stories come from "some other place." Frank would say, "I'm not even sure I'm the one writing it."

In David's poem the mysterious intentions of Marlowe or Spade are channeled through the Smith Corona typewriter which becomes the psychic medium connecting their misty world with Chandler or Hammett alive in another place and time. I considered David's poem to be a tribute to Frank and their kinship as writers. Like Barbara's short essay about the Promised Land, David describes the confusing wilderness, mediated by a typewriter, which exists between our conscious and unconscious minds.

What the Smith Corona Saw

That night, on a rock-strewn,
moon-dark beach, a silhouette,
rain-heavy in mist, stood.
Black onyx surf swept
across and across.

Earlier that night, back
in the city: He—
call him Marlowe or Spade—

murdered; pointed
cobalt gat and pulled trigger;
watched the body drop
next to the dumpster
in the wet, cramped alley
off the neon-splashed strip.
Maybe he—Marlowe or Spade—
knows why. Chandler or Hammett,
at his Smith Corona, can only
lift his fedora and scratch his head.

At the beach,
sharp, diamond waves
strike like an obsidian panther.
Chandler or Hammett types on.
He—Marlowe or Spade—
wades in, cutting
deeper and deeper.

During our sessions over the next several weeks Frank and I discussed his visit. It was a powerful therapeutic event. Frank said,

The evening and the session the next morning were magical. Each member had something constructive to say and it was humbling how much effort they put into what they said. I thought I'd entered a sacred space. It was a spiritual experience. It reminded me of my two visits to John of God at the Omega Institute. We met each other with open hearts. All my anger—they didn't say it was wrong. They took my anger onto themselves and they accepted me.

During the five months the study group met and discussed his work Frank was both apprehensive and flattered. That's what it's like to be the center of attention. This was the first time he'd written anything, and the first time his creative efforts were being judged by others. He had no context for understanding this experience. He believed I'd insulated him from the per-plexed bewilderment the group must have experienced reading his work. On the other hand, he was flattered that a group of professionals would take his work so seriously. Their insightful feedback showed him how carefully they'd thought about his work, which powerfully affected him.

I decided to write up the group's experience for this chapter. I asked each member of the group to send me their observations. Margo wrote to me,

> *I have been changed by this group and really by the whole experience. This has fit well into what started for me before Don's death continuing to the present; certainly, the life/death part. My reception of Don's continuing existence after death—dealing with serious issues with such fun simply allow for the opening of possibilities we are used to covering up and denying because being open demands too much energy and courage.*

Naturally, I asked Frank to write his account of the experience. True to form, Frank wrote an imaginative vignette exploring each of four possible outcomes of the evening dinner: "Assassination," "Hostile psychological entanglement," "No psychological entanglement," and "Successful encounter with psychological entanglement." Each of these differing outcomes contains the same introductory sequence of events: Alone in his room Nigel cuts his bald head shaving, in the hotel lobby Barbara affixes a bandage, then escorts him to the restaurant where they enter a private dining room, drinks are ordered, and dinner ensues. I circulated Frank's piece to members of the group.

Frank's vignette had a powerful effect on Barbara. His first story, "Assassination," identifies Barbara as a Mossad agent and ends with the waiter shooting Nigel in the right temple. This drove Barbara into a state of intense creativity. In a matter of days, she wrote counter versions of each of Frank's four possible outcomes. She was consumed by this activity declaring, *"All I want to do is write!"* Barbara was inspired. In each of her stories she was indeed a Mossad agent, codenamed Ancient Soul, assigned to the task of killing Nigel. Her stories were brilliant, playful, humorous riffs on Frank's somber melodies.

I'd known Barbara for years. She is seventy-years old, reserved and deliberate. I'd never seen such girlish playfulness in her. She'd become a different person. What produced this new self? Had she created a new Barbara, or accessed a part of herself from which she'd been dissociated? Naturally, I showed each of Barbara's pieces to Frank. He responded,

> *At first, I thought Barbara was mocking me in some way. Then, I thought about what she was writing, and I had the idea I'd inspired her. I'd have never thought that because my mind just doesn't work that way. But it's really quite a feeling to be an inspiration.*

Barbara agreed. Frank had inspired her. And, frankly, reading their vignettes side-by-side inspired me. Frank said,

> As I recollect that experience—the whole thing, the dinner, the group, writing this stuff up—I can't tell you how much this means to me. Remembering the experience actually scares me, it frightens me. It frightens me because it gives me hope, and you know how many times my hopes have been dashed.

I was struck again by the transformative power of love and imagination. Hope, of course, is a form of imagination. I was surprised by the many ways group members described love in their depictions of this experience. Barbara was inspired. Did her inspiration have anything to do with love? It looked that way.

I was curious about the final chapter in Frank's novel, his newfound hopefulness and the name of the restaurant, Pentimento, which hosted our dinner. The final scene of Frank's novel, *The journey west*, ends when a Norwegian pine tree crashes to the earth. Nigel leaves his house joining his dead son. Together they get on a barge heading west, presumably across the Nile. This seems like a prophetic image suggesting Frank's death. Apart from being reunited with his son, the image is bleak.

Pentimento is Italian for "repentance." It's also a term used in visual art. Pentimento refers to traces left in a painting indicating the artist changed his mind. For example, in a portrait the tilt of a head or a gesture may change. So, pentimento is about repentance and changing one's mind. I wondered if the hope Frank was feeling meant he was rewriting the end of his story. Perhaps Barbara was rewriting her story as well. It's interesting to find shifting states of mind expressed in the creative writing of Barbara and Frank as they describe a dinner occurring in place named for changing your mind. Was that coincidence, the product of suggestion, or synchronicity? Again, I thought about the curious way life unfolds.

Frank and I continued our work together on The Project for another three years. Frank wrote a second novel producing a seventy-thousand-word manuscript. Frank remained connected with the study group making three trips to Long Island for visits. He incorporated group members as characters in his new novel. He often remarked on how deeply moved he was by his connection with the group. He'd say, *"You don't know how much these people mean to me."*

In the summer of 2016 Barbara moved from Long Island to Richmond, Virginia, to live near her daughter who'd married and had a child. The following January, I began hosting the study group in my art studio using internet-based videoconferencing with a large video monitor so that Raul, Frank, and Barbara could participate from their locations in Hoboken, Woodstock and Richmond. Jennie, David, Margo and Tony (a new member) joined me in the studio. Frank now participated in the group as a paying member rather than as a special guest. The group met for an hour and a half on Saturday afternoons, every other week throughout the following year. As in previous years, I selected weekly readings. After ten weeks of videoconferencing Barbara dropped out as did Tony.

In the summer of 2017, I sent our proposal for *Psychoanalysis, intersubjective writing, and a postmaterialist model of mind* to George Hagman for consideration in the Art, Creativity, and Psychoanalysis series he was editing for Routledge. In August, George endorsed our proposal and forwarded it to Routledge for their review.

Frank continued to care for his wife, Signe, who was receiving chemotherapy for metastatic breast cancer. Frank and Signe had been together for nearly forty years. During this period Frank's mother, who lived with Frank and his family, died of cancer. Frank had been caring for dying loved ones continuously for fifteen years. He often described himself as suffering from battle fatigue. He'd say, "*I don't think I'm depressed—I'm just worn out. I feel like I can't take another day of this.*"

During the spring of 2018, Signe became increasingly frail and less mobile, requiring Frank to provide more care. In the last months of her life a dose of chemotherapy paralyzed her hand making it impossible for her to play the viola, one of her remaining pleasures. Group members asked Frank if he could get help caring for Signe. Frank didn't want strangers in his house or touching his wife. Frank was devoted to Signe and they were committed to her dying at home. On May 2 Frank told me, "*Signe will die today.*" That night was the worst of his life. Signe died early the next day.

The following morning at six o'clock Kate Hawes, Senior Publisher at Routledge in London, emailed George Hagman saying she'd like to make an offer to publish our book. An hour later George emailed me. I was in New York seeing patients. When I got the news, I emailed Frank between sessions. In our email exchanges over the years Frank had assumed the name of his character Nigel and I called myself Dizzy, an abbreviation of Dr. Distanziert.

Nigel, I heard from Routledge, the publisher. They're going to publish our book! Thank you. Thank you. I feel Signe and Anders had a hand in this. Dizzy

Dizzy, I was having such a difficult morning. Then your email. I just mentioned to you I really needed this book to be published, and it happened after so long. You're right. Their hands were in this. Wonderful. Holding on for dear life, Nigel

Nigel, hold on. We have a book tour to do. I guess the Charlie Rose interview is out of the question. I thank Signe for this. She's looking out for us.

Dizzy, I could deal with Charlie in his underwear. George has suggested the Woodstock bookstore. They are very strong on promoting authors from the Woodstock area. He believes we can setup a reading and book signing. I hope I'm not getting ahead of myself. Nigel

Nigel, excellent! I'm all-in. Here's the anonymous reviewer's comments about the book. Dizzy

Dizzy, I read the reviewer's comments and wonder, am I to be the faceless patient? Are we listed as co-authors? How will I be perceived? I'm scared now that I made a mistake. That I'll be plunged into a world I know nothing about. Will I be your Frankenstein monster? Brought to life by the hand of Colin Clive, or the hunchback Fritz doing his master's bidding? Suddenly I'm afraid I'll be terrifying the villagers. The misunderstood brute, given life by a half-crazed genius. Only to be consumed by his own inability to understand why he was reanimated. To be trapped and destroyed by the mob while you toast your success. The cocktail I consumed has revealed a landscape as bleak as James Whales. Nigel

That evening I wrote,

Nigel, I think your reaction is completely understandable and should be included in the book. It's built into the parts we're playing. These are inescapable things. That's why I think, if we do public presentations, we do them together. I think we'll get some opportunities like that.

The title page reads Dan Gilhooley with Frank Toich. Nothing has changed. Routledge will send us a contract. Royalties will be split equally between us. On a $50 book I think we'd each get $1.88. We won't get rich.

If you catch Charlie Rose in his underwear, it would make a great interview. Dizzy

The next morning, Frank emailed me.

Dizzy, I reread what I sent you and I love it. Yes, as I lay in bed and see her side empty, things seem bleak. Sometimes there is a part of me that thinks a public affirmation of my writing will be very satisfying. As usual, your understanding is spot-on. I'm crouched in a shell hole praying for a barrage to lift but it never does. What is a saving grace, now more than ever, is that I can look across the mud, surrounded by the smell of death and cordite, and see you crouching with me. Always, Nigel aka the Monster

I was struck by Frank describing me as Dr. Frankenstein, a half-crazed genius reanimating him after Signe's death. The Project started with a dream of waking up dead. Frankenstein was another version of waking the dead. I thought about unanticipated dangers associated with creating new life. In the Frankenstein story the fiend murders two and threatens Frankenstein's life when he fails to create a bride for him. The story ends with the doctor and monster trying to kill each other. Would new life emerging out of our book lead us to destroy one another?

Two weeks later Frank sent me a vignette entitled "The inferno" which I distributed to members of the study group. This was his first piece of creative writing since Signe's death. The magnitude of loss and fury Frank was experiencing was uncountable—emotional infinity. First, he watched his son die, then his mother, now his wife—unable to save them. Frank had said losing Anders was soul crushing. This was worse. Frank was now completely alone.

"The inferno" was composed of bleak images of a succession of protagonists—each an embodiment of Frank—near-death, fading in-and-out of consciousness. Each character was paired with a different member of the study group who ends up holding him in his or her arms. Several times the protagonist hopes the comforter will kill him to relieve him of his misery, but they each embrace him instead. At the next meeting of the study group Frank said he was embarrassed he'd put everyone in such a position. They must have felt obliged to hold and protect him. Margo, David, Jennie and Raul told Frank they loved him, as did I.

Chapter 31

Imagination, dissociation and *Nous*

Frank often says he doesn't know where his writing comes from, or even if he's the author of his stories. Images arise in his mind. Words and sentences appear on the page. But if Frank is not the creator of these stories, then where do they come from? Surely, they come from his imagination, but Frank believes they originate outside of himself.

At first Frank has no feeling of ownership of the story. But, like a dream, the story becomes richly rewarding after he's written it. When writing, Frank is in a mild dissociative trance which he thinks is akin to dreaming or automatic writing. Curiosity complements and fuels Frank's creative work. He likes to place his characters in historically accurate settings, and he does a lot of research trying to get the smallest details right. So, Frank's creative writing alternates between his curiosity mining the world for information, and his synthesis of this material in an altered state of consciousness.

As previously discussed, it appears telepathy is the basis for several parallels between depictions in Frank's novel and my life. For example, Frank wrote about a life-threatening experience two months before I experienced it. And Frank rendered a boy raised by a shell-shocked veteran whose memory of combat contributes to his suicide, which was my life growing up with my brain-injured father.

In addition to reading my mind, Frank's writing also demonstrates his unconscious access to a transpersonal body of knowledge. The most obvious example is Frank's character Watson Page who publishes a paper proving the existence of parallel universes. In Frank's story "Convergence," Page is informed by his doppelganger that the mathematical formulas in his paper actually map out the apocalyptic destruction of his world. Page's career is destroyed by a group of scientists in Copenhagen who are committed to a more conservative explanation of reality.

In my interpretation of Frank's story, Page appeared to be modeled on the life of Hugh Everett who, I discovered, was the originator of the Many Worlds theory. Everett's career in quantum physics was destroyed by Bohr and his associates in Copenhagen who regarded his theory as heretical. This caused Everett to go to work for the Pentagon where he spent a career calculating the probability of nuclear annihilation, mapping out the apocalyptic destruction of the planet. The similarity between Watson Page and Hugh Everett seemed obvious. But when I asked Frank about Hugh Everett, he'd never heard of him. Everett came as a surprise to him. I suppose it's possible that Frank learned about Everett years ago and forgot, but it seems unlikely he could have known about Everett's formulas predicting nuclear annihilation before Peter Byrne's biography of Everett published in June of 2010, just two months before Frank began writing "Convergence."

Or, consider Frank's character Mekes who Nigel is pursuing in the netherworld between life and death. Mekes is the center of all the action, but never actually appears in Frank's novel. His elusiveness makes him intriguing. We learn about Mekes through Max, his next-door neighbor. Mekes is the leader of a cult. He's done a scholarly translation of the *Egyptian book of the dead* and provides technical support for movie-like productions authored by his colleague, Chinese magician Ching Ling Foo, who is actually God. Using people's memories, hopes and dreams, Mekes creates alternate realities—sometimes past lives—which individuals in the netherworld experience as waking dreams. Working in concert with Foo, Mekes' most powerful skill is his ability to get inside peoples' minds, observing their thoughts and feelings. Mekes is a telepathist. Using this telepathically acquired knowledge, at Foo's direction he crafts alternate versions of individuals' realities.

I asked Frank how he came up with the name Mekes. He said it's an inversion of the Egyptian word "sekhem" which means "powerful" and is associated with ancient Egyptian healing practices. This is consistent with Frank's use of Khu, Ba, Ka and Ren which are all Egyptian mythological names for portions of the soul. Naturally, life after death focuses on the soul, and Frank's sees therapy as a healing practice. I was curious to find that "mekes" in Hebrew means "computation," to enumerate "the proportion to be paid." Mekes is phonetically spelled "meh-kes," the inversion of sekhem.

Based on the prominence of Zeno and Egyptian mythology in Frank's novel, I wondered who in the ancient world was associated with enumeration and proportion, took an interest in healing practices, was the powerful leader of a cult who could only be known secondhand, traveled the netherworld and experienced past lives, was focused on the immortality of the soul, worked for the divine, communicated with Chinese Magi, and had a scholarly knowledge of the Egyptian *Book of the dead*. My research (Burkert, 1972; Huffman, 2014; Kahn, 2001; Laks, 2014; Lloyd, 2014; Riedweg, 2005) found only one person possessed these ten characteristics: Pythagoras. How, I wondered, could Mekes *coincidently* possess ten characteristics of Pythagoras?

When I shared my interpretation with Frank, he told me he hadn't thought of Pythagoras when writing his novel. And, although he recalled learning about him in a history of mathematics course forty-five years ago, he wasn't aware of these specific details about Pythagoras' life. Indeed, shamanic and supernatural attributes like Pythagoras' memory of past lives and his ability to know the future, his miracle work, his trips to the netherworld, and bilocation don't usually appear in brief summaries of his life. These details, offered by his contemporaries, are dismissed today as folklore and are only found by reading Pythagorean scholarship. But in 530 BCE Pythagoras' supernatural abilities caused him to be considered semidivine, which is the role he plays in Frank's novel. In ancient Greece, Pythagoras' status was associated with his doctrine of metempsychosis (reincarnation)

> which transcends normal human ways of knowing, can find a guarantee only in supernatural experience, in the world of the divine or quasi-divine. If Pythagoras knew the facts about the fate of the soul in this life and the next, he must have had superhuman powers and faculties.
>
> (Burkert, 1972, p.136)

Of course, this is how Mekes appears in *The journey west*.

In the Pythagorean tradition there's no separation between science and religion, philosophy and the occult: "For here the uncanny and the arcane have been at home from the beginning" (Kahn, 2001, p.140). Furthermore, consider Mekes' affiliation with a Chinese magician, Foo. The fact that Pythagoras associated with Magi appears in his first biography written eighteen-hundred years ago, but the proposal that the Magi were actually Chinese shamans is a scholarly detail emerging recently, well after Frank's college days. So, where could Frank's knowledge of Hugh Everett and Pythagoras come from if not from Frank's learned experience? When writing in a dissociative trance, Frank seems to tap unconsciously into a body of human knowledge that transcends any individual mind, obtaining in-depth and up to date information.

Then there's Dr. Distanziert. In his pursuit of Mekes, Nigel repeatedly runs into Max and Max's Freudian psychoanalyst, Dr. Distanziert. I was curious about the character Frank created to represent me. Frank describes Distanziert as a Freudian analyst active in Berlin in the early 1930s who was captivated with Gestalt psychology, and who traveled to Vienna to study with an associate of Freud after completing his medical education. Were there any Freudian analysts who fit the bill? I did some research and found only one: Fritz Perls.

As a young man Perls served in the trenches of the World War I as a medical officer (Clarkson & Mackewn, 1993). Decorated for bravery, this traumatic experience fostered a lifelong interest in the arts and leftwing politics. After the war, Perls worked as an assistant to Kurt Goldstein at his Institute for Brain Damaged Soldiers where he was influenced by Goldstein's organismic theory. Perls' first analysis was a brief stint with Karen Horney in Berlin, thereafter moving to Vienna for a year to complete his psychoanalytic education. His most extensive analysis was with Wilhelm Reich in Berlin between 1931–1933. He fled Nazi Germany in 1934.

Perls regarded Freud as essential but considered the philosophy and methods of psychoanalysis obsolete. Perls was attracted to innovators like Horney and Reich, the active technique and mutuality of Ferenczi, and Jung's concept of active imagination. When Perls immigrated to the United States, he was associated with the Interpersonal School being developed by Harry Stack Sullivan and Clara Thompson. Perls had a charismatic personality.

I was unaware of Fritz Perls before reading Frank's novel, and researched Perls only because I considered him a symbolic stand in for me. It's curious to find numerous parallels between us. For example, my introduction to psychoanalytic theory began by reading four books by Horney. My father was a brain-damaged soldier and my early life was saturated with war stories. Tom's war experience combined with my artistic interests tilting me toward leftwing politics. Doing dissertation research, I was influenced by Goldstein's holistic conception of regression and self-actualization as an organic response to trauma. Like Perls, I admire Freud but consider the philosophy and methods of psychoanalysis to be obsolete. I've been drawn to psychoanalytic innovators like Spotnitz and Searles, have been influenced by Ferenczi's mutual analysis, Jung's active imagination, and psychoanalysts associated with the American Interpersonal School. I spent a career as a charismatic teacher. But most important, the psychic weather idea I developed at the end of the "Drawing" chapter could be seen as an elaboration of Perls' (1973) gestalt field theory concerning the relationship between individuals and their environment. Of course, I never thought of Perls in this context. A knowledgeable supervisor brought this to my attention.

The similarities between Perls and me are noteworthy. After researching Perls, I asked Frank what he knew about him. Nothing at all, and, of course, he had no awareness of my professional background. So, having no knowledge of either Perls or me, how could Frank select such an accurate representation of me? If this were an isolated example, it could be dismissed as coincidental. But Frank's novel is filled with this sort of thing.

Again, if his story writes itself, who is its author? Actually, Frank's novel tells us. It's reasonable to conclude that Ching Ling Foo and Mekes are representations of Frank's creative unconscious. Frank's imagination emerges within his telepathic mind. He has access to a vast body of human knowledge, and he works under the direction of a superhuman organizing force, Foo. After all, it takes a remarkable degree of order to create Watson Page, Mekes and Distanziert as mirror images of Everett, Pythagoras and Perls, each of whom was unknown to Frank. So, what's this organizing force Frank names Ching Ling Foo?

Frank considers the origin of his creativity to be the divine, or what psychoanalyst Wilfred Bion (1965) called O, "absolute truth and ultimate reality," the traditional definition of God (Bowker, 2014). Frank says, "That's how I write. I surrender myself to the divine." As Frank sees it, for unknowable reasons, a divine power shapes his stories. Foo is the compositional energy within his unconscious which organizes Frank's stories allowing him to create Mekes as a stand in for Pythagoras. Frank's belief in the divine as a compositional force is similar to James Grotstein's (2000) contention that dreams are authored in the unconscious by an unknown preternatural presence, Bion's O. Like philosophers in the ancient world, Grotstein proposes some dreams are gifts from God. Frank, likewise, considers the divine to be the organizing energy behind his stories. Indeed, seen from this mystical perspective the unconscious *is God*. Grotstein (2000) declares, "I believe that the unconscious is as close as any mortal is likely to get to the experience of God" (p.80).

Looking through Grotstein's lens, man's persistent rejection of unconscious experience is his manic defense against the experience of O. Grotstein (2007) says mankind is born with a "raw dread of O" (p.44). Could our ubiquitous fear of the unconscious mind—encountered throughout this book—ultimately be a fear of God? I'm not sure what to make of this. Frank possesses a broad and intense spirituality, but I'm not religious. I'm more observer than observant. Certainly, the qualities Freud (an avowed atheist) attributed to the unconscious—as infinite, omniscient, timeless, eternal, something unknowable which can't be directly observed, alien, awesome, and even terrifying—are all characteristics traditionally associated with God (Bomford, 1999; Otto, 1923). Seen from this perspective, Freud's preoccupation with the unconscious is a secularized version of man's traditional pursuit of God. If the unconscious is God, then mankind is semidivine just as Pythagoras proposed (Kahn, 2001). Freud, of course, would scoff at this expression of omnipotence. With an air of superiority, he'd dismiss the idea of himself as semidivine.

Additionally, Frank's creative imagination reveals just how impersonal and transpersonal the unconscious really is. In fact, Jung's colleague, physicist Wolfgang Pauli, used the term "objective" to describe the unconscious because it incorporates external reality while consciousness is deeply subjective (Atmanspacher & Fach, 2015, p.201). Of course, this is a much broader conception of the unconscious than the narrow intrapsychic world that Freud (1915) proposed a century ago.

But, if the unconscious *is* God, or contains God as Frank believes, and if it's transpersonal and reflects external reality as Pauli suggests, then does contact with the unconscious mind inevitably involve a loss of personal identity? It looks that way. Psychologist Etzel Cardena (1994) notes the "notion of 'dissociation' is indistinguishable from such terms as 'preconscious,' 'subconscious,' 'subliminal,' and 'unconscious'" (p.17). So, does dissociation occur each time we slip into an unconscious state? Certainly, Frank's imaginative writing takes place in a mild dissociative trance.

Dissociation appears to be characteristic of all creative activity (Asma, 2017; Csikszentmihalyi, 1996; Csikszentmihalyi & Csikszentmihalyi, 1988; Richman, 2014). Psychoanalyst Sophia Richman (2014) writes, "It is my contention here that dissociation is an integral part of the creative process, an essential aspect of making art" (p.66). When we are creative, we enter an egoless state of intense concentration in which we lose our sense of time, awareness of our surroundings, and our sense of agency and control.

Mihaly Csikszentmihalyi (1996), a psychologist studying creativity and optimal experience, describes a euphoric state of selfless immersion he calls "flow" which is the fertile arena for imaginative activity. Here's a statement by a composer, studied by Csikszentmihalyi in the 1970s, that characterizes flow:

> You are in an ecstatic state to such a point that you feel as though you almost don't exist. I have experienced this time and again. My hand seems devoid of myself, and I have nothing to do with what is happening. I just sit there watching it in a state of awe and wonderment, and the music just flows out of itself.
>
> (Csikszentmihalyi, 2004)

Of course, this is how Frank talks about his writing.

Csikszentmihalyi (1988, 1996) describes this altered state of consciousness as effortless and akin to trance. Flow is "done for the sake of doing it," and is therefore addictive. Paradoxically, the self grows through this egoless activity. This is similar to the process seen in symbiotic merger researched by Rachel Blass and Sydney Blatt (1996) where the loss of identity in symbiosis becomes the basis for the development of self. This is the ultimate version of the psychoanalytic concept of regression in the service of the ego (Kris, 1952). Frank notes that a contemporary of Pythagoras, the wise old Chinese philosopher Lao-tzu, is believed to have said, "When I let go of what I am, I become what I might be."

Imagination operates in both the conscious and unconscious minds. For example, while dreams arise in the unconscious, daydreams are consciously constructed fantasies. Jungian analyst and dream researcher, Robert Bosnak (2007), differentiates "true imagination" engaging the other in the unconscious from rational forms of confabulation. Bosnak writes, "Whereas embodied imagination facilitates a meeting with substantive alien presences through mutual intelligence, confabulation belongs to endless reconfirmation of pre-existing notions of self, holding otherness at bay" (p.67). Similarly, French historian of Islamic mysticism, Henry Corbin (1969, 1972), distinguishes between the phenomenological quality of the *imaginal*—visionary perception in an altered state—versus consciously created fantasies. Imaginal experiences are noetic; they are glimpses of a higher form of reality. In the Sufi tradition, these visions are accessed through what Corbin calls "creative imagination," and occur in an intermediate realm between material reality and God. So, the imaginal is not imaginary. Rather, "the imaginal is imagination on steroids" (Kripal, 2010, p.83). The imaginal is perception occurring in an unconscious dissociative state, while the imaginary is produced by conscious discursive thinking.

Imagination is at odds with existing knowledge. Imaginative creations spring spontaneously and fully formed from the unconscious—vibrant and vital, the embodiment of wisdom—while knowledge is usually developed from conscious, logical, deliberative reasoning (Rothenberg, 1979). Einstein famously asserts, "Imagination is more important than knowledge" (Isaacson, 2007, p.7). Einstein describes his imaginative process as preverbal and pre-symbolic, involving playful visual associations rooted in his body ("of muscular type"), and indifferent to logic (Ghiselin, 1952, pp.32–33). Knowledge, logic and reason maintain the status quo, and an important first step in creativity is leaving knowledge behind (Ward, Smith & Finke, 1999). Plato (1989a) says, a poet is "never able to compose until he has become inspired, and *is beside himself*, and *reason is no longer in him*" (p.220, italics added). The poet is inspired like "seers and prophets who deliver all their sublime messages without knowing in the least what they mean" (1989b, p.8). The poet loses himself, becomes possessed, is carried along by passion and madness, leaving reason behind. Plato (1989c) writes about "the superiority of heaven-sent madness over man-made sanity" (p.492). Powerful truths come from the poet's divine inspiration, allowing his mania to become mantic, or prophetic. That's how Frank writes about an experience two months before I have it!

Immanuel Kant (1951) declares, it's genius "and *not a premeditated purpose*, that gives the rule to the art" (p.189, italics added). Genius can't be taught, Kant says, because a genius has no idea what he's doing. The artist can't show how ideas form in his mind because he can't observe it happening. Creativity is invisible: we see its product but not the process. So, creative imagination originates outside reason and premeditation, outside self-awareness and conscious control. Moreover, imagination *leaps over* current knowledge. Imagination produces new knowledge in a nonlinear way (Oppenheim, 2013). For this reason, philosopher of science, Thomas Kuhn (1962), describes the products of imagination as "anomalous" and potentially "revolutionary."

Imagination has "a mind of its own." Investigating imagination, philosopher Stephen Asma (2017) notes, "The flow state is a reconnection with the *involuntary* imagination" which takes control of the creative process while the conscious self gives up agency to a form of blind processing (p.225, italics added). That's what Plato means when Socrates declares the poet is "beside himself." Imaginative, creative and intuitive actions are all initiated nonlocally. They represent emotional thinking done somewhere else by something else. We glibly claim the "something and somewhere else" is *our* unconscious mind, but we have no idea what the unconscious actually is, and the extent to which we can call it *ours*. Perhaps, like the Sufis, we should consider the unconscious an intermediate realm between material reality and God. If the unconscious is transpersonal and contains O as Bion proposes, then imaginative, intuitive and creative thoughts likely originate in the Other, and are therefore products of dissociation.

Dissociation, or the loss of personal identity, also occurs in altered mental states experienced in therapeutic processes. For example, each of the four clinical subjects studied in this book—Victor Race, Friedricke Hauffe, Leonie Boulanger and Bertha Pappenheim—all experienced dissociative states during which there was a loss of identity usually accompanied by amnesia. For example, Breuer (1895) describes Bertha's hypnoid state as "some kind of *vacancy of consciousness* in which an emerging idea meets with no resistance" (p.215, italics added). Like Plato's poet, in her hallucinatory trance Bertha was *beside herself*—indeed, Breuer describes her as a case of double consciousness. Furthermore, when psychoanalysts "become their patients," when they experience induced feelings and objective countertransference, at those moments they've lost their sense of identity. Like Bertha, they're experiencing double consciousness. So, creative and psychologically transformative processes involving the unconscious mind require dissociation from a conscious sense of self.

But Frank's statement, "I surrender myself to the divine," involves a deeper question of personal agency and intention in the world. When writing,

Frank gives up personal agency to an external organizing force (like Mekes and Foo) which structures his narrative. If intelligent life is solely capable of initiating purposeful action, does this mean Frank's divine is a kind of super-intelligence shaping his story? It looks that way.

I glance over at Max adjusting a laser tool in the corner of the studio. I ask, "Max, is there any Pre-Socratic writing about a divine mind as an organizing force?" I've come to rely on Max's knowledge of ancient Greek philosophy.

Max replies,

Oh, yeah, sure, Anaxagoras was a descendent of Parmenides and a contemporary of Zeno. He lived in Athens around the time of Socrates, but I'm not sure they ever met. He was a big deal in Athenian culture. He was the teacher of Pericles, Euripides, and the sculptor Phidias. One of his students became Socrates' teacher. So, yeah, I think he's perfect for your book.

Anaxagoras said mind is the motive force in the universe, causing matter to separate, mix and rotate. This whirling force organizes the universe. Kurt Godel, with his rotating universe, must have loved that, right? And those quantum guys—like Max Plank, Gene Wigner and John Wheeler who concluded mind is the root of everything—they're echoing Anaxagoras. He's the origin of philosophical idealism. Anaxagoras had the idea that "everything is in everything," the entire universe is present in the smallest seed, perfect for those fractal guys like Mandelbrot. And he wrote about multiple co-occurring worlds nested within our world, each made from the same stuff as ours, but each functioning differently, with worlds separated from and unaware of each other. Sounds like Hugh Everett, right? Are you getting the idea? This guy *knew something*.

Anyway, Anaxagoras proposed two forms of mind—what he called *Nous*—a great and pure cosmic super mind, and weak contaminated little minds that us creatures with souls possess. *Nous*, the cosmic mind, is immaterial, pure, and completely separate from the physical stuff of the world which always exists in forms of mixture. Mind is the ordering force in nature. It determines the form matter takes. Any quantum physicist would tell you that! *Nous* is everywhere causing everything. It's a powerful force making matter move. Newton would be in complete agreement with Anaxagoras! The cosmic mind is the only source of creation. It is discerning, contains all knowledge and controls everything possessing a soul. That fellow you talk about, Bion, his O is *Nous*. Knowledge obtained in our little minds is incomplete and sometimes wrong because we rely on perception. But even so, Anaxagoras says we can still get it right because—I love his phrase— "appearances are a glimpse of the unseen."

So, yeah, Anaxagoras would say Frank's stories are being written by *Nous*, the cosmic mind. No doubt about it. But, I'm not sure about the divine angle. Anaxagoras was agnostic. The divine twist probably originates in Orphic poetry, a religious cult that took up Anaxagoras's ideas.

Following Max's tip, I look up Anaxagoras (Curd, 2007, 2008; Marmodoro, 2017) and find he influenced Plato, Aristotle, Plotinus and Plutarch, who in turn affected the development of Judeo-Christian religions. Thirteenth-century Catholic saint, Thomas Aquinas, equated Anaxagoras's cosmic mind with God. Aquinas (1993) declared all knowledge descends from God and "only God can create" (p.309). This is certainly Frank's position. In *Creative intuition in art and poetry*, contemporary Catholic aesthetician, Jacques Maritain, describes a spiritual unconscious based on the philosophy of Aquinas. Maritain (1953) says we all possess an Illuminating Intellect, "an inner spiritual light which is a participation in the uncreated divine light," that "causes all our ideas to arise in us" (p.71, p.73). So, this conception of a cosmic or divine origin of creative imagination has a two-thousand-five-hundred-year old history in Western thought. It's an ancient belief with legs.

Thinking of a cosmic intelligence reminds me of Puysegur's work with Victor Race, a peasant who, when entranced, spoke as an educated person with great intelligence. I remember Puysegur saying of Victor,

> But my man, or perhaps I should say *my intelligence*, calms me. He is teaching me the conduct I must follow. . .It is a peasant, the most narrow and limited in this locality, that teaches me this. *When he is in crisis, I know no one as profound, prudent, and clear-sighted.*
> (Crabtree, 1993, p.43, italics added)

When entranced, Victor possessed an intelligence superior to Puysegur. Then there was Friedricke Hauffe, an illiterate peasant girl, who when entranced spoke in high German reciting Plato and Parmenides. Had Victor and Friedricke made contact with Anaxagoras' *Nous*?

Max responds,

> Yes, that's right. Where do you think I get *my* ideas? You think I'm so fuckin smart about these ancient Greeks. *I'm a work of fiction*! These ideas don't originate in me. They arise in me from another source. So, yeah, I'm tapping into a universal knowledge. Where do you think Anaxagoras got *his* ideas! How could a guy writing 2500 years ago be so in sync with twentieth century science? It's *Nous*, dummy!

"Okay," I say, "I'll think about that."

Maybe a super-intelligence shapes Frank's story, but to what purpose? In our specific example, why is there a central character Mekes who represents Pythagoras? Why is Pythagoras meaningful in Frank's recovery from the death of his son? Frank's novel suggests Pythagoras' beliefs about the immortality of the soul, healing, and his conception of Eternal Recurrence may be important for Frank's recovery. Pythagoras provides the conceptual basis for Frank believing he'll be reunited with his dead but immortal son, which is the main theme of *The journey west*. Pythagoras also stands for a different kind of knowledge drawn from Eastern and Western cultures, with no boundary between religion, science, and the occult, all informing a code of moral conduct. I find it significant that the Pythagoreans were a cult of listeners whose initiation began with a year of silence.

What about Hugh Everett's quantum conception of parallel universes? If a cosmic mind is structuring Frank's writing, what's its significance for Frank's recovery? Frank says the elemental takeaway from Everett's parallel universes, growing out of Schrödinger's equation, is that in one universe he and Anders are immortal. That's what you get for basing a theory on the full range of probabilities between life and death! Frank says Everett's multiverse conception provides for both apocalyptic annihilation and immortality. Both are available and may not even be mutually exclusive.

Finally, if a divine super-intelligence is composing Frank's novel, what should I understand from my apparent association with Fritz Perls? Distanziert is interested in the power of the gestalt to modify reality, which

I translate to mean "the power of imagination to alter physical states." Anaxagoras claims *Nous* is a powerful immaterial force causing matter to move. And in this book, we've repeatedly seen sick people cured by the immaterial force of imagination. Gassner acknowledged imagination was the basis of his exorcisms, scientists assessing Mesmer determined he cured patients through imagination, psychoanalysis was born out of Charcot's belief that mind alters matter, and Bertha's paralyzes were alleviated by her imaginative hallucinations.

For centuries scientists and religious figures have acknowledged the psychological basis of healing. For example, in 1608 a professor of medicine at the University of Louvain, writes, "the emotions are greatly alterative with respect to the body. . .Through them the imagination is able to transform the body" (Jackson, 1999, p.224). During the twentieth century, science discovered the placebo effect where meaning and expectation are the basis of powerful physical transformations (Brody, 2000; Frank & Frank, 1961; Harrington, 1997; Moerman, 2002; Wampold, Imel & Minami, 2007). Placebo proves Anaxagoras was right about *Nous*. For example, in the area of mental health, research shows eighty percent of the effect of antidepressant medication is caused by the mind (Kirsch, 2010). Psychotherapy researcher, Joel Weinberg (1995), identified five empirically derived factors common to all psychotherapy: Doctor/patient relationship, expectation, recognizing and mastering a problem, and explanation for therapeutic change. These are the same elements researchers Howard Brody (2000) and Daniel Moerman (2002) say stimulates the mind's natural placebo response. Illness is transformed by meaning and imagination, by our beliefs about the future. To an extent, we become the future we believe.

What's the emotional energy fueling imagination? Eros, Freud's instinct intent on promoting and preserving life. Mesmer proposed the source of cure was a life force passing between patient and clinician via invisible magnetic currents. Carl Jung (1953) declares, "Imagination is. . .a concentrated extract of the life forces, both physical and psychic" (p.278). Freud (1938) writes the aim of Eros "is to establish ever greater unities and to preserve them thus—in short, to *bind together*" (p.148, italics added). Distanziert clarifies, "A gestalt is a cluster of associated elements *bound together* to form a single meaning, like a face formed from many features." Using a psychic glue derived from love and "life force," gestalts link together mental representations to create our subjective realities.

Okay, but why should Frank be writing any of this in the first place? There's widespread recognition that creative activity is restorative (Chodorow, 1997; Forgeard et al., 2014; Hagman, 2005; Jamison, 1993; Richman, 2014; Rose, 1996; Sandblom, 1999; Ulanov & Ulanov, 1991). Painter, Paul Klee, says simply, "I create—in order not to cry" (Sandblom, 1999, p.192). Frank sees writing as a vocation of unhappiness, born out of painful emotions. Frank writes because he's miserable—plain and simple. Over the years writing has brought him relief. Graham Greene (1980) explains, "Writing is a form of therapy," a way of escaping madness, melancholy and panic (p.285). Psychologists James Pennebaker (1990, 1995), Stephen Lepore and Joshua Smyth (2002) have produced a body of research demonstrating the health benefits of expressive writing telling stories. In a diary entry Virginia Woolf (2003) notes, "Odd how the creative power at once brings the whole universe to order" (p.213). Anaxagoras agrees, "That's the organizing power of *Nous* at the heart of creativity."

Certainly, the integration Frank brings to his stories contrasts with the psychic disintegration he experiences in life. The content of Frank's virtual realities is more pleasurable than the awful reality which engulfs him. And the curiosity with which he searches the world for information about his characters is an antidote for his ruminations about loss and isolation. Finally, Frank's writing is expansive, opening him up to future possibility. Really, *anything is possible* in his writing. Dream researchers David Kahn and Tzivia Gover (2010), discuss the connection between dreaming and creativity:

> While dreaming we are not constrained by what we know is possible. . . while dreaming we benefit by *thinking the unthinkable and, importantly, believing it* and experiencing it. . .Dreams allow us to experience things beyond our abilities in waking reality, and beyond the laws of physical science and nature.
>
> (pp.193–194, italics added)

As in his dreams, when Frank is writing he's *believing the unthinkable, imaging the impossible*, expanding the creative potential of his life. Imagination makes the unthinkable possible, and the unbearable livable.

With the deaths of Anders, Signe and his mother, Frank's world was destroyed. What's left? Frank says, "I'm alone, totally isolated. Think where I'd be if I didn't have an imagination."

References

Aquinas, T. (1993). *Selected philosophical writings*. T. McDermott (Trans.). Oxford: Oxford University Press.

Asma, S. (2017). Blowing away the self: Creativity and control. In *The evolution of the imagination* (pp.176–226). Chicago, IL: University of Chicago Press.

Atmanspacher, H. & Fach, W. (2015). Mind-matter correlations in duel-aspect monism. In E. Kelly, A. Crabtree, & P. Marshall, (Eds.) *Beyond physicalism: Toward reconciliation of science and spirituality* (pp.195–226). Lanham, MD: Rowman & Littlefield.

Bion, W. (1965). *Transformations*. London: Maresfield Library.

Blass, R. & Blatt, S. (1996). Attachment and separateness in the experience of symbiotic relatedness. *Psychoanalytic Quarterly*, 65, 711–746.

Bomford, R. (1999). God and the unconscious. In *The symmetry of God* (pp.57–67). London: Free Association Books.

Bosnak, R. (2007). Kinds of imagination. In *Embodiment: Creative imagination, in medicine, art and travel* (pp.67–73). London: Routledge.

Bowker, J. (2014). *God: A very short introduction*. Oxford: Oxford University Press.

Breuer, J. (1895). Theoretical. In Breuer, J. & Freud, S. Studies on hysteria (pp.183–251). *Standard Edition*. London: Hogarth Press, 2, 3–309.

Brody, H. (2000). *The placebo response*. New York, NY: HarperCollins.

Burkert, W. (1972). *Lore and science in ancient Pythagoreanism*. Cambridge, MA: Harvard University Press.

Byrne, P. (2010). *The many worlds of Hugh Everett III: Multiple universes, mutual assured destruction, and the meltdown of a nuclear family*. Oxford: Oxford University Press.

Cardena, E. (1994). The domain of dissociation. In S. Lynn & J. Rhue (Eds.) *Dissociation: Clinical and theoretical perspectives* (pp.15–31). New York, NY: Guilford Press.

Chodorow, J. (Ed.) (1997). *Jung on active imagination*. Princeton, NJ: Princeton University Press.

Clarkson, P. & Mackewn, J. (1993). *Fritz Perls*. London: Sage Publications.

Corbin, H. (1969). *Alone with the alone: Creative imagination in the Sufism of Ibn Arabi*. Princeton, NJ: Princeton University Press.

Corbin, H. (1972). *Mundus imaginalis*, or the imaginary and the imaginal. *Spring: An Annual of Archetypal and Jungian Thought*, 18–41. https://archive.org/details/mundus_imaginalis_201512 (Accessed November 1, 2018)

Crabtree, A. (1993). *From Mesmer to Freud: Magnetic sleep and the roots of psychological healing*. New Haven, CT: Yale University Press.

Csikszentmihalyi, M. (1996). *Creativity: Flow and the psychology of discovery and invention*. New York, NY: Harper Perennial.

Csikszentmihalyi, M. (2004). Ted Talks: Mihaly Csikszentmihalyi: Flow, the secret of happiness. https://www.ted.com/talks/mihaly_csikszentmihalyi_on_flow?language=en (Accessed October 20, 2018)

Csikszentmihalyi, M. & Csikszentmihalyi, I. (Eds.) (1988). *Optimal experience: Psychological studies of flow in consciousness*. Cambridge: Cambridge University Press.

Curd, P. (2007). *Anaxagoras of Clazomenae: Fragments and testimonia*. Toronto: University of Toronto Press.

Curd, P. (2008). Anaxagoras and the theory of everything. In P. Curd & D. Graham (Eds.), *The Oxford handbook of presocratic philosophy* (pp.230–249). Oxford: Oxford University Press.

Forgeard, M., Mecklenburg, A., Lacasse, J. & Jayawickreme, E. (2014). Bringing the whole universe to order: Creativity, healing, and posttraumatic growth. In J. Kaufman (Ed.), *Creativity and mental illness* (pp.321–342). Cambridge: Cambridge University Press.

Frank, J. D. & Frank, J. A. (1961). *Persuasion and healing: A comparative study of psychotherapy*. Baltimore, MD: Johns Hopkins University.

Freud, S. (1915). The unconscious. *Standard Edition*. London: Hogarth Press, 14, 159–215.

Freud, S. (1938). An outline of psycho-analysis. *Standard Edition*. London: Hogarth Press, 23, 141–207.

Ghiselin, B. (Ed.) (1952). Albert Einstein: Letter to Jacques Hadamard. *The creative process: A symposium* (pp.32–33). Berkeley, CA: University of California Press.

Greene, G. (1980). *Ways of escape: An autobiography*. New York, NY: Simon & Schuster.

Grotstein, J. (2000). *Who is the dreamer who dreams the dream?* Hillsdale, NJ: The Analytic Press.

Grotstein, J. (2007). *A beam of intense darkness: Wilfred Bion's legacy to psychoanalysis*. London: Karnac.

Hagman, G. (2005). The creative process. *Aesthetic experience: Beauty, creativity, and the search for the ideal* (pp.61–83). Amsterdam: Rodopi.

Harrington, A. (1997). *The placebo effect: An interdisciplinary exploration*. Cambridge, MA: Harvard University Press.

Huffman, C. (Ed.) (2014). *A history of Pythagoreanism*. Cambridge: Cambridge University Press.

Isaacson, W. (2007). *Einstein: His life and universe*. New York, NY: Simon & Schuster.

Jackson, S. (1999). The use of imagination. *Care of the psyche: A history of psychological healing*, (pp.221–235). New Haven, CT: Yale University Press.

Jamison, K. (1993). *Touched with fire: Manic-depressive illness and the artistic temperament*. New York, NY: Simon & Schuster.

Jung, C. (1953). Psychology and alchemy. H. Read, M. Fordham, G. Adler & W. McGuire (Eds.) *Collected Works of C. G. Jung*, volume 12. Princeton, NJ: Princeton University Press.

Kahn, C. (2001). *Pythagoras and the Pythagoreans*. Indianapolis, IN: Hackett Publishing Company.

Kahn, D. & Gover, T. (2010). Consciousness in dreams. *International Review of Neurobiology*, 92, 181–195.

Kant, I. (1951). *Critique of judgement*. New York, NY: Macmillan Publishing Company. (Original work 1790)

Kirsch, I. (2010). *The emperor's new drugs: Exploding the antidepressant myth*. New York, NY: Basic Books.

Kripal, J. (2010). The book as seance: Frederic Myers and the London Society for Psychical Research. *Authors of the impossible: The paranormal and the sacred* (pp.36–91). Chicago, IL: University of Chicago Press.

Kris, E. (1952). *Psychoanalytic explorations in art*. Madison, CT: International Universities Press.

Kuhn, T. (1962). *The structure of scientific revolutions*. Chicago, IL: University of Chicago Press.

Laks, A. (2014). Diogenes Laertius' *Life of Pythagoras*. In C. Huffman (Ed.) *A history of Pythagoreanism* (pp.360–380). Cambridge: Cambridge University Press.

Lepore, S. & Smyth, J. (2002). *The writing cure: How expressive writing promotes health and emotional well-being*. Washington, DC: The American Psychological Association.

Lloyd, G. (2014). Pythagoras. In C. Huffman (Ed.) *A history of Pythagoreanism* (pp.24–45). Cambridge: Cambridge University Press.

Maritain, J. (1953). *Creative intuition in art and poetry*. New York, NY: Pantheon Books.

Marmodoro, A. (2017). *Everything from everything: Anaxagoras's metaphysics*. Oxford: Oxford University Press.

Moerman, D. (2002). *Meaning, medicine, and the "placebo effect."* Cambridge: Cambridge University Press.

Oppenheim, L. (2013). *Imagination from fantasy to delusion*. New York, NY: Routledge.

Otto, R. (1923). *The idea of the holy*. London: Oxford University Press.

Pennebaker, J. (1990). *Opening up: The healing power of expressing emotions*. New York, NY: Guilford Press.

Pennebaker, J. (Ed.) (1995). *Emotion, disclosure, and health*. Washington, DC: The American Psychological Association.

Perls, F. (1973). The gestalt approach. In *The gestalt approach & Eye witness to therapy* (pp.1–114). New York, NY: Science and Behavior Books.

Plato (1989a). Ion.In E. Hamilton & H. Cairns (Eds.), *The collected dialogues of Plato, Including the letters* (pp.215–228). Princeton, NJ: Princeton University Press.

Plato (1989b). Socrates' defense. In E. Hamilton & H. Cairns (Eds.), *The collected dialogues of Plato, Including the letters* (pp.3–26). Princeton, NJ: Princeton University Press.

Plato (1989c). Phaedrus. In E. Hamilton & H. Cairns (Eds.), *The collected dialogues of Plato, including the letters* (pp.475–525). Princeton, NJ: Princeton University Press.

Richman, S. (2014). Inspiration, insanity, and the paradox of dissociation. In *Mended by the muse: Creative transformations of trauma* (pp.54–78). New York, NY: Routledge.

Riedweg, C. (2005). *Pythagoras: His life, teachings and influence*. Ithaca, NY: Cornell University Press.

Rose, G. (1996). *Trauma and mastery in life and art*. Madison, CT: International Universities Press.

Rothenberg, A. (1979). *The emerging Goddess: The creative process in art, science, and other fields*. Chicago, IL: University of Chicago Press.

Sandblom, P. (1999). *Creativity and disease*. New York, NY: Marion Boyers.

Ulanov, A. & Ulanov, B. (1991). *The healing imagination: The meeting of psyche and soul*. Einsiendeln, Switzerland: Daimon Publishing.

Wampold, B., Imel, Z. & Minami, T. (2007), The story of placebo effects in medicine: evidence in context. *Journal of Clinical Psychology*, 63, 379–390.

Ward, T., Smith, S. & Finke, R. (1999). Creative cognition. In R. Sternberg (Ed.), *Handbook of creativity* (pp.189–212). Cambridge: Cambridge University Press.

Weinberger, J. (1995). Common factors aren't so common: The common factors dilemma. *Clinical Psychology: Science and Practice*, 2, 45–69.

Woolf, V. (2003). Friday, July 27th, 1934. L. Woolf (Ed.) *A writer's diary*. Orlando, FL: Harcourt.

Index